CLASSICAL MEMORIES/MODERN IDENTITIES
Paul Allen Miller and Richard H. Armstrong, Series Editors

Reflections of Romanity

DISCOURSES OF SUBJECTIVITY IN IMPERIAL ROME

RICHARD ALSTON
AND
EFROSSINI SPENTZOU

 THE OHIO STATE UNIVERSITY PRESS / COLUMBUS

Copyright © 2011 by The Ohio State University Press.
All rights reserved.

Library of Congress Cataloging-in-Publication Data
Alston, Richard, 1965–
 Reflections of Romanity : discourses of subjectivity in Imperial Rome / Richard Alston and Efrossini Spentzou.
  p. cm. — (Classical memories/modern identities)
 Includes bibliographical references and index.
 ISBN-13: 978-0-8142-1149-6 (cloth : alk. paper)
 ISBN-10: 0-8142-1149-6 (cloth : alk. paper)
 ISBN-13: 978-0-8142-9250-1 (cd)
 1. Latin literature—History and criticism. 2. Self in literature. 3. Subjectivity in literature. I. Spentzou, Efrossini. II. Title. III. Series: Classical memories/modern identities.
 PA6003.A45 2011
 870.9'353—dc22
                              2010039574

This book is available in the following editions:
Cloth (ISBN 978-0-8142-1149-6)
CD-ROM (ISBN 978-0-8142-9250-1)

Cover design by Laurence J. Nozik
Type set in Adobe Garamond Pro
Text design by Juliet Williams

♾ The paper used in this publication meets the minimum requirements of the American National Standard for Information Sciences—Permanence of Paper for Printed Library Materials. ANSI Z39.48-1992.

9 8 7 6 5 4 3 2 1

Για τα αγγελάκια μας,
το Βασίλη και το Στέφανο

Only connect.

E. M. Forster, *Howards End*

Contents

Series Editors' Foreword   ix

Acknowledgments   xiii

Chapter 1   Introduction. Talking to Strangers: Classical Readings and the Modern Self   1

Chapter 2   Home Alone: Terror and Power   27

Chapter 3   Death and Love: Rationality and Passion   65

Chapter 4   Private Partners and Family Dramas   107

Chapter 5   Living with the Past: Tradition, Invention, and History   141

Chapter 6   Imperial Dreams: Being Roman in a World Empire   193

Chapter 7   Epilogue   225

Bibliography   231

Index   241

Series Editors' Foreword

Talking to strangers can be dangerous. We tell our kids not to. They look so familiar, but looks can be deceiving. Who knows who these people are? Of course, the whole possibility of conversation depends on us not knowing these people, on a certain constitutive opacity and hence danger. If the other were completely known to us, if the other were not estranged from us, there could be no conversation, indeed there could no meaning. For the absolute presence of the self to the other would not only eliminate the other, and hence the possibility of our exchanging meanings in a conversation, it would also eliminate meaning itself. The possibility of one thing referring to another, of language and signification, is that those things not be the same. Thus in a sense we are always talking to strangers, and we cannot be ourselves or form meaningful existences for ourselves outside that conversation. But at the same time, stranger danger is real. The other always threatens the integrity of the same, the possibility of identity.

Richard Alston and Efrossini Spentzou offer us a conversation. It is one held between a variety of strangers, some stranger than others. It begins with the recognition that something strange is happening "in the historical period roughly defined by the reigns of Nero and Trajan (c.e. 54–117)." In the texts of what in a more self-confident time were known as "Silver Age" Latin literature—Lucan, Statius, Valerius Flaccus, Seneca, Tacitus, and Pliny—there is an evident unease. Latecomers in an age of relative peace and stability, immensely talented heirs of an immense tradition, they seek to carve out a place for themselves in the conversation that had become Latin literature. But when the script had already been written, on the political level by Augustus and his successors and on the literary level by Vergil, Horace, Livy, and the elegists, then how do you perform it with a degree of authenticity? One of the great problems, indeed, for the writers of the "long first century" is how do they perform Romanness authentically without falling into parody?

This predicament is one that is not unfamiliar to the inhabitant of the postmodern condition. We too live in a world where there is no outside, no alternative order whose essence we are meant to perform. For Tacitus, Pliny, and Seneca, what was the alternative to the Roman imperial order? They had received it and they could judge it, but they could not step outside it or remake it. They performed their status as *civis Romanus* always under the ironizing shadow of their own, structurally necessary bad faith. The citizen of the global economy faces the same dilemma: how to perform his or her own status as a citizen of the United States, the UK, Europe, or China, without falling into inauthenticity by accepting a Walt Disney commodified version of individual and communal identity, or irony by assuming inauthenticity as the theme of one's existence, or denial by adopting a fundamentalist refusal of that inauthenticity whether in its various religious or political forms. The Roman of the long first century thus becomes a good conversation partner for the postmodern reader: the inhabitant of a global system she inherited but did not make, who is consequently suspicious of the narratives that underwrite that system but still unable to replace them with new narratives no longer parasitic on the old.

These Romans, then, are our intimate others. They are people we can talk to because they are not us, but though strangers, they are not unintelligible. Instead they occupy that middle position that Socrates in the *Lysis* says makes friendship possible. The wholly good man and the wholly evil have no need of friends. The completely good man as a self-contained and perfect whole has no need of any other. He is the principle of self-identity, really more a god than a man. The wholly bad man, in so far as he would reject all good things, would also have no need of friendship, which all agree to be good. The friend, then, like the conversation partner will always be in part a stranger, but still recognizeable: the good but not perfect man, the bearer of a certain resemblance to ourselves, yet not our simple reflection. Alston and Spentzou make the strong case that the Romans of the long first century could be such friends and conversation partners.

As is common once we start talking to strangers, even while recognizing the dangers they present, their friends become our friends. The people whose conversation we already find most enriching in turn enrich the conversations of our new friends. In the case of Alston and Spentzou, these old friends, the friends from our own community, are Michel Foucault, Jacques Lacan, and

Jean Luc Nancy, among others. This delegation is not invited here into the text as a panel of experts, whose modern "theory" will elucidate the obscure object of desire that is antiquity. They are not a crack team of pathologists in an episode of CSI: Rome. They are invited as co-doubters, co-interregators of the self and its histories; they arrive with their own aporias and full of unfinished arguments; they join this conversation not as privileged savants, but as something more like "concerned citizens" in this world of worry that links us to our Roman conversationalists.

It is a strength of this book that Alston and Spentzou are not afraid of a conversation that bucks the settled confines of disciplinarity. Their threads of discussion wind through ancient texts spanning disparate genres, and pick up modern discussions already in progress. The reader will, for example, watch the panic of a falling emperor, consider the broad patterns of *amicitia* through Pliny's letters, contemplate the figure of Lucan's Caesar, and thence via Kierkegaard and Nietzsche, come face to face with the unique form of alienation the elite Roman of the first century faced: a discursive drought that left one caught between terms of friendship and mastery, susceptible to violent extremes (or at least their imaginative formulation), sudden loneliness, and social discontent. By looking to antiquity's loose ends, cracked foundations, and imagined terrors, the authors thread through a labyrinth of moments they allow to irrupt with their own force, uncontained by a safety net that would reduce such irruptions to the merely historical.

Reflections of Romanity serves this series well in that it offers an intelligent challenge to a settled pattern of antiquity's construal in the modern self. Classical education was long enlisted in a project of modern self-fashioning (for which the German word *Bildung* sounds so much more apt than our "education") that cast ancient culture as foundational, solid, natural, and especially *clear*. This is what supposedly made the ancients safe tutors for good European children for three hundred or so years. Hegel, as rector of the *Gymnasium* at Nürnberg, enjoined his audience to study antiquity as "the spiritual bath, the secular baptism that first and indelibly attunes and tinctures the soul in respect of taste and knowledge"; this study is not superficial, but requires an intense engagement so as to make us "at home in this [classical] world, the most beautiful that has ever been."[1] We are still, in a sense, struggling with this legacy of appropriation, where antiquity is that realm constituted in opposition to modern (and post-modern) doubt, corrosion, division, and dread. The human spirit, in Hegel's view, develops from primeval nature and flowers in antiquity, emerging "like a bride from

---

1. *Gymnasial-Reden*, I: Am 29 September 1809; translation by Richard Kroner (*G. W. F. Hegel: Early Theological Writings I* [1971]: 321–30), cited from the selection in *German Aesthetic and Literary Criticism*, ed. David Simpson (Cambridge, 1984) 201–202.

her chamber endowed with a yet more beautiful naturalness, with freedom, depth, and serenity"; the human spirit's profundity is no longer manifested "in confusion, gloom, or arrogance, but in perfect clarity."[2] Even in subsequent reversals of this idealist *hieros gamos* of antiquity and modernity, we still find a giddy clarity reached through excavating a deeply *un*serene Dionysian or Oedipal pre-history among the ancients.

What will happen to us when antiquity no longer comes forward as a natural and self-evident bride, but instead, as already riven with loss, poisoned by irony and inauthenticity, restless in its cultural discontent, unclear in its relation to history, nature, and the world? This book shows us we need not fear to face the ancients in their untimeliness and unclarity (their *untiquity,* we might say). If anything, we have more to gain by admitting that they too had their all too human struggles with being at home in the world. That is the basis for the discussion the reader will find here, one the authors and the editors hope will continue on into this new millennium. We will try to have the courage of our suspicions and to rethink antiquity as something as unsettling, confounding, and compelling as our own troubled age. Alston and Spentzou find the importance of antiquity lies in analogy, not genealogy; in this work, they seek out situational resonances, not timeless or foundational truths, in order "to find the human and humane in the spaces between the closed epistemes, and in so doing fracture those enclosures" (21). It is a passage to humanity through Romanity, a "history of the past for the present" that we are proud to present in this series.

2. See note 1.

Acknowledgments

This book is, amongst other things, about memory and recollection. Drafting our acknowledgments, we recall, in conversation, that first exchange in a corridor in the Institute of Classical Studies in London about research and what each one of us might do next, and the surprise we felt when we realized that we were thinking about shifting our research to the same period. And then more conversations followed, and then a project, and then a grant and then we started to research and write. Inevitably, schedules never quite matched. One of us would be working on our project, while the other was just finishing off something else. And then our lives and programs would switch. We brought to the project different skills and interests, different approaches and different voices, but for us the journey was not one of trying to amalgamate those separate voices into a coherent form, making one book from two studies, but of finding a third voice, of working our way into new modes of thinking and expression, of challenging the disciplinary boundaries in which we separately worked, and thinking afresh our understandings of the world we studied. We both, then, had to separate how we wrote and thought together from how we write and think as individuals, creating almost a separate dream of writing in which we wrote as each other, Efi as Richard, Richard as Efi, to make a new author. It may be that a discerning critic, if they can be bothered, and one who knows us both, might be able to pick through the text and assign original authorship to one of the Efi–Richard beings, but we have lost track. When words were scribed by one hand, the idea may have originated with the other. In that dream of writing, the fluidity of personality and the complexity of the relationship of the author with the text became very real for us.

Along this journey, we have reassessed, rethought, and re-engaged with our subject matter, both on the local scale of the literature and society of the early Roman Empire, but also our overall connection with classical studies. We found, somewhat to our surprise, that we were continually returning to the issue of the purpose of classical studies and that we kept arguing for a closer and more disciplined engagement with the classical past, that what happened in antiquity matters, not because of some general commitment to the history of other cultures nor because of the continuous reception of the classical past (both of which are important), but because the classical gives us a new/old perspective on the problems of our society and of being human. Although this engagement has often been uncomfortable, and we have at times faced incomprehension in an academia which is fond of genres and categories, our intellectual lives have been immensely enriched by this experience and we have emerged from this project invigorated and convinced of the value of classical research. Our hope is that our readers take this project for what it is, an engagement, an intervention, that is a jumping off point for discussion and not 'the last word.' Our need is for more conversations, more words and new debates, not conclusions. We have become convinced that in Rome of the early imperial period, there is a past that is worth listening to, struggling with, and understanding, a past that offers radical challenges to the present. Research is a voyage of discovery, and we are very grateful that almost ten years ago we bought the ticket, and embarked on this trip into the unknown.

We owe much to the enthusiastic support of our friends and colleagues. We carried this project into classrooms, seminars, meetings over coffee, or on the fringes of a conference. Several of these conversations were not even about our project per se. The regular seminars of the Humanities and Arts Research Centre (HARC) at Royal Holloway, University of London, especially in the period 2003–7, gave us an invaluable comparative literature forum and were vital in encouraging a radical approach. Ewan Fernie engaged with our ideas from a very early stage, helped us think through problems, and encouraged us to look towards unfamiliar sources of inspiration. Ruud Nauta and Onno van Nijf drummed up an audience of staff and students for a seminar at the University of Groningen, and their supportive responses at a crucial stage in the evolution of our ideas were more important than they can possibly have realized. Jim Samson read the whole manuscript for us and suggested many improvements, remaining positive and supportive all the way. We would also like to thank our students both at BA at Royal Holloway, and at MA in the University of London, on whom we have tried out our ideas over a number of years. Sometimes baffled, sometimes inspired, but always engaged, their responses and contributions have been entertaining and inspiring, demonstrating repeatedly the advantages of the link between teaching and research. So often their fresh eyes would see things in the texts that we had missed, and their responses would suggest different ways in which we could work through the problems that we were posing. Their openness to disciplinary diversity and their unwillingness to accept 'authoritative voices' enlivened seminars, and made teaching a reinvigorating experience. We also thank the Leverhulme Trust, who funded our research at a very early stage, and the Arts and Humanities Research Council, who provided Efi with a research leave extension that enabled us to complete a draft of the book of sufficient coherence that we could show it to publishers. The process of bringing this volume to publication has not been straightforward. We would like to thank Eugene O'Connor and The Ohio State University Press for their willingness to see this project for what it is and for their continuing support. The series editors, Richard Armstrong and Paul Allen Miller, who read the manuscript at a relatively early stage, demonstrated remarkable acuity in their comments and have, as a result, made this a much better book. Their commitment to the project was unwaivering, and we are enormously grateful. Of course we stand up, and take full responsibility, for the ideas, suggestions, and any pitfalls of the book.

FINALLY, the cover. We fell in love with this painting: the painting of an exile; color, fluidity, vibrancy. It tries to capture water in movement. Somehow that seemed entirely appropriate.

1

Introduction.
Talking to Strangers

CLASSICAL READINGS AND THE MODERN SELF

CONVERSATIONS IN THE TWILIGHT OF ROMANITY

The project that gave rise to this book started as a conversation; conversations marked its progress and this book is, ultimately, a form of literary conversation. The conversation started with a casual remark, a gesture of incomprehension on the part of a historian faced with a literary text. That admission drew a confession of confusion, and then an expression of worry. The conversation concerned first one and then another author writing in the historical period roughly defined by the reigns of Nero and Trajan (C.E. 54–117), which we might describe as the latter end of a 'long' first century C.E. We were in conversation with different texts, with the epistolography and *Panegyricus* of Pliny the Younger; the epics of Lucan, Statius, and Valerius Flaccus; the histories of Tacitus; the philosophical writings of Seneca and Epictetus; the *Satires* of Juvenal; the epigrams of Martial; the *Silvae* of Statius; and the parallel traditions of Greece, most obviously represented by Plutarch and Dio Chrysostom. Yet our separate conversations generated a similar unease. In many ways, these texts were familiar friends, continuing literary traditions that could be traced back sometimes over centuries. But although they looked like these older texts (the epics have their heroes and battles and describe the rise and fall of nations; there are poems and letters of love and loss and friendship; we have political histories of kings and leaders), the familiarity of the classical models was not enough to hide their individuality. In the epics, we saw a welter of violence and loss, families and states torn apart, heroes that seemed somehow unheroic, and gods (when they were present) who presided over appallingly bloody destruction. The comfortable world of Pliny's *Epistles* (at first sight so radically different from the epics and the ferocity of Juvenalian anger that it seemed to come from a different universe), with dinner parties, book readings, and friends and family, started to look a little tattered round the edges; there were doubts, and, sometimes, distrust and diffidence. Likewise Tacitus' conservatism and seeming adherence to the values of the Republican aristocracy slipped through the fingers as his characters engaged with the real political world and struggled to make sense of this new state that was the Roman Empire. Wherever we looked, there was an unease, a sense that unlike the familiar figures of the classical world, we were conversing here with characters who were nervous, shifting, demanding interrogation and yet eluding the questions through their superficial similarities to textual characters of another age; these were texts pretending to be what they were a century or so earlier, but which appeared to be masquerading in borrowed clothes. They said they were old friends, but had none of the easiness of familiarity. They were dislocated from traditions, not a new literature, but a literature uncomfortable in its old forms. Gradually we became aware that we were talking to strangers.

It is not immediately obvious why we should get such a concentration of unsettled texts in this period. Arguably, the great trauma of Roman history occurred at least ninety years earlier (49–28 B.C.E.); after seven centuries of Republican rule, the Romans engaged in a series of vicious civil conflicts. Wars were fought across Italy. Political opponents were murdered. Lands were confiscated and populations shifted. The old political system was torn apart and a new monarchic system established. A century later and the Republic was dead, the rule of the emperors unchallenged. The political system was, generally speaking, stable. There was a brief and destructive outbreak of civil conflict between C.E. 68–70, but this was not an event that threatened the social order. In that civil war, there was no great ideological conflict, no dispute over the meaning of Rome, nothing other than the brute politics of military conflict. The events of C.E. 68–70 merely affirmed the political consensus and the wars did not provoke any kind of social or cultural crisis. The years of Nero and of the Flavian dynasty were similarly relatively stable by most measures. There were purges under Nero and under Domitian, purges that were painful for the aristocracy of the period, but in scale they were nothing compared to the purges of the late Republic. It seems very likely that virtually all below the senatorial level and a high proportion of the nine hundred or so senators escaped the direct effects of these political disturbances. Other than in C.E. 68–69, Italy was not threatened by war.

The empire continued to expand throughout the period. It is difficult not to imagine that the empire grew richer in this extended period of peace, and that the rich especially benefited from this (slowly) growing world. The elites of Italy were probably more politically settled, wealthier, and more secure in their wealth than at any other time in Roman history.

In marked contrast to the unsettled texts of the latter decades of the long first century C.E., the politically disturbed period in the latter half of the first century B.C.E. saw the production of some of the great formative narratives of Roman identity, most notably Livy's mammoth *Ab Urbe Condita*, a history of Rome from its foundation, and Virgil's *Aeneid*, an epic of Roman foundation. The latter is the Ur-text of imperial Roman epic. It has multiple layers of meaning and multiple voices, and although the text can be (and has been) read as expressing doubts over the Augustan regime and is susceptible to pessimistic readings in which the future of Rome will be less than glorious, the narrative drive is overwhelmingly the subordination of the individual to the demands of fate. Aeneas may doubt, but fate drives him on and he never rejects that fate, with its implicit subordination of his individuality to the needs of the state.[1] Meaning is given to Aeneas, and by implication to all Romans, by this dominance of the state; although there may be a sense of loss in that sublimation of the individual, there is ultimately no choice and no alternative meaning available. Arguably, Augustan ideology created a new model of Roman identity, a model firmly rooted in the past, but also one which elevated loyalty to the state above other concerns and proclaimed the historical destiny of Rome. Opposition could mock and establish alternative modes of masculinity (especially in the elegiac lovers of Propertius and Ovid), but, ultimately, it was forced to position itself in relation to the models of Roman manhood foregrounded in the Virgilian epic. The powerful, directed vision of the state, given voice in the *Aeneid* and monumentalized in the Augustan transformation of the city of Rome, was a vision of Rome and Roman identity about whose validity one could argue, and against which one could mobilize literary and no doubt political resources, but it was a vision the power of which could not be denied. Individuals were placed in opposition to it or marginalized by it, but they were not adrift.

The *Aeneid*, with its foundational ideology of the Roman self, was quickly established as a literary classic. Later works defined themselves not just against its aesthetic and generic representation, but also its heroism and image of the Roman man.[2] But we have come a long way since the late nine-

---

1. For an elaborate exploration of the binding influence of the state and the ideals of public good on the epic story of the *Aeneid* see Conte (1986) 141–84.
2. See e.g. Syed (2005).

teenth century when scholarship called this body of texts 'Silver' Latin literature to emphasize its natural inferiority to the 'Golden' Augustan corpus.[3] 'Silver' Latin, especially in the past couple of decades, has attracted acclamation precisely for not being 'Golden'; for daring to breach the 'golden' rules of writing and expression and for developing a bold idiom reminding the modern readers of the fascinating and terrifying excesses and strength of modern Expressionism. One of the more eclectic, personal, and committed treatments is W. R. Johnson's *Momentary Monsters,* a book reveling in the exploration of the delusional, "nobly impotent," and comic heroes of Lucan's historical epic. Johnson speaks with relish of the "genuine inscrutability, a properly garbled obscurity"[4] of figures such as Pompey, and dismisses the weird episode of the snakes guarding the spring in the desert of Book 9 as a hollow victory of an empty man (Cato),[5] admitting the deep pleasure that he draws from the bathos, absurdity, historical unreality, and discord that dominate the muddled epic landscape. Aware of the long-lasting prejudice accompanying these 'late' texts, he issues a warning right from the start:

> Nor, of course, should we succumb here to the temptation of supposing that the *content* of the writers who lived and wrote in these and later reigns can best be understood in terms of literary conventions that excessive rhetorical training (is there such a thing?) and a mysterious passion for being decadent had ripened to rottenness. Pondering their nation's past and present, lacking the precious hindsight and apparent dispassion that help today's historians in their unwritings of Tacitus, the great post-Augustan writers tended to see *their* Rome and its history as terrifying and incomprehensible (though they were valiant in their efforts to comprehend it), and their unforgettable imaginations of the terror of history cannot be charmed away by the historian's or the rhetorician's appeal to decorum and coherence. Beyond even Tacitus, Lucan, in his angry, desperate wit, is least susceptible of all the imperial writers to the demands of sweet reason.[6] (emphasis in original)

Though our loci of dialogue with these texts are inevitably different, we have found in Johnson's personal tone and his commitment to the text a valuable precursor. We have similarly not tried to explain away the absurdi-

---

3. An attitude, however, that would survive throughout the twentieth century and be attested as late and in as prominent a context as, e.g., in Williams (1978) *passim,* and again Williams (1986) who sums up his overall attitude to Statius right at the opening of his article when he states that "Statius' most severe anxiety did not arise from political oppression; it arose from poetic oppressions, from a sense of the overpowering greatness of a predecessor" (207).
4. Johnson (1987) 85.
5. Johnson (1987) 47–55.
6. Johnson (1987) xii.

ties and intractability of the characters in our texts. Very much like Johnson, we found ourselves intrigued, captivated, and puzzled by these texts. Within the texts, and in their relationship to traditions and history, we found an overwhelming concern with the past, an obsessive backwards glance, an acknowledgment of the 'presence' of the past even as there is a distancing from it. Yet, reading the texts against their exemplars, noting the influences, creating a textual genealogy in which the deep structures of the texts become obvious, only pointed to a deeper issue. People write about what interests and worries them. Discourses center on the perceived problems in a society. And in these texts it seemed to us that it was the legacy of previous generations and the very traditions of Rome that were in question.

Although some texts, perhaps most notably Lucan's epic, may have been oppositional in the sense that they would not have given pleasure to readers in the imperial court, the majority of our other texts operate without obvious political dichotomies. Instead of grand political posturing, manifestos for change, the rhetorical brilliance of political battle, we find an unease, a striving for meaning, and a discomfort with inherited meanings which drove the writers to produce texts dealing with disruptions to the political and cultural system in which they lived. These concerns, in some ways familiar to many modern readers of the works, would appear to reflect an ideological uncertainty at the heart of Roman society, a sense that the hegemonic narratives no longer work. Traditionally, one might explain this on aesthetic or political grounds, attributing it to a discontent resultant from the formation of monarchy and the subsequent loss of authority and autonomy faced by the Roman political and literary elite, or a familiar (for classicists at least) sense of living in a postclassical age, after the glorious and heroic moment of a particular society. Yet, the issue, for us, is not just that there is something wrong in Latin literature of the late first century; it is rather that what is wrong escapes aesthetic and state-political spheres to be refracted across the social world. The difference is that between a dispute within a coherent political system and a sense that the system itself is bankrupt. In the former case, a dispute over who is most suited to rule might be violent, carried through in recrimination, and might lead to accusations of perversion of the political-moral order (accusing opponents of being womanish or slavish, etc.), but such reversals actually reinforce the hegemonic culture (suggesting that the good need to be manly and noble). In the latter case, however, the hegemonic codes seem empty, incoherent, or artificial. We are here talking about the difference between opposition and alienation. If one borrows from Marxist terminology, though the parallel is not exact, it is as if individuals recognize that they operate with a false consciousness. But unlike the Marxist parallel, for the Romans there was no 'breakthrough' into true consciousness. But if there is no obvious answer to which the texts are moving, no obvious source of this alienation, and perhaps even no agreed set of issues (and in this sense the literature of our period differs radically from that of the Augustan period), then we are left with something of a critical *aporia,* in which we are doomed to regard these literary works as rereadings of issues in other, clearer, and better understood literatures.

Yet, engaging with this literature, tracing its playing with forms, experimenting with approaches and connections, opening the critical field in search of new approaches, we have come, uneasily, to another set of intertexts, texts drawn from outside the classical world. We have found in these texts resonances pointing not just backwards, but forwards too. The very discomfort of our classical texts seemed to us increasingly familiar as we persevered. Whilst looking at the bloody battles of Lucan's *Pharsalia* or the grotesque holocausts of Statius *Thebaid,* we were prompted to think of modern American and, indeed, Japanese cinema's obsession with extremes, with horror, with everyday stories of obsessive folk slaughtering each other in almost unimaginable ways. Reading the spectacle in Lucan, one is brought to face the extreme in art, an almost cinematic representation of what is beyond. In Tacitus, we can see a 'difficult' relationship with the Roman state and Roman imperialism, an uneasy alienation from the empire of which Tacitus was a part, a distaste for the corruption and violence which seems an almost unavoidable part of empire. In all these, we perceived resonances, uncomfortable ones, with current imperial entanglements and with the distance that so many feel from their political culture. And yet, Tacitus' distaste is tempered by the sense that there is no other option, no alternative to the imperial system, and that Roman 'globalization' meant that there was no escape from the net of power relations in which the ancient authors were inextricably bound. With Silius Italicus' reworking of the Second Punic War, an epic retelling of national triumph, we note a disconnection from the past, a similar disconnection from the myths and triumphs of the nation, as if this was a story that should mean something, but ultimately did not, but in that not-meaning there was ultimately a powerful reading of history and of contemporary Rome. Pliny's *Epistles* show us the astonishingly comfortable and secure world of a rich Italian senator, yet Pliny seems so anxious about his place in history, so concerned that in the end his life might seem marginal and insignificant. Lurking within this near-perfect world is an existential angst, a search for meaning that seems deferred or denied. Pliny's self-presentation reminded us of the great heroes of modernist literature, somehow longing for another stage, another age, or even a death that would at least free them from the search for meaning.[7] Death also transforms Statius' *Silvae.* These were poems

---

7. See, for instance, Thomas Mann's *Buddenbrooks,* a portrait of a commercial family after the

for the occasion, almost party-pieces, erudite, sometimes laudatory poems for the emperor and for Statius' friends; yet they are from time to time distorted into great cries of grief for the loss of children and, memorably, for Statius' father. In such moments the facility displayed in Statius' poetic art fails, and from the incoherent roar of emotion a different and powerful form of poetry takes hold, as if in death Statius' voice finds life, breaking from the mundanities of the everyday into a more immediate, raw emotionality. In this we find an echo of the contemporary obsession with the emotionally authentic, with reaching out to connect, with finding the emotional point which will make us feel alive and together.

As we found no comfort with these texts, so they seemed uncomfortable with themselves, and in their discomfort we found echoes of our modern discomfort with the world. The texts were speaking to us, but they were speaking a literary language that was familiar from another seemingly radically different context. With a very different rhetoric and in very different social and political circumstances, texts from almost two millennia ago began to make better sense to us, as dramatizations of concerns and issues familiar from modernity. In our first-century C.E. texts, we found writers distracted and often remote from the traditional ideologies; we found writers trying to interact with a cultural world that has only a weak hold on them. Similarly, many of the key modern texts we turned to reflected a thorough unease, a discontent with civilization, which, however, exists alongside a consciousness of the benefits of the modern. As modern texts searched for an ideology which would give meaning to people's lives, an idea onto which individuals could hold amidst the economic and social transformations that afflicted the world, so we see our ancients struggling to make sense of their world, and to find a way of living that avoids sublimation by an ideology to which they can no longer entirely adhere.

The resonances between the antique and the modern are, in themselves, both remarkable and intriguing. Arguably, all historical study is contemporary, not in the crude sense that we, as historians, simply import our concerns and perceptions from the modern to the old, but in the broader sense that we write about what interests us, and that interest is inevitably shaped by the modern world. The discourses of history, through which we understand and decide what is important (and unimportant) about the past, are firmly part of our present.[8] Still, as we set out to study the ancient corpus we kept discovering pathways into the modern laid out for us in ways that seemed unusually clear. We wanted to know why these texts spoke this

---

heroic age of mercantilism, a family that sought meaning in the bourgeois morality and society of their small German town, and singularly failed to find it.

8. Collingwood (1994) 154.

particular literary language and why they had such powerful resonances, and so we took the risk (theoretical and methodological) to invite additional conversationalists, texts from the modern era.

Reading the texts while looking forwards, rather than backwards, is in many ways a counterintuitive process, and certainly contrary to many of the traditional mantras of the disciplines in which we have trained. It requires a certain suspension of disbelief and of long-learnt critical facilities, but it seemed that in so doing we found ways of reading that were both new and more 'honest.' Such a claim to honesty may seem surprising in an academic work. But we all come to texts with a heterogeneous reading experience and with an interpretative network derived from numerous, disparate sources. We are eclectic readers. Academic discipline is so often about a denial of eclecticism, ruling out readings, denying different perspectives, and inevitably limiting or obfuscating intertexts. And yet, of course, we all know the impossibility of such a task: we cannot unread all that we have read, nor unmake the linguistic parameters in which we are educated, any more than one can objectively experience a text. Instead, we open up the contexts, experiment with lines of thought, and embrace the eclectic. There is inevitably a certain 'delicacy' in the method; it cannot work within a scientific model of historical or literary study, and we cannot, and do not, make any claim that our readings have a monopolistic relationship to the truth. But by shifting critical paradigms, it seems to us that new possibilities are made available. Our task is not to close down critical perspectives, or to deny those already employed in the field, but to explore readings from this alternative critical location. In what follows, we make no claim that our readings are comprehensive; rather we think of them as exploratory and experimental essays grouped round a theme. The value of our approach seems to us to be that as we produced our readings, shadows of other perspectives and other readings suggested different narratives that open the way to a multiplicity of critical perspectives, and it is in this multiplicity that we do justice to the rich complexity of the literature of this period.

In some ways, this approach means also a step away from the traditions of theory in classics and ancient history. For we are not here applying 'theory' to a set of texts or taking a set of texts as illustrative of 'theory.' If there is 'theory' here, our usage of it is also loose. We read in the modern texts echoes and refractions of the concerns in the antique texts, and in reading the modern and the antique alongside each other (not through each other) we find commonalities, what one might call 'homologies' or similar 'shapes' in the texts. It is these homologies that allow us to think of the texts in new ways. To follow this course, we encounter a diverse range of modern writers. In this juxtaposition we cannot hope to explore the classical influences in their work, nor to establish an interpretative infrastructure around each writer. We cannot produce a comprehensive, encyclopedic discussion of literary, philosophical, and political issues from the different periods. Instead, our approach is often impressionistic, and always personal. We trace a path through the texts in the hope that others will find interest and plausibility in the route that we follow (and might even want to explore it further). Good conversations do not aim to find neat solutions. But good conversations (much like the *auseinandersetzungen* of continental philosophy) actively seek, as well as respect, differences: differences obligate us to converse and attempt to understand all parties and their—and our—perspectives a little better. That is, after all, the great benefit, and the ethical obligation, of talking to strangers.

TALKING ABOUT THE SELF

In the chapters that follow, our explorations circle around issues of selfhood and identity. This problem of the 'self' has been much explored in Western philosophy and it is, therefore, possible to write a history of perceptions of the self. Christopher Gill argues in *Personality in Greek Epic, Tragedy, and Philosophy* that antiquity had an "objective-participant model" of identity, which is to be contrasted with the subjective-individualistic self of the post-Enlightenment period.[9] Gill suggests that "to be a person" in the fullest classical sense is to live an ethically sound life, which is achieved through reason. Human nature is associated with rationality, which is objective and capable of representation in public debate. The wise man must engage in the community, both to reinforce his rationality and to benefit the community by providing a model of goodness and rationalism free from passion or distress and invulnerable to contingent circumstances.[10] In a later work, looking at the self in Hellenistic and Roman philosophy, Gill contends that a new self emerges, a "structured self," but that "structured self is shaped by the objective-participant model."[11] This self is a model for a structured society in that it is both an exemplar and a micro-form of society. The regulated structure of the self ties the self to the community; the self is fashioned as the community is fashioned. The objective-participant model promotes a selfhood that is shared, and therefore substantial and even verifiable.[12]

---

9. Gill (1996) 1–28, esp. 11–12.
10. Gill (2006) xvii.
11. Gill (2006) 343.
12. Robert Kaster (2005) 132–40, similarly argues that the ancient wise man seeks to become the *homo integer* whose life is characterized by steadfastness and constraint, by respect for the com-

Although there are countervailing tendencies, this self would enjoy a security drawn from the ultimate participation in an affirming whole that promises, and generally manages, to deliver order.[13] To put it in Aristotelian terms, classical man is seen as a political animal, whereas modern man is seen as an individualistic animal.[14]

Yet, such perceptions beg a wider question: would the history of understandings of the self be a history of the self? To presume that one can write a history of the self would mean that the self is structured differently in different periods. If one assumes that the self is a historical constant, part of the nature of being human, then the self would have no history. The problem is fundamental to our understandings of the relationship between history and the present, and, for our purposes here, the relationship between modernity and antiquity. If we are divided from ancient ancestors by a radically different experience of what it is to be human, not only does this process of reading across periods that we outlined above seem more problematic, but antiquity itself is rendered remote from the concerns of the modern, worth little more than a fable.[15] In trying to resolve this question, we were drawn to engage with the works of Michel Foucault, who would seem the most direct and obvious precursor for our work.

When we started this project, one of our aims was to understand better the Foucauldian interpretation of sexuality in *Le Souci de Soi,* the third volume in his *History of Sexuality*.[16] Yet although the specter of that final work of the trilogy hangs over the various chapters that follow, and Foucault is one of our main philosophical and theoretical interlocutors, it is, however, a specter difficult to place within our text. It is a somehow invisible and intangible presence, and in the main chapters there are few references to Foucault. In part, this results from a number of alienating features of the Foucauldian text. The relative absence of notes, of obvious secondary interlocutors, gives

---

munity, and by an awareness that his emotional needs are 'scripted' and approved by the ideological requirements of the Roman elite (which they, thus, support).

13. For more on the socially mobilized self of Plato and Aristotle see Taylor (1989) 115–26.

14. For an overview into the qualities and characteristics of the modernist self, cf. Cascardi (1992) 1–15. Cartesian ontology elevated a rationality that depended exclusively on the subjective individual and constructed the world (and society) as an 'other,' which tended to oppose or even oppress the rational individual. The ethical good lay not in communal benefits, but in the freedom of the individual. Cf. here John Gray (1995) 5, who, writing on liberalism, posits that Plato's *Republic* "advances what is, in effect, an anti-liberal Utopia. For in it the claims of individuality go unprotected and indeed unrecognised. . . . Plato elaborated one of the most systematic and powerful attacks on the idea of human freedom to be found in intellectual history." See also Leonard (2005) 158–89 for views of Socrates and individuality, and bibliography there cited.

15. Our response to antique texts would also be limited, since we could not inhabit the selves represented in the texts in any direct way and to imagine that we could, would risk anachronism.

16. Foucault (1986).

Foucault's text a 'purity' in its representation of the antique material that obscures the contemporary intertexts and, for us at least, the agenda being addressed. Further, volumes II and III of the *History of Sexuality* came late in Foucault's long and productive writing life, and mark a radical change in subject matter, an engagement with a period in which he had shown almost no interest. The problems of understanding the text appear to us to be worsened by the critiques of 'mainstream' historians, which focus on Foucault's treatment of the 'archive' of primary material and his 'anachronism,' and yet these seemed to us (as we came at the work a generation after his first reception) the points at which he was most conventional, precisely in emphasizing historical difference, and in honoring the historical specificity of the text.[17] We felt that Foucault places too much emphasis on historical difference thus obstructing our understanding of the resonances between antiquity and modernity, and, ultimately, we found ourselves in retreat from him, towards a self less historically bounded.

We came to this position as we worked through Foucault's view of history. In *Discipline and Punish* Foucault writes: "I would like to write a history of this prison, with all the political investments of the body that it gathers together in its closed architecture. Why? Simply because I am interested in the past? No, if one means by that writing a history of the past in terms of the present. Yes, if one means writing the history of the present."[18] Foucault explicitly denies here that he is writing the past in terms of the present, that is, writing into the past the concerns of the present, but claims that his history is a history of the present.[19] In his conclusion, he argues that "the prison transformed the punitive procedure into a penitentiary technique; the carceral archipelago transported this technique from the penal institution to the entire social body."[20] Incarceration came to function through a continuity of institutions, from the almshouses, the workshops, the schools, hospitals, and, one could add, asylums. Surveillance and discipline became general and institutionalized.[21] Although the particular panopticon envisaged by Jeremy Bentham was never built, a plethora of panoptica came to

---

17. Foucault (2002) 27; see also Foucault (1984) 101–20, on authorship. For critiques see, among many others, Castel (1994), who accuses Foucault of a "presentism," that is, a writing of the concerns of the present into the past; Chartier (1994) and Cohen and Saller (1994), who discuss Foucault's use and abuse of the historical archive; and Ransom (1997) on politics in Foucault.

18. Foucault (1977) 30–1

19. One wonders at the missing third option in this sequence, which would be to write a history of the past in terms of the past. That this is not even presented (though it would seem to be the goal of 'mainstream' history) suggests that it considered by Foucault either unworkable or merely antiquarianism and a waste of everyone's time.

20. Foucault (1977) 298.

21. Foucault (1977) 299.

dominate society. It is clear that this is not just a historical observation. Finally, Foucault declares that, "I end a book which must serve as a historical background to various studies of the power of normalization and the formation of knowledge in modern society."[22] The book is thus historical, but is about the history of the ideas that allowed modern society to come into being and which continue to inflect modern society. It recognizes that the ideas that are currently in circulation have a prehistory, a genealogy, which leads to them forming part of the discourses by which we understand our society.[23]

The issue of the history of the present appears in a different form in "What is Enlightenment?"[24] Taking a minor text of Kant's, a contribution to a journal, Foucault argues that Kant's description of Enlightenment as a break with tradition is also in itself a fundamental break with tradition. For Kant, Enlightenment is the triumph of reason over tradition, not that unusual a definition, but Kant develops the argument to claim that reason has a limited sphere of operation: though public debate must indeed be governed by reason, however, society must govern private action (reversing the normal assumptions of freedom of private reason). Kant thus accepts that reason is social. But if the social is dominant in reason, then reason (and hence philosophy) must be specific to a culture. Kant argues that the Enlightenment produces a socially and historically specific reason and Foucault suggests that this acceptance of historically specific philosophy was groundbreaking.[25] In fact, it made possible the writing of a history of reason divided into particular sociocultural periods, and this perception was central to Foucault's own historical projects. It follows that ancient rationality is as historically grounded as modern post-Enlightenment reason, and—as rationality is so closely tied to ideas of the self—that we are historically determined beings. The uniqueness of the present would seem to argue against the value of historical study (at least the study of any period before the Enlightenment). At face value, this is also a very strong argument for excluding modern theory from much consideration of the past and for trying, as far as is possible, to understand the past in its own terms and would accord with Foucault's contempt for "writing a history of the past in terms of the present."

---

22. Foucault (1977) 308.

23. It hardly matters that Foucault may not have reached the ultimate origins of certain ideas, and that certain other ideas, such as Bentham's panopticon, may never have achieved an architectural reality: they remain part of the genealogy of ideas that make up the modern

24. Foucault (1984) 32–50.

25. The issue of origins surfaces here. It does not matter whether Kant truly was the first to express this view, but it does matter that this view of the Enlightenment was expressed and by an authority such as Kant.

Foucault's article shifts from Kant to Baudelaire, arguing that the latter also saw in modernity the radical break from the past. That break gave the individual a certain freedom, a freedom to construct a self and to self-fashion, imagining the self in a hyperreality of art. This is a "heroization of the present" but one which does not "liberate man from his own being; it compels him to face the task of producing himself."[26] The Enlightenment provides a certain ability (though not a freedom) to act in emphasizing the uniqueness of today and in breaking the connection to the past. But although Foucault leaves open the question of the principles by which the individual should self-fashion, his comments on self-fashioning in the hyperreality of art pushes us towards an aesthetics of the self.

This is a bewildering trajectory, taking us from Kant's revolutionary perception of the historically specific nature of philosophy and rationality to a 'dandyism' in the fashioning of the self. Yet, this approach presents us with certain problems: although Foucault presents us with a society soaked with power, denaturalizing social relations, he also offers us a discourse which is strangely denuded of politics.[27] Further, in the focus on aesthetics, he takes an issue which has notoriously been regarded as an 'absolute,' untouched by time and social perceptions, and puts it at the center of his project.[28] The emphasis on aesthetics allows, it seems to us, an element of agency into Foucault's theory, but in turning to aesthetic choice, to a dandification of the self, the theory would appear to offer a 'free-floating' self that can break (with certain unclear limitations) from conventions enmeshed in the social-political world.

It is this intellectual itinerary that we were able to trace within *Histoire de la sexualité II: L'usage des plaisirs* and *Histoire de la sexualité III: Le souci de soi*,[29] which both focus on Greco-Roman antiquity. This change in subject matter is an intriguing shift for a thinker who consistently maintained a desire to write engaged histories of the present and seems elsewhere convinced that the Enlightenment marked a watershed in history. Things

---

26. Foucault (1984) 42.

27. Any ability to remake oneself or the present is limited by a historical determination manifested through the discourses that underpin the structures of power that make the modern. Through genealogical analysis, one can undermine those discourses, but there can be no revolutionary escape. Freedom, in any meaningful sense, is illusory for Foucault and thus cannot be the appropriate goal of political action. Foucault's politics are limited and localized (showing similarities with Heidegger) and anti-foundational (echoing Nietzsche). See Foucault (1987) 2–4; Foucault (1984) 46; Foucault (1978) 88–89; Ransom (1997). See Milchman and Rosenberg (2003a) for a series of discussions of the relationship between Heidegger and Foucault.

28. However, the link between aesthetics and ethics, giving rise to a 'new aestheticism' is prominent in much postmodern philosophy. See, for example, Badiou (2001); Gibson (1999); Joughin and Malpas (2003).

29. Foucault (1985) and Foucault (1986).

started falling into place for us as we came to appreciate this turning to antiquity as an attack by Foucault on the status of 'classical' psychoanalytical texts, especially Freud and his atemporal new science based on a timeless, or almost timeless, perception of ancient Greek myth.[30] Oedipus was famously deployed by Freud in order to 'naturalize' certain elements of family structure; since Freud embedded the development of the psyche in the family, the influence of social structure (history) on the psyche has been obscured. It is this apolitical psychoanalysis that Deleuze and Guattari (1984) attacked in a volume for which Foucault wrote a laudatory introduction.[31] Whatever one thinks of the transhistorical nature of the psyche, it was through such routes that antiquity was written into contemporary culture, always an element within modern and postmodern discourses, always there, but simultaneously always remote and divided from us; timeless, but chronologically bound.[32] The problematic status of antiquity, an eternal outsider, but always a privileged presence, means that it is available as an alternative subject position from which to explore the alien character of modernity. As Paul Allen Miller argues, "History from the poststructuralist point of view . . . is never simply an allegory of the present, in its re-presentation, but always its intimate other, the opaque kernel that lies at its heart and operates in its dispersion."[33] Antiquity is thus part of the discourse of the modern, and in writing about

---

30. For the importance of archaeology as a motif in Freudian thought, see Armstrong 2005.

31. Foucault's introduction to Deleuze and Guattari's *Anti-Oedipus* in 1972 aligned him with their anti-classical, anti-Freudian project. Deleuze and Guattari (1984) attacked the universalism that comes in placing Oedipus at the center of psychoanalysis and pour scorn on Freud's 'discovery' of Oedipus, seeing it as a perverse attempt to force psychoanalysis into the framework of Goethian classical education (p. 55–56). Oedipus allows the modern self to pose in classical clothing and establish itself as a transhistorical, natural construct. Instead, Deleuze and Guattari would see the self as produced, and sex not an enactment of the Oedipal dilemma, but "the fantastic theatre of Nature and Production" (49). For Deleuze and Guattari, like all objects of production the self is capable of being subject to Marxist critique. Foucault's engagement with psychoanalysis was a central element in his intellectual activity. *Folie et déraison. Histoire de la folie à l'âge classique* was published as early as 1961 and his first published work, *Maladie mentale et personnalité*, came out in 1954. In *The History of Sexuality I*, he concludes that the "history of the development of sexuality . . . can serve as an archaeology of psychoanalysis" (Foucault [1978] 130 and see also Toews [1994]). Myth also plays an important part in structuralist anthropology, which could be similarly subjected to Foucauldian critique. See Leonard (2005) 54–56.

32. See Armstrong (2005), who argues that the Freudian deployment of the archaeological metaphor led to an uncovering of classical strata within the psyche. See Leonard (2005) and Miller (2007) for extensive discussions of the twentieth-century French intellectual engagement with the classical world. It is possible to argue that the classicism detected within the Freudian psyche derives in large part from the *habitus* out of which psychoanalysis emerged. Lacan's suggestion (1977) 310, that the loss of the sense of tragedy would undermine the Oedipal self (quoted in Armstrong [2005] 5) would seem to suggest that the classical elements of the psyche were learnt. Armstrong's use of the biographical and his critique of Freudian 'suggestion' in his analysis (esp. 187–89) suggest that Freud's psychology is at the center of Freudian psychology and its classical emphasis.

33. Miller (2007) 17

the self in antiquity, Foucault is also writing a history of the present. And yet, Foucault argues that the selves (and sexuality) of the classical period were fundamentally different from their modern equivalents, constructed as they were around different types of discourse, thus challenging the atemporality of the self.[34] Freud is thus defeated in the heartland of his theory, antiquity, but the Foucauldian project is not just about demolishing the Freudian science, since *Le souci de soi* sees in Roman treatments precisely the aestheticization of the self that he calls for in "What is Enlightenment?" What we are left with is an uneasy sense that the resonances between antiquity and modernity are nonfoundational charades, an echoing of the classical past in modern *Kultur*, that works in large part because there is no foundational psyche and the foundational classicizing discourses produced the very psyche that was emerging through analysis.

This advocacy of an ancient mode of constructing the self complicates our understanding of Foucault's relationship to the classical past and in particular the issue of historical psychology. The psychology of Foucault is not a psychology beyond time. Psychology reflects the society in which the individuals live. And yet the classics are part of the genealogy of the modern, as an aesthetic mode, thus rendering resonances between contemporary and classical thought less surprising. Perversely, the very attempt to create the 'voice from outside' which would allow critique of the modern builds that voice into the system of discourses of (post)modernity. Yet more perversely, the positioning of the classical outside modernity, but as a high-status aesthetic opposed to the modern, allows an Olympian detachment from the modern to be built into modernity. But if the classical self does not survive into modernity through a genealogy of knowledge, Foucault offers it survival through analogy, and, we may add, through reinvention. By proposing a self which is chosen, the late Foucault offers an opportunity for the individual to turn to the classical aesthetics, and thus partially escape the constraints of the institutions of modernity on whose ability to shape the self he had written so powerfully. Yet, he would seem not to acknowledge that this stance aligns him with the Freudian position from which he was so obviously distancing himself.

In seeing the production of the self embedded in a series of discourses, Foucault tends to create flexibility and an uncertainty (as well as a considerable and almost worrying scope for agency) that has considerable appeal, both in methodological terms and in explaining resonances between ancient and modern texts. If in Foucaldian psychology there is very little beyond the

---

34. There is considerable doubt as to whether Freud meant his self to be atemporal. See Armstrong (2005) *passim*, but esp. 131–34 and the critique of Foucault therein.

text, all we have as classical scholars *are* the texts, the discourses in which the self was reflected and constructed (or scripted).[35] As far as we can see, there is a loss of confidence in our Roman scripts, a sense that they might, after all, be just scripts of identity devoid of any claim to authenticity, as if our authors had been reading Foucault. And yet, this is a hard doctrine. For if we care for our selves, build our selves through an assumption of roles, we are, it seems, obliged to make the proper ethical choices in constructing that self; and we are further obliged to face existential questions: is this what there is? What, if anything, exists beyond the discourses? We read Foucault in an uneasy tension with Sartre and Nietzsche, conscious of the inauthenticity behind any scripts of identity and sensing that inauthenticity opens the path to nihilism, conscious also of nihilism as a source of freedom, but also of destruction and alienation.[36]

In embedding the self in discourses, Foucault diminishes the importance of embodiment, a criticism that has also been leveled at Sartre.[37] The choices open to a male, powerful agent may be rather different from those available to women or to the children who appear as love-objects within classical sexualities. We see the body as indeed mapped by discourses, (de)sexualised, normalized, aestheticized, but also as a site on which biology and external powers work to limit the ability of the individual to shape her own aesthetics of sexuality. The very physicality and mortality of the body, its pains, its chemistry, its growth and decay, can (and must) be written into the discourses, since for discourses to have plausibility, they must account for the reality of the body. This is a fundamental limitation, for Man is not just a political animal, but is a being unto death, and as a being unto death we cannot forever relive our lives with different choices, escape our physicality and social conventions, and endlessly reinvent *personae* and associated histories. Death, or rather our limited physicalities, forces accommodations and requires us to bring together the strands of discourse that surround our persons to create a coherent personality, existing in time, space, and body. Death and the body take us also beyond discourses—beyond Foucault—and force us to return to the issue of what, if anything, is beyond. It is in this 'beyond' that we find the classics returning to psychoanalysis.

---

35. Archaeology would not appear to be useful in resolving the type of questions we are considering here.

36. See here Megill (1985). Famously, for Sartre the operation of analysis which turned the self into an object was an act of 'bad faith' which rendered the encounter with the other traumatic. Yet, since the self was not bound by the scripts of identity, freedom, equally traumatic as it might be, was ultimate. See Sartre (1958), especially p. 90; also 62–67.

37. See, e.g. Reynolds (2006) 69 and bibliography there cited.

TRACING THE COMPLEX relationship of Lacan to the classical canon, Miller suggests that Lacan found in Sophocles' *Antigone* a moment of beauty which transcends history: "Beauty for Lacan represents the perfect moment between life and death, a moment both articulated by and beyond time and desire, beyond any recognizable object. For Lacan, . . . the search for ethics leads above all to an aesthetics of existence, to the search for the beautiful life."[38] In her refusal to bow to the law of the city, in her drive to surpass social conventions and to become someone 'beyond' in her self-devotion, Antigone becomes the sublime individual, the very essence of beauty. In her extremity, Antigone embraces what Lacan names the Real.

At the heart of Lacanian analysis are three aspects of the self (the Imaginary, the Symbolic, and the Real).[39] These can be understood as dimensions, orders, or registers. As dimensions, they represent elements of selfhood which are indivisible. The dimensions are essential to the composition of the self as length, depth, and width are essential to an object. The self can be represented or felt in its three registers. The self is thus unitary, in the sense that it is one being, but tridimensional. The Imaginary is an 'identification' which occurs in infant development at about six months, in the "mirror stage," when an infant comes to recognize himself in a mirror and thus forms an 'identification,' and an ego "which will always remain irreducible for the individual alone."[40] The Symbolic gives a social meaning to the individual and establishes the individual in the network of social codes.[41] The third element of the triad is the Real.[42] The Real is made manifest in that

---

38. Miller (2007) 84.
39. Lacanian thought is famously opaque and understanding Lacan is not helped by the peculiar publication of his teachings. For a lucid introduction of the three Lacanian Orders, as well as significant concepts in Lacan's thought such as Lack, see Benvenuto and Kennedy (1986); Žižek (1991); Stavrakakis (1996).
40. Lacan (1977) 2. At this moment, the infant undergoes "the transformation that takes place in the subject when he assumes an image." The world of images is real since the images exist in the world and are reflections of reality. It is thus 'Imaginary' in its derivation from the 'imago,' but this Imaginary is a reflection of reality for the particular individual. As Lacan writes, this "state situates the agency of the ego, before its social determination, in a fictional direction, which will always remain irreducible for the individual alone." Yet, the Imaginary is a dimension of frustration since that 'I' is forever different, a reflection that works in opposite ways which correspond to the 'I' but are alienated from it. The Imaginary is thus an Ideal 'I,' which the individual cannot match. Further, the mirror is a metaphor and there is a multiplicity of mirrors alongside the literal ones. Other individuals, notably the mother, are also mirrors. For a coherent explanation of the Imaginary, see also Janan (1994) 18–19.
41. Lacan (1981) 20–28. The Symbolic requires a recognition of difference from the other, but is also constituted on the basis of a 'lack.' The subject is constituted in signifiers that provide a social location for the individual. And yet the individual is never just her Symbolic aspect, never just a combination of signifiers, and it is the failure of the Symbolic Order to adequately affirm an identity which constitutes its fundamental lack.
42. See Janan (1994) 17–18.

which is beyond description and social codes. For instance, in the Lacanian unconscious, dreams are comprehensible through the Symbolic order; they can be understood as streams of signifiers (and thus interpreted, but because the dream takes the form it does (it exists as a dream), those signifiers always exist in a dimension that is beyond the symbolic, a dimension in which the trauma is preserved and not codified.[43] That Real is beyond language and thus beyond analysis. It can be the sublime, the beautiful, or the terrible and the psychotic. It exists beyond convention and can force the individual to break free from the codes of society; but beyond those codes, beyond social location, there is terror and loneliness, a place of no sense, possibly also a place of no self, and of trauma and death.[44]

In the chapters that follow we regularly invoke the Lacanian model, in large part because its tridimensional form offers a means of negotiating the relationship between self and society which is more complex and nuanced; allows space for that which appears beyond discourses, for the expressions of terror and horror that we find in our sources; and breaks free from the bipolarities of self and society. Further, the Lacanian self is always in creative tension between the three dimensions. Whereas the social may make itself felt primarily within the Symbolic, the Real can render the relationship with society tense and shifting. Also, the 'lack' or the incompleteness in identifications in the Symbolic and Imaginary allows an energy to be manifested in social relations that always has the potential to disrupt, create friction, and encourage the manipulation or rejection of social codes. Dissatisfaction in the Symbolic and Imaginary encourages experimentation.[45] For Lacan the sense of unredeemable inadequacy in the core of selfhood is a trigger for the imagination in which the self becomes realized.[46]

This understanding of the self in which there is continuous dissatisfaction, continuous and integral lack, combines a transhistorical understanding (these elements are not inflected by history and would seem to be fundamental to the social human) and historical particularity since the self is inevitably affected by society, and one assumes that this affect will vary according to the particular arrangements of a society. It is also an understanding which generates a considerable energy in society, since society must be conceptualized as a sea of agents engaged in a competitive search for roles, trying and inevitably failing to reconcile their self-image with the social world, and

---

43. See Lacan (1981) 53–61.
44. In representing the human as a being-unto-death, we shall argue that it is in this Real that the human resides. Yet, in existing most powerfully in the Real (in the Reality of dreams for instance), there is a sense of life being in trauma, and madness. It is this paradox that emerges very powerfully in our texts.
45. Stavrakakis (1999) 13–39 describes this continuous process of re-identification.
46. Lacan (1977) 8–29.

hence being drawn into a tense relationship with that world. We will use the phrase 'symbolic economy' to describe this process of competitive engagement with the social world, of deals and exchanges, that strive to establish a relative stability.

The products of this symbolic economy are the discourses that in turn inflect the Symbolic order. But the 'lack' at the heart of the Symbolic means that the discourses never quite sit comfortably with us, are continuously disputed, and always in 'bad faith.' It seems to us that 'totalizing discourses,' discourses which seek to explain or exert influence over everything, are likely to most obviously expose this 'lack,' and more directly lead to alienation, since in symbolic economies in which there is significant debate, or significant friction between the various elements, it seems likely that alternate discourses might provide different scripts that would attract the disaffected.

And yet, in a paradoxical mode constituent of modernity, it seems to us that the emergence of new ways of behaving and living, which effectively means the creation of new scripts, is rendered insignificant since the modern symbolic economy renders all such variance part of its modernity, located within its grand scheme of knowledge, history, and place. Thus, the plurality of the modern tends to mean that all scripts are inauthentic, all part of a wider schema, and all in some way marginal. The modern is thus experienced by each and all of us in a desultory and marginalized fashion.[47] Thus the Foucauldian aesthetic choice becomes no choice, since all choice is compressed within modernity's monopolistic ideology.[48] Resistance at a psychological level may be possible, but at a political level it is not. At a psychological level that resistance would ultimately be alienation (even psychosis). In this observation, we are left in a quandary, and one that is in many ways particular to our modern experience. Yet, although the Romans worked down very different routes, it seems to us (as we will attempt to demonstrate in the following chapters) that our Roman characters are also marginalized, sometimes alienated, and in search of authenticity, adrift in a symbolic economy in which there was no safe or comfortable port.

The symbolic economy, with all its competing agents, has a certain delicacy in relation to the Real, which always threatens (and manages) to infiltrate, and the universal 'lack' in the integration of individuals into social systems renders all systems potentially unstable. Societies instinctively try to accommodate the Real and build it into their cultures, protecting themselves from fragmentation in the face of trauma. Discourses are thus the histori-

---

47. See Žižek (2000) 209 on the 'nonsubstantial' experience of modernity.
48. For Adorno and Horkheimer (1979), Western reason from Homer to fascism is monopolistic, absorbing all oppositions within its dialectic. Benhabib (1994) argues that redemption, specifically in memory, can exist only outside the historical continuum.

cally contingent means by which we ritualize the emergence of the Real so that it seems less dangerous, less disruptive. But what if the discourses fail? The power of discourses lies in their ability to generate commitment from individuals. People have to believe in the truth of their particular Symbolic Order, but if they do not, truth is drained from the symbolic. In these circumstances, what is left but to turn away from the Symbolic (as far as this is possible) and towards the Imaginary and the Real?

The Lacanian perspective creates a problem for political theorists. It follows from the pervasive 'lack' at the core of the social self, that a harmonious society can only be achieved by an immense act of power which has suppressed all individuals and forced them to accept their social roles. The harmonious society is thus like a great ocean rendered calm by a divine act, while underneath the surface great currents and whirlpools create a maelstrom of activity. Utopianism (whether liberal, Platonic, or of any other kind) is illusory and oppressive, reducing that individual friction and attempting to subsume the individual.[49] A true Utopia would, then, be not frictionless, a community of the wise in consensus, but always dysfunctional, always (in the phraseology of Jean-Luc Nancy) "inoperable."[50] Nancy's inoperable Utopia would consist not of individuals, but of singularities.

> Individuation detaches closed off entities from a formless ground—whereas only communication, contagion, or communion constitute the being of individuals. But singularity does not proceed from such a detaching of clear forms or figures. . . . Singularity perhaps does not *proceed* from anything. It is not a work resulting from an operation. [Singularity can only be felt] with the contact of the skin (or the heart) of another singular being . . . always *other*, always shared, always exposed.[51]

Nancy's singularities exist in common boundaries with other singularities. As long as singularities are able to maintain uniqueness in intimate contact, they can retain their status as singularities, whereas individuals exist in separation. A smooth amalgamation of individuals into a community with politicized relationships risks the loss of autonomy inherent in notions such as citizenship, and thus Nancy insists on the difference between 'being-

---

49. Stavrakakis (1999) 74 argues that the impossibility of harmony turns politics into an endless play of desire and frustration, "an unending circular play between possibility and impossibility, between construction and destruction, representation and failure, articulation and dislocation, reality and the real, politics and the political."

50. Nancy (1991) argues that a live community is unsettled, unsettling, questioning, in which the myths of a normally lost community have oppressive force. For other ways of politicizing Lacanian thought, see e.g. Žižek (2000); Laclau and Zak (1994).

51. Nancy (1991) 27–28.

in-common' and 'common-being.' Individuals can only achieve something approaching communality and freedom in a society in which difference is preserved. The most ethical political task is to maintain that measure of chaos so that community can be built on communication, but not on consensus; on difference, not on similitude. We find in his text an attempt to build a community beyond norms. In so doing, Nancy appears to us to develop a model of community which is based not in the communalities of discourse, but in something more immediate, and more primal, in the touch of singularities, skin on skin. Nancy's politics seem to us to be an attempt to imagine a polity in a deliberately fragmentary symbolic economy, in which relationships are based on nondiscursive elements, a politics of authenticity, a politics of the Real embodied in the touch. Whether this new form of politics is in any way practical is almost beyond the point; it is the urge for an alternative kind of politics prompted by the inadequacies of the symbolic economy that is significant, an urge that can fuel extremism, fundamentalism, but also more humane forms of political relationship. And repeatedly within our Roman writers, amidst the gloom and failure, the blood and violence, we read redemptive moments in which the politics of the personal seems almost possible.

It seems to us, then, that a Lacanian perspective raises fundamental problems for the Foucauldian project. We can certainly write a history of conceptions of the self, but that would be a very different project from the history of the self. The discourses of the self, the scripts, do indeed offer versions of a self to the symbolic economy but they far from exhaust it. If we were to take a radical position on the Foucauldian argument, as we understand it, we would argue that Foucault denies that which exists beyond the text, beyond the discourse, beyond the episteme, and in so doing emphasizes the 'constructed' nature of the human. It is this that allows him the radical freedom of choice in the care of the self, but it is also a road that takes us close to a nonfoundational nihilism and, in its disregard of the body, of the being-unto-death, and of the multidimensional, nondiscursive elements of the human experience, is ultimately dehumanizing. Foucault draws (relatively) hard lines between past and present, between antiquity and the modern, seeing only the slightest relationship between the humans of the Roman world and his contemporaries. Our response is to insist on the resonances between modernity and antiquity (while honoring the differences) and to find the human and humane in the spaces between the closed epistemes, and in so doing fracture those enclosures.

We look to antiquity not because it is part of the genealogy of the modern (or the postmodern). We do not believe that the modern is derived in any real and meaningful sense from the thought of late first-century writers.

We do not trace a genealogy from Lucan, for instance, to the postmoderns. For us, the importance of this period of history lies in analogy, not genealogy. Antiquity is a 'voice from outside' that resonates deep inside the body of modernity. We are interested in a genuine encounter, a meeting of texts and of readings. We see the analogy lying in precisely the incipient discontent, in a pronounced reluctance, or inability, to engage in the discourses of the social order, either hegemonic or oppositional, and in an eager search for meaning that takes the individuals beyond society and social ideologies. What we read in the Roman texts is a struggle to accommodate a lack in the symbolic economy, a struggle to accommodate a 'beyond' and still retain humane values. The Roman texts do not seem to us to be engaged in an obsessive desire to reconcile the social world, forever seeking to close the sutures of a wounded society, but to be exploring those ruptures and their possibilities. And instead of seeing in those ruptures the revolutionary moment, in which past and place are suspended, social order fails, and the self is suddenly free with all the disturbing implications of that freedom, the Roman texts offer us a less polarized version of the world and the self in the world.[52] In spite of all, authenticity and redemption lurk within our texts.[53] In reading across periods, we honor the historical differences between the two societies; but we take the risk of connecting, of recognizing a shared humanity faced with similar problems, of asserting that we are not forever separated by language and culture, by the differences of *habitus*. Our history is not antiquarianism, genealogy, or archaeology, but a history of the past for the present.

PROBLEMS AND METHODS

Our method throughout the following chapters is to follow threads. We start with an ancient text in which we find a problem, something that seems not to 'fit.' We then follow where that thread leads, through further ancient texts and into modern texts. Juxtaposing ancient and modern we found ourselves aligning texts of different periods and genres, using them as

---

52. Our Roman individuals find it almost impossible to sever their ties from the world, their place and time, which would seem to pre-echo Heideggerian thought. See Hammer (2008) for a discussion of Roman thought as 'being in the world.' See Mitchell (2001) for an extended discussion of Heidegger's theories of the self.

53. In a Heideggerian manner, the ripples of social and political change always reach the individual; but whereas Heidegger's politics confront us with a world slipping beyond control, our often bleak Roman narratives provide us with individuals who seem able to renegotiate their relationship to the community in the most difficult circumstances (e.g. Lucan's Pompey and Statius' Polynices). See Megill (1985) and Safranski (1998).

markers in a labyrinthine journey of exploration of the self, modern as well as ancient. For that exploration, we needed classical texts with 'loose ends' that revealed intersections from which we could turn in different directions. We veered away from polemic (the wild anger of Juvenal's narrator), and the jeweled epigram (Martial), and the systematic biographies (Suetonius). The Greek texts of the period also seemed to belong to a somewhat different story. Almost inevitably, Greek authors appear to have been less exercised by Rome's Republican traditions; one step further remote from the seat of empire and political power, the Greeks constructed their relationship to the barbarians in different ways. Unexpectedly, we found that the Greeks had significantly different concerns that could not be incorporated into our narrative. As we followed the threads, other texts, important texts, slipped away; they were not necessarily part of a different story, just lay along a different path towards a similar goal. To have followed all the possible paths and have mapped out the labyrinth would have risked losing the reader in a journey that is already complex enough.

We found our path through the epics of foundation (Lucan, *Pharsalia;* Silius Italicus, *Punica*), epics that dealt explicitly or implicitly with the Virgilian legacy; in the petty and realistic stories of family and friends, love and sorrow (Statius, *Silvae;* Pliny, *Epistulae*); through the complexities and ironies of Tacitus; and in the fantasy of destruction, the anti-foundational epic of Statius' *Thebaid*. In our readings, we try to show loyalty to the texts as events, with their capacity to surprise and shock. We are interested in where they exhibit problems, where they invite debates on identity.

Our aim is not to provide elaborate maps of the formal(istic) relationship between any two texts and we only infrequently depend on direct verbal echoes between texts. There is no dearth of such studies.[54] Ganiban's recent book-length study on the *Thebaid* takes the intertextual endeavor to a logical conclusion:

> Interpretation of the *Thebaid* is thus centrally concerned with the epic's engagement with the *Aeneid,* yet there is no consensus on what that engagement means. It is my contention that the need to understand the *Thebaid* as a reflection (either positive or negative) of Domitian detracts from a more fundamental dialogue. There is a significant political component to the *Thebaid*. It lies, however, not in the immediate context of Statius' irretrievable historical attitude toward Domitian and the Flavians, but in the

---

54. The case of the *Thebaid* is particularly prominent in this respect. See e.g. Hill (1990); Hershkowitz (1997); Pollmann (2001); Lovatt (1999) and (2005); Ganiban (2007) all offering nuanced suggestions on the significance of the intertextual resonances between Statius and previous texts, especially the *Aeneid*.

Thebaid's interaction with the presentation of kingship and the Principate in the heart of the *Aeneid*.[55]

Through such cross-readings, we are encouraged to looking 'back' towards an origin. The immediate meaning of the text becomes a cipher for a more fundamental, and displaced, meaning that is lodged somewhere in the past. In Ganiban's own concluding words: "[in its moral and political reinterpretation of the *Aeneid*, the *Thebaid*] offers one of the richest and more sustained readings of Virgil's epic."[56] And yet, when looking to shift the paradigms within which our ancient texts could be seen to function and convey meaning, one needs to look beyond this formal intertextual pursuit of the past. Further, we have not sought to create a great metanarrative for the literature of the period in which all texts find their intertexts and meanings, but tried to read the texts for their evident meanings, with due account for their literary allusions, their ironies and the generic and literary conventions of the period.

In this volume we read across genres. One could argue that in so doing we damage the integrity of the 'archives.' One text belongs to an archive marked "philosophers," another to "epic poets," another to "historians"; but there seems little reason why we should not disrupt the neat separation of ideas into discrete locales of knowledge. Although it seems to us overwhelmingly probable that Tacitus, for example, knew the text of Lucan, it is no part of our case to prove that Tacitus was a reader of epic poetry; what matters for us is that both (along with many others) were thinking about the historical legacy of the Republic. Once an idea is given voice and 'irrupts' into the world, its place within an archive seems of marginal importance.[57] The text 'lives' at the moment of its irruption, not as a note in the biographical history of the author, or a stage in the longer history of "literature."[58] Our interest is thus in problematics, and our method is focused on exposing those problems and trace the lines of thought that lie behind those problematics.[59] We thus

---

55. Ganiban (2007) 6.
56. Ganiban (2007) 232.
57. Archives are 'unnatural' compilations of material and always incomplete. Only a small proportion of the discourse of any period comes down to us and it is equally misguided to believe that what we have is a random representation of the thought of any period.
58. Reading the text against the author becomes problematic since it robs the text of its autonomy and gives an improper *a priori* status to the author as the ultimate and rational interpreter and source of texts. The author is not unimportant, acting as a type of marker for the text, and is thus part of the text and its reading, but the text is what is important. See Foucault (2002) 27 and Foucault (1984) 101–20, on authorship.
59. The suggestion that other texts will have other ideas which will confound the analysis is at sea. Emphasizing a particular problem does not means that there are no other problems circulating at the same time: the problem does not go away simply because one has not looked at every text from a period or archive or author.

make no attempt at completeness in our analysis. We have chosen texts that seemed germane to our purpose, and which spoke to us and seemed to be speaking to each other. These texts are themselves incomplete; they are contributions to a discourse, or even a series of discourses, and are thus inevitably in conversation with other texts, some extant, some lost. We are looking for cracks in the discourses, for problems and disagreements, and for the efforts to contain their destructive potential.

We have organized our examination into five essays. These are five 'scenes' or locales in which we can examine the operation and conception of the self. The book creates a type of topography of the self. In chapter 2, we look at moments when the self is in isolation. Our texts find these moments dangerous and disruptive, leading to horror and breeding selves which are amoral and nihilistic. In chapter 3 we find selves struggling with emotions often understood through philosophical lenses and regarded with suspicion. Our characters find that emotions can lead them out of isolation, either from a community or a deeper isolation of the self, and help them build new bonds in society. We follow this line into chapter 4, seeing how individuals invest in the conjugal relationship and how that relationship becomes a point of negotiation between the public and the private, between the individual and society, thus moving our focus from the space of the individual to the bedroom and to the house. In the penultimate chapter, chapter 5, we shift from space to time, looking at the way the discourses of selfhood were embedded in memory and a historical understanding; we see how the historical narratives explore the past as a place of nostalgia and resistance which individuals could use to distance themselves from the social codes of their contemporary world. Finally, in chapter 6, we consider the Roman individual in the world empire, an empire so vast and changing that narratives of local identity made limited sense.

There is an obvious progression in these five scenes, but that progression is not causal: we do not locate the cause of the 'crisis' in Roman identity narratives in politics or empire, any more than one could locate a single cause for the 'crisis' of modernity. In not giving primacy to the political games played around, on behalf of, and by, the emperor, we avoid having to categorize texts as for or against the regime, for or against the particular emperor, and thus allow the diversity of themes in the texts their full scope.[60] Social

---

60. This differentiates our approach from, for instance, Alain Gowing's (2005) *Empire and Memory*. Gowing's subtle approach exposes the conflicts within the understanding of history in the early imperial period, but when he comes to explain why these conflicts arose, he is trapped within the high politics of political postures and agendas. For instance, one can compare our treatment of Lucan on the Republican memory, and especially Caesar at Troy (see p. 168–69), with that of Gowing. Gowing concludes his discussion with the suggestion that "Lucan's concern with memory . . . looks rather . . . like an attempt to counter a political agenda that sought to devalue

power operated in many different spheres, people lived in many different social locales, and state-level politics is only a particular part of the matrix of political power and political culture.[61]

As reflected in our choice of conversationalists (and bibliography), we have consciously tried to shift the critical paradigm and open pathways of conversation with texts and genres from an altogether different era that spoke to us as classical scholars of the early twenty-first century. We believe that, through this shift in the critical paradigm, we have enabled further voices to emerge from the ancient texts, while also providing our modern interlocutors with a new perspective from which they can be tested and judged. The scenes illustrated in our book are connected by the search for a home, for a place in which the individual could be content, be it in isolation, in the conjugal relationship, in the state or in the past. They are connected by a restlessness and a sense of there being a problem, not the devastating problems of civil war, but the malaise of a society that has lost its certainties. It is that sense of malaise (and the ways the Romans and the moderns tried/try to think themselves out of it) that is the subject of this book.

---

the past" (100), whereas we argue that Lucan problematizes the relationship between Romans and the Roman tradition and thereby introduces uncertainty into a fundamental element around which Roman identity was constructed. We have no need to posit a historiographical-political school against which Lucan is writing. Ambivalence is a notable feature of imperial literature when it comes to politics. Our approach means that we do not have to reduce that ambivalence or produce a 'real' political meaning lurking within the text.

61. Albeit one that has tended to receive the lion's share in critical scholarship. For example, see recently Boyle and Dominik (2003): a rich volume of essays on culture in Flavian Rome with the emperor as the center point of the jigsaw, a focus painstakingly established in an extensive introduction by Boyle (2003) 1–67.

2

Home Alone

TERROR AND POWER

HOME ALONE

In his account of the year of four emperors in Rome, when we are approaching the final acts of the civil conflict, Tacitus takes us with Vitellius, the defeated emperor, on a last journey from his private residence to the imperial palace, a journey that reverses his surprising political trajectory. But on entering the palace, he finds it

> vastum desertumque, dilapsis etiam infimis servitiorum aut occursum eius declinantibus. terret solitudo et tacentes loci; temptat clausa, inhorrescit vacuis; fessusque misero errore et pudenda latebra semet occultans ab Iulio Placido tribuno cohortis protrahitur.
>
> empty and deserted, for even the lowest of the slaves had slipped away or avoided meeting him. He was terrified by the solitude and the quietness of the place. He tried closed doors. He shivered at the emptiness. Exhausted by his wanderings, and hiding himself in a shameful corner, he was dragged out by Iulius Placidus, tribune of the cohort. Tac., *Hist.* III 85

There is a profound emptiness here and a contrast, implied and understood, with the normal life of the emperor. Suetonius tells a similar story of Nero. Unable to persuade the praetorian guard to flee Italy with him, he returned to the palace and slept. He woke near midnight to find his guard gone. He, too, wandered the palace in search of his friends and servants, and finding none, cried "Ergo ego . . . nec amicum habeo nec inimicum?" (So, do I have neither friend nor foe?), before running from the palace in search of the Tiber and a theatrical watery suicide (Suet., *Nero,* 47.3).

The Emperor always had a crowd following him: attendants, slaves, friends. They begged favors, performed his wishes, advised him, informed him. The same could likewise be said of other powerful Roman aristocrats. The busy-ness of the aristocrat was the measure of his political position. Positioned at the center of a political and social theatre, his standing was reflected in the size of the crowds, and in the social standing of those who formed the crowds. An emperor invariably lived "on-stage." Vespasian received his first visitors as he woke in the early morning, and, on rising and dressing, would then meet a host of visitors who had come to pay him the early morning honor of the *salutatio* (Suet. *Vesp.* 21).[1] From that point onwards, the worthy emperor commanded political attention. He made himself accessible to senators and was surrounded by luminaries such as consuls, former consuls, generals, and other members of the elite. Such men were on hand to offer advice as the emperor dealt with the business of the day, but would also be there at night, when he dined and entertained, and in the morning when he woke. In contrast, our sources depict Claudius surrounded by his freedmen and wives, and Nero by actors, poets, and sexual partners, and by more sinister figures too. Philo records Gaius Caligula receiving the Jewish ambassadors when engaged in the seemingly equally important activity of arranging for the redecoration of one of his palaces. The ambassadors and (presumably) those in charge of the reordering of the palaces followed the emperor through the various rooms of the palace, engaging in intermittent debate about the situation in Alexandria, Jewish religious practices, and fixtures and fittings (Philo, *Legatio ad Gaium* 349–67). All around there was a crowd anxious to win his favor, eager to show their support, and pleased to show their approval of his witticisms. This crowd recorded the emperor's sayings and doings, rethinking his thoughts in search of his desires, and swamping the court with gossip.

This was not just a characteristic of the imperial court. Sejanus, Tiberius' all-powerful praetorian prefect, held morning *salutationes* whose popularity measured to perfection his political rise and subsequent fall.[2] Seneca, too,

---

1. The *salutatio*, the morning greeting, was a Roman social custom by which the lesser men would gather at an early hour to greet a great man in his house and offer service. The great man might then respond with gifts, invitations, or other benefactions.

2. At the very height of Sejanus' power, and just before his fall, there were conflicts before the doors of his house as people competed to get in to see the man who seemed to be emperor (Cassius Dio, LVIII 5.1–2). The crowds were so great that a couch collapsed under the weight of the audience (Cassius Dio, LVIII 5.5). As the messages from Tiberius became mixed, the people shunned Sejanus (Cassius Dio, LVIII 9.1).

on receiving permission from Nero to retire, stopped receiving the great numbers who had flocked to greet and serve him, though, in his case, the withdrawal of the crowds was willed by the philosopher-politician.[3] The crowd was a central element in the design of Roman life, monumentalized in domestic architecture.[4] The Roman was ideally in the midst of the crowd or receiving the crowd; he attended or was attended. Public and private dissolved in this convivial culture; the modern (equally idealized) boundaries are difficult to map onto Roman social consciousness.

The symbolism of Nero and Vitellius' wanderings through the palace is at one level easy to read: the disappearance of the crowd represented political failure.[5] There is an ironic contrast between the fawning adulation and the now empty corridors of power. But there is more drama here. We are in the realm of the historical novel. We are with Vitellius as he tries the doors of his palace. We feel his fear, his terror. We see him shudder. We watch Nero call out for his servants, listen to his cry of despair, see him run from the palace, knowing that he was heading for the river. Yet it is essential to the scene that there was no one to see Vitellius shudder when he entered a room and no one to hear Nero exclaim. It seems unlikely that Vitellius confessed his innermost feelings to his murderer as he was dragged out of his hiding place and only slightly less unlikely that Nero explained to those he met just what his intentions were and why he was so desperate. One might assume that it was fear of death that unmanned them, and left Vitellius cowed, confined to a small corner of his great house. But Vitellius knew he was going to die before he returned to the palace, for his war was already lost; and Nero's sudden suicidal urges suggest that it was not death he feared. The fictional intervention into these histories centers on what it must have been like for these men to be in solitude, focusing on their fear, their exhaustion, and, in Vitellius' case, their mental disintegration. We are not just witnessing a political disaster, but a psychological collapse, and although this could be the final insult for the fallen emperor (Vitellius' power gone, he faces death in terror and without honor, a last nasty stab at his character from a hostile tradition), there is a pathos here that goes beyond the political.

In this chapter we explore the tensions between individuals and the 'community,' delineating the operation of *amicitia*, the network of friendships that established social location, but also operated as a social technology, a means by which things got done in Roman (elite) society. We explore

---

3. See Tac. *Ann.* XIV 56; XV 45; XV 60.
4. Wallace-Hadrill (1988); (1994).
5. At one level, this exposes the emptiness of the political symbols that surrounded royalty. The emperor was not powerful because of the palace, but because of the people who surrounded him and did his bidding. Power rested in people.

'crises' within this system: a political 'crisis' caused by the concentration of power on the person of the emperor; a 'crisis' of representation in which dissimulation perverted the network of trust and communication; and a 'crisis' of rebellion, in which individuals rejected the limitations of *amicitia*. Such crises enhanced the potential for alienation, and we explore how various writers dealt with that potential. Seneca, for instance, appears to remake the networks, excising corrupt elements. Pliny would appear to invest more heavily in them, willing away the problems. And yet, there were more radical options. In Pliny and Lucan, we find heroic figures defining themselves not within the social system, but outside it, expressing a will to power over men, over nature, and even over history. Yet, this 'stepping beyond' comes at a price, an enhanced alienation that has the potential to dissolve into terror. That terror lurks in the portrayals of Domitian, the monster-emperor before whom all social and familial bonds are rendered as nothing, and is fictionalized in Lucan's Caesar. We chose to read Lucan's Caesar alongside twentieth-century experiences of terror, and the nineteenth-century philosophies of the extreme. Lucan makes clear the calamitous consequences of substituting *dominatio,* the radical individualism of the great man, for *amicitia,* as we have historical experience of the consequences of Caesarism substituting for liberalism.

AMICITIA: SYSTEM AND OPPOSITION

It is common for writers to return to the same themes time and time again. For some it is politics, for others religion, and for others love. For Pliny the Younger, it was friendship. His letters are to friends and about friends. He rejoices in his friends, retells their stories of him, recounts their dramas, helps them, entertains them and tells his audience (presumably initially comprising largely of his friends) all about his friends. Pliny lives for us in his reflections on his friends which were in turn supposedly sent to his friends. The occasional unsavory character walks across his pages, but for the most part this is a self-congratulatory, self-obsessed world of 'nice' people. Although if one delves deeper into the Plinian oeuvre, one finds some demons, there is a coziness about the letters which did not escape criticism.[6] *Amicitia* emerges through Pliny's letters as the dominant technology of social relations, effective in politics, administration, economic management and literary activity, and operating through a busy round of

---

6. See, e.g., Pliny *Ep.* IX 8 in praise of a fellow author who had written in praise of Pliny. In *Ep.* VII 28 we learn that such lavish praise has been seen as excessive and Pliny admits he may have made a happy error.

social events that worked to cement a social network and establish an individual's social location.⁷

These networks extended throughout the Roman political class and included the emperor. An emperor who was a friend to the senators established a network of relationships that allowed a certain style of politics. Augustus could, supposedly, remember the names of all the senators and would display this talent at meetings of the full senate. He visited the houses of senators and remembered and attended their family events until he reached a great age (Suet. *Aug.* 53). His behavior in senate meetings tended towards the informal, allowing senators to speak in opposition (Suet. *Aug.* 54). Further, when he sought to elevate the status of the senate by creating a timocratic bar, he gave his personal financial support to those whose wealth was insufficient to meet the new criterion (Suet. *Aug.* 40). All senators became his friends, and his network of friends extended beyond the senatorial class. Supposedly, Augustus monitored the wills of his friends with great care, and although he often ultimately returned inheritances to heirs, he valued the show of friendship that came with a legacy (Suet. *Aug.* 66).⁸ Leaving property to the emperor was an acknowledgment of an amicable relationship: an emperor might have every right to feel aggrieved if he missed out when the list of legatees was read.⁹

It is this Augustan model of imperial behavior that Pliny praises in Trajan. The *Panegyricus* makes much of Trajan's open and friendly manner, and contrasts his full halls with the empty halls of Domitian.¹⁰ Friends lingered in Trajan's presence and chatted with each other. Trajan himself rejected any sign that appeared to elevate him above the senatorial group. He refused blatant signs of divinity and avoided the title of *dominus*. It was just such

---

7. In politics, Pliny drummed up support for junior colleagues from his own friends (*Ep.* II 9; VI 6; VI 9). Other offices were also secured through indirect patronage: a friend recommended to a friend (*Ep.* II 13; III 2; III 8; IV 4; IV 15; VII 22), or alternatively a recommendation creating a new friendship (*Ep.* VII 31). Pliny himself relied on the friendship of powerful senior senators (*Ep.* II 1). For the round of social events (dinner parties, readings, official engagements), about which Pliny complained, see e.g. *Ep.* VII 3; VIII 9; IX 6.

8. For the importance of wills in cementing a social circle, see Champlin (1991). The freedom that the Romans enjoyed to bequeath their property and leave legacies to a wide circle of friends meant that the will could become an assertion of social status, recording one's friendships through a plethora of minor bequests, sometimes explained in the will itself (see, for example, Pliny *Ep.* VIII 18). The inclusion or exclusion of an individual was an issue of note for Roman society. Those who surrounded the deceased in life had every expectation of receiving an inheritance (*Ep.* V 1; V 7; VI 33) and the posturing in a will was such that Pliny notes that both he and Tacitus were regular beneficiaries of the wills of people unknown to them whose preference for literature was displayed in their disbursements (*Ep.* VII 20). Also see Frier (1985) 37–38 for litigation concerning wills.

9. Ejection from the position of friend of the emperor made an individual vulnerable to his enemies, see, for instance, Suet. *Aug.* 66.

10. Pliny, *Panegyricus* 48; 22–24; cf. Suetonius, *Domitian* 3.

a title that Augustus rejected, and Tiberius followed his example.[11] Vespasian likewise avoided symbolic elevation to the extent of living in a garden villa rather than in the palace and holding a *salutatio* in which his friends penetrated into his bedroom. There were no searches of the prospective visitors: all were his *amici*.[12] This elevation of *amicitia* was fundamental to the Augustan *principatus,* in which the emperor's power was a peculiar mix of the institutional and the personal.[13]

Pliny's emphasis on *amicitia* as an essential and successful bond within the Roman social system idealized his own society, which partly explains the criticism that it attracted. The world of friendships can be seen as a workable and stable social system. Members of the elite were bound together by ties of mutual loyalty and existed within a hierarchy in which the powerful and senior men supported their juniors, as they had themselves been supported by their seniors. Such men also extended their support to lesser figures within the social hierarchy, men from whom perhaps there may be no obvious return in services other than a public show of respect. The language of *amicitia* is comparatively status-free in that it can incorporate relationships of equal and unequal power: the lesser men around his home town of Comum who gained from Pliny's generosity were as much *amici* as were the great senators of his acquaintance. The Romans were very conscious of hierarchies and expected proper observance of social status: customs such as ranking guests by social status at dinner parties is sufficient proof of this, but inequalities between free men were cloaked by the language of friendship. Although Roman society maintained timocratic and hereditary distinctions that ensured a certain stability in the transmission of power and status between generations of a family, there was not a straightforward caste system. Rather than birth, *amicitia* played the determining role in social status. The individual was always determined socially by his place in the web of friendships. Because of the relative informality of this system (compared with class, office, or caste systems), we are almost certainly unable to understand its full nuances. It was through the manipulation of that network of friends that an individual rose to honor, and that in turn allowed him both to build new friendships and to reward old friends.

Amicitia ensured that individuals, in theory at least, could not rise seamlessly through the social and political ranks. In rising, an individual would accumulate a range of debts, but would also have to befriend individuals

---

11. Suet., *Aug.* 53; *Tib.* 27. This contrasts with Domitian who allegedly preferred to be called *dominus et deus noster* (our master and god) (Suet., *Dom.* 13).

12. Suet. *Vesp.* 12; 21; Cassius Dio LXVI 10 4–5.

13. Augustus (*Res Gestae* 35) denied that his superiority lay in statute or magisterial power, and claimed instead that it lay in *auctoritas,* a quality that mixed the charismatic with the bureaucratic.

and groups who acted as 'gatekeepers' to privilege. This kind of engineering could be particularly effective in ensuring social and political continuities and in excluding those who might threaten the system.[14] By controlling access to political status, those within the system could ensure that only those who shared similar world views would rise. *Amicitia* thus provided a relatively flexible technology of power that could be manipulated to elevate individuals beyond the social rank of their birth, but that also allowed the exercise of strongly normative forces. Individuals had to cultivate a nexus of friendships and adhere to social and political norms. The silken threads that bound everyone into the web of *amicitia* were pervasive.

Yet the system could go wrong. Domitian's reliance on a small body of close advisors, certainly towards the end of his reign, created a faction that divided the senate and encouraged a drift towards paranoia (see, for example, Juvenal, *Satire* IV). With an embattled emperor, *amici* were to be feared, as they were powerful and had access to the emperor, should their ambitions lead them to conspiracy. Many of those who seemed to have been closest to the emperor ended as enemies. Eventually, members of Domitian's own household, feeling their lives threatened, assassinated the emperor. All 'friendship' became unreal in such circumstances and a cover for the true political relationship, which was one of terror. Moreover, the perversion of *amicitia* into 'terror' crossed the boundaries of the court and fed into the houses of the elite. The use of *delatores* (informers) meant that *amici* could no longer be trusted (Pliny, *Ep.* I 12; Tacitus, *Agricola* 1–3). At such a moment, the system of *amicitia* collapsed.

Although the political crisis surrounding Domitian can be regarded as unusual, there is some reason to think that problems with *amicitia* were inherent in the political structure of Roman society. By its very nature, *amicitia* blurred distinctions between public and private. An individual, especially a person of power and relative independence, could choose friends from a variety of social locations. Although some friends would undoubtedly be 'respectable,' others were not necessarily so; however, once individuals were allowed access to the network of *amicitia*, it was very difficult to stop them accumulating power. Nowhere does this become more obvious than in the imperial circle. From the very advent of imperial power, Roman politics inevitably came to take on some of the characteristics of other monarchic systems, focusing on personal relations at court. In some other systems (ideally at least), those personal relations were carefully regulated so that the king's friends came to be drawn from the most powerful in the land, and access to the source of power could be rigorously controlled by convention.

---

14. See Lendon (1997) 30–73.

But perhaps because the Romans were inventing their system, there was no such ritual or organization. Hence, emperors could find friends or might look to find friends among groups whose status was questionable, such as actors and charioteers, women and slaves or the freed. The blurring of public and private meant that there could be no private domain for the emperor, but also that all of an emperor's relationships were pushed onto the political stage. Although this would seem to be an inevitable consequence of *amicitia*, such social technologies operate most smoothly when confirming rather than challenging conventional views of status. Once the technology is used in contravention of social norms, the validity of such technology is bound to be questioned.

A further element of tension was a "crisis of representation." Although mendacity on the part of political leaders is not restricted to the Roman imperial age, lying appears to have become something of an art form in the first century of imperial rule. Shadi Bartsch (1994) and Vasily Rudich (1993) both argue that dissimulation or 'doublespeak' became the language of power and dissent. In part, this was due to the *amicitia* system itself. In a system in which the emperor needed to be a friend to all the powerful and all the powerful needed to befriend the emperor, it was in no one's interest for any breach to become public. The dominance of the language of friendship and cordiality could mask animosities, and, what is worse, could be examined as if stereotypical cordialities were covert assaults. People lied, and everyone knew that they lied, but all pretended that the expressions of loyalty with which speeches were peppered, the statements of friendship which filled imperial pronouncements, and the honors freely granted by a loving senate and people were sincere. Speeches inevitably played to different audiences and were 'coded,' so that praise could be read as criticism. Deception and dissimulation not only affected the political order (where we are most likely to see it) but percolated through to social transactions. This explains, in part, the contemporary rage at "legacy hunting," a social practice that Pliny mocks mercilessly (*Ep.* II 20).[15] At death, a member of the elite would have very considerable resources to disburse, and legacies were one of the easiest and perhaps most efficient ways in which to accumulate wealth. Pretence in adopting friendly relations with an elderly and childless individual (*Ep.* IV 2) perverted the whole system of *amicitia*. No one could be sure whether a friend sought their company or their money: there was no litmus test of honesty.[16]

---

15. Pliny is by no means alone in this; cf., for example, Seneca, *Ep.* 68.10.
16. The culture of dissimulation caused Pliny significant problems when it came to his *Panegyricus*. The language of praise had been debased under his predecessors so that any praise that Pliny

Yet, the language of *amicitia* retained its hegemony and stepping out of the corrupted system risked social death. In *Epistle* 55, Seneca considers the villa of the noted Tiberian aristocrat Vatia. Vatia had lived in luxurious obscurity and thus been safe from the political machinations that brought down so many. Seneca explains that the exclamation: *O Vatia solus scis vivere* ("O Vatia you alone know how to live") became a political complaint of the persecuted who envied Vatia's escape from the troubles of the period. But Seneca comments *At ille latere sciebat, non vivere* ("but he knew how to hide, not to live"). Seneca's attitude to withdrawal was, however, somewhat ambivalent. *Ep.* 8, for instance, seems to portray withdrawal as being an unambiguous good; in *Ep.* 68, however, the position taken is rather more complex:

> Praeterea, cum sapienti rem publicam ipso dignam dedimus, id est mundum, non est extra rem publicam, etiam si recesserit, immo fortasse relicto uno angulo in maiora atque ampliora transit et caelo inpositus intellegit, cum sellam aut tribunal ascenderet, quam humili loco sederit.

> Additionally, when we give to the wise man public matters worthy of him (which is all the world), he is not outside public life even if retreats; he is perhaps moving from one small corner into greater and wider places, and, once placed in the heavens, he realizes in what a lowly place he sat when he ascended the tribunal or the chair of office.

Even if the wise man retreats from political office, he remains engaged, and perhaps even more so, though Seneca resorts to metaphor in explaining the sphere of activity (a broad [place] after the narrow corner of political life). Political life is thus only one way in which the wise can be of practical service to their fellow men, but in this there is also a distinction between the political sphere and the public sphere that is unusual in classical texts. The same argument appears in *de Tranquillitate Animi*. There Seneca argues that withdrawal can be a useful strategy, using military imagery to compare it to a tactical retreat by which the army and its honor are saved. When political involvement becomes difficult, the wise man seeks other opportunities to display *virtus*, such as literature, which is a *portus . . . in periculosa navigatione* (a port in dangerous seas).[17] Although the life of study is potentially

---

could invent might look like the "false praises" lavished on Domitian. His solution, that it was only under a great emperor that words can have their true meaning once more, was probably no more convincing then than it is now, and points explicitly to the crisis of representation. See Pliny, *Panegyricus* 1–4.3.

17. Seneca, *de Tranquillitate Animi* 4–5; 5.5. Withdrawal, however, was to be active and Sen-

isolating, the literary man will inevitably attract a network of friends. *Amici* will flock to the scholar-philosopher, for "even obscure virtue never remains hidden" (3.6). In *Ep.* 9, Seneca argues that a wise man should be content or happy without material or social resources: *Ita sapiens se contentus est non ut velit esse sine amico, sed ut possit.* ("So a wise man is happy in himself, not because he wishes to be without a friend, but because he can be"). When exiled or deserted, the wise man finds happiness in himself (*in se reconditur*), but *sine amico . . . numquam erit* ("he will never be without a friend"), which echoes *de Tranquillitate Animi* 3.6.[18]

Although Seneca concedes the theoretical possibility that the philosopher could exist in isolation and find reward in the knowledge of his goodness, he grounds his moral teaching in practical, social terms. The stoical good man exists in splendid confidence of his own rationality. Yet, Seneca's wise man exists within society. Withdrawal results not in abandoning the network of friends, but in reordering that network. The social and psychological identity of the wise man is maintained because he is not alone. Commitment to the public is the way to psychological health. Seneca argues that it is possible to have that network of friends and a degree of public involvement away from the political world. And thus *amicitia* can continue to work for the individual even when the political edge of the web is excised. Yet, each of these webs is in itself an instrument of power, which could hardly escape the attention of an emperor. A web which excised the political elite was a network of power from which the emperor was excluded, which was in itself a political act.

But the metaphor of a web seems to us to break down in one important respect. A web suggests a creative spider who sits at the center of the network and controls its various twitches, but what we have here was a web with many spiders, and one which bound the emperors as much as it bound everyone else. Offering the model of emperor as universal *amicus* in the *Panegyricus,* Pliny binds the emperor into the conventions of his day, subject to the judgment of the *amici*. Further, although someone such as Pliny might like to present the web as a pleasant home in which to situate himself, it was still a home that controlled him with the force of the opinions of his *amici,* bound him to a particular sense of social duty, and, therefore, restricted his freedom. However comfortable the club, it had its rules. *Amicitia* tended to pool power and worked to maintain the collectivity of the aristocratic

---

eca recommends study as a means of allaying boredom, whereas complete isolation is a recipe for listlessness and apathy (3.6).

18. The paradox that the wise man can be happily without friends, but obviously will never be so deserted, looks like an attempt to reassure an audience for whom social isolation is the stuff of nightmares.

network against the ambitions of any individual. The myth of the Augustan restitution of the Republic was that the power of the network was restored. Yet, this was potentially a difficult model for imperial government. Emperors could be restricted and even pressured by influential friends and this pressure might be burdensome, especially if there was good reason to doubt those friends' respect and loyalty.

The social conventions of *amicitia* thus created a network of ties that bound individuals into a social system and ideology. In his structuration theory, Antony Giddens argues that social systems are maintained by regular decisions of individuals to abide by, or break with, social conventions.[19] Thus Giddens sharpens our perception of the fragility of social structure as individuals develop an active relationship with the rules of social convention, analyzing and disputing the workings of a social system from within.[20] The rules of society may appear to be 'natural' to participants, indeed so natural as to be invisible, but they are also potentially subject to critique as being unfairly operated. As individuals compete, in one way or another, it seems very likely that in most complex societies the results of the workings of a social system would seem to some, perhaps even to the majority of the participants, unfair or restrictive. Thus, it is open to an individual to complain that someone else is not playing the social game properly, for instance, by hunting legacies, or that the rules of the game are at fault and by implication attempt to change or stand outside those social conventions.[21] Yet, even if one accepts that a particular social order is unfair or distorted, a social agent's options are limited; opting out of society is rarely an option and revolutions entail considerable risk. It is our contention that the texts that we are about to examine take a radical step, suggesting a more profound withdrawal than that discussed by Seneca. In so doing, they offer an alternative vision of a relationship between individual and society that is based on power in an unmediated and extreme form. That will to power resonates destructively in our texts and offers parallels with modern texts of alienation.[22]

---

19. See the exposition of the theory of structuration in Giddens (1984).
20. And in so doing, parallels Pierre Bourdieu (1977); (1990b) in anthropology and especially his own flexible web, the *habitus*.
21. There is an important distinction in Bourdieu's work between social rules of the kind that were studied by Claude Lévi-Strauss (1969), which appear to allow no flexibility, and social regularities: see Bourdieu (1990a), esp. 65. The concentration of power in the imperial person was very likely to produce what might be perceived as social irregularities which alongside the irregularities of representation might leave many disenchanted.
22. One could argue that the individualism suggested here should only be possible after the Enlightenment, with its emphasis on the autonomous thinking individual. Yet, the individual is a base unit for society, and when other forms of social organization break down the individual is an obvious unit around which to build a new society. We do not see individualism as a purely modern or capitalistic phenomenon.

CHAPTER 2

PLINY AT HOME:
VILLAS AND THE CONQUEST OF NATURE

Pliny's second book of letters mostly concerns public business of greater and lesser moment. We see Pliny "in the world," performing his public duty, dealing with the great affairs of state, looking after the interests of his friends, and maintaining his own legal interests and estates. But II 17, an extensive description of his seaside villa, breaks this sequence. For an individual intent on illustrating the social and literary whirl in which he spent his time and who so publicly displayed his friendships, Pliny's description of himself at home presents us with a startling image of the author in isolation.

The letter opens with a description of the villa's location, particularly in relation to Rome, but also to the coast and surrounding woods and meadows. Pliny then moves to an obviously impressionistic description of the architecture. We start with a hall, courtyard, an inner hall and then a dining hall, which brings us to the shore. There are two *cubicula,* an apsidal library, a further *cubiculum,* a corridor, and slave quarters. A third sequence of rooms involves another dining room and *cubiculum* and the baths. Pliny then describes the garden and drive, a garden dining room, a vine pergola, and then a long arcade. This arcade (long enough for a public building) leads to a suite constructed by Pliny himself. Here Pliny has rooms with views of the sea, the woods and nearby villas. Here also is a silent bedroom from which Pliny cannot hear his household. In this suite, he escapes from his house, particularly necessary during the riotous celebrations of the Saturnalia. Other than this mention of the festival, the description is notably short on occupants: it is architecture devoid of life. Although this mode of architectural description is familiar to moderns, it is not necessarily natural. Pliny could have described his household, the faithful servants (perhaps his librarian), the old dog who rose to greet him as he arrived, those who tended the surrounding fields, his neighbors. Indeed, instead of the house pictured at the center of a community, one comes to understand Pliny operating in a house without any obvious community; and when a community does surface in the riot of the Saturnalia, Pliny is isolated, separated from his household by an extraordinarily long arcade. The house then has two main foci; a main section with that central spine of hall, court, dining room, and associated baths (perhaps what we expect of a villa), and then the isolated small suite, in which the master seems to reside.

Pliny's isolation from his household also features in *Ep.* IX 36, which describes Pliny's everyday routine in his Tuscan villa. On waking, Pliny lies in darkness and silence, in which state he is removed and free and left to himself (*abductus et liber et relictus mihi*). Later, he sees his *notarius,* or secretary. Much later, he dines with his wife or a few friends, during which time a book is read. After dinner he might walk with members of his household, some of whom are educated. Sometimes his friends from neighboring towns visit and sometimes he sees his *coloni* (peasants). Pliny makes very little mention of other human interaction during his account of the rest of the day. His specific references to the company he keeps in the evening reinforces the impression that the rest of the day would mostly be spent alone.[23]

Pliny's attitude towards his household, those whom we might expect to form his basic community, was also ambivalent. In *Ep.* VIII 16, he shows sorrow and grief at the loss of slaves, an emotional reaction which he claims to have been controversial (cf *Ep.* V 19). Although some regarded slaves as no more than possessions, Pliny acknowledges his shared humanity with his own slaves. His slaves were not beasts but subjects, for "the household is a kind of state for the slave and an equivalent to citizenship" (*servis res publica quaedam et quasi civitas domus est*). Pliny could thus be seen as a domestic emperor.[24] Similarly, we see him in IX 36 engaged in pleasant conversation with selected members of his own household. Yet, his comments on the murder of Macedo in *Ep.* III 14 suggest that he held a distinctly illiberal view of his subjects. Macedo, described as *superbus* (arrogant) and *saevus* (savage), was attacked by a group of his slaves. Assuming that he was dead, they pretended that he had been overcome by the heat of the baths, and carried him out, whereupon he was revived by *fideliores* and the *concubinae* (some more loyal servants and the concubines) and lived long enough to give evidence of his attack. The slaves fled.[25] Pliny complains:

> Vides quot periculis quot contumelis quot ludibriis simus obnoxii; nec est quod quisquam possit esse securus, quia sit remissus et mitis; non enim iudicio domini sed scelere perimuntur.

---

23. In IX 40, he claims to have very much the same routine while at his Laurentine villa, which tended to be his winter residence, though in the Tuscan villa he was awake earlier. There is a notable contrast with *Ep.* III 1 in which Pliny provides us with a conspicuously idealized description of the lifestyle of Spurinna, whose mode of life he would seek to emulate, he claims, should he reach old age. Notably, in his retirement Spurinna is surrounded by people. He is, in Pliny's view, deserving of this *otium*, but Pliny himself cannot claim this prize at his age for fear of being accused of "crimen inertiae" (the crime of laziness). One wonders whether Spurinna's sociable retirement is a feature of the political life of a past age, and therefore also a nostalgic image beyond the grasp of Pliny.

24. Extending the metaphor is both discomforting and informative. If Pliny is thinking of himself as emperor, his slaves would be roughly in the position of his *amici*, his control over them analogous to that friendly parental authority which Trajan of the *Panegyricus* was supposed to hold over the senators, which would be a kindly view of slavery. But this metaphor would also render the senators happy slaves, and (Emperor) Pliny's response to revolt (see below) would seemingly be to slaughter all the senators. Thus, Pliny slips easily into tyrannical violence.

25. Radice (1963) translates *Diffugiunt servi* as "The guilty slaves fled." It is difficult to understand this adjectival injection other than as an embarrassed explication of the rather vicious sentiments that followed.

> You see to how many dangers, how many abuses, how many insults we are exposed. No one is able to be safe because he is indulgent and mild, for masters are destroyed not by judgment but by wickedness. Pliny, *Ep.* III 14

Pliny claims that Romans dominated households of potentially wicked and untrustworthy slaves by the threat of brutality. Pliny's sympathy lay firmly with Macedo: *non sine ultionis solacio decessit ita vivus vindicatus, ut occisi solent* ("he died not without the comfort of revenge, so he was avenged while alive as they died in the usual fashion"). Although Pliny presents himself as a *mitis dominus* ("soft-hearted master") in I 4, ruling the household through fear makes analogies with the imperial position uncomfortable and any possibility of an amicable relationship with the slave *familia* remote.

The isolationist Pliny appears in other contexts, nearly always surprising:

> Ridebis et licet rideas. Ego, ille quem nosti, apros tres et quidem pulcherrimos cepi. "Ipse?" inquis. Ipse.
>
> You will laugh and you are allowed to. I, that man you know, have captured three boars and fine ones. "Him?" you ask. Him. Pliny, *Ep.* I 6

Pliny goes on to explain the delight of hunting, pointing out that he took his notebooks with him: "For the woods and the solitude and the silence itself, which is necessary for hunting are a great spur to thought." He was fond of hunting (*Ep.* V 6; 18; IX 10; 16; 36) and also depicts it as Trajan's sole relaxation (*Panegyricus* 81.1). For Trajan too, hunting was not a sociable activity, but rather a solitary escape from the business of the world.[26] Hunting can of course be a social activity: a preparation for military activity in which a team works together to conquer nature, an economic activity, a form of pest disposal, or an arena for heroic activity, for civilizing nature and clearing away the monsters who lurk in hidden places. It can, in short, be a form of colonialism, and one could see Pliny and Trajan as the direct heirs of Odysseus, Theseus, and Hercules. But the analogy quickly breaks down. For Pliny's boars are not monsters that threaten the farmlands of civilization. Rather, the hunt is a conquest away from the social world; a pursuit of solitude; an act of heroism achieved in and through withdrawal from society, and it is the withdrawal more than the conquest that is its aim. This may be mock-heroism with Pliny, but is true heroism with Trajan, a heroism that places man alone in nature.

The second great house description in Pliny comes in *Ep.* V 6, devoted

---

26. This contrasts with, for instance, Ovid's hunter, Actaeon (*Metam.* III 131–252). It is the loneliness of his digression that exposes Actaeon to danger. In his isolation, he encounters dangerous forces that turn him from man to animal.

to Pliny's Tuscan villa, a description in which the architecture is lost in the descriptions of the gardens and the environment. The letter's premise is that Domitius Apollinaris has been worried about Pliny staying on the notoriously pestilential Tuscan coast in the summer. Pliny reassures him. The villa is not coastal, but sits at the foot of the mountains in an environment so healthy that grandfathers and great-grandfathers of youths are common. He talks next of the area: a plane neither too wet nor too dry, ringed by mountains, wooded slopes, vineyards, meadows, corn fields with excellent natural irrigation, a navigable river by which the produce of this earthly paradise can be transported to Rome. Then he turns to his house.

The description of the house is far less detailed than that of II 17. Pliny places initial emphasis on a south-facing colonnade: a long marble line marking off and defending the cultural world from the world of nature, a structure from public architecture in a private house. Before this, however, there was a terrace on which Pliny's household practised the dark arts of topiary, the hedges cut into the shapes of animals. Pliny's description of the architecture of the house is interspersed by mention of the trees and fountains that ornamented the open spaces between the clusters of rooms. Yet, Pliny's pride seems most excited by the *hippodromos* (the horse-riding yard). This is described as a large formal garden planted with box hedges and plane trees to give it a basic shape, open to the center and yet surrounded by a network of paths. Further trees provide shade and variety. Lawns, more topiary, this time spelling out Pliny's name, and that of the gardener, artist and patron signing their work, culminated in a less obviously formal section of the garden. This area contained a rural dining room which, in a startling flight of fancy, had a large marble fresh-water pond, regulated so that it was always filling and never overflowing. At Pliny's allegedly frugal dinner parties, the lighter offerings were floated across to the guests in dishes shaped as ships or birds. Within this dining area was a *cubiculum* in which there was a smaller, yet more distant room, surrounded by vines, in which, reclining, one could imagine being asleep in a wood, but a wood unthreatened by rain.

Such a description offers parallels with II 17 in providing us with an image of Pliny isolated from his household, sleeping in a remote corner of his villa, but it is more startling for the contrivances by which Pliny (who claims to have had some responsibility for the design of the villa and its gardens) manipulated his environment. Pliny appears to make every effort to place himself in nature, his grotto giving him, as he lay sleeping, the impression of living in a wood, surrounded by the water fountains trickling around him.[27]

---

27. There are clear parallels in Statius' villa descriptions in the *Silvae*, most notably *Silvae* I 3, on the Tiburtine villa of Manilius Vopsicus. The more notable architectural feature of the house is that it is divided in two by the river Anio. In lines 20–23, the Anio is described as tumbling above and

Returning to II 17, we can read it not just as a portrayal of Pliny and his household, but as a literary representation of an architectural display. The sequencing of rooms is a means of staging the experience of the house. The textual visitor is drawn to the heart of the house, a dining room (*triclinium*) that opens onto the shore and can even be splashed by the sea when the wind is sufficiently strong and in the right direction. In this dining room, nature and culture meet. Nature, and in particular the untamed sea and shore, are captured in a variety of vistas.[28] A second dining facility (a *cenatio*) also had sea views (*latissimum mare longissimum litus villas amoenissimas possidet*: "it overlooks the greatest expanse of sea, the widest stretch of shore and the finest villas"). The description turns quickly to another *triclinium*, this one sheltered from the sea and with views over the garden. The garden has a pergola of vines, mulberry trees, and fig trees, and is encircled by a box hedge. Pliny is describing a wooded courtyard in the midst of his house, a cultivated nature surrounded by his buildings.

Pliny's private suite had views of the sea, the surrounding villas and the woods, described by Pliny as if he were examining a landscape painting: *a*

---

below the villa but running smoothly inside it so as not to disturb the poetic and musical snoozing of Vopsicus. Newlands (2002) 119–53, sees I 3 as an example of "imperial pastoral." This is, she suggests, an alternative space which exists apart, but somehow in relation to the imperial court and its patronage.

28. There are obvious parallels with *Silvae* II 2, an extended praise-poem for the villa of Pollius Felix. The villa is described as "a high spectator over the Neapolitan Sea" (3), but the wildness of the sea is controlled by Pollius and the gods.

> ante domum tumidae moderator caerulus undae
> excubat, innocui custos laris; huius amico
> spumant templa salo. felicia rura tuetur
> Alcides; gaudet gemino sub numine portus;
> hic servat terras, hic saevis fluctibus obstat.
> mira quies pelagi: ponunt hic lassa furorem
> aequora, et insani spirant clementius austri
> hic praeceps minus audet hiems, nulloque tumultu
> stagna modesta iacent dominique imitantia mores.

> Before the house, the dark-blue ruler of the rising waves watches as a guard of the innocent household and it is his shrine that is sprayed with friendly salt. Alcides protects the fortunate fields. The harbor rejoices beneath the twin spirits. This serves the land, the other controls the savage turbulence. There is a wondrous peace on the ocean. Here, the weary sea loses its fury and the wild south wind blows more gently. Here, the dangerous storm dares less, and the pools lie quiet, disturbed by no tempest, in imitation of the customs of the *dominus*. Statius, *Silvae* II 2, 21–29

In lines 52–60, Statius rejoices in the ability of Pollius to destroy mountains, house the wilderness, and construct a forest. The very rocks themselves are made over to the will of Pollius. The views from the windows capture the landscape. Newlands (2002) 154–98 argues similarly that the poem represents a triumph over nature and suggests that in elevating Campanian villa culture, Statius is offering an (Neopolitan) alternative to conventional Roman military triumphs.

pedibus mare, a tergo villae, a capite silvae ("sea at the feet, villas in the middle, woods at the head"). The emphasis on nature as a prospect is tempered by Pliny's fondness for the *tecta villarum* (the villa buildings) that ornamented the shoreline and formed a quasi-urban landscape. Pliny's preference for tamed nature also appears in his brief description of his two villas on Lake Como, named Tragedy and Comedy (IX 7). Tragedy stood on a promontory above the lake, while Comedy was on the lakeshore itself, washed by the lake's waves. Here we see an architecturalization of a natural environment. The naming of the villas makes them literary, as much creations of the ego of their owner as his literary works.[29]

Pliny's literary and highly artificial pastoral could be dismissed as play-acting, but it also uneasily and explicitly looks back to Virgilian pastoral.[30] Pliny has created his own, highly artificial, self-consciously literary, pastoral world, from the grotto in which he resides and sleeps to the painted landscape in which his villa is set. Moreover, and unlike the landscapes of Virgilian pastoral, this is an environment in which the author is in control. He maintains the buildings, the trees with their delicate shadows, and the water that trickles through the fountains of his estate. Topiary is an extreme example of man exercising control over nature. Turning trees by an act of will into animals smacks of hubristic tendencies, a metamorphosis executed on a living thing through the will of the owner. Yet more egomaniacal is the turning of trees into direct representatives of Pliny's identity, the letters of his name. The gardens display the power of Pliny over nature: a *dominus* who makes nature his slave.[31]

In its inherent fragility, pastoral undermines the contemporary and manifests nostalgia for a mythic past of idealized values. Apprehensive of change, pastoral is a literary form which creates a distance, or even escapes from the society in which the genre is composed. It reacts to the contemporary by searching for an unchanging world, or at least for a lyrical past in which elements of the old moral and social order are preserved. But even this pastoral paradise is not enough for Pliny, who finds freedom cut off from the world, in deep contemplation. Instead of selfhood resting on the social location of the individual affirmed through *amicitia*, Pliny experiences selfhood in isolation.

Of course, Pliny's writing is hardly unitary. He appears to 'toy' with differing models of selfhood, which suggests to us that for all the constraints

---

29. This artificial nature and tamed ruggedness has a parallel in Pompeian wall paintings with their fondness for landscape and a highly artificial combination of architecture and nature.

30. Pliny compares his description in *Ep.* V 6 with the density of description in Virgilian epic and Homer (and also Aratus). *Silvae* III, 1 on a construction of a temple to Heracles similarly emphasizing the heroic nature of villa construction

31. *Silvae* IV 3 provides a spectacular instance of the epic imperial conquest of nature.

of the Imperial age, an aristocratic Roman was presented with ideological choices.³² We detect in Pliny's writings a model of selfhood in which the self is located within a world of friends and shared social values, juxtaposed to a self that is a more autonomous wielder of power. The radical nature of this *dominatio* is shown by the treatment of pastoral in these texts. Whereas traditional pastoral presents a world in which the individual lives in harmony with nature, Pliny's pastoral is one of heroic triumph over nature. This new Roman hero does not subsume his identity to the needs of the Roman state, or to a Roman community, or even to the dictates of individual fate or a heroic code, but stands as an individual above the natural order. This is a model of heroism very familiar from the modern world: a model of the hero who stands against nature, who overcomes the world through force or charisma, and has come to be associated with cults of personality and, indeed, with terror. This unsettled and unsettling territory draws us to connect Pliny's seemingly convivial world with Lucan's *Pharsalia,* where we find a terrifying dramatization of the potential of the asocial power that emerged in Pliny's letters.

FROM POWER TO TERROR: CAESAR AS A TRANGRESSIVE HERO

In contravention of the epic tradition, and certainly in contrast to the *Aeneid,* Lucan's *Pharsalia* is an epic without an obvious hero, destiny, or target, which is filled with a violent intensity that seems to systematically destroy places and people, and the values that they represent. Dramatizing the war that resulted in the founding of Empire, the poem forces upon its readers a welter of destruction and *furor* at the heart of which is Caesar.³³

Pompey and Caesar are introduced in an ominous passage in Book I (129–57) in which they are both compared to Aeneas and, through him, to each other. A shadow of his illustrious name, Pompey is likened to a lofty oak in a fruitful field—conjuring the image of firm Aeneas resisting Dido's (and her sister's) lures as an oak with strong roots in *Aeneid* IV 438–46. However, unlike that image of a determined Aeneas who is about to head off to found a new people and embrace a glorious destiny, Pompey's oak has no roots and is about to fall, thus accentuating an impression of infirmity

---

32. In this there are parallels with the Foucauldian account (see pp. 10–16).
33. For a sociopolitical reading of "Roman madness" personified primarily by Caesar, and secondarily by Cato, see Hershkowitz (1998) 197–246, following on from Ahl (1976). She locates the reason for the chaos we meet in Lucan's world in an extreme, misplaced, unrepublican explosion of *virtus* rendered by its own wild energy into *furor.*

and weakness which suggest that the age of Pompey is passed. The oak serves also to contrast the epics. Instead of an epic of foundational triumph, the *Pharsalia* is a story of a fall. Instead of the birth of a nation, we have *Götterdämmerung*.[34]

From the rotting Pompey, we turn to the rising Caesar. His imagery conveys fierce and indomitable energy and culminates in a thunderbolt that flashes through the clouds:

> . . . Sed non in Caesare tantum
> nomen erat nec fama ducis, sed nescia virtus
> stare loco, solusque pudor non vincere bello;
> . . .
> . . . inpellens, quidquid sibi summa petenti obstaret.
> Qualiter expressum ventis per nubila fulmen
> aetheris inpulsi sonitu mundique fragore
> emicuit. 1. 143–53

> But not so with Caesar: he had not only the name and fame of a general, but unlimited energy too; his only shame was to conquer without war . . . driving back whatever might stand in his way. . . . Just so strikes the thunderbolt propelled by the winds through the cloud, as the crashed heavens and shattered atmosphere resound around it. . . .

The lightning speed and deafening noise match the cosmic impression that Aeneas exacts when hurling his spear at a defeated Turnus in the final scene of the *Aeneid*: *Telum Aeneas fatale coruscat, . . . et corpore toto eminus intorquet . . . nec fulmine tanto dissultant crepitus . volat atri turbinis instar . . . hasta* ("[Aeneas] brandishes his lethal spear and . . . hurls it with all the strength of his body from afar . . . and [hurled rocks] do not crash with such a thunderous rattle; the spear flies ... like a black tornado" [12. 919–24]). The comparison again serves to contrast the epics and the heroes. The attack on Turnus is a moment of doubt in the *Aeneid*, a critical crux in its reading. The destructive force of Aeneas is fuelled by passion, by *furor*, and the killing of Turnus is morally questionable. The slaughter raises the specter of a Roman state in which (civil) violence will weave destruction into its fabric at the very moment of its foundation. It is this destructive spirit, the moment of possible heroic failure, which is recalled in Caesar's introductory simile. Yet, Caesar's aggressive thunderbolt triggers Lucan's epic, while

---

34. For a systematic exploration of the inverted formulas in Pompey's journey eastwards in the *Pharsalia* compared with Aeneas' journey westwards in the *Aeneid*, see Rossi (2000) with a special reference to the image of the oak (573–74).

Aeneas' unsavory charge brings the Virgilian epic to an end. Caesar could thus be seen as the hero who carries on the story where Aeneas has left it, rendering the *Aeneid* as a sort of direct prequel to Lucan's *Pharsalia*.

Bartsch's reading of the *Pharsalia* has argued for an intimate connection between the political strife of the collapse of the Roman Republic and the mental disintegration of individuals. Bartsch's strategy is to read the extensive, unusually detailed and brutal somatic violence in Lucan's text as a metaphor for a general breakdown of boundaries, as they are traditionally used to define, or better secure, the self:

> The scope of [the] violation of boundaries extends outward to the universe as it extends inwards to the body; microcosm and macrocosm reflect the dissolution of all normative limits.... Somatic, natural, political, and legal: the demarcations that make things what they are are clearly under siege in the *Civil War*.[35]

Whereas other authors might focus on the dying light of the eyes, Lucan plunges us into the viscera of death. Physical rupture not only represents the destruction and loss of life in civil war but also the disintegration of subjectivity. The bodily detail that fills the accounts of battles reflects a horror at that physical destruction but also a breakdown of the somatic container of the self. The soldiers' viscera are an ultimate personal transgression in a long series of transgressions that connect the political and the bodily.

This bodily interlacing of individual and state appears in the very first acts of the war, the crossing of the Rubicon. The scene is replete with violence and even some resonances of rape. A brook in the summer, the river is swollen (1. 213–19) and exceptional strength and determination are demanded for the crossing, as if nature herself stands against Caesar (1.220–22). A vision of the goddess Roma as a disheveled, distraught woman appears to Caesar the night before the crossing:

> Ingens visa duci patriae trepidantis imago
> clara per obscuram voltu maestissima noctem
> turrigero canos effundens vertice crines,
> caesarie lacera nudisque ... lacertis. 1. 186–89

And in the dark night a clear image of his distraught country appeared to the leader, with most unhappy face, her white hair pouring forth from a head adorned with towers, with tresses torn and naked shoulders.

---

35. Bartsch (1997) 17–18.

Pausing momentarily, Caesar overcomes his anxiety (1. 192–94) and presses on, yielding nothing to either divinity or nature. His transgression is not solely physical.

> Ut adversam superato gurgite ripam
> attigit, Hesperiae vetitis et constitit arvis,
> "hic" ait, "hic pacem temerataque iura relinquo;
> te, Fortuna, sequor. Procul hinc iam foedera sunto." 223–26

> When he reached the bank opposite, having crossed the swollen stream, he stopped on the forbidden Italian soil and "Here," he said, "here I abandon peace and humbled law; You, Fortune, I follow. Now let us be distant from agreements."

Hardly has he set foot on the other, forbidden, side of the Rubicon when he disdainfully announces his contempt for law or treaty.[36] Nature, the gods, the epic traditions of Rome, law, and community all stand against Caesar, and Caesar stands against them.

What impresses us most in the scene of the Rubicon's crossing is the magnitude of Caesar's provocation. His transgression takes him beyond the Rubicon, beyond contemporary values, and beyond the limits of the customs and laws of Rome, and into a new epic world. The world of the *Pharsalia* is amoral in that it is devoid of transcendental essences (such as gods) and universalizing moralities. The epic could be described as nonfoundational since it shows little sign of defending or arguing for fundamental social or moral values that could provide social grounding. There is no "moral code of the warrior," no consistent devotion either to the state or to some metaphysical ideal. Caesar's only driving force appears to be his need to break from containment, to triumph over all around, to achieve power, to transgress. He becomes a force that crushes all that gets in his way, a thunderbolt that exists not like a force of nature or as a weapon of the gods, but as the power of a man. This manifests itself in a relentless, uncontrolled and frenetic energy that rages against delay and avoids rest.[37]

---

36. On the banks of the Rubicon, Caesar dispenses with any "anxiety of influence." The last act of the *Aeneid* was to promise peace through Turnus' slaughter, and Law was a foundational element of the Roman state. Both are dismissed by Caesar. Compare Caesar's careless trampling over the old ruins—and history—of Troy at 9. 964–79, and see Rossi (2000) 588 and 588fn74 for further discussion of this passage.

37. In Book I, Caesar is compared to a sling and an arrow (1. 228–30), as he manifests his *celeritas* in conquest (1. 467–68). As Pompey flees Rome, Caesar is consumed by rage at a temporary lull in the war. He resents the interlude and cares nothing for victory if it means postponement of war (3. 48–52) and uses the pause to spread war to Sardinia (3.52–70). Notably, he refuses triumphal

A key moment comes at the end of Book V. A large part of Caesar's army is stranded in Brundisium, held back by bad weather, while his advanced guard is in Epirus. This division of forces prevents him from mounting an assault on the Pompeians. Nature has again turned against him. Caesar rages against the delay and attempts to persuade his fleet to put to sea, unsuccessfully (476–91). When all threats and cajoling have failed, he decides to cross the Adriatic from Epirus to the Italian port of Brundisium in a dinghy with the near-impossible aim of leading his stranded troops' back to the Greek coast (497–503). He rouses a poor boatman from a hovel on the shore, and persuades him to launch his boat. The boatman is skilled in reading the weather and warns of a storm, but agrees to be guided by Caesar's will (for he has little to lose). As they set out, the heavens themselves tremble (560–67). The boatman's courage fails and he begs Caesar to turn back, but Caesar is defiant. He is protected by the gods; he will stand against heaven's orders. His own person will overcome the power of sea and wind (579–93). Then, the storm breaks on the boat. The waters of all the seas are thrown together by the wind and the waves reach up as if to touch the stars (594–693). Caesar is now moved and comes to expect death, glorying in the magnificence of the storm sent to destroy him. In the face of the conventional fear that he would remain unburied, and thus never find rest, he hopes for just such a fate. He has no need for tomb or pyre, but wishes his death to remain unresolved, so that all may fear his return (654–71). Yet the sea throws him not to his death, but to his troops, and he returns to the shore he had recklessly left earlier in the night (672–77). His soldiers meet him on the shore and berate him for abandoning them and for the foolishness of his attempted crossing. He is beyond their comprehension (682–702).

This incomprehension in the face of Caesar is characteristic. At the siege of Ilerda, Caesar hemmed in a group of Pompeian soldiers. They are kept from the plains by Caesar's cavalry, and a trench is dug to shut off their water supply. The soldiers face certain defeat, but instead of surrender, decide to charge Caesar's lines and meet their deaths in battle. Caesar's troops are ordered to refuse battle and the Ilerdan troops throw themselves against the ramparts in vain (4. 253–75). Caesar explains this unusual tactic:

" . . .
En, sibi vilis adest invisa luce iuventus
iam damno peritura meo; non sentiet ictus,
incumbet gladiis, gaudebit sanguine fuso.

---

processions (3. 73–79) since a triumph would be a ceremonial closure of the breach in the moral order that is war. Caesar is averse to peace and consensus.

Deserat hic fervor mentes, cadat impetus amens,
perdant velle mori." Sic deflagrare minaces
incassum et vetito passus languescere bello[.] 4. 276–81

"Look! Here come young men, holding themselves cheap, hating life, destined to die at my loss; they will not feel the blows, they will fall upon the swords, they will rejoice at the shedding of their blood. Let this passion leave their minds, let the mad impulse fade; let the wish to die be lost." Thus by refusing battle their threats burned out in vain and their stifled suffering was weakened. . . .

Exhausted, they are captured and brought before Caesar, who, with a face betraying no emotion, shows *clementia* where it is least expected, and frees the soldiers, much to their bewilderment (4. 344–81). He recognizes the passion in the soldiers and the excess of emotion that has driven them forth. This excess elevates them above the ordinary, an elevation that Caesar will not tolerate. He exhausts their passion by forcing it to break on the rock of his ramparts. His unpredictability and refusal to be bound by expectations triumphs: the defeated soldiers are refused the resolution that would have given their madness purpose and their defeat is to be sent home quietly, their opposition and fury rendered meaningless before the greater passion that is Caesar. While Caesar's own soldiers are reminded of the indeterminacy characteristic of their leader, Pompey's soldiers are robbed of their desired resolution.

Caesar invades to make the present chaotic and transgresses the revered, regulated past in posing disturbing possibilities for an indeterminate future. As when he stood by the edge of river Rubicon in Book I, or on the Adriatic coast in Epirus daring the wild sea in Book V, Caesar stubbornly resides on the edge, in constant engagement with the uncharted territory that lies before Rome. There is "an excess" to Caesar that can hardly be adequately represented. He breaks free of all conventions and ensures that he can neither be completely understood nor controlled. His unpredictability is linked to his refusal to cease activity. To pause and accept victory would mean allowing society to come to a balance and assign due roles to victors and victims. Caesar could then be incorporated into the ideological order and the story of his wars would be given its appropriate conclusion. But Caesar hates peace as well as the laws that maintain and come along with that peace. Caesar, the individual, the alpha and omega, is not (ever?) ready to accept a societal settlement. His energy and ambition drive on the narrative of the *Pharsalia*. He pits himself against nature, embracing conflict with the divine. His intoxicated, near-demonical intransigence and his refusal to be settled render him both monstrous and creative. He exists in a triumph of the will, as a ghastly, indeterminable force that both disrupts and haunts.

Nowhere does this inexplicable force leave a greater imprint than on Caesar's own soldiers. As the civil war unfolds, Caesar's troops lurch from horror to adoration as they face their enigmatic leader. Early in the epic, with Rome nearly in sight, Caesar gathers his soldiers. The soldiers are agitated. An uneasy silence spreads across the army as the soldiers catch sight of their leader (1. 296–98). Caesar then explains the reasons for the war, aiming to rouse his troops for battle. He compares his invasion with that of Hannibal (1. 304–5) as an attack on Italy, presenting himself as a second historic threat to Rome and recalling the first epic of Roman foundationalism, Naevius' *Punica*. Yet, Caesar justifies the war by claiming his personal dues, the blessings of fortune that run with him, and the weakness of the aging Pompey. Although he lists the crimes of Pompey and asserts that the soldiers have a legitimate claim for reward following their efforts in Gaul, the war is justified at least as much by the opportunity for power. The speech ends and we look to the audience.

> Dixerat; at dubium non claro murmure volgus
> secum incerta fremit. Pietas patriique penates
> quamquam caede feras mentes animosque tumentes
> frangunt; sed diro ferri revocantur amore
> ductorisque metu. 352–56

> He finished; but the doubtful crowd murmurs indistinctly with uncertain whispers. Pietas and the ancestral gods break their aroused spirits and minds made fierce by slaughter, but they are recalled by their hideous love of the sword and by their terror of their leader.

Love of country (*Pietas patriique penates*) is here juxtaposed with love of violence (*amor ferri*); love of the ancestral gods (*penates*) is replaced by terror of their leader (*metus ductoris*). Momentarily, Caesar's soldiers waver between their patriotic feelings and their thirst for blood, between the values of the traditional order (home, family, tradition, religion), so obviously represented by the ancestral gods (brought by Aeneas from Troy), and their fear of their leader. It is that fear that threatens to replace all those other values of community, leaving Caesar as the only loyalty. Yet what holds them to Caesar is not love, but terror, an emotion which is not bonding and social, but individual and atomizing. Each individual is locked in a profoundly personal and powerful relationship with the force that is to rule them.[38] In this moment

---

38. The charisma of the hero stands in opposition to the rules of the community, setting up

of doubt, as the troops waver between Caesar and community, the centurion Laelius, ironically described as a man who was honored for the saving of Roman lives, asserts their loyalty to Caesar:

> "Si licet," exclamat "Romani maxime rector
> nominis, et ius est veras expromere voces,
> quod tam lenta tuas tenuit patientia vires,
> conquerimur. Deratne tibi fiducia nostri?
> Dum movet haec calidus spirantia corpora sanguis,
> et dum pila valent fortes torquere lacerti,
> degenerem patiere togam regnumque senatus?
> Usque adeo miserum est civili vincere bello?
> Duc age per Scythiae populos, per inhospita Syrtis
> Litora, per calidas Libyae sitientis harenas:
> Haec manus, ut victum post terga relinqueret orbem,
> Oceani tumidas remo conpescuit undas,
> Fregit et arctoo spumantem vertice Rhenum:
> Iussa sequi tam posse mihi quam velle necesse est.
> Nec civis meus est, in quem tua classica, Caesar,
> Audiero. Per signa decem felicia castris
> Perque tuos iuro quocumque ex hoste triumphos:
> Pectore si fratris gladium iuguloque parentis
> Condere me iubeas plenaeque in viscera partu
> Coniugis, invita peragam tamen omnia dextra;
> Si spoliare deos ignemque inmittere templis,
> Numina miscebit castrensis flamma monetae;
> Castra super Tusci si ponere Thybridis undas,
> Hesperios audax veniam metator in agros;
> Tu quoscumque voles in planum effundere muros,
> His aries actus disperget saxa lacertis,
> Illa licet, penitus tolli quam iusseris urbem,
> Roma sit." 1. 359–86

"If it is allowed," he exclaimed, "and it is lawful to expound the truth, we complain that your patience, so long extended, has lessened your strength. Did you lack faith in us? While warm blood flows in these bodies breathe

---

a dynamic that reverses the relationship in the *Aeneid*. When Aeneas' personal attraction failed to inspire, the distant goal of the formation of a community could be mobilized to rally the troops. Aeneas' performance in the first scene of the epic is programmatic. Aeneas galvanizes his soldiers with a mention of the grander destiny that is awaiting them (*Aen.* 1. 187–209), and, significantly, omits lavish praise of his own self, and especially his personal standing and capabilities as a leader, unlhike his famous predecessor, Odysseus, in similar circumstances (cf, e.g., *Od.* 12. 201–33).

and move with hot blood and arms are sturdy still to hurl the javelin, will you suffer the degeneracy of politics and the kingship of the senate? Is it so terrible to win a civil war? Come, lead us through the Scythian peoples, through the inhospitable shores of Syrtis, through the hot sands of thirsty Libya. To leave a conquered world behind, these hands curbed the Ocean's swollen waters with oar and broke the Rhine, white with icy whirlpools. I need both power and will to follow your orders. For he against whom your trumpets sound, Caesar, can be no fellow-citizen of mine. I swear by the standards prosperous over ten campaigns, by your triumphs over every enemy that if you bid me plunge my sword into my brother's heart or my parent's throat or the full womb of my wife, I will do it all, though with unwilling hand; if you bid me despoil the gods and set alight the temples, the flame of our military mint will melt the divinities ; if you order me to pitch camp by the waters of Etruscan Tiber, will I enter the fields of Hesperia as a bold surveyor; whichever walls you wish reduced to the ground, the ram propelled by these arms will scatter the stones, even if Rome is the city which you have ordered to be destroyed."

Caesar is elevated to a mythical, quasi-divine status as the foremost *gubernator* (helmsman) of the Roman people. Yet, this is a leader who will not reaffirm the values of community and family but annihilate those bonds of love. Blood and love are opposed in the offer of Laelius to kill his own brother, slaughter his pregnant wife and unborn child. The *gubernator* of Rome is to be served through the very destruction of Rome and its gods: all are to fall before the triumph of Caesar, a triumph that is to bring the world and, especially, its wastes under the sway of Caesar. Immediately and in this spirit, Caesar's troops invade.

The loyalty of the soldiers is tested once again in Book V. The setting is a mutiny which exposes further the allure and repulsion that the soldiers feel for Caesar. Caesar's soldiers are being led to Brundisium, where they will embark to cross the Adriatic in order to chase Pompey. But they are increasingly weary. They waver in almost exactly the same way that they wavered in Book I. Lucan explains this loss of resolution:

> . . . seu maesto classica paulum
> intermissa sono claususque et frigidus ensis
> expulerat belli furias, seu, praemia miles
> dum maiora petit, damnat causamque ducemque
> et scelere inbutos etiamnunc venditat enses.
> . . .
> Non pavidum iam murmur erat, nec pectore tecto
> ira latens; nam quae dubias constringere mentes

causa solet, dum quisque pavet, quibus ipse timori est
seque putat solum regnorum iniusta gravari,
haud retinet. Quippe ipsa metus exsolverat audax
turba suos: quidquid multis peccatur inultum est. 5. 244–48; 255–60

Perhaps the short interruption of the trumpet's gloomy sound and the cold, sheathed sword had expelled the fury for war from their hearts; perhaps the troops rejected cause and leader while seeking greater prizes and again put forward for sale their swords stained with crime.

No longer was there fearful muttering and anger concealed in one's secret heart, because what tends to bind doubtful minds together (while each one fears those to whom he causes fear, and each one believes that he alone is aggravated by the tyrants' injustices) no longer held sway. The bold crowd relieves itself from its fears: the transgressions committed by many go unpunished.

Emboldened by their numbers, the soldiers rage at Caesar:

Imus in omne nefas manibus ferroque nocentes,
paupertate pii. Finis quis quaeritur armis?
Quid satis est, si Roma parum est?
. . .
Usus abit vitae, bellis consumpsimus aevum:
ad mortem dimitte senes. En improba vota:
non duro liceat morientia caespite membra
ponere, non anima galeam fugiente ferire
atque oculos morti clausuram quaerere dextram,
coniugis inlabi lacrimis, unique paratum
scire rogum; liceat morbis finire senectam.
. . .
Nil actum est bellis, si nondum conperit istas
omnia posse manus. Nec fas nec vincula iuris
hoc audere vetant.
. . .
. . . ingrato meritorum iudice virtus
nostra perit: quidquid gerimus, fortuna vocatur.
Nos fatum sciat esse suum. Licet omne deorum
obsequium speres, irato milite, Caesar,
pax erit. 5. 272–74; 276–82; 287–89; 291–95

We advance to every crime, causing harm with hand and sword, and yet pious due to our poverty. For what end to the war do you aim? What is enough, if Rome is not enough for you? . . . The time for enjoying life is now past, we have consumed our lives in fighting: dismiss us, old men, to die. See how perverse our prayer is: allow us not to lay our dying limbs on the hard turf, not to rattle the helmet with our escaping spirit, to seek a hand to close our eyes in the moment of our death; and slip away amid our wives' tears and to know the pyre is prepared for one body alone; let us end our old age through sickness. . . . Nothing have the wars achieved if he has not yet appreciated that our hands are capable of anything. Neither duty nor the bonds of law limit our audacity. . . . Our virtue is wasted when we have a judge who feels no gratitude for our services: all we have achieved is called "luck." Let Caesar learn that we are his destiny. Even though you, Caesar, hope for absolute service from the gods, if your troops are angered, there will be peace.

Such an uproar, we are told, would frighten the toughest of leaders (5. 300). But Caesar, shocks his soldiers (and the readers) with his reaction. Entirely unruffled, he sees the crisis as a boon (301–2). He exults in his frenzied troops, goads them to ask for more atrocities and love war without a hint of hesitation (307–8). He would give them the temples of Rome; he would allow them to rape the wives and daughters of the senators. Only the sanity of his uncontrollable troups gives him reason to fear (309). He exhibits a fearlessness that inspires fear, and his voice threatens the mutinous troops (5. 317–8):

> . . . Tremuit saeva sub voce minantis
> volgus iners, unumque caput tam magna iuventus
> privatum factura timet, velut ensibus ipsis
> imperet invito moturus milite ferrum.
> Ipse pavet, ne tela sibi dextraque negentur
> ad scelus hoc, Caesar: vicit patientia saevi
> spem ducis, et iugulos non tantum praestitit enses. 5. 364–70

The passive crowd trembled before the ferocity of his threatening voice, and so great an army is scared before a single man—a man they sought to depose—as if he could command their own swords and could direct the steel against the soldiers' wishes. Caesar himself fears lest spears and limbs will be denied him for this crime; but their compliance overwhelmed the hope of their harsh leader and offered up necks, not just swords.

The soldiers' despair at their never-ending toils is transformed into a self-destructive urge to serve: they offer their throats in his service, inebriated by

Caesar's energy. The troops are overwhelmed by his intensity, and mesmerized in their inability to comprehend their leader. The more inexplicable and excessive a figure he cuts, the more alluring his character seems to be.

To make any sense of Caesar's enigma, we have to appreciate the psychological extremity of the scenes we highlighted above. Caesar fears a slackening of the destructive pace of his war because any pause would allow the soldiers to reinvent their community. They revolt because a temporary respite allows them to see beyond their alienation and their corporateness gives them confidence. They now desire those very pleasures of community they had previously rejected: the religious rituals of death that negotiate communal and individual loss, the caring hand to close their eyes. They long for emotional comfort and connection to those wives whom they were previously willing to slaughter. The soldiers have proved themselves to the great Caesar by embracing his extremity to this point: their rediscovered communal instinct now wishes to bring an end to his excess. But Caesar rejects peace. As the glorious individual, Caesar is incommensurate with a community that cannot accommodate his genius. He thus threatens to kill the leaders of the mutiny and to discharge all who wish to go. Gradually, he disengages them from each other and, ultimately, wins them over by proclaiming his individual power and by threatening them with exclusion from the genius that is Caesar. Before Caesar, each individual is as nothing. The same choice is offered to them as in Book I: community or Caesar. It is a choice between humane values and inhumane greatness, what we might describe as the mundane (or everyday) and History. And the soldiers yield, defeated in the face of a daemonic leader far beyond their rational capacity to understand. As in Book I, they embrace Caesar and offer themselves to death on his behalf.

Caesar exists beyond the conventional, a self-enclosed leader whose appeal is neither to the community nor exactly to individualism. In fact, Caesar sublimates the ordinary individual within his own greatness. Those individuals willingly give themselves to slaughter in support of the great historical figure who can bestow meaning on their lives in the triumph of his individual power. They ride to war not for the great idea, but for the idea that is the great man. Caesar renders the individual as nothing beside him. He is inexplicable and sublime.

KIERKEGAARDIAN FANTASIES, NIETZSCHEAN NIGHTMARES: READING CAESAR AS THE SUBLIME

Encountering Lucan's Caesar opens up numerous critical paths. The *furor* of the founder of empire allows us to read him against Aeneas, as an epic anti-hero and the bringer of ruin to all that Rome had built. We could polarize and politicize the narrative. Yet, Caesar's transgressions are not just personal, a phenomenon of political corruption; they also represent a systemic overthrow in the Roman world. So much in this epic exists beyond norms. The most obvious potential point of stability, the Republican past, does not seem to work for this epic (see chapter 5 below). The poem does not heroize that past and the representative of the Republic, Cato, is as flawed as Caesar (see pp. 118–19). Instead of trying to find a stable moral point, a critical Olympus, from which to view Lucan's Caesar and the Roman world, we choose to read the epic from a point of instability, from Caesar, who is the present and the future of the epic. History speaks through Caesar, as the inexorable fate of the Roman world, but a History that is unstable and irrational, unconventional and transgressive. This History is an Absolute, and thus in itself a manifestation of the sublime.[39]

Yet, it is not the sublime that, at first glance, is most obvious in our text, but the abject – and not just to us. Shadi Bartsch has recourse to the abject to explain the extreme somatic violence of the *Pharsalia:*

> [The a]bject [is] a bodily part or product that both is and is not identifiable with the self and other because it has been severed or separated from its origin. The abject thus includes all bodily emissions, all substances that pass from being part of us to being . . . "other" and often taboo . . . . From the point of view of the individual, [abject] is neither subject (me) nor object (part of the outside world) but something in between; it disrupts our most basic conceptual categories. . . . The disturbing quality of the abject arises precisely from this uncertain status, for it necessarily confuses our sense of the limits that define us against that which is not-us. . . . "[The abject] . . . is what disturbs identity, system, and order, disrupting the social boundaries demanded by the symbolic."[40]

As Richard Kearney suggests,

> [The abject] signals that borderline experience of something monstrously disturbing which fills us with both repulsion and attraction. The admixture

---

39. The term was famously coined as an aesthetic distinction, generally believed to convey an elevation of style beyond the ordinary, by pseudo-Longinus in his rhetorical treatise *On the Sublime* dating probably from the first century C.E. As we will see in our discussion of Caesar below, in modern times the sublime has had, and continues to have, significant impact as a philosophical proposition.

40. Bartsch (1997) 19. The horror and abomination of the abject as a formative influence on subjectivity is the subject-matter of Kristeva (1982), the story of Céline but also a powerful study of the anxieties concentrated at the borders of identity. See, e.g., 11–12; 154–55; 133–45; 206. On this see also Lechte (1990) 158–67.

of disgust and ecstasy is typical of our uncanny response to the abject. . . . "The abject shatters the wall of repression and its judgements," writes [Julia] Kristeva. It returns the ego to its genesis "on the abominable limits of which, in order to be, the ego has broken away. . . . " That is why abjection is intrinsically related to perversion and transgression.[41]

The abject is, however, closely related to the sublime in that both cause an agitation which takes the individual beyond self. As Immanuel Kant puts it in his *Critique of the Aesthetic Judgement:*

> For while taste for the beautiful presupposes and sustains the mind in restful contemplation, the feeling of the sublime carries with it, as its character, a mental agitation connected with our judging of the object. . . .[42]
>
> In presenting the sublime in nature the mind feels agitated, while in aesthetic judgment about the beautiful in nature it is in restful contemplation. This agitation (above all at its inception) can be compared to vibration, i.e., with a rapid alternation of repulsion from, and attraction to, one and the same object. If [a thing] is excessive for the imagination (and the imagination is driven to [such excess] as it apprehends [the thing] in intuition), then [the thing] is, as it were, an abyss in which the imagination is afraid to lose itself.[43]

Kant receives the sublime in a thoroughly ambiguous and apprehensive manner:

> A liking for the sublime in nature is only negative (whereas a liking for the beautiful is *positive*): it is a feeling that the imagination by its own action is depriving itself of its freedom, in being determined purposively according to a law different from that of its empirical use. The imagination thereby acquires an expansion and a might that surpasses the one it sacrifices . . . and is indeed seized by amazement bordering on terror, by horror and a sacred thrill.[44]

The abyss in the depth of which imagination is faced by the prospect of its own loss is a place where control is absent and, for Kant, control is an essential part of rationality and freedom.[45]

---

41. Kearney (2003) 89–90, with a quote from Kristeva (1982) 15.
42. Kant (1987) 247 [P.101, § 24].
43. Kant (1987) 258 [P. 115 § 27].
44. Kant (1987) 269 [P. 129 § 29].
45. This lack of control loosens the bonds of social convention and places the individual on the margins of society. Marginality can either result from or cause the sublime, and thus horror is

For Kearney, the sublime

> is a category for dealing with experiences which are beyond categories. . . . [It] is indeterminate and indeterminable and inspires in us the peculiarly contradictory feelings of "pleasure and pain, joy and anxiety, exaltation and depression." . . . [It] is that mark of the unforeseeable and incommensurable which flouts our rules of reason, and ultimately reduces us to silence.[46]

When silence is the appropriate response to an experience, we are in the realm of the ineffable, the unrepresentable.[47] In a discussion on the aesthetics of the sublime, Jean-François Lyotard suggests that the sublime is

> . . . a pleasure mixed with pain, a pleasure that comes from pain. In the event of an absolutely large object—the desert, a mountain, a pyramid—or one that is absolutely powerful—a storm at sea, an erupting volcano—which like all absolutes can only be thought, without any sensible/sensory intuition, as an Idea of reason, the faculty of presentation, the imagination, fails to provide a representation corresponding to this Idea. This failure of expression gives rise to a pain, a kind of cleavage within the subject between what can be conceived and what can be imagined or presented. But this pain in turn engenders a pleasure, in fact a double pleasure: the impotence of imagination attests a contrario to an imagination striving to figure even that which cannot be figured. . . . Here is then an account of the sublime feeling: a very big, very powerful object threatens to deprive the soul of any "it happens," strikes it with "astonishment" (at lower intensities the soul is seized with admiration, veneration, respect). The soul is thus dumb, immobilised, as good as dead. . . . The sublime [is] no longer a matter of elevation (the category by which Aristotle defined tragedy), but a matter of intensification.[48]

Lyotard's description of the mesmerizing effect the sublime has on the soul, prompts us to search back at the beginning of the epic for the struggle (end

---

frequently associated with the socially and geographically marginal.

46. Kearney (2003) 92 with a quote from Jean-François Lyotard (1988) 92.

47. The critics struggle—perhaps appropriately—with the ineffable and its inchoate ethics, in ways reminiscent of the bewilderment of Lucanian Caesar's own internal and external audiences. For example, Gibson (1999) works on the ways textual silences and, generally, the unspeakable shadows over a text liberate it from the closural pressure of representationalism. In contrast, reflecting on the unrepresentability of the Holocaust, Haidu (1992) explores the ethical conundrums presented to us when, by silence, we tacitly accept the radical incomprehensibility of an event. On this see also Kearney (2003) 88–89.

48. Lyotard (1988) 98–100.

failure) of the people of Rome to make sense of a Caesar absent but looming large and threatening over them. In the terrified citizens' imagination, Caesar is not like a storm at sea or an erupting volcano, but unfamiliar stars and a "sky burning with flames, shooting stars flying sidelong through the empty skies, the hair of a threatening star, and a comet signalling a change in power on earth . . . a silent thunderbolt . . . strik[ing] the ancient site of Latium" (1. 526–35). And the people of Latium sense the enormity and "each gives strength to rumour through fearing, and they dread calamities of their own making that have not been confirmed" (1. 484–86). They fear "unutterable things" and know that "worse than [their] fears will soon come" (1. 634-35). Dread accompanies, and annuls, expression.

In the first clash of the war, Caesar's men seize Ariminum in the early morning and wake the citizens with their military trumpets. In confusion, the menfolk seize their rusted and ancient weapons which lie next to their household gods and rush to meet the threat, but as Caesar's standards are recognized and they see Caesar himself, they freeze. The hushed terror that afflicts them resembles Lyotard's "eloquent silence":

> Ut notae fulsere aquilae Romanaque signa
> et celsus medio conspectus in agmine Caesar,
> deriguere metu, gelidos pavor occupat artus,
> et tacito mutos volvunt in pectore questus. 1. 244–47

> When the glint of Roman eagles and standards was recognized and Caesar was seen high in the middle of the column of troops, they grew rigid in fear, terror seizes their frozen limbs, and they rehearse silently in their hearts mute complaints.

The flurry of activity as the menfolk of Ariminum rush to the defense of their city is emblematic of Caesar's power to dismantle and to transform. In the face of the ineffable Caesar the weapons, long consecrated by their connection to the household gods, have no power; their vitality has been sapped by age just as surely as Pompey's oak totters. The frenzied preparations for battle are a quintessential epic locus. In Book II of the *Aeneid*, the Trojans rush to battle, as news of the Greek invasion spreads. Furious and desperate warfare follows, narrated by Aeneas, who was partly participant and partly observer.[49] In contrast, the sight of Caesar in the forum at Ariminum means that there is no desperate and futile slaughter. Caesar's appearance stops the action. In the face of the sublime, even the powerful conventions of epic are subverted.

---

49. See, e.g. *Aen.* 2. 313–27; 347–69.

Caesar is thus the unstable point of stillness in the epic. History is made in his presence and, as Lucan's preface to the epic suggests (1. 33–64), History suspends all moral and aesthetic judgement when it comes to Caesar. This suspension stems from the historical purpose of the civil wars (or "fate") which is to secure the Neronian age, and thus the wars become a fortunate inevitability in the historical progression. It is obviously tempting to read the preface as exculpatory and ironic, covering an attack on the imperial regime with a fig leaf of panegyric, but it seems to us possible to read in the preface a claim for the triumph of History. Nero and Caesar would thus be depicted as manifestations of History and thus beyond conventional categories of moral and aesthetic value. The individual through whom History acts takes us to the heart of modern historical philosophy, to Hegel's World Historical Individuals, but, more strikingingly for us, to Kierkegaard and Nietzsche.

In *The Book on Adler,* Søren Kierkegaard wonders:

> What are then the dialectical relations between a) the *universal* and b) the *single individual* and c) the special individual, that is, the extraordinary? When the single individual only reproduces the established order . . . then . . . [he is] the normal individual, the ordinary individual . . . his life by no means devoid of spirit because of this. . . . As soon, however, as the single individual lets his reflection move him so deeply that he wants to reflect on the basic presupposition of the established order . . . he is rejecting the *impressa vestigia* [footprints] of the established order, [and] is *extra ordinem* [outside the order] on his own responsibility. And when the single individual continues along this road and goes so far that he does not as the ordinary individual *reproductively renew the life of the established order within himself* by willing, . . . but wants to renew *the life of the established order by bringing a new point of departure* for it, . . . then he is extraordinary. That is, this then becomes the place allotted to him, whether he is justified or not; here he must be victorious and here find his judgment—the universal must exclude him.[50]

Kierkegaard claims that an extraordinary individual can exist and should exist outside normal social and moral constraints and can only be judged by his (and, we would add, her) unique criteria:

> Either a person should want to serve the universal, the established order, express this, and in that case his merit becomes proportional to the faithful-

---

50. Hong and Hong (eds.) (2000) 419.

ness and scrupulousness with which he knows how to conform himself to it, knows how to make his life into a beautiful and rich and true reproduction of the established order—or he should be an extraordinary in earnest, and then he, *extra ordinem,* should step out of line, out of the ranks where he does not belong. . . . It is *the point of departure* that makes the difference between the ordinary individual and the special individual.[51]

The extraordinary individual (extraordinary in the sense of being beyond order, but also with an implication of being beyond reason) steps beyond the moral *ordo* and, in this transgression, Kierkegaard finds something admirable. The *impressa vestigia* of society mask oppression and in transgression there is an escape and a realization of the full potential of the individual. The only measure against which an extraordinary individual can be judged is the individual himself. Mark Taylor argues that:

> Kierkegaard is convinced that . . . the journey to selfhood cannot culminate in spiritual community but must be a solitary sojourn that separates self from other . . . "isolation is a condition sine qua non, an indispensable condition." Since identity does not arise from internal relation to otherness, but is a function of contrast with or opposition to otherness, "spirit is exactly this: not to be like others." The Kierkegaardian formula for authentic selfhood "constantly is: individual in opposition to the others."[52]

This constant journey is the key, and arrival becomes the enemy of selfhood, since arrival (peace) brings an end to conflict and an incorporation of the self into a social system. As Taylor puts it, "to remain under way is to immerse oneself even more deeply in the ineluctable ambiguities, the irresolvable contradictions and the irreconcilable oppositions of concrete existence."[53] The Kierkegaardian hero must reject social convention in order to achieve full individualism and humanity. In so doing, the extraorindary individual becomes by definition isolated and lives in transgression of social and cultural norms. This theory has a binary foundation: the self is perceived in opposition to society. By extension, the sublimation of the individual into the social order becomes a sort of social death, a dissolution of the individual in the conventions of social order.

---

51. Hong and Hong (eds.) (2000) 420.
52. Taylor (2000) 179. The context here is a very engaging comparative study of Kierkegaardian isolation and Hegelian dialectics as two opposing and complementary journeys towards the realization and cultivation of subjectivity (141–80).
53. Taylor (2000) 179.

This transgressive tendency is taken to extremes in Friedrich Nietzsche. Nietzsche attacks liberalism since liberalism tends to advance the happiness or, at least, the material benefit of the greatest proportion of the human population as being the universal good.[54] In this way, there is a democratization of spiritual and moral values and an elevation of materialism to a philosophical position. The absence of struggle and questioning within liberalism creates the last man, huddled in comfort, protected and warm, but in spiritual lethargy, unable to achieve individualism because of their sublimation to the democratic society. Liberalism produces comfort, but man is unable to evolve to the next stage and to achieve his potential, and thus undergoes the spiritual death feared by Kierkegaard.[55] If we see these "individuals" as lost in a crowd, and incapable of achieving their potential, their value is considerably reduced. Further, if one rejects conventional values, such as the sacredness of human life, then these lesser humans become mere tools, objects on which History can work. In Nietzschean thought, History is driven by Great Men, who make their own worlds: Napoleon, Cesare Borgia, and Julius Caesar seize opportunities for power that break with convention, overthrow the moral values of their world, and build a world anew, but rather than the imposition of that new symbolic economy, their motivation is the achievement of power.[56] History becomes the story of great, radical, transgressive males generating change irrespective of human cost.

In perceiving the social values of the industrial age as a dead hand that limited and oppressed, Nietzsche sought the liberation of an elected few and hence denied full humanity to all, obvious in his praise of the exceptional and his deliberate obscurantism: not for him a mass market; he was writing for a small select group. His writings preach a transcendental and primitive authenticity. In *Thus Spoke Zarathustra* (1883–1885), he cast himself in the role of the primitive and archaic Eastern prophet whose obscure and quasi-religious sayings were to generate confusion and intense commentary. In this late work, he continues a theme from an early work, *The Birth of Tragedy* (1872) in which, like Schiller and others, he sought authenticity in classical Greece, but in Dionysian inebriation rather than Socratic rationality. Authenticity resided in passion and power. Thus, Nietzsche longs for

---

54. Schacht (1983) 362–65.
55. Detwiler (1990) 69–73.
56. See Detwiler (1990) 134. There is a potential circularity in reading Lucan's Caesar against Nietzsche since Neitzsche idealized Caesar, along with his namesake Cesare Borgia. The historical accuracy of Nietzsche's view of Caesar is somewhat beyond the point, since he came to stand for an idea in Nietzschean philosophy, that of the Great Man. If one were to take a conventional historical view on Caesar, drawing from Cicero, Suetonius, and Sallust and, obviously, Caesar himself, there is very little that might have allowed Nietzsche to find in Caesar the radical iconoclast that he imagines. Yet, if one were to start with Lucan, the Nietzschean Caesar has a clear literary precursor.

war—the great testing ground of manhood.⁵⁷ War, provided it does not destroy, is the teacher of freedom, the honer of courage, the maker of men. In the anarchy of war and conflict, the power of the individual can rise above social and moral constraints. Here again, we find echoes of Lucan. Lucan's soldiers gave up their families for the love of blood, for pain and the violence of war in which they, as bodies and individuals, came to feel. Their bodies are not turned into the repositories of deadened consciousnesses, for that would cheapen their loss. Their bodies feel the pain of death, and in their violent experience of blood they feel that they are alive. Here, there is a further connection with the abject, with something brutal and primal, with an essentialism of humanity stripped of social convention. In their passion for blood, Lucan's men become real.

Nietzschean primitivism and aestheticization of war led (by devious paths) to the mechanized slaughter in the mud of Flanders as Lucan's Caesar's embracing of passion led, rather more directly, to the wholesale slaughter in the *Pharsalia*. Nietzschean individualism elevated the superhuman above the system, and thereby created the subhuman, *untermenschen* expendable in the great progression of the individual.⁵⁸ Here, we see Lucan's Caesar's cavalier willingness to sacrifice those around him, and their willingness to be sacrificed, as a manifestation of this divided destiny. Caesar is valued by the gods—all others are expendable: their glory only existing in their contribution to Caesar's greater mission. And in their deaths, they are willing, desiring victims of Caesar's transcendent greatness. Yet, the nature of the Caesarian destiny is obscured: what is the mission? Is there any *telos* other than the triumph of Caesar, the triumph of History?⁵⁹

Nietzsche, Freud, Marx, fascism, and state-communism can all be seen as manifestations of a discontent within modernism. It is possible to trace that crisis into the postmodern movement. Yet, here we face a fundamental problem. There can be little doubt that the modern age delivered one of the most materially successful and powerful social formations the world has ever seen; the sum of wealth, by virtually any measure, is higher than at any previous stage in human history. The political and material triumph of modernist liberalism over three centuries has been so complete that recent thinkers on the right have argued that not only is it the hegemonic ideology but it also exercises an ideological monopoly; there is no more ideological discussion worth having.⁶⁰ Yet, discontent with the modern emerges not just in the

---

57. Detwiler (1990) 94–95.
58. See Behler (1996) for a discussion of political readings of Nietzsche and individualism.
59. Cf. here *Pharsalia* 3. 103–12. The Fathers are still present in the Senate in a semblance of political activity. But their power and civic identity is lent to Caesar (or, more precisely wrenched from them by Caesar) and put to the service of his wishes. Caesar becomes the state and the state reflects his values.
60. See Fukuyama (2002).

margins where the poor and hungry struggle for their very survival, but among the warm, sheltered, and well-fed, among Nietzsche's last men. The circumstances of the discontent that we see in modernity are very different from anything that could be found in antiquity, and yet the resonances that we have detected in the literature of the late first-century C.E. suggest that the educated elite, though similarly comfortable to their modern counterparts, also faced an alienation that led to the creation of such an exceptional character as Lucan's Caesar. Faced with what seems by most estimates to have been an astonishingly successful symbolic economy, the Romans of the late first century appear susceptible to gestures of extremity. That desire for exception is not limited to the moment of revolution, when the state comes tumbling down around the emperors, and we are given the chance to witness the scale of the psychological and political trauma caused by sudden loneliness. We see it also in Pliny, possibly the most sophisticated exponent of *amicitia* as an ideological system that we find in Roman literature, sometimes slipping out of the system he so lavishly and lovingly portrays. It drove Pliny from the luxury of his villa to a cherished isolation and to a pursuit of solitude in a pretend countryside. Pliny's villa descriptions offer an alternative conception of the role of the great man, not a man who stands in the midst of his community, but one who stands against nature, a man who can control sublime forces. Pliny's isolation and his flirtation with *dominatio* are not limited to a moment of crisis: they rather speak of a gnawing sense of unease and uncertainty with the received ideologies of Rome.

Lucan seems convinced that the rampant and unconstrained megalomania of his Caesar was ultimately a bloody nihilism. This was not spectacular prescience on his part; although he did not have the historical experience of fascism, he did experience Roman totalitarianism. The ancient texts we discussed in this chapter exhibit varying degrees of a desire to overhaul society, but rejection of the social order was not a viable political solution. The Roman elite may have played with *dominatio* on their estates and in their villas, but they were also aware of the short step from *dominatio* to terror and the destructive consequences of that step. It is abundantly clear to anyone who reads Pliny's *Panegyricus* with its attempts to portray the emperor as a universal, quasi-divine *amicus,* that Romans were in need of a new political ideology. Caught between *amicitia* and *dominatio,* they also needed a new way of constructing the relationship between the individual and society. It is, however, not obvious what this new process of conceptualizing the individual's place in the community might be. Caught between two failing systems, one has a certain sympathy with Pliny's decision to lock himself away in his room in the dark.

3

Death and Love

RATIONALITY AND PASSION

THE BOOK GROUP COMPLAINS

In *Ep.* V 3, Pliny writes to Aristo to defend himself in response to a report of a literary discussion held at Aristo's house. The discussion centered on Pliny's poetry. There were some "who did not disapprove of the writings themselves, but castigated me [Pliny] in a friendly and straightforward manner, since I wrote and recited them." Pliny responds: "I admit I write verse which is not always serious. I also listen to comedies and watch mimes and read lyric and appreciate Sotadic.[1] Additionally, sometimes I laugh, I joke, I play. I can briefly summarize all these types of innocent escapes; I am a man."

It is not immediately easy to see why Pliny is under attack, nor why he should consider it worth defending his reputation. Pliny notes that the attack was not on the poetry itself, which was regarded as respectable, but on the fact that he was the author. Later in the same letter, he produces a long list of authors of high moral repute who had engaged in the production of light verse: M. Tullius (Cicero), C. Calvus, Asinius Pollio, M. Messala, Q. Hortensius, M. Brutus, L. Sulla, Q. Catulus, Q. Scaevola, Servius Sulpicius, Varro, Torquatus, C. Memmius, Lentulus Gaetulicus, Annaeus Seneca, and Verginius Rufus. To this impressive list he added Divus Julius,

---

1. "Facio non numquam versiculos severos parum, facio; nam et comoedias audio et specto mimos et lyricos lego et Sotadicos intellego; aliquando praeterea rideo iocor ludo, utque omnia innoxiae remissionis genera breviter amplectar, homo sum." Sotadics were a form of obscene verse. The manuscript tradition has "Socraticos" as the predominant reading, but that has made no sense to editors.

Divus Augustus, Divus Nerva, Tiberius Caesar, and (though in a different category) Nero. Pliny has here gathered together many leading political figures of the Republic and added a sprinkling of approved emperors. These *viri* demonstrate what Pliny describes in *Ep.* VII 4 as *sales humani* (humane wit).[2] Such a list affirms that the political aristocracy of the late Republic and early Empire found relaxation in literary composition and that the *literati* were also the political men. This makes perfect sense in the cultural milieu of the late Republic, and it seems unsurprising that Pliny, a senator with a literary bent, should wish to cast himself in this mold.[3] Yet, unless Pliny misleads us, this was an issue that aroused some contemporary disquiet.[4]

Pliny returns to the theme in VII 4 and even treats us to one of his poems.

> Cum libros Galli legerem quibus ille parenti
> ausus de Cicerone dare est palmamque decusque
> lascivum inveni lusum Ciceronis et illo
> spectandum ingenio quo seria condidit et quo
> humanis salibus multo varioque lepore
> magnorum ostendit mentes gaudere virorum
> nam queritur quod fraude mala frustratus amantem
> paucula cenato sibi debita savia Tiro
> tempore nocturno subtraxerit. His ego legis
> "cur post haec" inquam "nostros celamus amores
> nullumque in medium timidi damus atque fatemur
> Tironisque dolos, Tironis nosse fugaces
> blanditias et furta novas addentia flammas?"

> When I was reading the books of Gallus in which he dared to give
> to his father the palm and glory won from Cicero
> I found the wanton games of Cicero and
> saw that talent with which he laid aside serious matters and
> in which he showed humane wit and much varied charm
> such as pleased the minds of great men
> For he complains that Tiro by wicked tricks defrauding his lover
> of the kisses owed to him for a little dinner,
> has drawn away the hours of darkness. I, reading these,
> I say "Why after this do we hide our loves

---

2. There is a difficulty in the translation here *sal* can mean good taste, whereas "humanus" carries both the implication of "human" and some, but not all, of the meanings of "civilized."

3. For the mix of literature and politics in the period, see Woolf (2003).

4. Roller (1998) and Hershkowitz (1995) both argue that Pliny is engaged in a literary game.

and fear to speak out and talk of
the other Tiro's guile and our Tiro's shy seduction
and the intrigues by which he adds new passions?" Pliny, *Ep.* VII 4

The poem is included in a letter to Pontius, who had seemingly wondered why a serious man (*severus homo*) such as Pliny would write such stuff, thus triggering a complex exercise in literary allusion: the poet Gallus celebrates his poet-father's emulation of another poet (Cicero), and, in so doing, inspires our poet (Pliny) to emulate the earliest poet (Cicero). To whom should the palm be awarded in this multilayered competition of poetic greatness? The literary artificiality is also obvious in the expression of homoerotic sentiments. Pliny's lover Tiro is explicitly and obviously a literary echo of Cicero's efforts, which in turn echo Greek traditions of amatory poetry. Pliny's answer to Pontius's question is entirely literary. He is inspired by poetry and seeks fame in writing poetry: there is no sense that he is driven by sexual desire for the apparent object of his affection. In fact, it seems not to cross Pliny's mind that he is being asked about sexual desire, and the letter and poem appear to play on the deferral of a passionate meaning. The passion is enclosed in a poem about a poem about a poem in a letter about poetry. Pliny plays on this literary obscurity with the language of deceit, sly seduction, and hidden love. His letter cuts a firebreak between literature and reality. Yet, the text ends with the uncertainty of a question. Why should Pliny be ashamed to write such poetry? The problem for us is not whether Pliny was passionate, but why his display of (literary) passion should arouse disquiet and cause the book group to write.

Pliny's somewhat defensive claim that great men could entertain (literary) passion would appear not to reflect a very real anxiety. Pliny is confident in his defense, and the amassing of a whole series of virtuous Romans on his side merely strengthens and gives context to his argument that noble Romans can also engage in lighter poetry. What Pliny is playing with is a perceived contast with the seemingly hegemonic Roman ethical and philosophical teachings of stoicism. Although there is a lightness of tone that matches the lightness of poetry, that ironic distancing would seem to allude to more serious and fundamental issues.[5] Stoic *apatheia* (a distancing from the assaults of sorrows and emotions) emerges in the Hellenistic period as

---

5. This is a subject that has aroused considerable philosophical debate in recent years. See, e.g., Sihvola and Engberg-Pedersen (1998); also Gill (2006) 207–90 on the different attitudes towards passion within Stoicism. For Aristotle's views on emotion see, indicatively, Fortenbaugh (2003); Cooper (1992); Frede (1992); Striker (1992). On the modern revelance of stoicism, see Williams (1997) 211–13.

a shield of the self.[6] Although the sage should be a model of virtue for the community, he should also maintain a strategic distance from that community so that, if disaster occurs, it will not have the power to affect his *ataraxia* (calmness).[7] The Younger Seneca illustrates this willed distance for his contemporary Romans: when asked about the potential of moderate emotions, his answer is unequivocal: *nostri illos expellunt* ("Our group would drive them out" [*Ep.* 116]); moderate emotion could open the person up to stronger emotion and is thus to be avoided. Seneca's comfort to those disheartened by the task of rejecting all emotion is to proclaim that they must have strength.[8] Upon a friend's death, the wise man is advised to find another friend (*Ep.* 63.13). Even a woman should not grieve for too long, because nothing becomes hateful more quickly than grief (*Ep.* 63. 13). In the *ad Marciam* Seneca concentrates on the idea that grief has no purpose, as *in aeternum fixa nulla miseria mutatur* ("no wretchedness can change what is fixed for eternity" [6.2]) and argues for the benefits of death, whose prospect should lead us to value our children and greedily enjoy our time with them (10.4). Moreover, death is both an inevitability (*ad Marciam* 21) and the means to "cross to freedom" (*ad libertatem transire*) (*ad Marciam* 20.3). It is a release from the dangers of the world (21.3) and from the skin and face and hands all of which are chains of the spirit. (24.5) The *ad Polybium* continues in the same vein. Grief is useless. If one grieves for the lost one, how does one know that they continue to feel? And if they do continue to feel, they are probably in a rather more pleasant situation than they were (9.1). Mortal life is anyhow spent "*in carcere*," echoing the imprisonment imagery of the *ad Marciam*.

Cutting emotional ties is a means of self-preservation in a world which is irretrievably hostile. Separation is the route to emotional health. Epictetus takes this to a logical conclusion: the whole method of care for the self, avoiding emotional disaster, is to regard oneself as passing through and not to form strong attachments to people and things that are only temporarily with us.

> At no point say about anything "I have lost it" but that I have given it back. Your child dies. He is given back. Your wife dies. She is given back. Your farm is confiscated? So this too is given back. But an evil man took it! What is it to you how the giver took it from you? Provided he gave it

---

6. See, e.g., Brennan (1998).
7. The dilemma between engagement with and distance from social turbulence is much debated by Stoics, though not as much as by their modern commentators. Foucault (1986) 81–95, and Veyne (2003) esp. 58–66.
8. See also Inwood (1997).

to you, manage it as if it were another's, like travelers at an inn. Epictetus, *Encheiridion* 11

Even one's body is separate.

> Disease is an impediment of the body, but not of the will, unless the will consents. Lameness is an impediment of the leg, but not of the will. And say this to yourself at everything that happens to you, for you will find anything to be an impediment to something other, but not to you. Epictetus, *Encheiridion* 9

Nevertheless, Epictetus argues that Man is a social being. Humans are bound to their fellow citizens as if they are part of the same body and good cannot be achieved if we do not see ourselves as part of a community (*Encheiridion* 200–1). Seneca expresses very similar views when he argues that emotion is destructive because of the damage it does to community. To approach the community through emotion would be to deny the rational capabilities of the community. Thus, anger is inhuman. To subject someone to anger is to deny their rationality and thus their humanity. Paradoxically, the stoic self of rationality can be separated from all that surrounds it, social difficulties, fortune, wealth, family, friends, and body, and yet it is a self that is connected to society, bound not by ties of emotion or passion or love, but by duty. On the one hand, the freedom of the rational self is elevated to supreme importance so that all that surrounds it is unimportant except that which impinges on the freedom and exercise of rationality; on the other hand, the rational self is a social self, therefore ethical dilemmas are the order of the day for the wise man as he strives to fulfill his social duties. For example, the good man is called to make the judgment as to whether it is better to condemn the bad or whether that will lead to yet more evil. So the man at Caligula's court who dines with a happy smile on the very day that Caligula has killed the man's son (*De Ira* II 33) acts rationally in that he has judged that this is how he must save his remaining son. The man whose children have all been killed by a tyrant and who then praises that tyrant acts irrationally because his actions do not correct the behavior of the tyrant. Ultimately, Seneca himself was asked to make such a decision: faced with the tyranny of Nero, he chose to take his own life in protest. Is this dispassionate response the correct course for the wise?

This tension and presumed opposition between emotions and rationality resound throughout Western culture, and Seneca's treatment of the tension has been recently and influentially revived by Martha Nussbaum. In her representation of Senecan ethics, Nussbaum recounts the story of the liberation of a Nazi death camp through the childish eyes of Elie Wiesel, which was transmitted to her by a colonel at West Point.

> On the day the Allied forces arrived, the first member of the liberating army he saw was a very large black officer. Walking into the camp and seeing what there was to be seen, this man began to curse, shouting at the top of his voice. As the child Wiesel watched, he went on shouting and cursing at the top of his voice for a very long time. And the child Wiesel thought, watching him, now humanity has come back.[9]

The story fits nicely with the stoic duty in the face of evil in society. All would agree that the soldier should react by seeking to punish those responsible and one would expect that the Senecan judgement here would be that those responsible should be killed in order to demonstrate to them the errors into which they had fallen. But should the soldier have simply sighed on seeing the piles of dead, proclaimed that man is mortal, and set to work to honor dispassionately the humanity of the guards by killing them? Nussbaum argues that Seneca's response would, in fact, have been more complex. In a society in which there are manifest wrongs, Seneca, according to Nussbaum, gives direction:

> The official conclusion is that it is always possible to avoid anger, whether by mild detachment or by suicide. But the twistings and turnings of the text contain a far more complex message. For "step back and laugh," "don't see too much," is hardly the advice Seneca gives, when the chips are down in an extreme case of family love and honor. These things matter, and it is slavish not to let them matter. Whether in angry resistance or in the quasi-anger proper to suicide, he confronts them, curses ready to hand, more Weisel's soldier than his own incurious hero.[10]

Nussbaum here appears to be denying that emotional detachment means an intellectual or social disinterest, and instead suggests that intellectual and social commitment requires some form of ethical 'anger.' She sees Seneca's suicide and his advice to others to avoid the worst of tyranny by death or other means as manifestations of an engaged social outrage. What binds the Senecan self to society is a sense of duty which is manifested in a detached and dispassionate responsibility for others. Seneca's own martyrdom, thus, can be read as a witness to the tyranny of Nero and, therefore, a rational,

---

9. Nussbaum (1994) 403.
10. Nussbaum (1994) 437.

educative act, carrying with it the possibility of good, as well as also demonstrating the freedom of the spirit over all constraints. Thus, in a situation of difficulty, the correct response is to use rationality to assess the situation and the correct course of action to follow is the one that will produce the greatest good. This allows for a form of righteous pseudo-anger, perhaps even benevolent violence, which the Stoic can turn either onto others or onto himself. Even in suicide and the moment at which the wise man despairs (in a rational—and not emotional—act) of the social order, it is rationality that triumphs: thus at the moment of his death, Seneca philosophizes and does not "rage, rage against the dying of the light," as the Welsh poet Dylan Thomas famously exhorts his dying father to do.[11] Following this reading, we can understand the soldier's cursing, in the story of Elie Weisel, as a manifestation of dutiful stoic condemnation.

But we can read Elie Weisel's story differently. Most of us can—thankfully—only imagine how the camp prisoners felt as they were brutalized, starved, diminished in every way, and treated as animals. Their lives were of the deepest unimportance. They were people who had seen and experienced the most appalling atrocities and yet had learned to avoid anger and confrontation for fear of terrible retribution. What, then, did they feel when this huge black man, this blaze of color, energy and force, his color being of relevance in a North European context in which those of African extraction were extremely rare, his size presumably contrasting with the physically reduced in the camp, arrived among them and started to curse? We might understand the ferocity as an expression of a deep anger that someone had done this to other human beings, or of revulsion at the abject nature of death and suffering that was all around. Whichever the case, this anger was an expression of the soldier's connection to those other human beings and a gesture of human or humane inclusion for those who were under attack. To be angry was not to dehumanize the guards, but was to humanize the inmates. Anger becomes a sign of a revolutionary moment, when the society of the camp was overthrown, and a hope for and a connection to a new society that lay beyond the confines of the camp. But the anger also shows that to be human was to relate, not just rationally (for the good of social order), but emotionally and directly, in a way which was deeper than rationality, and beyond the social. Anger, in this instance, becomes a way of 'touching' others, a form of the friction that Nancy envisages as the means of connecting in his utopian "inoperable communities" (discussed in chapter 1). In the extremity of an obviously evil society, passion offers the possibility of a human community.

---

11. Thomas 1971, "Do not go gentle into that good night."

In this chapter, we explore the problematization and possibilities of passion in our texts. We follow manifestations of unworldly passion in Lucan's *Pharsalia*, examine suicide and women in mourning from Statius' *Thebaid*, and look at presentations of grief in the more realistic literature of Pliny's letters and Statius' *Silvae*. In the presentation of the extremities of grief we see a social discomfort which is in part related to philosophical doctrines. But we broaden our perspective to look beyond the philosophical hegemony of stoicism—in no sense do we wish to create a dichotomous reading of the texts as stoic or anti-stoic. Instead, we look at how passion creates the possibility of stepping outside the social order, and in this we return to ideas of the Lacanian Symbolic and Real. Grief becomes for us Kristeva's Semiotic, an outbreak of the Real that disturbs to the point of destruction an individual's social being.[12] And this is, of course, a general issue of emotion, especially in extremes, since trauma destabilizes self and in so doing has the potential to destabilize society. In our account however, we also read grief as having the potential to create social unity. This is achieved along two entirely separate and contradictory paths. On the one road, the codes of society provide the scripts through which grief can be expressed, and thus given shape and place in the symbolic economy. These scripts, or rituals, can thus reinforce a sense of self through containing the Real, and thus strengthening the Symbolic. It is our contention, however, that our texts display a repeated failure of ritual, and the impossibility of language as a container of the Real. In these instances, we find further examples of the dislocation of the social self that we discussed in the previous chapter. But here these dislocations to not result in an anomic isolation of the great man; rather, in grief, there seems to emerge a rediscovery of social bonds and of a shared humanity, a humanity that rests not so much on shared rationality, but in a recognition and sharing of emotion that exists outside and in opposition to social convention.

EPIC EMOTIONS

The destructive and alienating power of grief is a prominent feature of the epic literature of this period. In her exploration of lament in Lucan, Statius, and Silius, Elaine Fantham goes as far as arguing that lament replaces traditional forms of conflict in epic. No longer the exclusive realm of soldiers waging a series of coded confrontations based in long-established stereotypical behaviors, the battlefield is regularly filled with wailing, uncontrollable

---

12. See Smith (1998) 14–29 and also 100–101 for a detailed discussion.

females.¹³ The predominance of lament, especially in Statius' *Thebaid*, is such that it threatens the epic code, exposing the futility of valor.

> These recurring speeches of mourning by the poet and his personages are a measure of the dead heroes' worth, so their iteration drives home Statius' message that this worth has been misused, and the grief is greater than the glory. These heroes have died for nothing. There is no new liberty, no heroic code of values, to celebrate . . . [Statius'] intensive use of lament [is] an instrument of condemnation, a verdict on human creed, cruelty, and folly. Lament has triumphed over heroics and put them to shame. Small wonder that the *Thebaid* had no Roman successor.¹⁴

Whereas epic has a tradition of presenting a model of heroism that finds meaning in fame and the claims of history, grief overwhelms the epic stage. In so doing, grief renders the achievements of men meaningless or empty; it undermines the epic genre and the normative codes enmeshed within it. There is an energy associated with mourning that subverts the epic. Rather than providing closure, allowing a coda to the action and the wounds of society to be closed, we find grief stopping the action, rendering onlookers voiceless. Grief provides no resolution, but it both exposes and enacts destruction.

We start with two incidents from Lucan as examples. In Book II, long before the arrival of Caesar's troops, grief and terror have overcome Rome. The intimation of "great disasters" (2. 16–17) afflicts citizens and the symbols of social and political order are laid aside.¹⁵ At this moment, our attention is drawn to the *matronae* of Rome:

> . . . Cultus matrona priores
> deposuit, maestaeque tenent delubra catervae.
> Hae lacrimis sparsere deos, hae pectora duro
> adflixere solo, lacerasque in limine sacro
> attonitae fudere comas votisque vocari
> adsuetas crebris feriunt ululatibus aures
> nec cunctae summi templo iacuere Tonantis:
> divisere deos, et nullis defuit aris
> invidiam factura parens. 2. 28–36

---

13. The disproportional narrative and psychological weight of lament in the *Thebaid* is a frequent concern of recent scholarship. Lovatt (1999) esp. 140–46, discusses lament as an incomplete and unsatisfying closural trope in the epic; Pagan (2000), however, views the lamenting aftermath of Book XII as a open-ended hiatus that allows a new turn to be imagined.
14. Fantham (1999) 232.
15. *Latuit plebeio tectus amictu omnis honos, nullos comitata est purpura fasces* ("every magistrate lay low, clad in ordinary dress, no purple robe accompanying the rods of office" [2. 18–19]).

> . . . The matrons laid aside their former cothing and in grieving bands occupied the sanctuaries. Some spattered the gods with tears, some hurled themselves face down onto the hard floor. They, stunned, loosened their torn hair on the sacred threshold and assaulted with shrieks ears accustomed to be addressed with frequent prayers. And they did not all lie in the temple of the great Thunderer. They divided the gods and every parent had an altar at which to complain.

At first sight, the *matronae* fit within the expected norms of mourning: their matronal finery is put aside, they crowd the altars, they wail and tear their hair, all recognizable and ritualistic forms of denial and destruction of the social self. Nonetheless, their wailing is unsettling. They visit every temple, but in reproach, and not in supplication.[16] They operate in hostility to the gods and can do so because, in this instant, there is a suspension of the normal political order:

> Nunc o miserae contundite pectora matres,
> nunc laniate comas neve hunc differte dolorem
> et summis servate malis. Nunc flere potestas,
> dum pendet fortuna ducum; cum vicerit alter,
> gaudendum est. 2. 38–42
>
> Now beat your breasts, miserable mothers, now tear your hair; and do not defer your grief, storing it for the greatest calamities. Now while the leaders' fortune is on the balance, you have the power to weep; once one of them becomes the winner, you must rejoice.

The rituals of grief normally occurred within specified times and locations. Yet, in this case, the mourning is in advance of loss, thus escaping the designated time and place. The whole city and all the temples are captured (in itself a reversal) by the grieving women. The ordered calendar of divine–human interaction is upset. And it is not just one family that leads the mourning, a mourning that would reassert the social status of the family in relation to the city, but all the *matronae,* and in this democratic moment there is a loss of hierarchy and identity. Grief threatens to engulf Rome; only empire will (perversely, since then there is death) return the women to

---

16. Cf. indicatively here Crotty (1994) with an extended discussion of the figures and rites of supplication in the Homeric epics as a benign, if complex, force leading to the integration of warring elements within a single broader pattern. It is interesting to notice, in contrast, the ambiguous role and success of the traditional channels of supplication followed by the the lamenting Argive women in the *Thebaid.* On this compare Braund (1996), Dietrich (1999), and Lovatt (1999).

their houses. Emotion overwhelms the social world, making redundant all systems of representation and languages of order (in this case symbolized by the practices of the temples). When a new leader will be declared, order will suppress grief to obscure and thereby deny the appalling cost of establishing a new regime. Thus, this hiatus must be seized by the women: the outbreak of community will be denied in the imperial order.

Our second episode comes from Book I. In lines 673–95 we see a possessed *matrona* charging through the streets of Rome relaying prophesies, until, overcome, she collapses. Her prophesy is not a verbal message from the god to the people of Rome, but a verbalization of a vision that the people of Rome cannot see, and which she cannot meaningfully narrate. The *matrona*, "roaming through shocked Rome," recalls a Bacchante racing down from Pindus' summit (674) and spreads panic among the already terrified crowds. The *matrona*-Bacchante is a potent illustration of a rupture in society: her behavior is pre-Symbolic and in her possessed state, she edges into the realm of the nonhuman. As *matrona* she was a guardian of Roman moral and familial values, a keeper of societal order, but as Bacchante she becomes an irruption of the Real into Roman public space.

The prophesy has an order comprehensible to the reader informed of the history of the civil wars, but is incomprehensible to the possessed and to the crowd.[17] The matron is whisked from the snow-covered ridges and steep crags of Thrace to the Nile, and then back to the Pyrenees. She comments on a distant vision of the battle of Pharsalus and the fate of Pompey, but meaning is obscured. Her words work towards representation while at the same time defying all the fundamental rules that could make this representation communicable; we have images, but without the narrative structure that would allow us to make sense of events. The prophesy thus represents History for the reader and it is the force of History that sweeps the woman across the Roman world; yet this History of the future is bewildering. Nothing within the comprehension of the immediate audience can make sense of what she sees. Temporal and spatial boundaries are transgressed in what may look like madness, and in the horrified observation of madness it is the Roman crowd who are excluded from History, from the spaces of their empire, and left to observe passively exhaustion, collapse, and the peace that befalls the woman as the book comes to an end.

Terror, dislocation, and wild Maenadic forces overwhelming social conventions are also features of the treatment of grief in the *Thebaid*. In Book III, after Eteocles has treacherously attempted to ambush Tydeus (his brother's brother-in-law) and thus caused the death of all but one of the fifty

---

17. Thus neatly illustrating the idea that one reader's history is another person's madness.

soldiers who were sent to kill the latter, Maeon, the sole survivor, makes a long, dramatic speech before the Theban king. At the culmination of his condemnation, Maeon kills himself. The suicide releases the Theban audience: parents, wives, and children stream from the city heading for their dead.

> At nuptae exanimes puerique aegrique parentes
> moenibus effusi per plana, per avia, passim
> quisque suas avidi ad lacrimas miserabile currunt
> certamen, quod densa gradu comitantur euntes
> milia solandi studio; pars visere flagrant
> unius acta viri et tantos in nocte labores. 3. 114–19

> Now fainting wives and children and ailing parents poured out of the city across the plains and the pathless spaces; everywhere they run in piteous contest, each hastening to their tears, and as they go, a crowd of thousands accompanies them eager to comfort; some are burning to see the deeds of this one man and the great labors of the night.

Outside the controlled environment of their city, there are no coherent groups; mourners mingle with curious onlookers, who need to see the carnage with their own eyes. They have no leader and do not form a collective; they are simply responding to emotion. We are provided with an assortment of stories, including that of Ide.

> At vaga per dumos vacuique in pulvere campi
> magna parens iuvenum, gemini nunc funeris, Ide
> squalentem sublata comam liventiaque ora
> ungue premens—nec iam infelix miserandaque, verum
> terror est lacrimis—per et arma et corpora passim
> canitiem implexam dira tellure volutans
> quaerit inops natos omnique in corpore plangit
> Thessalis haud aliter bello gavisa recenti,
> cui gentile nefas hominem renovare canendo,
> multifida attollens antiqua lumina cedro
> nocte subit campos versatque in sanguine functum
> vulgus et explorat manes, cui plurima busto
> imperet ad superos. 3. 133–45

> Ide wanders through the scrub and in the dust of the empty plain, great mother of youths, now twins in death, her dirty hair released, her cheeks

bruised and scratched, not unhappy and pitiable now but terrible in her grief, as through all places, through the weapons and bodies, dragging her white hair across the hard soil, she seeks in vain her sons and laments over every corpse. So a Thessalian, rejoicing in a recent war, whose evil people chant to raise the dead, haunts the plain at night, raising her many-headed light of ancient cedar, and turns the dead crowd over in their blood searching the spirits for whom, when burnt, she will command those above.

Having lost her sons, Ide is transformed from "Great Parent" to a woman bruised and smeared with dirt, unable even to locate or recognize those who were her children. She is also transformed from Theban to Thessalian, from the object of communal honor to an object of terror.[18] Her lament cannot provide closure and reconciliation. She is a sinister force, equipped with a witch's chthonic powers. Her voice rises from the plain of death in a necromancy that stretches beyond representation, beyond language, and beyond death. Her magical grief reverses the order of the world, as she herself is revolutionized, transformed from matron to witch.

In her extremity, Ide is removed from her fellow mourners who may equal her in grief, but seem, at least at first, drawn to the restorative powers of ritual.

> Nec minus interea digesta strage suorum
> hic Cthonium coniunx, hic mater Penthea clamat
> Astyoche, puerique rudes, tua, Phaedime, proles,
> amissum didicere patrem, Marpessaque pactum
> Phyllea, sanguineumque lavant Acamanta sorores. 3. 169–73

> Meanwhile no less do the rest lament, as the dead are divided: here his wife for Chthonius, here his mother Astyoche cries for Pentheus, and your adolescent boys, Phaedimus, have learnt of their father's loss. Marpessa washes Phylleus, her promised one; his sisters wash blood-stained Acamas.

The preparations for the respectful cremation of the bodies, the affectionate way they are being looked after, the gentle reminders of the ties of familial love that link the dead to the living who tend them, allow the scene to slip faintly but perceptibly towards the ritualistic. In so doing, the chaotic flight to the battlefield begins to take shape and develop order. The rituals join the living and the dead to the long sequence of ancestors and descendants

---

18. Lovatt (1999) 140–43, offers an extensive reading of this textual mode of demonization in Books III and XII of the epic.

who have performed the same rituals, and will have the rituals performed for them. The wild energy gives way. In the culmination of this transformation, as the grieving relatives stand by the pyre, as if reluctant to accept its fiery completion (3. 176–77), sage old Aletes comes to the center of the scene, his age and wisdom making him a spokesman for tradition and community, assigning to him a voice of authority by which he could bring meaning to the deaths and establish the dominant narrative by which the deaths can be understood and reconciliation begin.

Aletes provides consoling words for the bereaved (*consilium infaustum dictis mulcebat Aletes* / "Aletes was soothing the inauspicious company with words" [3. 178]). His oration starts with a reassuring reference to the ancestors: *saepe quidem infelix varioque exercita ludo fatorum gens nostra fuit . . .* ("our race has often been unhappy and exercised by various games of fortune . . . " [3. 179–80]). Reminding us of the inclusive, participatory, traditional character of funeral rites, Aletes recalls past tragedies and their role in the affirmation of collective identity; the Thebans are no strangers to calamity. Famous Thebans, such as Athamas, Agave, and Niobe have caused destruction by hubristic behavior and have met with divine punishment. Aletes remembers those moments of mourning, when his tears mingled with those of his parents and they were joined in their grief by the whole citizen body. All is redeemed in one sentence: *illa tamen superi* ("but those were deeds of the gods" [3. 201]). Again, a little later, discussing Actaeon's punishment by Diana for desecrating her chaste pool, divine order offers redemption: *sic dura Sororum pensa dabant visumque Iovi* ("such hard lot the Sisters spun; so it seemed right to Jove" [3. 205-6]).[19] Aletes' history of past Theban grief shows that erstwhile mourning was able to bolster a sense of social cohesion, prompting the community to contemplate the depravity, or at least misdirection, of individuals and thus depart from the funeral with a renewed communal awareness. Those deaths are given a narrative meaning that reinforces communal values and provides reconciliation. And yet, the old man's narration has an unexpected twist. The stories are not a prelude to

---

19. In his version of events, any hint that Actaeon may not have deserved his punishment, as his encounter with naked Diana and her nymphs may have been a mere accident, is entirely missing. Contrast Ovid *Met* 3. 173–76:

> Dumque ibi perluitur solita Titania lympha,
> ecce nepos Cadmi dilata parte laborum
> per nemus ignotum non certis passibus errans
> pervenit in lucum: sic illum fata ferebant.

> And while the Goddess of Titanian descent was bathing in her usual spring waters, suddenly, the grandson of Cadmus stepped into the grove, as he was wandering with uncertain steps through the unfamiliar woods, giving a break to hunting.

a new reconciliation; they simply illustrate the lack of public meaning and communal solidarity in the present grief.

> . . . nunc Regis iniqui
> ob noxam immeritos patriae tot culmina cives
> exuimus, nec adhuc calcati foederis Argos
> fama subit, et iam bellorum extrema dolemus. 3. 206–9

> But now on account of the evil of a wicked king, we have lost blameless citizens, so many of the nobility of our land; and as yet no rumor of the crushed treaty has reached Argos, but already we mourn the losses of war.

Unlike past disasters, this grief has no divine balm that may be applied. No promise for new order can soften the raw pain. Instead, the promise is of more death, more war, and more lament. There can be no closure, and the rituals must fail.

To understand better Aletes' summation, we return to Maeon as he enters the city (3. 33–57). Thebes is waking as he comes within sight and the city is shaken violently out of its morning stupor. Maeon's lacerated face is barely recognizable, but as he beats his breast and wails, he provides unmistakable signs of disaster (42–44). Afraid to ask, the Theban women start howling, dreading the answers to the questions never posed (53ff). Verbal representations prove shamefully inadequate, and at the same time ultimately unnecessary, to explain the situation. Wailing transmits what needs to be communicated. Like the *matronae* of Rome, the women of Thebes mourn before they know their loss. Their reaction comes before any official narrative, and before meaning is asserted.

Eteocles receives Maeon in the great hall (58–59). But that meeting also does not bestow a public narrative on events. What grieves Maeon most is neither his ordeal nor his wounds, but that death was snatched away from him (*crudelem veniam atque inhonorae munera lucis* / "this cruel favour, this present of dishonored life" [65–66]). Maeon abuses Eteocles and the compromises, corruption, and oppression that have sustained his authoritarian and immoral leadership (69–77). In anger, Eteocles orders his guards to apprehend the traitor, but before the guards have a chance to stop him he unsheathes his sword and plunges it deep into his chest. His death is almost immediate (81–93).

Maeon's speech and suicide, like Aletes' address to the Theban mourners, denies reconciliation. His actions refuse the comfort of familiar narratives of sacrifice and loss. He avoids being engulfed by a social ideology in which he has lost faith. He is not going to be the honored survivor of an ill-fated mission of which the nation should be proud. His outburst, another puncture in the self-assurance of Eteocles' regime, ensures that the dead are not assimilated by the dominant ideology. Nor, unlike Caesar's soldiers, is he to be sublimated by the hero-king, given meaning by a Nietzschean superhero. By standing against Eteocles, Maeon cannot be portrayed as a national hero. By taking his own life, he further disrupts the process of mourning: better to be dead than live in Thebes; better to be dead than part of the national narrative. If he is not a hero, neither is he the nation's shameful coward; his suicide guarantees his courage. His condemnation of the waste of life in the ambush makes it very hard for anyone to present him as the nation's enemy. He avoids easy representation and assimilation.

A line from the opening of this episode may now be read differently. As Maeon approaches the gates of Thebes, "his face could be hardly seen and his identity was still uncertain" (*necdum ora patent, dubiusque notari* [42–43]). This refers to the physical distance between Maeon and the the Thebans, but we come to realize that Maeon will preserve this distance, and lack of recognition. He refuses a place in the social codes; he refuses the easy ascription of an identity by the powerful in society; he denounces a society that is hiding behind narratives. The rituals (and the narrations therein) with whose help the symbolic economy manages emotion are overwhelmed by the power of Maeon's grief and suicide. Exempting himself from the social encoding of the heroic, Maeon demands a reevaluation of the deaths of his fellow warriors. By his indictment of Eteocles' regime and the ploy that sent fifty Theban citizens to death, he pulls the dead away from an establishment in need of heroes. Maeon refuses meaning in and from grief, and denies the people's collective right to appropriate the deaths; these should remain shocking and pointless, beyond narratives and conclusions. There is no common awareness around which to gather the people, only a pointless, inexplicable waste of young life sacrificed for an irreligious war in a battle condemned by the gods (71–72). Maeon denies himself and the city the right to collective mourning and thus keeps the responsibility for the dead alive; he refuses to close down meanings and consign the event to history (the place of the dead past). Maeon does not feel entitled to mourn.

MOURNING BECOMES THE KING

In this refusal to be integrated into a hegemonic historical narrative, Maeon's death must remain unresolved, a perpetual challenge to the regime and, more broadly, the city. As the mourners outside Thebes refuse reintegration into the myths of the city and reject the closures of ritual, the emotional outbreak enables the Real to emerge, unsettling the symbolic economy not only in the wastes outside the city but also in its heart, with a full-blown assault on the kings, old (Oedipus) and new (Creon) alike, that changes them forever.

Oedipus returns to the narrative at the eleventh hour (and in the eleventh book). We are prompted to recall the opening scene of the poem: the old, decrepit king cursing his sons (Eteocles and Polynices), family, and homeland and retreating into isolation, accompanied only by Vengefulness.[20] Eleven books and oceans of blood later, Oedipus is still sealed off from society. But as news of his sons' deaths reaches him, he rises to rejoin the world. His reappearance is spectral:

> . . . Qualis si puppe relicta
> exosus manes pigri sulcator Averni
> exeat ad superos solemque et pallida turbet
> astra, nec ipse diu fortis patiensque superni
> aeris . . .
>
> . . .
>
> talis init campum, comitique extrema gementi
> "duc," ait "ad natos patremque recentibus, oro,
> inice funeribus!" 11. 587–95

> So the Ferryman of torpid Avernus, hating the ghosts, his boat abandoned, might emerge to the world above and disturb the sun and pale stars, though he himself is not able to endure the air above for long. . . . So does Oedipus enter the plain and cry to his wailing companion, "lead me to my sons and lay their father on their fresh corpses, I beg."

Everything in this scene jars; every angle emphasizes the deepest discord. A creature of the Underworld, blind but unable to bear the light, Oedipus staggers onto the battlefield. The tyrant who had in Book One called destruction upon the world, thus setting in motion the events that led to this present trauma, is now a pitiful, frail figure, dependent on his escort, his daughter Antigone.

> . . . nec noscere natos
> adloquiumque aptare licet; dic, virgo, precanti,
> quem teneo? Quo nunc vestras ego saevus honore
> prosequar inferias? 11. 611–14

---

20. See 1. 49–52.

> I cannot recognize my sons or adjust my words to suit the moment. Tell me, girl, I pray, whom do I hold? With what honor can I, so savage, follow your funeral?

Unable to honor, or name, his sons, or to assume his social position as mourner-in-chief at their funeral, Oedipus' inadequacy dominates the scene. Not only was it all but impossible to reach the place where the two brothers lay, but when it is finally reached, words are barely possible and even holding the bodies proves difficult.

> Nec vox ulla seni: iacet immugitque cruentis
> vulneribus, nec verba diu temptata sequuntur,
> dum tractat galeas atque ora latentia quaerit[.] 11. 601–4

> No sound from the old man. He lay and groaned on their bloody wounds and though he tried for long, words would not come, while he pulled at their helmets, seeking their hidden faces[.]

And yet, as their corpses lie in the makeshift graveyard, barely distinguishable from the surrounding debris, enveloped in silence and almost indiscernible to their blind father, the two brothers escape the distortion of a (respectively) idealized and demonized remembrance. They lie next to each other, indistinguishable, in their own right. The city (or at least the authority of the city) has not reached them, embracing one as the hero as it rejects the other as the foe.

Unsurprisingly, the city authorities usurp the scene, and the bodies. Relishing his new-found power, Creon makes a regal entrance. Oedipus and Creon (the old and new king, respectively) meet in front of the Orgygian gates. Oedipus defies the law and the king, but the new power overcomes the emotional force of the blind former ruler, who is exiled afresh (c. 11. 665–761). Thus, order triumphs over grief, politics over emotions, and it seems as though the Real will be dominated. Yet, the victory of the Law is always fragile, always holding within it the memory of the wordless mourning, and of the spectral king reduced, but restored to his family. In that moment of despair, Oedipus achieves an ethical value that restores to him a latent power. Creon's act of political authority can never erase that specter; merely banishing it beyond the city leaves it as an absent presence, haunting any attempt to build a new order.

Before too long, Creon himself is assaulted by grief. He must arrange the funeral of his son, Menoeceus, and he seeks to inscribe this event within a public narrative of heroism:

> At non plebeio fumare Menoecea busto
> rex genitor Thebaeque sinunt, nec robora vilem
> struxerunt de more rogum, sed bellicus agger
> curribus et clipeis Graiorumque omnibus armis
> sternitur; hostiles super ipse, ut victor, acervos,
> pacifera lauro crinem vittisque decorus
> accubat: haud aliter, quam cum poscentibus astris
> laetus in accensa iacuit Tirynthius Oeta. 12. 60–67

But the King, his father, and Thebes would not allow a plebeian pyre for Menoeceus and they built no common pile of cheap timber to him, but raised a martial mound of chariots and shields and Argive arms of every kind. He lay prominent as a victor over his enemies' heap, his hair decorated with ribbons and laurel, the peace-bringer, as the rejoicing Tirynthian once lay on the pyre of Oeta summoned to the stars.

Pan-hellenic myth and the history of Thebes are enlisted to lend meaning to this funeral. Young Menoeceus becomes the victorious hero, a quasi-legendary figure and the property of Thebes. But then, Creon subsides. The ritual he himself has devised fails and it no longer seems to Creon sweet and honorable to die for one's native land. Creon needs his son back, and is prepared to reject the state. His regality evaporates in grief.

> . . . venientia qui nunc
> gaudia et ingratum regni mihi munus acerbas!
> Tu supremum convexa licet coetusque perenni—
> credo equidem—virtute colas, mihi flebile semper
> numen eris: ponant aras excelsaque Thebae
> templa dicent; uni fas sit lugere parenti
> et nunc heu quae digna tibi sollemnia quasve
> largiar exsequias? Nec si fatale potestas
> Argos et impulses cineri miscere Mycenas,
>   . . . cui vita . . . et sanguine nati
> partus honos. 12. 74–84

[oh son of mine] . . . now you make bitter every joy that comes and the unpleasant duties of my office. Now, for your undying courage, you can sit high on the vaulted heaven; for me, though, you shall always be a god that brings me tears. Thebes raise altars and dedicate high temples, but it befits your father to mourn alone. And now, alas, what worthy rites, what fitting procession can I bestow? None, not even if I had the power to mix your ashes with fateful Argos and ruined Mycenae, . . . whose life . . . and honorable status is owed to my son's blood.

Creon's hopeless impotence mirrors that of Oedipus. Kingship is now a burden, trapping Creon within the confines of official duty, and that official space seems hollow and meaningless. Thebes may build altars and construct stories of public respect in Menoeceus' memory, but Creon needs to grieve alone, stripped of the trappings of power, and even then the rituals of grief are without force. He sheds his royal insignia and indulges in "unregal," uncontrolled behavior. But a king who distorts the composed public posture that he has cultivated so meticulously up to this point, is not a welcome sight. His own creations expel him; Creon is rushed inside by his guards (*abreptum comites in tecta ferebant* / "his men tore him away" [104]).

Yet, even with the departure of the kings, this is a crowded field of lament. The departure of the powers of the symbolic economy leave the field open to women. The stage is taken next by Polynices' Argive wife, Argia. Her very appearance on the field is a problem. For she is, here, a queen in a hostile land, bereft of family and with only one servant. She has escaped her own community, drawn on by "a vast desire" and "a prophetic spirit."[21] In her grief, Argia replays visions of Polynices, first as a guest of her father, then as her groom, then as her tender (elegiac) lover-husband, and finally as a sad warrior leaving his beloved and glancing back at her from the distance with sorrowful eyes (12.188–91). She tries to keep him close, alive in her imagination. Then Polynices returns to her dead and naked begging for burial (12. 191–93). She recognizes him from a cloak that she had given him herself, a poignant sign that the dead prince is still hers. But Argia hastens to *his* territory and *his* home; as she approaches his seat of power, she addresses him as a guest would, engaged with him in a relationship of reciprocity: *venit ad Thebas Argia tuas; age, moenibus induc et patrios ostende lares et mutua*

---

21. 12. 203–4. We first see the widowed Argia as part of a group of grieving Argian wives and mothers who have been prompted by Ornytus to seek help from Theseus, the king of Athens. But Argia recognizes inside her a strength that demands an altogether different form of expression. She distances herself from the rituals of supplication and sets off to Thebes. She wishes her female companions well and takes her leave. She needs to take on the Law-of-the-Father:

> . . . nec surda ferae pulsabimus urbis
> limina: sunt illic soceri mihi suntque sorores
> coniugis, et Thebas haud ignoranda subibo.
> Ne tantum revocate gradus: illo impetus ingens
> Auguriumque animi. 12. 200–4

On the gates of that fierce city I'll not beat unheard. There dwell my husband's parents, there his sisters; I shall not enter Thebes to be ignored. And do not call me back. Vast powers and a prophetic spirit drive me.

redde hospitia ("Argia has arrived at your Thebes, come, take me inside the walls, show me your ancestral seat, reciprocate with your hospitality" [12. 325–28]).[22] As Polynices had found a home and family in exile, so Argia now makes the long journey to Thebes in search of her alternative family and home.[23] She marches on to claim her rights as guest, wife, and family member, and since Polynices is of the regal line, she marches on to be united with the land of Thebes.

When Argia finds Polynices' corpse and stands alone before his broken body, her mind turns to those significant others, the other family from whom Polynices was exiled, but with whom some part of him still remained, part of the condition of exile. And as some part of Polynices was also absent, away from her, he was always hers, but not quite hers:

. . . nullasne tuorum
movisti lacrimas? Ubi mater, ubi inclyta fama
Antigone? Mihi nempe iaces, mihi victus es uni!
. . .
quid queror? Ipsa dedi bellum maestumque rogavi
ipsa patrem, ut talem nunc te complexa tenerem.
12. 330–37

Did you not move any of your loved ones to tears? Where is your mother? And where is renowned Antigone ? For me alone you lie, for me alone you were overcome. . . . But why do I complain? I gave you war, I pleaded for it to my sorrowful father—to hold you now in my arms like this.

Yet, hardly has Argia uttered her complaint, when a shadow emerges from the darkness; after a moment's hesitation, Argia realizes that the newcomer is Antigone. Antigone is initially keen to engulf Polynices within her own world; *her* love is proved slothful, *she* is shamed to have come second to this field of mourning (384–85). In Antigone's first address to Argia, love and grief for her brother are so exhausting, so devouring that she and he have become one: *mea membra tenes, mea funera plangis* ("the limbs you clasp are mine, the death you mourn for is mine, too" [383]). She takes possession of the body through identification. But soon, what appears to be a competition for the exclusive right to mourn subsides, and Argia and Antigone, two

---

22. For more on this narrative of hospitality, see chapter 4 below.
23. As Polynices was received by Argia's father in Argos, fleeing his homeland, family, and army, so Polynices now receives Argia to his other life and other land, which he had promised to her in Book 3. 360–62 and which she never tried to make him forget (see pp. 112–17 for the relationship between Polynices and Argia).

women from the two opposing sides of the conflict, mingle their tears and their stories as they mourn husband and brother. Tales and woes are shared: the narrative of loss of Thebes needs to accommodate the narrative of loss of Argos, and that of Argos make space for that of Thebes (12. 389–90). But these are tales which are largely private, not even transmitted to us as readers. They elude, and remain untouched by, official narratives. Ultimately, Argia renounces her conjugal right to emotional attachment and surrenders Polynices to Antigone:

> Per . . . conscia sidera iuro:
> non his amissos, quamquam vagus exsul, honores,
> non gentile solum, carae non pectora matris,
> te cupiit unam noctesque diesque locutus
> Antigonen; ego cura minor facilisque relinqui. 12. 393–97

> I swear in the name of the stars that witnessed us. . . . He did not long for his lost honours, or native land, though he was wandering exile, or his beloved mother's embrace, but for you alone, and of you he spoke day and night, Antigone. I counted less, he left me easily.

Argia's act of love is to give up Polynices to his sister, that is, yield to the family, but not to the city. Argia honors her husband in his difference from her, in his status as exile and lover. In so doing, she refuses that integration for which she came, and ceases, by an act of love, to be conjoined to Polynices and his household. The bonds of hospitality give way to a deeper bond that she has built with Antigone, whose response is lost, interrupted by an increasingly worried Menoetes (Argia's loyal attendant) (404–5).

The whole episode is articulated by a series of 'failures,' a series of non-happenings. When the two women, prompted by Menoetes, at long last turn their attention to the task in hand, hurdles appear before them; with Polynices' body washed and anointed, the two women in vain seek live remnants in the pyres all around them (415–19). After a frantic search one remaining funeral pyre is found and that barely alive. But Polynices' body is expelled from that pyre: *primos ut contigit artus ignis edax, tremuere rogi et novus advena busto pellitur* ("as soon as the devouring fire touched the body, the pile shook, and the newcomer is driven from the fire" [429–31]). The narrator offers an explanation. The unfriendly pyre was that of Eteocles (420–23); the hostility of the two brothers held strong even after death.

Argia plays the leading role in this defiant as well as indefinable act of mourning: *longius Argia reminiscitur actos* ("Argia spoke for longer reflecting on the past" [391]). She is more comfortable with words than Antigone, reversing the roles in Sophocles' *Antigone*.[24] Statius' Argia is filled with semiotic energy and fuelled by an urge to ensure that her husband does not get devoured either by her desire or by the State. Throughout this encounter, Polynices is always kept a few steps away, never really within her embrace. He has always been somebody else's: his father's, her father's, his army's, and now Antigone's. Argia's self-effacement and self-denial at the moment of grief keep Polynices' otherness alive and present.

In contrast with Sophocles, Statius' Polynices seems to remain unburied at the end of *Thebaid*. Theseus kills Creon and, in so doing, may be seen to restore order, but the memory of Polynices' unburied body still disturbs. Images of lacerated bodies permeate Statius' epic and are an often latent but enduring source of threat to the State. Creon is transfixed by the sight of the decaying bodies of the Thebans, some limbless, others with frightening wounds, and others torn away by the river (11. 276–78), but all retaining the power to shock and disrupt.

Like grief, disgust invades representation and lies outside its control. It leaves a mark through distortion and disfiguration which is unspeakable, inexplicable, but present in language, in thought, in expression. From all the breaches through which the eerie but ever present Real contaminates the fixity of the Symbolic, disgust before a dead body, and especially a violated body, is indescribable and thus immensely potent. Rather than a rational 'anger' that restores the symbolic values of the community, the visceral abject, the rotting of the corpses, produces a horror and a grief which overcome the State, and the rituals of mourning. Whereas mourning is supposed to restore or establish identity and social roles, the Kristevan notion of the abject[25] once more reminds us of the precarious boundaries of identity and of any systematic order. Corporeality and mortality are deeply uncomfortable reminders of the unpredictable, uncontrollable, and unclean that threaten from within meticulously constructed systems of signification.[26] The brutalized corpse, signifying the violence of loss and the absolute difference between life and death, can pierce the certainties; showing that we are all beings unto death. The corpse is "intolerable," as it "exists at the very borders of life" and "shifts the border into the heart of life itself."[27] In the

---

24. In the play, two women agonized over Polynices' body, Antigone and her sister Ismene, with Antigone clearly dominating. The goal then was the burial of Polynices' body: an act of defiance, yet an act performed in the name of the Law-of-the-Father that was violated by Creon's edict forbidding Polynices' burial. See, among many others, Žižek (2004) 52 on this.

25. Already touched upon in chapter 2, in our attempt to explain the unfathomable transgression embodied by Caesar in Lucan.

26. For an illuminating account of the centrality of the corpse within the Kristevan notion of the abject, see Gross (1990) 80–103, esp. 86–93.

27. Gross (1990) 92.

failure of ritual, bodies and the grief on the battlefield retain their power to distress, and in this retention there is both power and a loyalty. This loyalty is to the 'event' of the death and, indeed, to the dead, in refusing words and resolutions. The power is expressed in the the ability of the dead to disturb. Thus even Lucan's Caesar, breakfasting before the dead of Pharsalus, is eventually forced from the field, conquered by the dead whom he conquered in life.[28] Creon's very first act upon becoming a king is to order that the Argive dead are to remain unburied (11. 661–64), but it is this denial of ritual that brings about his downfall. The lacerated bodies that permeate the epics proclaim a viscerality, a physicality, a fleshiness, that makes man ultimately meat, and destroys the sophistications of political ideology. By means of their own horrific dismantlement the massacred soldiers are reduced to pitiful shadows of selves destroyed in the political aporia of the war and, in their anonymity and in their democratic, anarchic decay, they are rendered untouchable, free, and powerful.[29] As with the Roman *matronae,* as with Maeon, it is in death, in timelessness and out of all order that the people achieve power and negate the forces of empire.

AUTHENTICITY AND ORDER: PLINY AND STATIUS AT THE FUNERAL

There is a temptation to draw a distinction between realistic literature and the high epics of the period. One clearly cannot treat different genres in the same way. Certain genres have a distant relationship to the social world, a distance that allows the exploration of sometimes extreme ideas: in cinematic terms, science fiction, horror, and the violent thriller may treat serious social issues (violence, alienation, social exclusion, sexuality, identity), but the nonrealistic genre often allows those issues to be explored in a very stark fashion. One could imagine a historian, armed with only nonrealistic cinema, believing that the early twenty-first century populations lived in terror of technology, mystical monsters, mass murders, and apocalypse, whereas more realistic genres reflect a more complex and less absolute world. Most of us would, we think, rate our chances of being bitten by the undead as quite low in our list of concerns, though in cinema land this appears to be a serious

---

28. The dead bodies pollute the water and the stench chases him away. Lucan interjects: *Has trahe, Caesar, aquas; hoc, si potes, utere caelo. Sed tibi tabentes populi Pharsalica rura eripiunt camposque tenent victore fugato* ("Drink these waters, Caesar, breath this air, if you can. But the rotting hordes rob you of Pharsalian fields, they rout the conqueror and possess the plains" [7. 822–24]).

29. Compare here Pompey's faceless body washed ashore in Egypt in Book IX, and see pp. 136–37 for our comment.

problem, especially if you happen to be relatively young. One could read the Latin epics in this light, draining from them much of their power as social and political commentaries and seeing them as a literature of the extreme created in a world of banality and comfort. Yet, in the 'realist' literature of the period, notably Pliny's letters and Statius' *Silvae,* the same issues of excess in grief emerge repeatedly. It is our contention that the focus on grief and the rituals of death in this literature reflects social concern. In this literature, we have a prime example of a discourse forming around an issue which is of great concern to various members of society. What we find in this literature is not a uniformity of treatment, either within an author's output or even within a particular poem, but a fissured approach, as if the writers are trying out various responses to the problems they face. And it is this anxiety that we connect to the epic literature studied in the last sections.

In *Ep.* VIII 16 Pliny writes to Paternus about an outbreak of disease among his slaves which had led to the death of several of the younger men.[30] Pliny manages to find consolation in having freed at least some before death and allowed others to make a will, which he honored, provided that the goods they had assembled were distributed within the household. In spite of this obvious, albeit limited, act of kindness, Pliny is still worried.

> Sed quamquam his solaciis adquiescam, debilitor et frangor eadem illa humanitate, quae me ut hoc ipsum permitterem induxit. Non ideo tamen velim durior fieri. Nec ignoro alios eius modi casus nihil amplius vocare quam damnum, eoque sibi magnos homines et sapientes videri. Qui an magni sapientesque sint, nescio; homines non sint. Hominis est enim adfici dolore sentire, resistere tamen et solacia admittere non solaciis non egere.

> But although I am pacified by these consolations, I am weakened and broken by that same humanity which pressed me to allow this right. Not that I wish, however, to become harder. I am not unaware that some call a disaster of this kind nothing more than a loss, and that such men seem to themselves to be great and wise men. Whether they are great and good, I do not know; men, they are not. To be a man is to feel pain, to resist such pain and allow comfort nevertheless, but not to be without need of comfort.
> Pliny, *Ep.* VIII 16

This letter follows some of the basic conventions of the philosophical literature of *consolatio.* Nevertheless, the critique is explicit. Those who neither

---

30. See *Ep.* VIII 19 for Pliny's further worries about this outbreak of disease and also for his finding consolation in literature.

grieve nor feel pain at such events are less than human, even if they consider themselves to be philosophers. Pliny advances emotion as the mark of humanity, which is manifested in two ways. The first is in the pain of the loss, which presupposes some recognition of a shared humanity with the slaves; Pliny places himself in the position of the emperor, dominating the *civitas* of the *domus,* and, like the emperor, he expects to feel sympathy for those who were his subjects. The second relates to consolation. In Pliny's view, to be a man is to show the need for comfort. Pliny's letter concludes

> Est enim quaedam etiam dolendi voluptas, praesertim si in amici sinu defleas, apud quem lacrimis tuis vel laus sit parata vel venia.
>
> For there is even a certain pleasure in grief, especially if you weep in the arms of a friend, who will receive your tears with praise or indulgence. Pliny, *Ep.* VIII 16

The act of grieving is in itself social and reinforces the bond between friends. The duty of a friend to console is thereby displayed and so the philosopher who refuses to grieve refuses *amici* the right to console. Pliny would seem to be establishing grief and consolation as essential human needs, but rather than seeing grief as tearing apart the very fabric of the self and erupting violently into the social world, Pliny's grief reinforces the world of *amicitia* and affirms a comfortable sense of selfhood.

Grief keeps appearing throughout the collection. In *Ep.* V 16 Pliny tells Aefulanus Marcellinus of the death of the younger daughter of their mutual friend Fundanus. She died when betrothed and the accumulated goods and finery for the wedding were used for the funeral, adding to the poignancy. His daughter's loss has transformed Fundanus:

> Est quidem ille eruditus et sapiens ut qui se ab ineunte aetate altioribus studiis artibusque dediderit; sed nunc omnia quae audiit saepe quae dixit aspernatur expulsisque virtutibus aliis pietatis est totus. Ignosces laudabis etiam si cogitaveris quid amiserit.
>
> He is indeed a learned and wise man who from his youth has given himself over to higher studies and arts; but now everything which he has often heard, which he has said, he rejects, and, casting aside his other virtues, he is completely consumed by *pietas.* You would forgive, praise him even, if you knew what he had lost. Pliny, *Ep.* V 16

Pliny then provides some advice for Aefulanus Marcellinus.

Proinde si quas ad eum de dolore tam iusto litteras mittes memento adhibere solacium non quasi castigatorium et nimis forte sed molle et humanum.

If, then, you send letters to him in his so understandable sorrow, remember to apply comfort not as if castigating nor too strongly, but softly and with humanity. Pliny, *Ep.* V 16

Fundanus is a philosopher whose philosophy has deserted him. Pliny's response is to emphasize the humanity of Fundanus. The loss of his personal discipline is a loss of those qualities (*virtutes*) which would make Fundanus a *sapiens*. Nevertheless, a single virtue remains, *pietas*. Grief has the power to overturn the disciplines of a lifetime, and this brings unease to the stoic Marcellinus. Pliny defends Fundanus through this identification of grief with *pietas*. Grief is thus given an altogether different epic quality to the transgressive danger it poses in the *Thebaid*.[31]

Pliny also presents us with an example of 'bad' grief in a description of an emotional display by Pliny's enemy, Regulus. We hear of the death of Regulus' son in IV 2 and it is discussed again in IV 7, but we first come across the unfortunate boy in II 20. *Ep.* II 20 concerns the hunting of legacies, at which Regulus was allegedly a master. Pliny tells the story of how Regulus won the affection of a certain Verania by consulting soothsayers to procure her good health, securing her credulity by swearing oaths on the life of his son. In IV 2 that same son is dead. Pliny is not polite about Regulus' reaction: *amissum tamen luget insane* ("he mourns the loss madly"); *nec dolor erat ille, sed ostentatio doloris* ("this is not grief, but the show of grief"); *vexat ergo civitatem insaluberrimo tempore et, quod vexat, solacium putat* ("he troubles the city at the most unhealthy time and, because he troubles, he thinks it a comfort"). *Ep.* IV 7 continues the theme:

Placuit ei lugere filium: luget ut nemo. Placuit statuas eius et imagines quam plurimas facere; hoc omnibus officinis agit, illum coloribus illum cera illum aere illum argento illum auro ebore marmore effingit. Ipse vero nuper adhibito ingenti auditorio librum de vita eius recitavit; de vita pueri recitavit tamen. Eundem in exemplaria mille transcriptum per totam Italiam provinciasque dimisit.

It pleases him to mourn his son. He mourns as no other mourns. It pleases him to commission as many statues and images of him as possible. He busies the workshops: this portrays with color, this with wax, this in bronze, this

---

31. Compare, also, *Ep.* VIII 23 which presents Pliny himself overwhelmed by grief.

in silver, this in gold, ivory, marble. Recently he even recited a book on his life to a huge audience he had gathered; the life of a boy, but he recited it. The transcript has been copied thousands of times and he has sent it out through the whole of Italy and the provinces. Pliny, *Ep.* IV 7

Regulus is subjected to criticism, but it is very difficult to see how his display of grief differs from that expressed by, for instance, Fundanus. Fundanus' grief was *pius*, while Regulus' mourning is *insane*. Regulus' attempts to memorialize his son with statuary, paintings, and in literature is excessive, but in II 17 and III 10 Pliny describes honors offered to Cottius, son of Vestricius Spurinna and Cottia, which include a statue and a literary work composed by Pliny himself.

Pliny seems to find the philosophical teachings on grief inadequate and therefore defends the grieving against putative charges from the philosophically minded. For Pliny grief is natural, a marker of human feeling, but also *pius*, a mark of the Roman hero. Grief is *pietas* as it reflects the duties and bonds towards those one loves, especially family members, but also allows social bonds to be reinforced through the rituals of consolation. To be *pius*, grief must be public, which excuses the statue and literary masterpiece in honor of Cottius. The statue to the boy is public and, implicitly or explicitly, acknowledges the *pietas* of Spurinna whose official duties kept him away from his family when his son was dying. The statue is for the public good, encouraging those who would fulfill their duties towards the state by offering them *fama*. Nevertheless, if grief becomes socially troublesome, and a mere parade, one ends with Regulus.

For Pliny, grief is a sign of virtue because it serves the community.[32] It does so by providing moral *exempla* of proper familial and social relations, and in allowing those social relations to be reinforced as the friends and family console each other. Although he differs from the philosophers, Pliny wishes to bind the unregulated flood of feeling—the traces of the Real, *pace* Kristeva—into the symbolic economy, through the constraints of *pietas*. If grief breaks free from those constraints and threatens to disrupt the city (as in the case of Regulus), Pliny is repelled. Social convention regulates Pliny's own grief. In VIII 16, faced with the death of his slaves, Pliny congratulates himself that he has freed some and allowed the wills of others. There is, however, an important constraint on the bequests as they are allowed only within Pliny's own household. The slaves are ultimately constrained by their

---

32. *Pietas* is a virtue notably absent from Regulus' moral character. One may compare *Ep.* II 20, the account of Regulus' false oath on his son's life, with the finer feelings of our hero, who did not send his literary recollection of Cottius to his parents for fear of disrupting them on festive days during which religious or official duties would fall (*Ep.* III 10).

status as dependents of Pliny and have no social identity other than that of being members of Pliny's household. Their ability to contract to social relations is limited by the authority of the master. Further, the focus of the letter is not on the slaves, either dead or bereaved, but on what Pliny feels. Yet, alongside this conformity, we must place his annoyance with Regulus, who not only causes irritation in excessive display, but also seems to display an absence of unmediated emotion. The force of Fundanus' authentic, unassimiliated grief, however, impresses Pliny, even though he feels the need to cloak it with *pietas*. The irruption of the Real is desired and feared: it holds power and an authenticity.

Looking beyond the stylistic debates,[33] we find a very similar negotiation between authenticity and *pietas* in the several depictions of grief in Statius, *Silvae*. The different treatments of grief reflect not only the brutal levels of mortality in a pre-industrial and almost pre-(medical) scientific society but also a social unease, not necessarily about death, about which there is relatively little concern, but about the process of grieving. The *Silvae* juxtapose seemingly serious poems on grief with parodic treatments. *Silvae* II 1 concerns the death of Glaucias, slave of Atedius Melior. *Silvae* II 4 and II 5 relate to the deaths of Melior's parrot, and of a lion, whereas II 6 is a *consolatio* on the death of a slave of Flavius Ursus. In *Silvae* III 3, Statius provides a *consolatio* to Claudius Etruscus, an imperial freedman, on the death of his father. In V 1, again addressed to an imperial freedman, we have the death of a wife. The poetry becomes more personal with V 3, in which Statius writes of his father, and V 5, of which we have only an initial fragment dealing with the death of a slave-boy whom Statius had taken to heart. In what follows, we shall take II 1 as our key example.

Silvae II 1 is an attempt to console Melior, to whom the whole book was dedicated, for the loss of the boy Glaucias, and its dramatic setting is alongside the glowing pyre. Melior is shown as hating the poet (7), at which point Statius claims:

Intempesta cano: citius me tigris abactis
fetibus orbatique velint audire leones.

My song is poorly timed. Sooner would a tigress robbed of her cubs or a widowed lioness listen to me. Statius, *Silvae* II 1. 8–9

---

33. Statius' *Silvae* are works of very obvious artifice, littered with classical allusions, and set up as *pièces d'occasions*, supposedly composed *ex tempore*. The critical tradition seems mainly preoccupied with style and form. See, for example, Gibson (2006); van Dam (2006); Hardie (2006); Smolenaars (2006).

Not sated with images of wildness, Statius talks of *demens luctus* (mad grief) (10–11) and then

> Nemo vetat satiare malis aegrumque dolorem
> libertate doma. Iam flendi expleta voluptas.
> Iamque preces fessus non indignaris amicas?
> Iamne canam? Lacrimis en et mea carmina in ipso
> ore natant tristesque cadunt in verba liturae.

> No one forbids you to sate yourself with adversity and be overwhelmed openly by pain and grief. Now have you enough of the pleasure of weeping? Now, exhausted, do you not reject the prayers of a friend. Can I now sing? But the song in my throat swims in tears and sad erasures fall on the words.
> Statius, *Silvae* II 1. 14–18

This fleeting "*nemo,*" no one, recalls the philosopher for whom grief is an indulgence.[34] Statius then considers some standard *topoi* of *consolatio:* he proclaims that he, the poet, could be the person to restore rationality through his song, that a friend can bring the bereaved back to the world and remind him of the pleasures of friendship. After that, he turns around his philosophical-poetic consolatory persona. Far from being the rational, supportive friend, the poet himself is struck down by the loss and becomes the bereaved's partner in grief, with the uselessness of words neatly symbolized by their physical effacement, washed off the poet's tablets by a flood of tears. Yet, refusing consolation, refusing to be brought back into the ordered world, is to deny the efficacy of ritual. Ritual cannot rebind Melior to the community and the alternative to the community is a disordered isolationism that is animalistic. Thus, Melior becomes and remains a wild tigress and a lioness, losing both his gender and his humanity in grief. This is the route to madness, but, in impotence, the poet will join him. If Melior is mad, then so is the poet.

This madness was a spectacle displayed at the funeral, a "black procession" culminating in a pyre on which heaps of incense were burned and over which the wailing spirit of the dead boy presided (19–22), a truly disturbing image. Melior is held back from plunging into the flames by Statius and the fathers and mothers present. Such parents share a collective grief at the death of a collective son, but are all overpowered by Melior's display, in which Statius, though restraining and offending by restraining, is a *comes* (comrade) (23–25). The funeral is a parade of Eastern exoticism and the financial reach of the imperial elite, with flowers of Cilicia, herbs of India, perfumes of

---

34. Compare the opening lines of *Silvae* II 6: *Saeve nimis, lacrimis quisquis discrimina ponis / lugendique modos* ("Too cruel is he who judges tears and sets boundaries to grief").

Arabia, Pharos (Egypt), and Palestine (160–62). Melior's extravagance seems an attempt to consume his now "hated wealth" (162–65). The *placidissimus* Melior is now a savage, tearing his clothes and throwing himself to the ground. In the grip of unrestrained grief, he is destroyed by an emotion so strong that all others are lessened by it. The natural parents of the boy are reduced to witnesses of the grief of Melior, who abandons the posture of the (clean) public man hitherto offered to the world. The expense of the funeral and his attempts at self-immolation are manifestations of an urge towards self-destruction. Nevertheless, we are not encouraged to be critical; Melior's loss of sanity is a shared experience.

At the end of the poem, from 208, Statius returns to the conventional *consolatio,* asserting that death is normal: we are mortal, a sentiment that we find in Seneca. But more startling is the final *consolatio.* Glaucias can pass between the land of the dead and the present and thus console Melior in person. It is possible that Statius is imagining a ghostly visitation, that the boy could escape death, reminding us of the disturbing image of the child's spirit wailing over the pyre from earlier in the poem. Only in overcoming the boundary between life and death will Melior and Glaucias find peace.[35]

One of the central themes of the poem is status and Statius performs some extraordinary social gymnastics in order to change the status of Glaucias.[36] After the description of the maddened Melior, attention shifts briefly to the rest of the funeral party.

---

35. The juxtaposition of the emotional heights of the *consolatio* for Glaucias with the consolation of II 4, on Melior's parrot, might give pause for thought. This last is an *hommage* to Ovid, *Amores* II 6, on the death of Corinna's parrot, which is itself a parody of Catullus. Both Ovid and Statius use the opportunity to play with the ideas of *consolatio,* Statius' poem following a very similar structural pattern to that of II 1 on Glaucias. Statius carefully structured the poems in each book of the *Silvae,* and it would be naïve to assume that he was unaware of the possibility that II 4 would be read in conjunction with and as comment on II 1, or, indeed, the *consolatio* in II 6. Nevertheless, as a poetic exercise, publishing parodic examples of a genre alongside seemingly serious attempts could be seen as an act of bravado, displaying expertise in poetic diction rather than necessarily undermining the messages of the more serious poetic exercises. Indeed, the *Praefatio* of Book II, addressed as it is to Melior, explicitly instructs us to read II 1 conscious of the chronological gap between the act of *consolatio* represented in the poem and its publication. The prose *Praefatio* makes it clear that chronological distance from the events of II 1 might open the poem to greater critical attention and, indeed, attack, presumably not for its poetic diction, but for the themes expressed. Thus, Statius shows concern that the emotional outbursts displayed at the funeral in the poem could cause criticism. The mock *consolatio* of II 4 and the *Praefatio* itself may, in some way, offset that criticism by demonstrating that Melior achieved equilibrium and was once more able to appreciate literary sophistication.

36. Compare II 6 in which the dead boy Philetos (possibly a convenient literary name) is elevated above the servile. Philetos was free in mind rather than by lineage (11–12), greater in spirit than in blood (22–23), a son such as was the desire of Greek and Latin women (24–5), an object of manly heroism, Philetos' nobility is displayed through heroic comparanda, with which Statius bombards us (25–57).

> erant illic genitor materque iacentis
> maesta, sed attoniti te spectavere parentes.
> quid mirum?
>
> The natural father and his sad mother were there grieving but, astonished, the parents watched you. What wonder? Statius, *Silvae* II 1. 173–75

That sense of wonder is shared by the parents of the deceased, who are reduced to spectators at the funeral of their offspring. The natural father is described as the *genitor*, whereas Melior is the *pius altor* (pious nourisher) (1. 69), a *dominus* (1. 80), who chose his *nat[u]s* (son 1. 87), and whom the boy made his *pater* (103). Statius' language diminishes the natural father (merely the *genitor*) and builds for Melior a claim for paternity. Hence, the grief is changed from being grief for a slave boy into grief for a son. The grief has thereby been brought within the immediate family to become an act of *pietas*.[37]

Pietas also takes center stage in V 1, which focuses on Priscilla and the imperial freedman Abascantus, their lifelong relationship and the former's death and funeral. Once more, Statius uses the excuse of the *consolatio* to recount the career of Abascantus. Statius manages to provide Priscilla with one of the most unrealistic deathbed speeches one could wish for, in which she finds consolation for her death in the fact that Abascantus has risen so high in the imperial house and serves Domitian (176–93). Abascantus himself is restrained from suicide only by the thought that he must serve the emperor (207–8), and such faithfulness is a greater love than that which Priscilla and Abascantus shared. Even their matrimonial love, "a most chaste passion, deserves approval from the censorial master" (the emperor) (41–42). Statius presents a pretty portrait of Priscilla the Apulian or Sabine wife (the latter surely recalling Horace, *Odes* III 6. 33–44) who rushes to set food on the table as the light fades and to tend to her spouse returning from a day at the plough (122–26). The sophisticated diplomat who managed Domitian's provincial and foreign affairs becomes the simple, poor farmer, an image that must be dangerously close to parody, but one which enabled Statius to establish the couple as an ideal of a previous age, an age of peasant agriculture and *pietas*, of honest labor, and of morals such as those the censorial Domitian sought to restore. Abascantus' grief—expensive and suicidal—was embedded within Roman traditional values and images. There is an attempt

---

37. Similarly, Ursus displays extravagant emotion outdoing relatives in his grief for Philetus in II 6, and, as the pyre consumes spices in a display of extravagant and conspicuous consumption (80–88), Philetus is ennobled beyond his origins. The exceptional character of Philetus transcends those normal social boundaries.

to stabilize grief, bring it within the social codes, and make it rational by the application of *pietas*. With Priscilla and Abascantus, this display of virtue is almost Virgilian. The images used seem self-consciously archaic with its sublimation of personal feeling due to loyalty to the emperor. The archaism of the portrait of this modern Apulian husband and wife could be seen as an attempt to claim that Aenean *pietas* was still possible and that the moral certainties of a mythical bygone age could be maintained. Nevertheless, the uncertainties of the poem stem from the same archaism. Not only does *pietas* triumph to the extent that Priscilla is made with her dying breath to exhort her spouse to erect a statue to Domitian, but Statius, faced with the discomforting fact of her previous marriage, grants her a second virginity (l. 45–56). In the end, Abascantus is forced to deny grief in order to return to the service of the state. By inserting *pietas* into the scene, Statius attempts to bind the grieving into the symbolic economy. But, ultimately, *pietas* fails.

The poems seem to dramatize a tension between *pietas* and grief, but offer parallels with Pliny's reading of grief as potentially at least *pius*. And yet, the social gymnastics seem unconvincing and the focus shifts from a socially comforting reaffirmation of the moral order to the *mira*, the wonders on display. This wondrous manifestation of emotion signals the failure of *pietas*: although Abascantus is urged to return to the service of the emperor, as Pliny finds comfort in the arms of his friends, Melior finds no rest in the rituals. The funeral itself becomes a wonder, and the transformation of Melior from literary sophisticate to madman is a metamorphosis to rival Ovidian fantasies. The destruction of wealth is as of nothing compared with the destruction of self, and the ghastly, spectral image of Glaucias haunts reader and mourner. The very boundaries of death are transgressed in this extremity. The "wonder" recalls the sublime, the transgression of the settled symbolic economy so powerfully represented in the self-control of the *dominus*. Transgression here is the right of the master and the funeral displays the power of the trespassing *dominus* who possesses the slave boy even in death. Melior is accompanied by a crowd of onlookers as well as by the natural parents. The grief and ensuing loss of control are displayed before the entire community. This was madness shared, even elevated. In showing the breakdown of culture, the collapse of all that made these men great in their communities, and the ultimate failure of their value-systems, grief elevates these men to wonders. Their very extravagance draws our sympathy and that of the crowd. The unchartered emotions of the grief-stricken puncture the individuals' established relationship to societal norms. In their authentic, unregulated desolation, the mourners transcend social conventions; they become great.

In V 3, Statius writes of his grief at the death of his own father. There is no discussion of *pietas,* no attempt to confine that passion. Even as he expresses his grief poetically, Statius claims that his poetic talent, and all else that he has learned from his father (also a poet) and his career has been lost. His old voice is broken and he has to find a new authentic voice. He longs to found a temple for his father, to build a new pyramid, to construct a shrine such as that founded by Aeneas for Anchises, to found new Olympic games, to plant a sacred grove. His grief urges him towards new myths and symbols that will transcend and reject the symbolic economy of his time. All that is left when his voice has failed, when the great symbols of his age are no longer effective, is his love for his father.

The expressions of grief in the *Silvae* create a complex and difficult landscape. In grief, the achievements of the cultured world are suspended, or destroyed. Boundaries of time are transgressed. Death itself can be suspended. There is horror and awe. Words lose their power and society is threatened with dissolution. In the shadow of this grief, *pietas* is reasserted as if to reconnect with order, and to explain and justify a grief that seems beyond explanation. But ultimately, it is not *pietas* that offers restitution, but love, which allows a connection with the departed to be honored, a loyalty to the dead to be maintained, and at least a partial restoration to the community.

THE EMOTIONS STRIKE BACK

Seneca's primary evidence for the nature of anger is that it distorts the face and body (*De Ira* 1). The wise man controlled his features and thereby demonstrated his severity and his moral excellence. The rational spirit came to dominate the body, restraining and defeating emotions, and that rationality was displayed through the disciplining of the somatic self for all to see. Rationality was thus not just an intellectual stance, but also and predominantly a social one. In fact, the claim for the supremacy of rationality was, in itself, a political claim. Pliny's *severus vir* placed emotion in the service of the community in displaying and reinforcing social ties. Roman elite males could afford to dally with emotion as long as it did not threaten their position. Thus, the literature of homoerotic love becomes the plaything of the great. Although the Tiros are depicted as powerful, able to use trickery on their desiring lovers, the object of love remains subordinate, the guiles used only to stoke the flames of sexual passion towards what seems an inevitable, if delayed, off-stage consummation. The poetry is an implausible courtly charade, given that Pliny is not attempting to seduce a young boy from the gymnasium or the elegaic mistress (who could famously exclude her lover or swap her affections), but a dependent member of his own household.

The *puer* serves the *vir* and his coquettish guiles merely add to the latter's delight. Pliny mourns his slaves so that he can be consoled. This dominant male ego turns emotion to his service and his poetry and letters display his cultured, sophisticated enjoyment of resources. The letters are in themselves acts of power in which the dependants and the emotions are subordinated sometimes beneath layers of literary artifice.

Yet when probed further, much of the grief and love discussed in this chapter cannot be explained away; the art here is not the ephemeral representation of aristocratic dalliance. The grief on display in the fictional and realistic discourses is too often threatening or, at least, is seen to overcome social norms and conventions. This grief is not in compliance with the symbolic economy; this non-compliance, this refusal to reintegrate and to make peace with the symbolic economy is, as we have repeatedly noted, a failure of ritual. Rituals provide a normative structure, perhaps even a narrative script, for the individual who grieves; thus self-harming, deforming the body, tearing of clothes can all be represented as normal and normative parts of the rituals of grief in certain cultures, even if they appear extreme to those outside the cultural system. Further they provide a recognizable structure which allows those not grieving to associate with the grieving. Though such rituals throw the mourner in turmoil, they are not a threat to the symbolic economy. In fact, rituals protect both the symbolic economy by framing and constraining the deforming outburst. Grief, of course, continues beyond the rituals, but that does not mean that the rituals lose their efficacy. Rituals mark stages in a psychological torment; they are regularized manifestations of emotion in which the extremities of emotion, moments when the social codes do in some way break down and the self is manifested in society in a different light, can be socially sanctioned and limited within the temporal and physical space defined by the ritual. With the help of ritual, extreme emotions can reinforce social codes, building the event which caused the outburst (a death, a falling in love) into the discourses of society. Rituals may enact authentic feeling, real emotion, and, indeed, be a way in which the Real is co-opted into society.

Nevertheless, rituals are moments of social danger. The rituals of a wedding, for instance, display a new series of social relationships to a community, and allow the community to lend its blessing to those social relationships. A wedding can be thus a display of status and power, which might have very little to do with the newly married couple as individuals. But in such display, there is inevitably a social negotiation which may in certain circumstances result in conflict. A wedding provides a framework in which (often) two families can negotiate the transition that brings some kind of unity to disparate social organizations. Funerary rituals can provide the space for similar negotiations, displaying social status and conformity to social ideologies. They also provide a framework in which grief can be managed and death given meaning. A funeral establishes a narrative structure for the trauma of death.[38] Yet, at some point the manifestations of grief in a funerary context have the possibility of moving beyond the socially controlled emplacement of the Real within rituals, and into a dark realm that threatens social order. In our view, far from reinforcing the symbolic economy, the rituals of grief that we have encountered in this chapter repeatedly expose its fragility. Grief is a most powerful form of affect. Affect ruptures meaning as imposed by the structures and strictures of the Symbolic order and, as a powerful form of affect, grief in our texts destroys hierarchies, disturbs the rules of time and place, and transforms identities.[39] Isobel Armstrong suggests that this destabilization in powerful emotion (affect) has a visceral corporeality.

> Affect belongs to an economic principle of energy and discharge with a drive to kidnap representation. It is forever seeking representation. Affect makes us feel alive. . . . Affect moves between the visceral body and consciousness. The body is the spectator of affect. A noticing of affect is a noticing of the body which speaks, both confirming ownership of the body by consciousness and disowning consciousness—my body: *it* speaks. But a silent body is psychic death, and the invading terrors of dissolution arise from the silent body. Psychic life, on the other hand, depends on the *surprise element* of affect. Affect tears the barrier of repression, seizes, assaults and subjugates the subject. Affect rises, erupts, from the interior of the body *without the help of representation.*[40]

Subsequent to its emergence, affect finds representation in what Kristeva has called the Semiotic. The Semiotic, often residing within music, visual art, or poetry, provides an arena in which the Real and the Imaginary leave traces. Its unpredictable domain houses energies that challenge the regimented expressions of the Symbolic.[41] Central to Kristeva's understanding of socialization is the conviction that 'infra-verbal' manifestations of the ineffable, inexpressible Real explode into the ordered world of the Symbolic. Rituals may also be seen as traces of the Semiotic incorporated within the

---

38. *Consolatio* literature similarly provides a narrative in which grief can be understood.
39. For an analysis of the aesthetic and ethical disruption caused by affective states to the complacent body of dominant culture, see Armstrong (2000) 108–48, who builds on the work of Green (1999) on the destabilizing potential of affect.
40. Armstrong (2000) 117.
41. The vibrant presence of the Semiotic within (and before) the Symbolic in Kristeva's work is presented with remarkable clarity by Smith (1998) 14–29. For the "semiotic disposition" in poetry and art in general, see Lechte (1990) 65–87; 123–56.

world of the Symbolic, perceived as the very channel through which the sublime, frightening, awesome Real makes a fleeting appearance in the midst of the regulating Symbolic. For all its self-assured attempts to police signification, the Symbolic is never immune from the Semiotic.

Semiotic traces, indirect reflections of the Real, slip through fissures in the seam of the symbolic economy of society, confronting the rational, disembodied self with its corporeal, irrational roots. The corporeal is the site of feeling through which the world is experienced. Thus, the experiences of the sea, or of art, or of music can be analyzed and discussed, turned into a discourse, but they need to be experienced bodily for there to be any hope of understanding. Traces of that bodily, Real experience then affect the construction of that experience within the symbolic economy. Social relations must again make reference to the bodily and emotional experience of personal contact. Thus, any attempt to construct a symbolic economy in which individuals can be located in direct relationship to each other, is bound to be affected by the Real and contain traces of that Real. As the Symbolic Order cannot exist as a pure and pristine world of individual rationality, the symbolic economy must exist as a world of rituals, management strategies by which the Real can be contained and made meaningful within the boundaries set by society. Yet, this symbolic economy is by no means a fixed, uncontested entity. Rituals can also be usurped by resisting agents, to challenge and dispute aspects of the political operation of power.[42]

The symbolic economy is in continuous, systemic contact with the personal, and an ongoing dialectic between the individual and the social, between the personal and the political, means that the symbolic economy is always in flux. Yet, symbolic economies show resilience and adaptability in spite of all the pressures to which they are subject, and societies do not live in a state of continuous revolution. Various explanations suggest themselves to us. We could argue that power is at work, threatening, disciplining, and cajoling the subjects into maintaining the symbolic economy. We could argue that individuals seek contingent advantage. If we want to continue to operate socially, we need to follow the rules and adhere to the rituals of the symbolic economy. Individuals also have a heavy psychic investment in the symbolic economy, and the price of change, the potential destabilizing of the Symbolic Order, is too high to pay. Individually and collectively, we

---

42. One has to be careful not to confuse struggles over the management of political authorities, as seems to be the norm in contemporary Western politics, and crises within a society's ideological structures. For instance, the conflicts of C.E. 68–70 in Rome appear to have had little ideological motivation and thus to have posed minimal threat to the symbolic economy of Rome, but events such as the industrial revolution, and arguably the fall of the Roman Republic, far more complex in their operation and wide-ranging in their effects, could be seen as challenging pre-existing symbolic economies.

get over trauma. Life, it seems, goes on. Yet, in the desperate, fictionalized worlds of Lucan's *Pharsalia* and Statius' *Thebaid,* the symbolic economy is not so much breached as exploded. The result is a welter of blood. We may wonder why in the mid-to-late-first century, these poets sought to create such striking images of worlds which had lost all sense of order and had gone so horribly wrong. We may similarly wonder why in late-twentieth-century America, at a point of unprecedented wealth, individual freedom, and national confidence, so many of its cultural products depict its treasured youth being destroyed by monstrous forces. The cult of the horror film is as inexplicable as late-first-century Latin epic. The horror of the sublime not only threatens, defying the rules of science as much as the Lucanian and Statian versions defy the rules of myth and history, but also offers a vision of a world in which the symbolic economy may exist, yet is divested of authority. One could read the bloody and visceral outcomes of this negation of the societal rulings as a terrible warning of what might happens if the Symbolic Order is overturned (if we allowed teenagers freely to sate their sexual desires or if we overthrew the political balance): psychic anarchy results with all the monsters of our dreams stalking the land. The world of the Real is far from paradise.

The Imperial epic poems, we could argue, dramatize a crisis which in its very awfulness drives the reader into the safety of the symbolic economy: whatever its failures, it has to be better' than the anarchy of the Real. This would explain the strongly normative character of much of American horror. Although it may seem to come at a high cost, restoration of the symbolic economy could be necessary in order to live, seeking accommodation with the hegemonic ideology which will inevitably be controlled by the predominant political power. Thus, one response to this breach in the symbolic economy is to reinforce that symbolic economy, to adjust to the wound and to heal, to reshape itself so as to accommodate the loss and to build it into the constitutive narrative of the symbolic economy.[43] Thus Eteocles wants to give a civic meaning to the slaughter and incorporate the story into the civic stories of loss, but Maeon tears apart the possibility of reconciliation with his own narrative and his own violent and provocative assertion of the Real. The grieving women by the pyres are lulled by the rituals towards accepting the societal encoding of mourning, before Aletes reminds them of the differences between their losses and those that have made up the symbolic economy of Thebes. In the realistic literature, Pliny and Statius seem to be developing a new *pietas* which will bind this outpouring of emotion to the

---

43. Though at a level of individual psychology, the semiotic incorporates the Real into the Symbolic Order, leaving traces of the former in the latter.

symbolic economy, but Statius' mourners are not convincingly assimilated within the new structure. Melior does not get over the grief for Glaucias, but his love returns to him in ghostly form. An apparition from beyond this world brings him peace, whereas Statius' own father is mourned afresh by the poet, some considerable time after the death.[44] In each case, the love refuses settlement, and the bereaved remain true to the event of the death of the loved. *Consolatio* can be refused and by refusing *consolatio* the revolutionary force of the Real is maintained, questioning and upsetting the fabric of the Symbolic.

To maintain the power of emotion and refuse reconciliation runs the risk of perpetuating not just grief, but also hatreds and angers and thereby continuing conflicts infinitely, creating an emotional storm that will abstract the individual from all social contact. This perpetuation of grief and anger risks plunging us into the world of the *Thebaid* with its endless bloody conflicts. If there are only two choices available, nihilism, madness and violence in the Real, or the symbolic economy of rational liberalism, then there is no choice. Yet before we abandon ourselves (and our literary characters) to the comfort of a restored, imperial Symbolic, we can reverse the dialectic. What the Real allows us to see in ourselves and others is not just the affect in itself (the anger and the grief), but the humanity that lies within. Furthermore, these semiotic outbursts, so important in the Kristevan map of the self and society, may not only be destructive, but also pleasurable. Ultimately, they affirm humanity; they are emergences of the impulsive and the authentic in a social world which regulates, but also alienates, the individual.[45] By maintaining loyalty to that essential humanity that we are allowed to see through the fault opened by the Real, we can come to respect and conjoin with others. In the midst of the anarchy and blood, despite the traumas and disasters, nearly always these classical fictional stories find moments of redemption and love. By the light of the pyres, we see individuals united in mourning, and, what is more, we can unite with them, even those most corrupted and isolated. Eventually, when all else is lost, we can respond as humans to human loss and to human love. Pliny's complaint that Regulus did not really grieve but merely showed grief, points to a yearning for authenticity, not satisfied. When Melior collapses at the funeral, his friends and the crowd rally to him. Statius' tears erase the ritualistic script; he can only hold his friend and weep with him, joining him in the shared humanity uncovered by the Real.

---

44. Similarly, Philetus is reborn in another to bring comfort to Ursus in *Silvae* II 6.

45. Rupture and its akin notion of revolution are fundamental elements in Kristeva's understanding of dominant cultural structures. Chanter and Ziarek (eds.) (2005) offer an inspiring critique of Kristeva's revolt culture and its psychic, political, and aesthetic effects.

Looking for ways to make more sense of the unsettling mourning that we witnessed in this chapter, we encounter the austere ethics of Emmanuel Levinas, for whom selfhood rests on a series of identifications with the social world beyond our making and our understanding. The key word for us here is 'alterity': the very otherness of those via whom we define ourselves preserves a sense of self only as long as that alterity is maintained. But, in Levinas' thought, the alterity does not mean disengagement. The relationship with the others demands continuous engagement so that their otherness can be respected and preserved and so that the others, and hence the subject, preserve their identities (selfhoods) in this world of alterity. One can never complete the process of identification and must always feel the 'tension' and 'lack' at the heart of identity by which alterity is preserved.[46] In *Otherwise than Being* Levinas calls for a radical unselfconsciousness:

> The ego is not just a being endowed with certain qualities called moral which it would bear as a substance bears attributes, or which it would take on as accidents in its becoming. . . . It is a being divesting itself, emptying itself of its being, turning itself inside out, and if it can be put thus, the fact of "otherwise than being." . . . To be oneself, otherwise than being, to be dis-interested, is to bear the wretchedness and bankruptcy of the other, and even the responsibility that the other can have for me. . . . The self is through and through a hostage, older than the ego, prior to principles.[47]

Levinas depicts a self whose only commitment is to communicate with the non-ego, which, however, and crucially, "precedes any relationship of the ego with itself," and also precedes "the auto-affection of certainty, to which one always tries to reduce communication."[48] This communication is an adventure of subjectivity but not one seeking the reenforcement or at least the recovery of self-consciousness. Instead, it leads to openness, and exposes the self-in-the-other to risk of loss, dispossession, and unlimited guilt in the face of one's inability to fulfill one's obligation towards the other. Finally, this "openness is not complete if it is on the watch for recognition. It is complete not in opening to the spectacle of the recognition of the other, but in becoming a responsibility for him."[49]

In this ethical perspective, loyalty to the other cuts across all other forms

---

46. There is no conscious choice involved in this responsibility; it does not stem from a sense of a self that extends to the other. Rather, this responsibility substitutes for the essence of a self. What is more, the responsibility is never fulfilled and therefore never concludes or meets with success. A fundamental sense of failure is constitutive of an austere and unassimilable self.
47. As selected by Hand (ed.) (2000) 106–7.
48. Hand (ed.) (2000) 108.
49. Hand (ed.) (2000) 109.

of subjectivity. The self-location within a symbolic economy is rendered null by the loyalty shown to the other. The emergence of the Real in our texts makes possible not a restoration of the ordered world, a return to the laws of society, but a contrary and oppositional loyalty to the other. Lucan's grieving *matrona,* break free from time and place, seizing the moment in a democratic, nonhierachic collective loyalty to those about to die; their temporary conquest of Rome resists the momentum of the epic as it builds to Caesar's conquest and an imperial settlement. The women of Thebes and the grievers of the *Silvae,* wrest themselves away from the symbolic economy and from the state, resisting the comforts of familiar narrations. Maeon's angry, irreconcilable, unfinished, lonely grief attempts to preserve the alterity of the dead, protecting them from coercive participation within bankrupt social codes.[50] Loyalty to the other becomes the revolutionary moment, and in that there is a glimpse of a new society (often of mourners) in alienation from the old.

Let us return to the American soldier liberating the concentration camp. In this most malevolent of places a hideous but all-powerful symbolic structure held sway. But the soldier's anger brings forth the collapse of this economy, bursting open the channel for the restoration of a strong and forceful humanity to the inmates of the camp. Ultimately, this anger is a way in which we can see through the eyes of the soldier, the Jews can see through the eyes of the soldier, and we can see afresh through the eyes of the Jews. Thus we are all joined in a common human experience and, ultimately, in shared responsibility. Once that is achieved, we are committed to connect continuously in order to understand that shared humanity. In anger, there is freedom and liberation. But to maintain that freedom is a hard task. How do we stop the trauma closing, the symbolic order restoring itself around a victimhood that once more separates and divides humanity, with the camp declared a terrible aberration, a kind of anti-place.[51] This is a hard task. It binds us to an ever renewed engagement that prevents us from ever condemning events to history. Senecan rationality rushes to place the

---

50. Spargo (2004) provides illuminating literary and theoretical background reading here, with a study of several poignant examples of ethical failure, or even resistance, to grieve in Anglo-American elegiac poetry.

51. In the modern world, we are overwhelmed by examples of how grief and trauma are re-formed to construct social identity and selfhood. Trauma is particularly powerful in this regard, with memories of genocide, forced migration, slavery, and war lying behind the identities of many modern nations or ethnic groups. A unique injustice can define a group as different from all others, creating for them a unique identity and a symbolic economy all of their own. Shared trauma can be powerful in creating communities and politicians have often seized on assaults and threats to the memories (real or imagined) of a community in order to enforce social discipline, to quieten dissenting voices, and to build powerful symbolic economies that will allow the regulation of societies and, too often, the traumatic exclusion of individuals and groups from those newly re-formed societies.

dead in the past, arguing that death is inevitable and that new friends will replace the old ones. It does not allow for the responsibility towards the other to be continuous and for the passions of loss and love to remake one's identity. We have seen how Seneca and Pliny fail to question the injustices of their social system, devaluing slaves, women, and barbarians. On the other hand, in Statius we witnessed love crossing the boundaries between free and enslaved, as well as between life and death. Love allows a woman, Argia, to make the great journey to the battlefield on which her beloved lay, allows her to give up that beloved to his sister. There is a drive in the *Silvae* and the *Thebaid* that dismantles conventional social stratifications, urging the individual to locate their sense of being not in their own status (which is ultimately meaningless) but in their emotional connection with another.

4
Private Partners and Family Dramas

REMAKING LOVE: PLINY, STATIUS AND ELEGY

After the highly artificial treatment of the poetry of homosexual desire, discussed in the previous chapter, Pliny's very next letter continues the theme of love.

> Incredibile est quanto desiderio tui tenear. In causa amor primum, deinde quod non consuevimus abesse. Inde est quod magnam noctium partem in imagine tua vigil exigo; inde quod interdiu, quibus horis te visere solebam ad diaetam tuam ipsi me ut verissime dicitur, pedes ducunt; quod denique aeger et maestus ac similis excluso a vacuo limine recedo. Unum tempus his tormentis caret, quo in foro et amicorum litibus conteror.

> It is incredible how I am dominated by desire for you. Love has the greatest responsibility here, but then we are not used to absences. So I lie awake most of the night with you in my mind. Then, during the day, at the time when I usually see you, my feet lead me, and that is the best way to put it, to your suite, but then, sick and sad, and as if excluded, I retreat from your empty threshold. The one time without this torture is when I consume myself in litigation for my friends in the forum. Pliny, *Ep.* VII 5

A prose love elegy is being offered to us in which Pliny takes the twin roles of the husband and the excluded lover (*amator exclusus*). His mind is so restless that he cannot sleep. He is led by his feet and not his mind. Emotion dominates the poet's physical state which in turn dominates his mental state. Since his desires are not sated when he arrives at the threshold of his wife's empty room, he is sickened and saddened.

The elegiac clichés recall programmatic elegies, such as Propertius I 1 which proclaims the poet's physical and emotional enslavement to love and the heartless *puella*. Such poems set up a twofold subversion: of the freedom of the Roman aristocratic male and of the dominance of the male over the female. However, turning the world upside down by reversing polarities can paradoxically preserve conventions by adhering to the polarized categories. Being a slave to love, for example, was not necessarily an attack on slavery or on contemporary gender values. Yet, Pliny's letter places these poetic conventions in a new context, that of the relationship between a respectable Roman senator and his wife, thus bringing the socially disruptive elegiac *topoi* into the heart of the respectable household. But even this slavery does not represent an obvious disruption of the dominant political order. Overwhelmed by love, Pliny still finds respite in the forum, in a clear departure from the typical elegiac tendency towards the subversion of such public landmarks.[1] The polarities between elegiac and conventional masculinities are thus eroded in Pliny, and this realigns the subversion of elegy.[2]

Statius also plays with the conventions of elegy in a song to celebrate the wedding of the poet Stella to Violentilla (I 2).[3] The poem opens with an account of the Muses as they descend from Helicon, immediately highlighting the metaliterary nature of the poem. The Muses are led by Venus (described merely as the "Aenean mother [*genetrix Aeneia* (11)] and *petulans Elegea* [impudent Elegy (7)] limps among them, attempting to represent herself as their tenth sister (7–10). The image of Elegy attempting to win a place above her station is probably intended to be comic,[4] with her limping recalling both the metrical qualities of the poetry, and Vulcan, whose limp and erotic association with Venus had comic potential. Further, the reference to the dignified Aenean epic demeans elegy (and could be read as an allusion to the literary history of the Augustan period in which elegy competed with

---

1. See e.g. *Tristia* IV 10 with Ovid casting aside his rhetorical career when his speeches turn into verse, or Catullus 10 where the poet and his friends, the new poets, (in)famously use the forum for a subversive pursuit of girls and not for a conventional pursuit of politics.

2. Pliny shows himself to be a master of all literary forms, moving effortlessly between poetry and prose. Arguably, his prose elegy shows his literary ability to produce elegy within the epistolary genre. For Ovid, the Augustan elegist, however, oratory and poetry are incompatible. One could potentially also read Ovid's 'difficulty' with prose as a further claim to subjugation to love, again in stark opposition to Pliny.

3. Though the *Silvae* also contain more conventional descriptions of love, buried in depictions of matrimonial bliss and conventional family units. See, for instance, Pollius and Polla (*Silvae* II 2) or Statius' own parents (*Silvae* V 3).

4. And also to remind us of Elegy's other famous appearance in Ovid *Amores* 3.1.

epic). Statius seems to be gently attacking elegy. It is only at this point that we are told that this procession is bridal (11), and thus elegy's presence (the poetry of adulterous love) becomes anomalous. The metapoetic treatment of the wedding becomes a major theme of the poem.

> Cedant curaeque metusque.
> cessent mendaces obliqui carminis astus
> fama tace: subiit leges et frena momordit
> ille solutus amor: consumpta est fabula vulgi
> et narrata diu viderunt oscula cives . . .
> . . . Pone, o dulcis, suspira, vates
> pone: tua est. licet expositum per limen aperto
> ire, redire gradu: iam nusquam ianitor aut lex
> aut pudor. Amplexu tandem satiare petito,
> contigit, et duras pariter reminiscere noctes.

Let cares and fears give way. False suggestions of clever poems cease. Rumor, be quiet. That once unbound love obeys the laws and chews the reins. The tales of the crowd are ended and the citizens see the kisses so long narrated. . . . Lay aside, sweet poet, sighs, lay them aside, prophet: she is yours. You are allowed through the open door openly, to take the step again. Now there is no doorman, law, or shame. He who has sought satisfaction in an embrace, reach out and remember as well those hard nights. Statius, *Silvae* II 1.26–30; 33–37

Statius is, as is fitting for a wedding song, in playful mood. The elegist Stella has his courtship of Violentilla played out to elegiac *topoi*. His love is illegitimate, sung in typical elegiac style by the *amator exclusus,* shut out of his lover's house. Statius alludes to scandal and public disapproval, again a common elegiac trope, a scandal created or furthered by the outpourings of the broken-hearted poet.

Augustan elegists played on the fiction of their own relationships so that autobiography and poetic invention are inextricably intertwined in their verse. The tension was increased by the use of pseudonym. Their loves always retreated from public gaze, becoming a story. Similarly, Stella gallantly used a pseudonym, Asteris, to disguise the object of his affection. As with the elegists, Stella's love was not for an innocent girl but a *docta puella,* a woman of sexual experience. The elegists achieved sexual union with their loved ones, and Stella's poetry seems to have alluded to a consummation of the love. Yet the message is mixed. The kisses are narrated, the poems mendacious, leaving open the possibility of a nonconsummation. But in the marriage there is a concentration of sexual images so obvious as to suggest parody. Love submits, chews the reigns. The door, so long closed, is now open. Nobody prevents the poet from entering and he is urged to reach for his girl and remember his erstwhile, elegiac frustration. What was elegiac, covert, and narrated now becomes epic (blessed by the Aeneadic mother), viewed but unspoken. The unreal has become real. The published sighs of the poet become (unpublished) embraces. The relationship has escaped the poetic sphere and entered the public sphere, but in ceasing to be poetry, it becomes private. Yet, Statius urges Stella to remember his elegiac self in the lawful embraces of matrimonial love; the *amator* survives in the husband. Similarly, the citizens are expected to remember the illicit passion in viewing the licit kisses and affections shown by the newly married couple. Elegiac love is brought within the norms of imperial society, but its disruptive force is still fondly remembered.

A striking metamorphosis is accomplished within the poem. Statius takes the dangerously erotic and oppositional elegy and turns it into a joke. He takes the erotic and illicit relationship between the poet and his *puella* and makes it legitimate through marriage, transforming the *puella* into the *matrona*. The poet turns out to be destined to become a senator Stella (1.174–81), the widow remarkably becomes the virginal bride, the poetry of opposition turns into the stuff of historical epic. Yet love remains in Stella's passion and Violentilla's blushing.[5]

Tamed, the powerful and disruptive force of erotic love is harnessed and mollified in ways that mirror the treatments of grief by Pliny and Statius in the *Silvae*. The *docta puella*, the well-taught, promiscuous, dangerous girl of Augustan elegy thus blends into the respectable *docta matrona*, the well-taught, virginal, faithful, and conventional wife of the late first century C.E.[6] Whereas the *puella* of Augustan elegy thrived in separation from, and opposition to, the public world of marriage within which a married couple participated in the community and fulfilled their public roles, the *puella-matrona* that emerges in Pliny's and Statius' writings exists in a space between the public and the private. In Pliny's letters love develops in the bedchamber and is then displayed to the public through his prose elegy, linked to the forum in which he finds respite. In Statius, public and private are also complexly interlaced. Yet, as the elegiac ideal of the Augustan poets reversed the polarities of the traditional order, so the incorporation of that

---

5. In spite of the fact that this was a second marriage for Violentilla (1. 137), Statius grants her a restored virginity, comparing favorably with those of famous virginal innocents from the Roman past (I 2. 241–46).

6. See Hemelrijk (1999) 79–86, for the difficulties the *docta puella* faced in becoming the *docta matrona*.

ideal into the Roman family, in the case of Statius and Pliny, questions and alters the relationship between the conjugal couple and the social world. The development of an elegiac conjugality creates a new model of the conjugal couple and a new kind of social space in which the former can negotiate their relationship with the public.

In this chapter, we trace conjugal relationships and the importance of the intimate spaces of the bedchambers across our genres. In the *Thebaid*, Argia, Polynices, and Adrastus stand for an intimate family group which provides an emotional and ethical center for the poem. In the *Pharsalia*, the empty heart of Cato's marriage is contrasted with the love between Pompey and Cornelia, and we read that love as offering a personal redemption for Pompey. Yet, the epics do not leave the intimacy within the bedchamber. The love that animates Argia, Polynices, and Adrastus is a major dynamic force in the story, leading Adrastus to the destructive war. Love reaches beyond the bedchamber into the world of war and politics, the world of epic. That world is presented in brutal colors, dominated by a mob whose political loyalties are to an outdated and harsh moral code, whose spokesmen reflect an unthinking mass mentality, from which the thoughtful and informed of Argos shy away. Although eventually they come to the same conclusion, and History eventually sweeps them up, Adrastus and his family act in ethical loyalty, and that is their tragedy. Similarly, for Pompey and Cornelia communal Rome is a difficult place from which they are effectively exiled. Pompey moves as History's plaything, swayed by the various communities of Romans he encounters, unable to act of his own volition and seemingly unable to affect events until after Pharsalus. Only then, when the battle is lost does he reject History, rejoin his wife, and recover his self. In this redemption, he is embraced by a new community (Lesbos) and through Lesbos he has the hope of a reconciliation with Rome. In his last days, he ceases to be a general of imperial Rome, and offers us instead a new social model, an anti-imperial society of lovers, that survives his death. The ethical flow from the bedchamber to society allows a reformulation of society, perhaps only a fleeting one, since History does, in the last instance, triumph.

If the epics suggest a certain reading of the conjugal relationship and society, Pliny's letters concerning his wife provide a very different picture. Although there is a seeming intimacy, it is one in which the demands of the public, the *mores* of society, dominates. The "ethical flow" is not from the bedchamber to society, but in the opposite direction.

The texts of love suggest a problematic relationship between the affectionate couple and society. At the very least, the interest that we see in conjugality in these different genres suggests a problematization of conjugal love in the late first century C.E. The texts provide two or perhaps three different models of the relationship between the conjugal couple and the social system. In conclusion, we continue the Levinasian themes of the previous chapter, but this time work through the ideas of Jean-Luc Nancy to assess how and why conjugality has such a powerful resonance within the texts. In so doing, we discern in our texts an ethical individualism embedded in the respect for the other.

TALES OF LOVE: INTIMATE POLITICS IN THE *THEBAID*

In Book II, as war over the throne of Thebes between Eteocles (resident and in power in Thebes) and Polynices (a voluntary exile, married to Argia, daughter of Adrastus, king of Argos) comes closer, Argia and Polynices steal away to their bedchamber in the palace in Argos.[7] Polynices spends a sleepless night, but tries to hide his worries and tears from Argia, who, nonetheless, understands his anger (2. 319–33) and voices her concern:

> Utque toris primo complexa iacebat
> aurora pallore virum, "quos, callide, motus
> quamve fugam moliris?" ait "nil transit amantes.
> sentio, pervigiles acuunt suspiria questus,
> numquam in pace sopor. Quotiens haec ora natare
> fletibus et magnas latrantia pectora curas
> admota deprendo manu? Nil foedere rupto
> conubiisve super moveor viduaque iuventa,
> etsi crudus amor necdum post flammea toti
> intepuere tori: tua me, properabo fateri,
> angit, amate, salus. tune incomitatus, inermis
> regna petes poterisque tuis decedere Thebis,
> si neget?" 2. 333–45

As she lay on the bed in the first pale light of dawn embracing her husband, she said "What thoughts of flight do you consider, shrewd one? Nothing eludes lovers. I feel the sighs sharpen your sleepless complaint and sleep brings no peace. How many times I have stretched my hand to feel your face swimming with tears and your chest heaving with great qualms. I am not moved by the breaking of our marital treaty, nor the thought of early widowhood, though our love is raw and the flames of our bed have not cooled: I will be quick to speak, your safety concerns me, my love. Will you

---

7. The intertextual web of this episode is examined by Hershkowitz (1997).

seek the throne unarmed, without comrades, and could you escape your
Thebes, if he [Eteocles] refused you the throne?"

The threads of private intimacy and public duty are entangled in Argia's anxieties and public and private are set against each other, but not as mutually exclusive spaces. The princess of Argos expresses her passionate love, worthy of an elegiac heroine, but these private and interior passions (though expressedly inferior as motives) reinforce her political (and military) rationality.

Polynices' comforting reply similarly mixes love and politics and with a warm embrace and tender kisses that dry her tears, his soft, sweet words offer reassurance and a dream of a future together.

> solve metus animo, dabitur, mihi crede, merentum
> consiliis tranquilla dies; te fortior annis
> nondum cura decet. Sciat haec Saturnius olim
> fata parens, oculosque polo demittere si quos
> Iustitia et rectum terris defendere curat:
> fors aderit lux illa tibi, qua moenia cernes
> coniugis et geminas ibis regina per urbes. 2. 356–62

> Put fear away. Believe me, a calm day will come for counsels as is due. Cares beyond your years do not befit you. Should, one day, the Saturnian father know my destiny, and if Justice cares to turns her eyes from heaven and defend rights on earth, perhaps the day will come when you will see your husband's battlements and you will pass through two cities as queen.

Behind this image of Argia, queen of Thebes and of Argos, lurks the ghost of Helen of Troy walking on the battlements of the besieged city (in *Iliad* 3), seen and admired by two armies. Alongside her stands Dido, the Aeneadic Helen, whose infatuation destroys the regality that had so impressed the Trojan leader in *Aeneid* I. Helen and Dido make an infamous link between love and the doom of a city. In these earlier epics, lovers are causes of war. It is a bleak palimpsest, but it is overwritten by Polynices' story line. In an attempt to escape from the epic plot of the *Aeneid,* Polynices suggests a narrative in which the lovers stay together, unifying the two communities in Argia and in her love for Polynices.[8] In this fantasy world, elegiac love triumphs over epic and the couple's bedchamber proves the place in which

---

8. Another character from the *Thebaid* who stands for love, Hypsipyle, works in this against an engendering of conflict (as detected by Keith [2000] 65–100) in Latin epic, whereby the female tends to be associated with (barbarian) conflict and the male with (Roman) order.

the fundamental rift between the two domains is healed. As the world of politics crosses the threshold of the bridal chamber, the concerns of the world beyond reach Argia and Polynices' bed, invading the intimacy of their private space. Yet, from their bed, the two lovers conjure up solutions for their peoples' problems and offer a gentle vision of the future. So armed in tenderness, Polynices has to re-cross the threshold of his "beloved room" to seek out Tydeus, his brother-in-law and ally.

Tydeus and Polynices had met in combat in Book I when they fought each other as strangers before the gates of Argos (1. 401–34) (see p. 181). But their differences have been set aside and friendship has blossomed between them (2. 364–66). They are now both married to Adrastus' daughters, Deipyle and Argia. Adrastus joins the princes, the princesses appear to have their say, and they all deliberate on the proper course.

> Fit mora consilio, cum multa moventibus una
> iam potior cunctis sedit sententia, fratris
> pertemptare fidem tutosque in regna precando
> explorare aditus. Audax ea munera Tydeus
> sponte subit; nec non et te, fortissime gentis
> Aetolum, multum lacrimis conata morari
> Deipyle, sed iussa patris tutique regressus
> legato iustaeque preces vicere sororis. 2. 367–74

> There was a long consideration in their council with many shifts of sentiment, but now one plan seemed better to all, to make trial of his brother's good faith and seek by negotiation a safe return to the throne. Bold Tydeus volunteered for this duty. And then Deipyle tried with many tears to delay you as well, the bravest of Aetolia's sons, but a father's orders, the assurance of the safe return of an embassy, and the just prayers of a sister won her over.

This is a political decision debated within the family; a father, his sons-in-law, and his two daughters all speak and that decision is informed by the love within the family. We thus have a portrayal of a functional and largely happy family who allow those private feelings to cross into the public sphere.

TOWARDS THE END of Book III, an exhausted Tydeus returns from the mission for which he volunteered in Book II and relays his version of the Theban ambush.[9] The news throws Adrastus into turmoil. For seven days he

---

9. Cf. also chapter III with discussion of the reactions to this ambush at Thebes.

keeps to his room agonizing over whether to go to war (3. 440ff). While the city rages all around him and prepares for conflict, Adrastus stands apart, his anguish reflecting his appreciation of the gift of peace and his bitter knowledge of the seductive influence of war on younger, more impetuous men.[10] Nonetheless, a leader must eventually engage with his subjects and Adrastus returns to the public.

His first action is to consult the seers, Amphiaraus and Melampus (3. 450ff). They perform the necessary rites (3. 460–98), but the catastrophes they foresee plunge them into despair. Deploring their own prophetic skills (*piget inrupisse volantum concilia et caelo mentem insertasse vetanti, auditique odere deos* / "They regret intruding in the council of birds and probing the mind of forbidding heaven, and hate the gods that heard them" [3. 549–51]), they recall the simplicity of the Golden Age when men did not need to know the future (3. 559–62). And then they run away, tearing off their priestly garb and choosing retreat; the one to the solitude of his house, the other to the wildernesses of the countryside.

> Ille nec aspectum volgi, nec fida tyranni
> conloquia aut coetus procerum perferre, sed atra
> sede tegi, et superum clausus negat acta fateri;
> te pudor et curae retinent per rura, Melampu. 3. 570–73

> [Amphiaraus] will suffer neither the sight of citizens nor a conversation in private with the tyrant or in a gathering of the nobles but shuts himself up in his dark residence and, closed up, refuses to declare the deeds of heaven, while shame and anguish keep you, Melampus, in the countryside.

Rejecting the current age, both men retreat into a mythic other world, a pastoral universe or a Golden Age free from prophetic skill. Unlike Adrastus, who knows that he must return to the public and worries as to how he might influence that public, the seers cling to an impossible hide-out. Amphiaraus holds his silence for twelve days, keeping in suspense princes and people (3. 574–75). Much like the old wise king, the two seers find it difficult to play a role in a society on the verge of catastrophe. But in their absence, the public stage becomes an arena of uncontrollable passions.

> . . . iam suprema Tonantis
> iussa fremunt agrosque viris annosaque vastant

---

10. By keeping his silence, Adrastus contradicts inherited, (mainly) archaic models of epic leadership. Montiglio (2000) 46–115 explores the Homeric epics as a locus where *logos*, speech, voice are all highly valued and silence is encountered with apprehension as a sign of doubt and helplessness.

> oppida; bellipotens prae se deus agmina passim
> mille rapit; liquere domos dilectaque laeti
> conubia et primo plorantes limine natos:
> tantus in attonitos cecidit deus. 3.575–80

The Thunderer's highest commands roar out, emptying the fields and ancient towns of men. The War God gathers massive crowds before him. Happily, they leave their homes, the beloved wives, their children weeping at the doors. The god struck so powerfully the frenzied people.

In this frenzy, Capaneus appoints himself the voice of the people. He is described as a prince of ancient lineage (3. 600–1), and thus a recognizable descendant of the archaic heroes of the Homeric epics. Yet the hubris that threatened the old heroes' virtue is Capaneus' *modus operandi*. For him justice is an annoyance and the gods a despicable trap (3.601–3). In front of Amphiaraus' doors, where the people have gathered for a proclamation of the omens, Capaneus asserts a vision that is cheered by delirious crowds: a story of war, valor, and conquest. This unsavory manifesto is deliberately aristocratic, with Capaneus pouring scorn on the lowly birth of the priest, questioning his manhood, and offering a vision of a community in which identity and masculinity are forged on the battlefield. Even though Amphiaraus, stung by the criticism, warns that the path down which Capaneus leads the Thebans will end in death, the community is lured by the offer of a collective identity, a common understanding and a common cause.[11] There is an exuberance in the crowd that overwhelms the individual dissenting voice. The gate provides a symbolic boundary. Amphiaraus does not cross the threshold to bring his understanding into the public arena, and so that arena comes to be dominated by a traditional thirst for battle. By the time he is forced to speak, the opportunity for communication across the boundary has been lost. The fierceness of the crowd has rendered the outside dominant and relegated the inside to inaudibility.

Night falls and the jingoistic crowd subsides. Attention returns to the bedchamber. Argia once more endures Polynices' grief. As dawn approaches, this torture proves unbearable (3. 678ff) and she seeks refuge in her father's chamber. A moving scene develops, with Argia in her father's embrace, holding her baby son, Thessander: three generations united. In the pre-dawn light, a moment in which the world pauses and holds its breath, the family is united. Public concerns give way to intimate interactions. Argia is driven by love of Polynices. She cannot suffer his sorrow and shame, a sorrow and

---

11. We are reminded of Lucan's lament of the loss of the individual amidst the carnage of the battle in 7. 617–37.

shame that will pass to Thassander, and asks her father for war.

> . . . Tu solus opem, tu summa medendi
> iura tenes; da bella, pater, generique iacentis
> aspice res humiles, atque hanc, pater, aspice prolem
> exsulis; huic olim generis pudor. 3. 695–98

> You alone can help; you hold the greatest right to cure. Give war, father; look on the low state of your fallen son-in-law, look, father, here at the exile's child; one day will he be shamed by his birth!

And yet the war will be joyless. Argia is filled with sorrow at the prospect of parting from her love. She fears that she will regret her request. When dawn comes, Adrastus, his mind made up as a result of his daughter's intervention, rises and moves from the elegiac world in which the decision for war is made, into a sea of troubles.

The episode in Adrastus' bedchamber leaves behind a lingering expression of deep discomfort with the community. The community denies the power of the emotions of the bedchamber, those threads that bind together the family. The scenes of love occur in interstitial times, when the city is neither awake nor asleep. Only here, in a time out of time, can love speak. When dawn comes, the lovers must part as the world of the city comes to dominate. In this moment Argia longs for the bedchamber, and to return to the time of love. However, the force of the epic world, the community and its values triumph. Argia's love cannot save her husband. Emerging from contemplation in his rooms, Adrastus cannot convince the crowd to drop their epic values for elegiac ones. The community emerges as the tyrant, a controlling force with destructive potential. The elegiac world is haunted by the community and its values, and eventually has to give way.

Adherence to collective values threatens the community and the individual with death and destruction. With Capaneus, the older codes of the community are given voice, but the heroic code is shown as hollow. In spite of traditional Roman morality seemingly resting on just such an unwritten, traditional code, the *mos maiorum,* the ethical stance in this instance seems to rely on the recession to the bedchamber.[12]

---

12. Cf. here Hypsipyle's story, i.e., her refusal to sacrifice her father in accordance to the biddings of her community, as recounted by herself in *Thebaid,* Book V. Like Argia, Hypsipyle appears in the *Thebaid* as an alternative to the destructive potential of conformist communties. It is intimacy and a private bond with her father that enables her to rise to civic maturity, challenging the community voice, defrauded and twisted as it has become by the collective rage-turned-madness of her bent-to-revenge fellow citizens.

CHAPTER 4

TALES OF WAR:
GENERALS AND THE COMMUNITY IN THE *PHARSALIA*

This tension between politics and love, the city and the bedchamber, also features in Lucan's *Pharsalia;* it is, in fact, a significant element in the depiction of two of the main figures, Cato and Pompey. The contrast between them is stark. We first encounter Cato in Book II. Caesar has already crossed the Rubicon and is heading towards Rome, a city by now in panic. When Brutus knocks at his door at dawn, Cato is ready. But dawn for Cato is not the in-between time of intimacy. Instead, he glories in his community and offers himself to Rome. Yet, his speech takes a somewhat surprising course.

> Sidera quis mundumque velit spectare cadentem
> Expers ipse metus . . .
> Otia solus agam? Procul hunc arcete furorem,
> O superi, motura Dahas ut clade Getasque
> securo me Roma cadat . . .
>   non ante revellar
> exanimem quam te conplectar, Roma; tuumque
> nomen, Libertas, et inanem prosequar umbram. *Pharsalia* II 289–90; 296–97; 301–3

Who would want to see the stars and the world end staying free from fear? . . . Shall I alone have peace? Gods, keep such madness far from me when the Dahae and Getae are moved by this disaster, I stand safe as Rome falls. . . . I will not be torn away before I embrace your lifeless body, Rome, and follow your name and empty shadow, Liberty.

Cato yearns for death in battle, a death that will purify Rome, and he wishes to become a sacrificial victim for the good of his people.

> Me solum invadite ferro,
> me frustra leges et inania iura tuentem
> hic dabit, hic pacem iugulus finemque malorum
> gentibus Hesperiis: post me regnare volenti
> non opus est bello. *Pharsalia* II 315–9

Let the sword strike me alone, I who vainly defend the laws and empty rights. Let this throat give peace and an end to evils for the People of the West: after me he who wishes kingship has no need of war.

Cato appoints himself a representative of the old order, an order that he knows is doomed. Emphatically, he does not endorse Pompey, either as an individual or a general. Pompey is also aiming at sole rule and Cato's presence in his army is designed merely to confuse his message, to give a sense of Republicanism to the Pompeian cause.[13] His reason for fighting is nihilistic: to join with the destruction of the world. Although he hopes for personal destruction for the sake of his community, his participation in the war will bring evils to Italy that will only end in his defeat. On the very same day, Cato's former wife, Marcia, turns up at his modest house (2. 238). Cato had famously given up his fertile wife to Hortensius, a friend in need of descendants. Hortensius has died and Marcia returns from the funeral seeking a new marriage to Cato. But, exhausted by her procreative efforts, she asks only for "the empty name of wife" (*da tantum nomen inane conubii* 2. 341–42). She rejoins Cato not in joy, but to be closer to the perils of war. There are to be no festivities for the wedding, no rituals, and no sex (2. 360–80). Cato believes himself created for the world (2. 383); therefore, he has banished personal pleasure from his life (2. 390–91). The bedchamber will be barren in this nihilistic marriage.[14]

Pompey is a very different figure from the nihilistic Cato. We see very little, and learn even less, of him in the first few books. He is introduced to us as the old oak, a shadow of his old name, deprived of the public adulation to which he had been accustomed.[15] We might expect an imposing

---

13. That Pompey cannot convince should not surprise us, but it has intrigued Bartsch (1997, esp. 73–100) who puzzles in front of the unlikely 'canonization' of the aging hero in the later stages of the poem, and then decides to see Pompey (or at least his name) as the only possible anchor for an ideological statement in this world, the hero of an "effective history rather than objective history; namely the kind of history that is precisely oriented toward the production of a response" (140).

14. After this episode Cato disappears from the narrative for several books and we do not meet him again until Book IX. By then Pompey has lost the battle of Pharsalia and Cato becomes leader of the remnants of the Pompeian army. He assembles the troops in Libya and then decides to march across the desert to join with a client king. The march through the Libyan desert is an ultimately grotesque episode. Cato responds to the prospect of the suffering with a long semi-suicidal speech in which he proclaims his desire to walk on uncharted territories and meet poisonous snakes; he competes with his soldiers in withstanding heat and thirst, and the glare of sun; he rejoices in the price of courage (9. 379–406). Lucan finishes the scene by describing Cato as *securus* (9.410), even though his death is predicted. The adjective can mean "tranquil" or "calm," but it can also mean "careless" or "free from worry." The march through Libya is a disaster. The army is hit by a sandstorm (9. 445–92). Their water is lost, but they continue in desperate thirst. The soldiers encounter serpents (9. 619–937), and Lucan dwells on the snakes for more than three hundred lines (on which, see most recently Eldred [2000]). Yet this punishment is in a lost cause. The reader was informed of this before the march started, and the soldiers find out when the army reaches the oracle of Ammon (9. 564–86). In a useless commitment to death, and to the lost Republic, Cato sacrifices his soldiers, who have followed him devotedly but to whom he shows no personal feeling.

15. For more discussion and scholarship on other aspects of this introductory image, cf. chapter 2.

individual intent on public honor, yet we get a ghost who slips from Caesar's grasp towards the end of Book II (660ff) and flees Italy at the start of Book III (1–7). The dramatic focus shifts from Caesar to Pompey at the end of Book V (722–815). But even at this stage we do not meet Pompey, the general, leading his troops to war. Instead we meet Pompey the lover, proffering his tender farewells to his wife as he sets out for battle. Pompey prefers to postpone his destiny, to indulge in gentle delay and sneak time from fate (*blandaeque iuvat ventura trahentem indulgere morae et tempus subducere fatis*) (5. 732–33).[16] He prefers the company of his Cornelia to presiding over his army. When the time of parting eventually comes, Cornelia collapses and has to be carried onto her boat. The book ends with a portrait of the lonely Cornelia, miserable in the marital bed.[17] The power of "lawful Venus" pulls Pompey outside the conventions of martial epic and into a secluded, elegiac world (5. 727–28). Cornelia may be the lawful wife, a *matrona*, but she is divorced from her beloved by war, her status lost (764–65).[18] Instead of waiting patiently for her husband to return, the *matrona*, like the elegiac *puella*, is reduced to despair in the absence of her lover.

As the story progresses, Pompey appears reluctant to play his part. Sluggish and disconnected from his soldiers and officers, he increasingly withdraws, but as he retreats we start to understand more of him. In Book VI Caesar's attempt to surround the Pompeian army at Dyrrachium backfires and his army sustains heavy losses. As a depleted Caesar withdraws to Thessaly, Pompey's officers try to convince their leader to return to Rome. But Pompey refuses:

> . . . "Numquam me Caesaris," inquit
> "exemplo reddam patriae, numquamque videbit
> me nisi dimisso redeuntem milite Roma.
> . . .
> . . . Dum bella relegem,
> extremum Scythici transcendam frigoris orbem
> ardentesque plagas. Victor tibi, Roma, quietem
> eripiam, qui, ne premerent te proelia, fugi?" (6. 319–29)

---

16. In stark contrast to Aeneas, and his (in)famous haste to leave Dido and Carthage in *Aeneid*, Book IV (see, e.g., 4. 280–82), once his destiny has been made clear to him by Mercury.

17. The double motif of heart-rending separation at the beach, and abandonment in the cold marital bed recalls Ovid's *Heroides*, a corpus famously engaged with an extended elegiazation of epic heroines. See, for example, *Her.* 1. 7; 2. 91–99; 121–30; 10; 7–16; 25–36.

18. The private and informal nature of the liaison between Pompey and Cornelia had already been condemned, by Julia, Pompey's previous—and now late—wife and Caesar's daughter, in her apparition in Book III (3. 23). Julia calls Cornelia a *paelex*, a concubine, and Cornelia later reiterates the characterization (8. 104–5). Batinsky (1993) discusses the topic within the broader framework of Julia's overall ideological significance.

"Never shall I return to my land in the style of Caesar," he said. "Never shall Rome see me return unless I disband my army. . . . I will cross the edge of earth, the Scythian ice and the burning plains, to banish war. Rome, shall I destroy your peace as victor when I fled in order to to prevent battles from striking you down?"

Pompey refuses to return to Rome, but his exile is a communitarian act and his isolation has ethical value. Here his tactics are at last explained. There were historical precedents for a march on Rome (recalled in 6. 302–3) and such historical narratives offer a template by which the community could understand individual actions and by which individuals could negotiate their relations with the community. But Pompey refuses to subsume his ethical responsibilities to the strategies approved by history. Such a refusal challenges conventions and asserts individuality.

Book VII opens with Pompey asleep and dreaming of the applause he will receive in Rome, once more the darling of his community. Yet, this is a community from which he is currently isolated. When dawn comes, he returns from his dream-like union to the reality of his alienation: an angry crowd of soldiers confront him, demanding battle (7. 1–100). Eventually, Pompey allows himself to be persuaded. The soldiers take up arms and, as Pompey unleashes them, they cease to be soldiers, becoming a crowd ruled by anger.[19] His lack of resolve means that he has lost control of the situation and that the crowd comes to dominate the political sphere.[20] By evading his role as general, Pompey's individualism strengthens, but his political position disintegrates. Yet still there is the dream, the image of a Roman people who do not rage at him but applaud him in the theater. The dream appears to have almost more reality for Pompey than the soldiers who face him. In his alienation, it is only in dreams, the element of the psyche beyond his control, beyond the control of anyone, in which he can be restored to the community. Pompey's dream dissolves before the anger of his troops, but its memory hints at a different kind of future.

After the battle, Pompey flees to Lesbos where he is reunited with Cornelia. There, he realigns his identity and, remarkably, stands out against History, proclaiming that rather being known as Pompey the Great, "he would

---

19. The text here reads *arma permittit populis frenosque furentibus ira laxat* (7. 124–5). Inelegantly translated, this would be: "He allows the people weapons and anger releases the reins for fury." Notably, the soldiers are here *populus*, a crowd without discipline, which recalls the slightly earlier image of Pompey in the theater. Also, it is anger, not Pompey who releases the soldiers onto the fields.

20. Pompey, in marked contrast to Cato, fears the bloodshed of battle, but is unable to control his soldiers. It is as if the sphere of the public is so brutal that only a brutalized individual can exert authority.

prefer to be unknown to all nations" (*Cunctis ignotus gentibus esse mallet* [8. 19–20]). He regrets his successes in the Sullan wars, against the pirates of Cilicia, and his conquest of the Hellenistic states (8. 24–26). Cornelia faints as he arrives on Lesbos, pale and covered in dirt (8. 54–66), and, Pompey, so long passive, leaps from his ship and rushes to his love (8. 62). Although her attendants are unable to help her, Pompey takes Cornelia up in his arms and blood returns to her cheeks; she revives in his embrace (8. 65–68). Now Pompey speaks:

> . . . Erige mentem,
> et tua cum fatis pietas decertet, et ipsum,
> quod sum victus, ama. Nunc sum tibi gloria maior,
> a me quod fasces et quod pia turba senatus
> tantaque discessit regum manus: incipe Magnum
> sola sequi. 8. 76–81
>
> Raise your spirits, let your *pietas* contest with fate and love me because I am defeated. Now I am a greater glory for you, because the rods of office and the pious crowd of the senate and the great band of kings are taken from me: start following Magnus, alone.

In defeat, Cornelia is urged to *pietas,* but a *pietas* that contends with History. Pompey gently ushers Cornelia into a life that will no longer be in the shadow of Fate/History. For the first time in the epic we get a flavor of the charisma of Pompey. Suddenly, he seems freed from the geriatric weakness of the old oak. Cornelia responds by offering her life for the safety of her spouse (8. 96–105). But the extremity of the moment takes its toll:

> . . . Sic fata iterumque refusa
> coniugis in gremium cunctorum lumina solvit
> in lacrimas. Duri flectuntur pectora Magni,
> siccaque Thessalia confudit lumina Lesbos. 8. 105–8
>
> So she spoke and sinking back into her husband's lap, she reduced all eyes to tears. The heart of hard Magnus turns and Lesbos blurred the eyes that were dry at Thessaly.

Durus Magnus sheds his epic armor. The warrior becomes the lover and, free from the cares of public duty, he affects the gathering audience. The people of Mytilene pledge their loyalty afresh, not to the general, but to the *tantus maritus* ("so great husband" [8. 111]). It is through the guardianship of

Cornelia that they gain honor, and they beg Pompey to stay for a single night as by doing so he will make the city a place of worship for all ages and for all Romans to come in pilgrimage.[21] The couple have become capable of blessing the island and providing it with a religiosity similar to that given to sites of the epiphanies of divinities. Further, Pompey's and Cornelia's elevation as lovers allows the former to regain a popular acclaim which had earlier been confined to the unreality of his dreams. And yet, Pompey reluctantly refuses the offer of the people of Mytilene. He fears the retribution of Caesar, and thus, for the sake of the community, decides to leave (8. 129–46). The Mytilenians are sorrowed by Pompey's departure, but regard Cornelia's leaving as the loss of one of their own. Cornelia had become a part of the community, enjoying a firm bond with her hosts (8. 147–58). Love and its experience have led to the rebuilding of communal bonds.

Pompey starts life in the *Pharsalia* as a hapless figure: He fails as a conventional epic hero. He fails to take command of his army. He fails to lead his troops. He is led by circumstances and by those around him. In political matters, he is disconnected from the collective and unable to influence the flow of events. It is as if the great general is divested of any power over the community. But he is revitalized as a lover. His relationship with Cornelia transforms his identity. Cornelia, too, reaches her potential in love as the Roman *matrona-puella*. Their public recognition is achieved only when Pompey and Cornelia lay aside their pasts and traditional political roles and become defeated lovers. Pompey stresses to Cornelia that it is her Roman duty to reject the historical situation and find her identity and community in love. Pompey and Cornelia can be seen as rejecting the symbolic economy through their love, in a way that recalls the shattering of this economy through grief that we explored in the last chapter. But in comparison to those affective states, Pompey and Cornelia's feelings for each other have a more complex effect. Rather than simply creating a violent rupture, the couple's love reinscribes them into the public sphere and reunites them with the community from which they had been severed. In Mytilene, they are to be joined by locals and by future Roman, passionate lovers. In turn, Pompey and Cornelia respond with care to the people of Mytilene. Whereas Caesar cares for none other than himself, and Cato strides towards his death and the end of the Republic over the bodies of his own soldiers, Pompey wants to avoid bloodshed and save the people of Mytilene. Whereas Caesar has no love and Cato's marriage is empty, Pompey and Cornelia enjoy their passion and emerge from that passion not as self-indulgent lovers, but with

---

21. *Fac, Magne, locum, quem cuncta revisant saecula, quem veniens hospes Romanus adoret* (8. 114–15).

a renewed loyalty to each other and to the community. Pompey without Cornelia is alienated, very much as Cato and Caesar are separated from their communities; but Pompey with Cornelia feels, and acts upon, an ethical bond to those around him.

A SOCIETY MARRIAGE: PLINY AND CALPURNIA

In the imperial epics we have seen that the conjugal bond had repercussions in the world beyond the bedchamber. The bond either directly affected behavior in the public sphere or provided an ethical grounding which affected relations with the community. Correspondingly, it becomes possible for the social world to cross the threshold of the bedchamber and reach into the conjugal relationship. It is this second reading of the marital relationship which is negotiated in Pliny's depiction of his marriage with Calpurnia. Although elegiac elements are retained, the relationship with Calpurnia is shown as an integral part of Pliny's social world, shaped in critical ways by society. For Pliny, the elegiac moment is not an escape from a social world, an island that will be assaulted and eventually overcome by society; the elegiac moment is a defining feature of a relationship that is in its essence subsumed by the social. This reading of Pliny's conjugality is fundamentally different from Foucault's perception of these letters as displaying a new conjugality and a "relational role" between husband and wife.[22] For Foucault, these letters formulate the male as "an ethical subject" within the relation of conjugality, whereas we see this is a far more prominent feature of other texts. Reading Musonius Rufus, Foucault suggests that the conjugal bond has supplanted familial systems and friendship networks as part of a privileging of this relationship.[23] We do not see this model of conjugality of Pliny; rather we see his conjugality as reinforcing and reinforced by other social networking systems.

Pliny displays Calpurnia in a number of letters (*Ep.* IV 1; 19; VI 4; 7; VII 5; VIII 10; 11). As we saw at the start of this chapter, VII 5 is modeled on elegy but distorts some fundamental elements of the genre. As with VII 4, Pliny's love poem to Tiro to which this letter is juxtaposed (see pp. 66–67), the power dynamics of the relationship are subverted almost beyond restoration by the *pater-amator*'s dominance over his own household. Pliny can hardly be made the *amator exclusus* by an incorruptible doorkeeper or his wife's dalliance with another lover. Indeed, the elegy can be made con-

---

22. Foucault (1986) 80.
23. Foucault (1986) 163.

vincing only through (the artifice of) his wife's absence. Pliny's love objects exist within a sphere that he dominates. He does not need to pay any regard to their finer feelings, court their affections, or compete with other suitors. Instead, the love of the slave can be nonchalantly set alongside the passion for the absent wife, both ultimately passive recipients of the attention of the master-lover, and both ultimately reflections of, and subordinate to, his desires and needs. Pliny does not raise the status of the elegiac lover by making her a wife and giving her a social identity (doing away with the *noms de guerre* that protected blushes in much love elegy). Rather he reduces her by placing her within his household, where she becomes continuously available and lacks the means to close the door by which she might exclude her passionate husband.

Calpurnia's suppression is the predominant characteristic of her presentation. Although Calpurnia first appears in IV 1 (of which more below), we get more detail on her and Pliny from IV 19, a letter to Calpurnia Hispulla, Calpurnia's aunt. The letter opens with an expression of piety:

> Cum sis pietatis exemplum fratremque optimum et amantissimum tui pari caritate dilexeris, filiamque eius ut tuam diligas, nec tantum amitae ei adfectum verum etiam patris amissi repraesentes, non dubito maximo tibi gaudio fore cum cognoveris dignam patre dignam te dignam avo evadere. Summum est acumen summa frugalitas; amat me quod castitatis indicium est.

> As you are a model of piety and you loved that best and most loving brother of yours with a devotion equal to his, and you love his daughter as if she was your own, and you are indeed so much more than an aunt to her in filling the place left by her late father, I do not doubt that it will be a great joy to you when you know that she is worthy of her father, worthy of you, and worthy of her grandfather. She is very clever and very simple in taste. She loves me, which is an indication of her chasteness. Pliny *Ep.* IV 19

Calpurnia Hispulla is *pia* and devoted to her niece and her brother. Calpurnia herself displays *frugalitas* (simplicity in taste), *castitas* (chasteness) and *dignitas* (honor). These virtues stem from her family (her father, aunt, and grandfather), and love (*amor*) grows from these virtues. Pliny returns to the same theme at the end of the letter.

> Nec aliud decet tuis manibus educatam, tuis praeceptis institutam, quae nihil in conturbernio tuo viderit nisi sanctum et honestumque quae denique amare me ex tua praedicatione consueverit.

> It is only fitting that having been brought up by your hand, and taught by your precepts, and having seen nothing in your company unless it was worthy and honorable, she should come to love with me on your commendation. Pliny, *Ep.* IV 19

Calpurnia is the creation of her family and the embodiment of its virtues, and it is this body with which Pliny is joined in matrimony.

Pliny goes on to elaborate on the various manifestations of this dutiful love. Calpurnia has started to study literature as a direct result of her care for Pliny. She has copies of Pliny's works which she reads and even memorizes. She shows concern whenever Pliny appears in court and joy when he has finished speaking. She is a composer taught by love and has set his verse to music. One wonders whether this *magister amor* (teacher love) does not recall those elegiac *magistri amoris* (teachers of love) who inculcated rather different skills in the Augustan period, thus adding a subversive elegiac reference into a letter replete with images of respectability. Calpurnia is very much the object here, shaped by her aunt into the girl who can be married to Pliny, and further shaped by Pliny.

Starting his fourth book of letters with a letter on Calpurnia would seem to advertise that the marriage marked a new stage in Pliny's life.[24] Sherwin-White argues that the new marriage may have been as late as C.E. 104, when Pliny was in his early forties.[25] Calpurnia Hispulla was probably a little older than Pliny, young enough to be advised by Pliny's mother, old enough to provide Pliny with guidance. There was, thus, a close social relationship between the Calpurnii, the Plinii, and Caecilii (Pliny's father's family) that stretched back at least fifty years and probably longer, since all were established families in the relatively small town of Comum.[26] Pliny's marriage to Calpurnia was thus a classic case of a lineage marriage: a marriage arranged because of the social relationship between the families rather than any particular romantic tie. Further, the marriage was clearly brokered by Calpurnia Hispulla, to cement a female friendship previously broken by death. Pliny was Calpurnia's first husband and we could reasonably presume at least a twenty-five year age gap between Calpurnia and Pliny.[27] Pliny is

---

24. An earlier marriage ended with the death of Pliny's first wife in C.E. 96–97, coinciding with the accession of Nerva (*Ep.* IX 13).
25. Sherwin-White (1966) 264. Pliny's date of birth is established as 61–62 by *Ep.* VI 20.
26. Sherwin-White (1966) 69–70.
27. In *Ep.* VIII 10, which was probably written c. C.E. 107 and thus several years after the marriage, Pliny refers to Calpurnia as sufficiently young to be unaware of the symptoms of pregnancy. This might suggest that Calpurnia was married in her early teens and it seems possible that Pliny's extended period of bachelorhood (uncharacteristic given that it was the duty of Roman men to be married) may have been because he was waiting for Calpurnia to reach marriageable age.

drawn into describing the relationship using the language of love rather than duty, but his explanation of Calpurnia's love for him (other than mentioning family loyalty) is that Calpurnia did not love him for his age (*aetas*) or his body (*corpus*), as these will wither with time, but for his *gloria,* a decidedly public virtue.

Calpurnia's first appearance in the collection comes in the programmatic IV 1, addressed to her grandfather, Calpurnius Fabatus, who had held various local offices in Comum and a number of minor military offices.[28] He was likely to have been an elderly man, probably in his seventies at the time of his granddaughter's marriage. Pliny opens the letter emphasizing the mutuality of feelings:

> Cupis post longum tempus neptem tuam meque una videre. Gratum est utrique nostrum quod cupis mutuo me hercule.
>
> You wish after a long time to see once more your granddaughter and me. We are both pleased you want this, and the feeling is certainly reciprocated.
> Pliny, *Ep*. IV 1

Presumably recently married, the couple is portrayed as a domestic unit, feeling as one and speaking with one voice. This letter reveals Pliny's respect for his grandfather-in-law, showing pleasure at the favor shown by the elderly man to the couple. Although Calpurnius was a person of local prominence, Pliny, as a senator who had enjoyed high office in Rome, outranked him. Pliny's attitude shows the respect due from a younger man to an older man and a senior member of his wife's family. It was thus a display of *pietas,* which indeed is the theme of the letter. Although Pliny represents himself and Calpurnia as desperate to return to Fabatus, the happy couple first have to perform a religious duty at Tifernum. Pliny laces the letter with otiose details about his relationship with the town, before adding that he is due to dedicate a temple and that any further delay would be "inreligiosus" (irreligious). Pliny excuses his delaying in fulfilling a piety in visiting Fabatus with a contrasting piety towards the gods.

In several other letters, Pliny presents Fabatus as a stern and reproachful relation, prone to reminding Pliny of his duties.[29] This treatment of Fabatus

---

28. *Inscriptiones Latinae Selectae* 2721. Fabatus was an associate of L. Junius Silanus who was condemned under Nero. Although charges were brought against Fabatus, he was reprieved (Tacitus, *Annales* XVI 8).

29. In V 11 Pliny congratulates Fabatus on the building of a portico in the name of Fabatus himself and his son. In VI 12, Pliny responds to a number of "open-hearted" (*aperto pectore*) letters, which Fabatus now somewhat regrets. Pliny, however, regards the imperious tone in which those letters appear to have been written as reflecting his incorporation into Fabatus' family as a quasi-son

culminates in two letters on Calpurnia's miscarriage (VIII 10; 11). The letters sent to Fabatus and Hispulla contain exactly the same information and the inclusion of parallel letters invites comparison.

To Calpurnius Fabatus, his wife's grandfather

> Quo magis cupis ex nobis pronepotes videre, hoc tristior audies neptem tuam abortum fecisse, dum se praegnantem esse puellariter nescit, ac per hoc quaedam custodienda praegnantibus omittit, facit omittenda. Quem errorem magnis documentis expiavit, in summum periculum adducta. Igitur, ut necesse est graviter accipias senectutem tuam quasi paratis posteris destitutam, sic debes agere dis gratias, quod ita tibi in praesentia pronepotes negaverunt, ut servarent neptem, illos reddituri, quorum nobis spem certiorem haec ipsa quamquam parum prospere explorata fecunditas facit. Isdem nunc ego te quibus ipsum me hortor moneo confirmo. Neque enim ardentius tu pronepotes quam ego liberos cupio, quibus videor a meo tuoque latere pronum ad honores iter et audita latius nomina et non subitas imagines relicturus. Nascantur modo et hunc nostrum dolorem gaudio mutent. Vale.

> I know how anxious you are for us to give you a great grandchild, so you will be all the more sorry to hear that your granddaughter has had a miscarriage. Being young she did not realize she was pregnant, failed to take proper precautions, and did things best not done. She has atoned for her error by a great lesson which critically endangered her life. So, that although you must inevitably be hurt to be robbed of a descendant already on the way in your old age, you should thank the gods, though they denied you the child for the present, for saving your granddaughter. They will surely grant us others, and we are more certain in this hope given the evidence of fertility though this was insufficiently successful. I am now advising you in the same fashion as I encourage myself, for your desire for great-grandchildren cannot be keener than mine for children. Their descent from both of us should make their road to office easy; I can leave them a well-known name and an established ancestry. Let them only be born and turn our present grief to joy. Pliny, *Ep.* VIII 10

To Calpurnia Hispulla

> Cum affectum tuum erga fratris filiam cogito etiam materna indulgentia molliorem, intellego prius tibi quod est posterius nuntiandum, ut prae-

---

rather than as a grandson-in-law. Similarly, VII 11, concerning the sale of some inherited property to a friend, is also framed as responding to a reproachful letter.

sumpta laetitia sollicitudini locum non relinquat. Quamquam vereor ne post gratulationem quoque in metum redeas, atque ita gaudeas periculo liberatam, ut simul quod periclitata sit perhorrescas. Iam hilaris, iam sibi iam mihi reddita incipit refici, transmissumque discrimen convalescendo metiri. Fuit alioqui in summo discrimine,—impune dixisse liceat—fuit nulla sua culpa, aetatis aliqua. Inde abortus et ignorati uteri triste experimentum. Proinde etsi non contigit tibi desiderium fratris amissi aut nepote eius aut nepte solari, memento tamen dilatum magis istud quam negatum, cum salva sit ex qua sperari potest. Simul excusa patri tuo casum, cui paratior apud feminas venia. Vale.

When I think how you love your brother's daughter more tenderly than a mother, I realize that I must announce first what came after, so that happiness may come first so that it forestalls and leaves no place for anxiety. Yet, I am afraid that after relief you will turn to fear again, and so you will rejoice that she is free from danger but at the same time shudder that she was endangered. Now, she is happy. Now, she starts to feel herself restored to herself and to me, and judge the crisis by the journey to recovery. For it was indeed a great crisis—I hope I may safely say so—though no fault of hers, except of her age. Hence, she miscarried, sad proof of unsuspected pregnancy. And so although you still do not have what you want, a grandchild to your lost brother, who shall be a solace for your loss, remember that this is rather postponed than denied. We can hope for a child from her since she is saved. Meanwhile, explain this to your father, for indulgence is easier among women. Pliny, *Ep.* VIII 11

Pliny opens the letter to Hispulla with mention of the latter's love for his young wife, and then concentrates on the health of Calpurnia, showing concern about her ill health and relief at her recovery. The fertility is evidence that a child will come who will be a consolation for the loss of Hispulla's brother, a new life restoring a lost one. Hispulla is to mollify the old man. In the letter to Fabatus, Pliny ascribes blame to Calpurnia (allowable given her youth) for not taking proper precautions. A child born to Calpurnia is to be a continuator of Pliny's name and a man who will rise to high office on the back of the prestige of Pliny and Fabatus, who have already carved out a political career for the yet-to-be-conceived infant. There is no doubt that Calpurnia will bear male offspring. Fabatus is consoled by the prospect of a "public man" who will represent Pliny and himself on the political stage, while Hispulla is to hope for a new family member to replace her brother.

The two letters are crudely gendered. Pliny displays his awareness of the different emotional capacities and interests of his audience, female and male. This balance is somewhat upset when Hispulla is asked to explain the events to the old man, thus being cast in the role of the teacher, the person with the more accurate understanding. As with other aspects of Pliny's dealings with his wife's family, it is the women who seem to broker knowledge and thus influence and shape the family's behavior, and Pliny's recognition of this is striking. Gender is, however, insufficient by itself to explain these contrasted approaches; we cannot receive these letters as Pliny's display of his femininity. The difference of reaction between Fabatus and Pliny is due not to gender, but to age. Combining age and severity, Fabatus is constructed as an old-fashioned Roman male, a stereotype to be set against the degeneracy of the modern. But it is Fabatus who is to be taught the true way by his daughter; his knowledge and understanding are inferior. Fabatus' problem is not his old age, but his anachronistic attitudes. The contrast emerging here is not between the good old ancient and the modern debauched, but between Fabatus and Pliny, and in this there is a recognition of a change in the rules by which relations between the genders were played out. Both Pliny's distance from the age-old severity and his pseudo-elegiac relationship with Calpurnia offer a modified version of masculinity and gender relations.

With Calpurnia, Pliny is remaking the elegiac *puella*. The "girl" who was able to overturn hegemonic ideologies to wield power in Augustan elegy, is sculpted into a model of family piety in Pliny's presentation. Calpurnia is shaped by her aunt, her chastity, *pietas,* and honor. She is instructed to love in the best interests of her family and is instructed by love in learning those skills with which she is to express her love of Pliny. Calpurnia is made into a traditional *matrona* given the sophistication of the *docta puella;* but, unlike the *docta puella*, this particularly young *matrona* loses power and independence by her learning. She cannot be a figure who stands in opposition to the conventional *mores*, and as Pliny is able to subsume his love in the demands of public life, so Calpurnia is led to love by the demands of her family. Her love also has a clear public orientation: Calpurnia loves Pliny because of his *gloria*. In VI 7, Pliny offers us a quintessentially elegiac trope of embracing the letters, taken as substitute for an absent body, but this trope is distorted by the fact that these essentially private letters are not missives of intimate communication shot straight at her heart, but published (and polished) works of art.[30] Calpurnia embraces the letters of a man of letters. Calpurnia

---

30. The elegiac formulation of his relationship with Calpurnia in Book IV continues into Book VI with letters 4 and 7. In Book VI, Calpurnia is in Campania for her health, while Pliny is in Rome, detained by his duties. In VI 4, there is an anxiety caused in part by Calpurnia's illness, but also by a moral concern that the famed luxuries of the region would corrupt her. This implicit worry is answered by VI 7 in which Pliny tells us that Calpurnia claims she was feeling Pliny's absence, but that she found consolation in his writings, which she not only rereads but holds by her side. Pliny also holds her letters as a physical, as well as verbal, manifestation of his beloved. There is an obvious literary artifice at work here.

loves not the body for which the letters are traditionally a poor substitute, but the literary fame of Pliny, the public face of the man. Calpurnia is thus embracing her true object of love: the public persona of Pliny, whereas the corporeal, with all its uncertainties and infirmities is notably absent. Their love is therefore pure, completely integrated into the symbolic economy and almost divested of any elements of the Real.

Yet, the letters to and about Fabatus also make clear that Pliny wishes to distance himself from the traditional, aged paterfamilias. By putting the miscarriage letters together, Pliny is able to show his emotional and literary versatility. He can talk the language of the old (male), but he can also talk the language of the new (female), and indeed be drawn to the latter. With this correspondence Pliny suggests both the possibility of choice in behavior and a consciousness of change. That social change would seem to necessitate a renegotiation of relationships within the family and within the household. Yet these letters cannot be described as showing anxiety about his familial relationships; Pliny exerts power and, if anything, would seem to be displaying his mastery. He may be a slave to love, but he is always able to overcome his feelings. He may worry about Calpurnia in Campania, but she is shown to be loyal. He may clash with Fabatus, but Pliny is always right, always dutiful, and always more in control.

LOVE STORIES: A KISS IS JUST A KISS

The texts that we have examined in this chapter refuse simple explanations. We cannot see in these texts a new conjugality which operates, as if in some zero-sum game, to leach out the power and importance of other social networks (familial, amicitial). The public–private dichotomy, which is so central to modern perceptions of the self in society, is here transgressed by the conjugal unit, constantly private, constantly public. The couple cross from the bedchamber to the city and from the city to the bedchamber. The bedchamber exists within the city, but the city can be remade from the bedchamber, and it is this capacity to remake the city that renders the space of the bedchamber powerful. Power can emerge from the bedchamber, from the conjugal relationship itself, and is not necessarily controlled or constricted by social codes. Whereas Pliny does write those social codes into the heart of his conjugality, conjugality is in itself potentially a resistant force to social codes, and it is this aspect which seems to emerge from our epic texts. This requires some explanation, however, for it would not seem to fit with social models which see the origins of power in the individual or within the city. This power appears to come from a different source.

We have observed in our texts, time and again, a society that is created in systemic tension between individuals in negotiation with social codes. We see a Lacanian narrative in this: for Lacan the individual was himself formed as part of this negotiation through the Symbolic Order. It is, in fact, the negotiation between individual agents, all in tension with Symbolic Orders, that allows society and the symbolic economy its dynamism. And yet, the Levinasian line of the previous chapter suggests to us that individuals find their selves only through a dynamic engagement with others. This Levinasian view is, it seems to us, compatible with a Lacanian view of selfhood, since the 'other' is a key element in the making of the Symbolic Order and also in the Mirror stage. But if we take the Levinasian view, the individual's ontological relationship with the 'other' prevents that individual from ever being singular, since selfhood must always exist in relation to others. This plurality of individualism creates a complexity in the interrelationship of the social and the individual, for it is far from certain that the key referential other from whom one derives one's sense of identity need be the 'other' of the city (the societal other); familial or conjugal others could provide that reflected difference-similarity essential for the formation of selfhood. Selfhood is as likely to be achieved in the conjugal unit as in the wider community, and if the wider community, operating through the symbolic economy, denies or is in opposition to selfhood, then the conjugal-familial unit becomes a likely source of resistance and self-fulfilment. We are thus faced with a society whose individuals realize their selfhood in the confines of a delimited social relationship (be that the family or the conjugal unit), leaving the potential for discrepancies and turmoil wide open. In other words, ethical responsibility, conflict, and alienation go hand in hand in a bewildering mix of social roles and positions. In this complex web of relations between individual, self, other, and society, we grapple with far more diverse patterns than those envisaged in conventional Enlightenment, and indeed Aristotelian, views of the political society. To understand how this might work, we turn to Jean-Luc Nancy, especially his theories of the "singular-plural" individual and the "inoperable community."

Nancy draws a distinction between individuality, a separate anomalous isolation of the self, and singularity. Singularity can only be achieved through an ever-renewing negotiation with others (the plurality). As with Levinas, that plurality is integral to singularity.

> Being singular plural: in a single stroke, without punctuation, without a mark of equivalence, implication, or sequence. A single, continuous-discontinuous mark tracing out the entirety of the ontological domain, being-with-itself designated as the 'with' of the Being, of the singular and plural,

and dealing a blow of ontology.... This co-essence puts essence itself in the hyphenation—'being-singular-plural'—which is a mark of union and also a mark of division, a mark of sharing that effaces itself, leaving each term to its isolation *and* its being-with-the-others.[31]

There is not a singularity without a plurality, but there is not a plurality without a singularity. There is no being without the singular, and there is no being without plurality. The plurality emerges as a phenomenon of being in which the singular is essential, but that essential singularity is always distant because it has within it an 'origin,' a fundamental distancing from the rest of the world.[32] Nancy is thus exploring the paradox of a relational ontology which postulates that singularity is communal, while at the same time understanding that to exist is to be separate from the other. One could describe this as a paradox (and hence a trauma) of being.

Society, in Nancy's view, is a union of such singular pluralities.

The unity of the world is not one: it is made of a diversity, and even disparity and opposition. It is in fact, which is to say that it does not add or subtract anything. The unity of the world is nothing other than its diversity ... the mutual sharing and exposition of all its world—within this world.[33]

This diversity creates a tension that cannot be resolved. Binding that community together too closely risks the suppression of individuality.[34]

Nancy asks:

What is a community? It is not a macroorganism, or a big family (which is to assume that we know what an organism or a family is ...). The *common*, having in-common or being in-common, excludes interior unity, subsistence, and presence in and for itself. Being with, being together and even being 'united' are precisely not a matter of being 'one.' Within *unitary*

---

31. Nancy (2000) 37.
32. There is a discrete but salutary distance in the heart of each human association, always there between us and the origin and explanation of all things. Nancy relates it to the curiosity that we instinctively feel when faced with the unassimilable difference between ourselves and others: " ... the origin is the punctual and discrete spacing *between us, as between us and the rest of the world, as between all beings.* We find this alterity primarily and essentially intriguing. It intrigues us because it exposes the always-other origin, always inappropriate and always there, each and every time present as inimitable. This is why we are primarily and essentially *curious* about the world and about ourselves" (Nancy [2000] 19).
33. Nancy (2000) 185.
34. Nancy (2000) 189. Any attempt to provide an overarching ideology (a law of the world) by which diversity can be eliminated is doomed since individuals are always distancing themselves from the community: "The law of the world is an infinite tension with regard to the world itself."

community [*communauté une*] there is nothing but death, and not the sort of death found in the cemetery, which is a place of spacing or distinctness, but the death found in the ashes of crematorium ovens or in the accumulations of charnel-houses.[35]

Community is always in the making. Societies must exist in dialectic tension with the singularities which comprise that society. Communities are thus fundamentally 'inoperable,' and to render communities operable would be to turn the cemetery into the charnel house. A hegemonic ideology, be it liberal, fascist, or Roman, risks creating alienated individuals and suppressing the pluralities that allow singularities to flourish.

We can detect such a discomfort with the crowd (the unitary society) in Statius' *Thebaid*. Inflamed by Capaneus, the Argive crowd adopts a belligerent stance with regard to Thebes, celebrating its unitary characteristics and deploring the dissenting voice. Political leadership and ethical judgement, however, stand apart from the unitary community in which it is impossible to show loyalty to the other. In the *Thebaid* the rejection of communal morality entails separating the individual from tradition and, indeed, history as a source of ethical judgement.[36] Accordingly, the individual needs to make ethical decisions based on the current circumstances rather than on a received and traditional code. This could, in some instances, lead to a moral relativism or even immorality, but in the *Thebaid* we have found that it encourages an ethical decision-making. Recognizing their connection to an other, the characters in their public role are motivated by love and driven by that love to ethical judgments.

This play between public and private, morality and intimacy, communicability and incommunicability is a fundamental element in psychological and literary responses to love.[37] On the one hand, private love (forbidden love) can claim an intensity that nourishes absolute separation. Hidden love can remain stubbornly beyond rationality and social convention, beyond the watchful and controlling eyes of society, and retain a purity of sorts, but the inevitable counterbalance is that, by remaining hidden, love has to be controlled. Such love is thus limited in its ability to affect the environment

---

35. Nancy (2000) 154–55.
36. In a Roman context, this in itself is surprising. Rejecting the values of the community runs counter to an ideological tendency to glorify the old and portray society as being in decline from the time of the ancients. Such conservatism would be easily recognizable in Roman moralizing texts of the Augustan period. Yet, as we shall see in the next chapter, History is in itself an issue of choice.
37. For a literary history of the evolving social semantics of love, see Lunhmann (1986). Whether an ideal of solidarity or an all-absorbing passion, love for Luhmann is a communicative code that challenges the social framework with its improbabilities and individualizing excess, ultimately laying down its own partial, nontotalizing laws.

around it. Hidden love may be intense, but it cannot transform. Investing in separation means that such love can never be a site of opposition by which to affect the public sphere, since engaging in the public sphere would inevitably destroy that private isolation which it has so alluringly created. Private love is thus safe and subject to the symbolic economy which ultimately circumscribes its possible realm. But, by its very nature, love exists in (social) space. Whereas grief, anger, and fear can all exist internally, love stretches out from the body in innumerable tiny adjustments to the love object. Pertinently, Julia Kristeva conceives of love *as* action, as enactment.[38] If love is enacted, it needs a stage, and in its performance on that stage there is an impact. Such performances are essentially ideological in that they create certain social patterns, or shapes in society, and even without speaking the performance of love, the acting of an intimate relationship is by its nature constitutive of ideology. That performance has the potential to be yet more powerful, for in the realization of love and the opportunity for creating the bond with the other is the possibility of the creation of a self, a singular-plurality without reference to the symbolic economy. Even if a love that dare not speak its name is forced to remain silent and perhaps never reaches consummation, it will still leave an indelible mark on social interaction in a distant staring or a failed attempt at communication. However ferociously the lovers might defend its private nature from prying eyes, to retain an absolute privacy for staging love is a contradiction in terms. Even if one discreetly closes the door of the bedchamber behind the lovers, the bedchamber still exists within the house, and the closed chamber door exists within a more public arena. The moment the couple enter the chamber, a relationship is born within that potentially affects relationships outside the chamber. Love becomes a private story made famous (cf. Statius on Stella), and so encounters the symbolic economy. In spite of best efforts, the community is always forcing the door of the bedchamber and juxtaposing the communal with the conjugal, the latter altered at the moment of, and as a result of, this juxtaposition just as the former is potentially transformed. The bedchamber is thus, potentially, a revolutionary space, a generative space in which social singularities are formed, people who may step out from that space transformed and filled with revolutionary energy. Yet, it is abundantly clear that the revolutionary potential is rarely achieved.

This revolutionary potential seems to lurk within our epics, not just within the Argive royal family in the *Thebaid*, but also in the *Pharsalia*. While not precisely succumbing to the morals of the crowd, Cato eliminates

---

38. Kristeva (1987). See also Lechte and Margaroni (2004) 64–72, with further commentary on love as enactment and pointed references to Luhmann (1986).

his individualism in the service of the myths of the community. But Pompey's trajectory is more complex; he spends much of the epic in isolation in the midst of the community and in powerlessness before the crowd, but is revived when he rejects the public *persona* of the general and the burden of his illustrious history in order to embrace Cornelia. United with Cornelia, he is able to take ethical decisions. The enactment of his love on the public stage (ultimately on the beach at Lesbos) is the trigger for Pompey's reintegration within a community. Although this ability of love to reconnect the individual to the community is less explicit in the *Thebaid*, Polynices' (albeit futile) vision of Argia on the walls of Thebes as a queen in communion with her new citizens results from the intimacies of their relationship. The bedchamber seems an essential basis for an ethical engagement with society.

The radical nature of such a link for the Romans can only be appreciated when set in the context of the furore which surrounded trials *in cubiculo* (in the bedchamber) and the political influence of the women of the imperial family. Our sources castigate Claudius for holding treason trials *in camera*, surrounded by his slaves and womenfolk. The slaves and women are perceived to hold undue influence, distorting the legal process for personal, sometimes sexual, but always immoral purposes. Those accusations extend beyond the trials to the general political influence of Claudius' wives. It must have been perfectly clear to most Romans that when the doors of the imperial bedchamber were shut, what happened within was not necessarily fair or just. In this way, the imperial bedchamber was not obviously the wellspring of morality. Yet, our reading of the epics would seem, implausibly, to suggest that those subject to the summary justice of the bedchamber were rather more likely to receive an ethical trial than those facing the judgment of the crowd.

Sadly, History gets you in the end. As Polynices marches to war and to his death, so Pompey meets his own end on the sands of Egypt. If the story terminates there, we are faced with a bleak vision of the world, in which love is a mere pause, a momentary escape from the harsh realities of history, no more real than dreams of pastoral utopias. However, dreams offer a salutary open-endedness. Pompey pursues his dream by fleeing continuously, and this constant flight turns gradually into an ability to keep out of the encodings of the system and its rigid polarizations of the world. In love and fleeing to the margins, Pompey attracts increasing fame and respect, both previously denied to him when he was at the epicenter of the public arena. Just as with Argia and Polynices, love strengthens Pompey's and Cornelia's ethical power and public stature. Ultimately, love enables Pompey to satisfy his yearning for public acceptance. And even when defeated in battle, he is still not Caesar's victim. Codrus, the loyal soldier, may deplore the lowly state of the pitiable tomb he has managed to erect for his leader's mangled body (8. 814–22), but the facelessness of his decapitated body (8. 710–11) and this very unprepossessing tomb render Pompey symbolically unrepresentable. He cannot be fixed by the narratives of history and is thus capable of resurrection in different forms, most notably as a symbol of love to whom, the narrator assures us, the Romans will turn in the ages to come. Those Romans who seek an alternative model to the untrustworthy, imperial Caesar or the hopeless, Republican Cato will find it in Pompey, the lover. Gradually, imperceptibly, Pompey's diffident marginality has turned into his greatest attribute. His flight resists the new imperial ideology. Honors pour in after his death, but Pompey's faceless body and inconspicuous tomb guarantee his everlasting fame, as they elude the banality of a symbolic economy that is failing or subjugation to a new world order.

Yet, this revolutionary potential of conjugality is rarely manifested. In large part, this is due to the social pressures brought to bear on the lovers. Foucauldian discourses provide scripts through which the relationship is structured and the particularity of that relationship, and the singularity of the lovers, can be subsumed. Whereas we have mostly discussed conjugality as a form of liberation as seen in the epics, conjugality could also be a form of control. Pliny's Calpurnia does not emerge as a liberated singularity in her relationship with Pliny. She moves from being the cipher of her aunt to becoming the cipher of Pliny. She never achieves the power and independence of the elegiac *puella,* because she both loves out of familial duty (subsuming her self to the idea of the family) and commits herself to love the public man (subsuming her self to Pliny). Yet, this is not just a patriarchal dominance. Calpurnia is dominated by the public idea of Pliny. Their relationship is thus deeply imbued by the public, making their love almost a matter of ideological choice.

Nothing is simple here. We can neither see the tensions in these depictions of conjugality and family as a straightforward shift of power away from the public sphere to the individual, nor accept neat dichotomies between traditionalism and an avant-garde, public and private, societal and conjugal as a background to these stories. We cannot divide these presentations into two discrete groups and uncover a great ideological divide at the heart of Roman intimacy. Categorizing and labeling the different relationships we have explored in this chapter simplifies, reifies, and creates artificial oppositions. Nevertheless, throughout these texts we have detected unease and even disenchantment with received tradition. This ranges from the rejection of traditions within the *Thebaid* and *Pharsalia* to Pliny's uncomfortable relationship with his wife's grandfather and the societal values the old man is made to represent. After several decades and a few generations of Imperial rule, the values of old Rome no longer work convincingly. One might think that the rejection of a hegemonic ideology would lead to opposition, which might invert that ideology; the opposition would thus mirror and reverse the hegemonic ideology and create a dichotomy in society. But this can only be a short-term strategy. The choice between values that do not work and an absence or an inversion of values is no real choice. Instead, in the texts that we studied in this chapter we see a drive to reform community and communal relations that steers away from the ideological impasse.

A consuming love attracts by its simplicity. *Romeo and Juliet* opposes the warring factions in the city of Verona with the simplicity and passion of love and thus, in a Kristevan explosion, love attacks the dominant order and forces its realignment, even if belatedly; love can be a force which resists control and exists in opposition to the hegemonic order. We have discovered this latent opposition in our texts, perhaps carried over from the elegiac tradition. Alongside this, we have also followed the advancement of conjugality as an alternate ideology. At one and the same time, we have love as the destroyer of bonds to society (elegiac love), society as the binder of love (Pliny and Calpurnia), and love as the bond to the social (Cornelia and Pompey). Yet, these models overlie each other, existing as possibilities within the literary and ideological construction of a relationship, too unclear to represent ideological schools.[39] The conjugal and societal exist in dialectical tension, so that power can cross the threshold of the bedchamber in either direction. Yet, this dialectic establishes the bedchamber as a site of power, a place of possible resistance, and a place which the symbolic economy must both acknowledge and deal with. Acknowledging that the bedchamber is a stage in which power relations are formed, relations which can escape the chamber and influence the symbolic economy or even form the basis of resistance, further problematizes the relationship between conjugality and community. The bedchamber offers an opportunity not just for withdrawal from society, but also for the creation of singularities and the building of microcommunities that will oppose and affect the wider symbolic economy.[40] Once the bedchamber is

---

39. The very existence of choice upsets the Symbolic Order by highlighting the fact that it is not God-sent or a natural state. This could be represented as a crisis of authority in the Symbolic Order of a kind which not-infrequently gives way to deep-seated anxieties about an individual's place in the world, which might manifest itself in a search for a totalizing ideology to bring new certainties to an uncertain world.

40. There is a difference here with many modern representations of the home-society divide. The presentation of fictional worlds with bankrupt communal ideologies suggests a lingering dissatisfaction with the real world and its values. But instead of imagining worlds that stem from the bedroom, authors tend to turn to other normative structures which would provide them with a 'true' moral direction and through which they might negotiate a relationship with society. A withdrawal from the community fed late Victorian attempts to recreate "family values" and in particular to promote the home and the woman of the house as the locus of morality. Yet, such "family values" were defined,

closed, no one knows what goes on within, and when it opens, those who emerge are charged with its energies, transformed and less controllable in the social sphere. This is why Pliny tears the walls of his bedchamber down for us to look in. His bedchamber is also a stage in which love (and power) are enacted, but it is a stage that he controls and that is fully subservient to the *dominus* and his Symbolic Order. Taking down the walls of his bedchamber shows the world that nothing resistant goes on within, that his masculine power is unchallenged and unquestioned, and that the symbolic economy reigns supreme.

With Argia and Polynices, and especially with Pompey and Cornelia, we see individuals who use the conjugal and familial to connect with the others and, more broadly, with the community. In so doing, they do not lose their identities in the ideologies of state and tradition, but preserve those identities, often in conflict with traditional ideologies. By choosing to love, they find redemption and a new relationship with the community stemming from that responsibility for another individual. Conjugality and the love within the family offer a basis for a community that will rival the wider social organizations and thus can act as site of resistance. In their singularity-plurality, the characters explored in this chapter find ethical direction, a selfhood that allows them to reconnect with the societal other. Yet this is a hard road, not least because the bedchamber has to exist within society. There is no rule-book by which the individuals can be guided, not least because the very existence of a rule-book would jeopardize that essence of loyalty to the singularity of the other that is honored in the relationship. The respect for the other has to be continuously chosen and renewed, which includes understanding that other's engagement with society. Such engagement is both an ethical and existential necessity. Polynices, Argia, and Adrastus all face difficult choices. All these stories end on a somber note and the power of the hegemonic symbolic economy seems to triumph and crush all before it. The ideology of the community is the destroyer that brings death to the lovers and those around them. The triumph of the symbolic economy snuffs out the brief resistance of the bedchamber. History gets them in the end. To live for the other is to continually remake a relationship and to exist in continuous struggle with the fixity of identities in the symbolic economy. Pliny's way may abandon selfhood, and certainly Calpurnia loses, or is never able to attain, her singularity, but it was certainly easier than the paths taken by Pompey and Argia. Yet, even if these tales are, ultimately, dark, the contrast makes the fleeting moments of light in domestic happiness even brighter and

---

and defended, against the outside world. They were explicitly faithful to tradition, centered around the feminine and in opposition to a male, commercial, and modern world. See Tosh (1991).

harder to miss. Lucan claims that Romans and the people of Mytilene will remember the dedicated lovers long after their destruction. He offers a dream of Romans on a pilgrimage to Lesbos, an island of love, reuniting Pompey and his people through that love. This image establishes the hollowness of the symbolic economy that Cato and Caesar are fighting to maintain or transform. That hollowness is a symptom of dislocation, dissatisfaction with a world in which the symbolic economy is overwhelming and powerful, perhaps untouchable by mere mortals. There is, then, in the dream of Pompey returned to the theater, in the pilgrims to Mytilene, and in Argia as the new Helen wandering the battlements of Thebes, a faint sense of hope that society could be remade and made better, a hope that resists the painted paradise of Pliny's literary universe, a hope that remains in dreams of love. One cannot read the epics without seeing the deep and fundamental discontent with a world that destroys the individual. In worlds going to hell, only the dream of love lingers on.

5

Living with the Past

TRADITION, INVENTION, AND HISTORY

CICERO RENATUS: HISTORY AND MEMORY IN PLINY

By the ninth book of his letters, Pliny seems obsessed by *fama* (fame). For Pliny, *fama*, unlike our fame, was not transient; it was his ticket to immortality, and in a world of transience his immortality was to be earned through literature. In a letter to Valerius Paulinus (IX 3), Pliny speaks of having "the prize of immortality before his eyes" (*praemium aeternitatis ante oculos*) and claims that "all men must judge between their immortality and mortality" (*omnes homines arbitror oportere aut immortalitatem suam aut mortalitatem cogitare*). He is preaching to the converted, since Paulinus, so Pliny claims, is similarly engaged in a quest for literary immortality. This desire drives Pliny's frenzied literary activity and features repeatedly throughout the book. In IX 36 and 40, he describes his daily routines in his Laurentian and Tuscan villas, which from dawn until bed were dominated by study and composition. This activity was "leisure," *otium*, but, as he explained to Calvisius Rufus in IX 6, it was fundamentally different from the unproductive *otium* of the games. A related theme is the contemporary reception of Pliny's writings and character. Augurinus is praised for his writings on his friends, not least Pliny himself (IX 8). Geminus is thanked for telling Pliny that his books sold in Gaul (IX 10). IX 13 centers on Pliny's description of a speech in which he launched an attack on the prosecutors of Helvidius Priscus. Although Pliny had frequently alluded to his friendship with members of the "opposition," the collection had on the whole avoided dealing with the details of his political activities in the Domitianic period and its immediate aftermath.[1]

This letter (IX 13) provides a historical commentary on Pliny's speech, and asserts his historical importance. It can be no coincidence that the next letter encourages the historian Tacitus to focus on his own posthumous reputation, and thus continues with what appears to be a central preoccupation of Pliny. After a short sequence concerning a spell in the country, IX 18 returns to literary themes; Sabinus has been studying Pliny's light poetry and asks for more. Pliny will send some, but only in small doses, as befits a light poet. IX 19 neatly conjoins a discussion of Pliny's literary output (the letter is an exegesis of *Ep.* VI 10) with a discussion of *fama*, focusing on the manner in which the reputation of great men is preserved and transmitted (see below). The next letter (IX 20) shows how Pliny divides his time between supervising the grape harvest and his literary work, with literature absorbing most of his attention, and the occasion for the letter is a grateful response to Venator's critical appreciation of his publications. Even though seemingly descriptive, the letter is in the tradition of didactic literature on agricultural themes. Another letter (IX 23) centers on the fact that his *fama* is such that he can be recognized by his works and modestly reports that his speeches provoke spontaneous applause, while also claiming that being ranked with Tacitus as a literary figure is a far greater honor. Appreciations of Pliny's writings form the basis of IX 25 and 26. In IX 28 it is announced that Voconius Romanus, for whom Pliny petitioned for senatorial status (X 4), is writing a biography of Pliny, and in IX 29 Pliny complains that the diversity of his writing probably prevents him attaining excellence in any one field, explicitly a *captatio benevolentiae* for Pliny's latest work. In IX 31 Pliny thanks Sardus for his kind published comments (though it is unclear on what aspect of his friend Sardus decided to inform the world). Only at this point do the themes of the book move away from Pliny's own reputation.

Although the genre of epistolography is bound to put some emphasis on the individual, especially if one writes personal letters rather than philosophical disquisitions, the egoism that runs through Book IX comes as a surprise. Pliny's concern for his reputation suggests that he recognizes some kind of problem. The nature of that problem becomes clearer when we look at IX 2, where Pliny responds to Sabinus' encouragement to follow the example of Cicero:

> neque enim eadem nostra condicio quae M. Tulli, ad cuius exemplum nos vocas. Illi enim et copiosissimum ingenium, et par ingenio qua varietas

---

[1]. There are a few exceptions, e.g., Ep. I 5.

rerum qua magnitudo largissime suppetebat; nos quam angustis terminis claudamur etiam tacente me perspicis.

our condition is not the same as that of Marcus Tullius, to whose example you call me. For he had both a great talent and supplied that talent with a great variety of important matters, but you know without my mentioning it, how we are confined within narrow boundaries. Pliny. *Ep.* IX 2

As ever, Pliny's letter is densely written. The "narrow boundaries" (*angustis terminis*) are drawn from the critical reception of poetry and describe the contrast between the broad canvas of epic and the narrower scope of neoteric composition, in whose pure waters Pliny dabbled.² Pliny is restricted to the neoteric style because the subjects available were considerably less dramatic than the crises at the end of the Republic which formed Cicero's subject matter. Pliny falls short of Ciceronian epic, not because of any lapse on his part, but because of the different eras in which the two authors operated.

The attentive reader should here recall Book I, when Pliny introduces himself and stakes his claim to a literary territory. I 1 to Clarus proclaims that Pliny's publication of letters is casual, in response to the request of Clarus to make public any letters that may be written with a little more care (*si quas paulo curatius scripsisse*). Pliny thus represents his letters as "real": in other words, written for real correspondents and on real issues that emerged in their day-to day lives. This differentiates Pliny's collection from Seneca's letters, for instance, which were short philosophical treatises and probably always intended for publication. Thus, there can be little doubt that Pliny was inviting comparison with the Republican orator and epistolographer.

In II 2 Pliny discusses his literary masters, Demosthenes, Calvus, and especially *nostri Marci,* our Cicero. The occasion for the letter is his planned publication of a speech. He claims that the subject matter of the speech (which we do not know) encouraged him to higher rhetorical flights. The claim here is bold. Pliny offers himself up as the new Cicero. Yet, the confidence of these early assertions has lessened by Book IX. In this latter stage of his writing career, Pliny wonders whether he can attain the status of the great writer, not for any deficiency of talent, and certainly not because of lack of labor, but because of the constraints of the time. Pliny is asking two fundamental questions: is it possible to be great in these modern times and, more fundamentally, to what extent is the individual constrained by history.

---

2. Pliny further uses this epic-neoteric division to differentiate between his life and that of Sabinus, his correspondant, who served with the legions.

In the texts that we explore below, we find a crucial ambivalence towards history and memory. These are not presented as 'givens,' sets of facts to be recalled and recorded, but as malleable, subject to political concerns and capable of falsity, though not obviously subject to falsification. The classical discussions present the issue not as whether history is 'right' or 'wrong,' but whether history is 'appropriate' or 'inappropriate,' a concern that has perhaps more in common with discussions of collective memory than with conventional historical philosophy. The history that emerges is 'of the present': a central element in the formation of contemporary selves and society. In this we find support in the Heideggerian emphasis on time as an ontological element, especially as it is developed in Deleuze's notions of Aion and Chronos. These provide us with a means of distinguishing between time as universal and absolute (the time of physics and geology) and time as a human construct. Chronos is the framing conception of time in which other social conventions exist; it is the epistemic frame for a society. In these classical histories of the present, the issue is not what is history, but which history, and how and why one puts the *caesurae* in the historical record that would separate one temporal frame (Chronos) from another. Further, once one accepts the history of the present as the frame in which social and political life exist, to what extent can that frame be resisted? Is Pliny, for instance, a prisoner of his Chronos? For some (Tacitus and Lucan) the Caesarian revolution broke the flow of historical time, establishing a new epoch (Chronos). In so doing, the possibility of time being made anew was advanced, and in this possibility there is a continuous revolutionary potential. If time can be remade once, it can be remade many times. But the revolution also created a time before the current epoch, and the relationship between that earlier time and the current epoch becomes problematic and a potential site of resistance. The Caesarian revolution exists as both a historical event and an act that changes the nature of those events on either side of, and the significance of time around, the act. The significance of that change is fought out in the discourses of history. In these discourses of time, the narration of history is a profoundly political-ideological act. The issue is hardly one of political faction, with an imperial or conservative group in contestation over modes of political activity, but is an ontological statement about the time in which individuals exist. Contemporary history can be narrated so that, in the hands of Pliny, the Republic becomes part of the history of the present, whereas with Tacitus contemporary history is separated by a powerfully argued *caesura* between Republic and Empire. For Tacitus, and, we argue, for Lucan, seeing the Republic as part of the history of the present is in error, a political act that ensures a dislocation from the present epoch; even for Pliny, as we have seen, the Republic is a site of nostalgia that establishes a crisis of belonging. There are clear parallels here to the way in which collective memory is used to establish the identity of the collective, while simultaneously imprisoning peoples within the past and often in invented 'primordial' conflict. Maurice Blanchot's solution to these problems, a forgetful memory in which a choice is exercised over the act of remembering, seems to us an improbable suggestion, and one that is offered and fails in the *Thebaid*, while, by contrast, Alain Badiou offers us a harder, but more realistic road in which loyalty to the event, an equivalent to loyalty to the other discussed in the previous chapters, effectively and continuously remakes Chronos, establishing a perpetual revolutionary moment. It is this course that the epics suggest is almost impossible: History will, in the last instance, triumph. But in living in awareness of the possibility of difference, and of Chronos as an artifice of the present and not the natural time of Aion, there is a glimpse of the freedom denied, and a possibility of loosening the hold of time.

CONSERVATIVE HEROES: FREE MEN IN AN IMPERIAL AGE

In the wonderful world of Pliny's wonderful friends, some are marked out as more wonderful than others. The first of these (in order of presentation) is a philosopher, Euphrates (*Ep.* I 10). Pliny sees the presence of Euphrates as evidence of the flourishing of literary studies in Rome, immediately differentiating the present from the bad old days of the Domitianic period.[3] Euphrates is praised for his literary style, for the power and subtlety of his reasoning, and for his appearance. This model philosopher, whom Pliny first met in Syria and who carries a Greek name, is also a good Roman, as shown by a fertile marriage to the daughter of Pompeius Iulianus. And then the letter changes tune. Pliny claims that he never has time to hear Euphrates. He is bothered by official business, and the tedium of *honores* is set against the wisdom of philosophy.[4]

It is Euphrates, himself, who consoles Pliny:

> adfirmat etiam hanc philosophiae et quidem pulcherrimam partem, agere negotium publicum, cognoscere iudicare, promere et exercere iustitiam, quaeque ipsi doceant in usu habere.

---

3. Cf *Ep.* I 13. In the context of our debate here, we wonder whether Pliny considered the Domitianic period an aberration, and thus the "present time" was a restoration of normal order. By contrast, see the unclear meaning of "present time" in Tacitus, *Agricola* 2, but which cannot be seen as a restoration of the pre-Domitianic era.

4. This picks up a lament from the previous letter (I 9) about the *negotium* (business) of Rome compared with productive *otium* which he enjoys in his Laurentine villa. Pliny hangs a precept on the end of the letter: *Satius est enim . . . otiosum esse quam nihil agere* ("For it is better to be at leisure than to do nothing").

> He affirms that even this is a part of philosophy, and the most fine part, to engage in public business, to sit in judgment, to expound and exercise justice, to put into use what is taught. *Ep* I 10

Euphrates thus affirms the virtues of the political life. His own small contribution to public life was in the fathering of children. Similarly, Euphrates is depicted as the son-in-law of another man worthy of emulation, a man with a distinguished career of office-holding. Euphrates speaks against Pliny's instinct, which is to prefer *otium* to *negotium* by elevating *negotium* above *otium*. We are supposed to infer that by his continuous activity, Pliny performs his duty as a philosopher as well as his duty to the community and state. It can hardly be a coincidence that the next letter in the collection (I 11), one that appears to add very little in terms of content, is addressed to Fabius Iustus, who had already appeared in the *Letters* as an important political actor in the aftermath of the assassination of Domitian (I 5), but who was also the addressee of Tacitus' *Dialogus*. The fundamental issue of the *Dialogus* was whether it was better to live in retirement from the political world. Pliny's response is clear: the good man should engage in political life, and that it is, indeed, possible to be great in the imperial age.

Of course, this answer is only a partial solution and raises a number of further practical questions, most notably that of how the good man should engage in politics. Pliny's response follows a traditional Roman model of ethical writing. He provides in his letters answers to this question in a traditional Roman manner, through the use of *exempla* who would act as models both for emulation and for the judgment of moral behavior. In what follows, we examine three of these *exempla*, Corellius Rufus, Titinius Capito, and Verginius Rufus, and then we look at certain members of the so-called "philosophical opposition."

Pliny shares his reminiscences of Corellius Rufus in *Ep.* I 12 on the occasion of the latter's death. Rufus' death was self-inflicted to relieve him of the suffering caused by what appears to have been some form of advanced circulatory problem. Pliny visited him after he had become bedridden sometime during the reign of Domitian. Corellius sent all from the room, including his wife, and then told Pliny that he prolonged his life only to outlive the *latro* (bandit) Domitian. Pliny claims that he would have acted against Domitian if illness had not made such conspiratorial opposition impossible. Pliny presents the suicide as following more or less directly on the death of Domitian and as bringing an end to thirty-five years of pain and disease.[5]

---

5. There are reasons to think that Pliny is improving the account here. Corellius appears elsewhere in the *Epistles*. In IV 17, Pliny represents Corellius as one of his foremost sponsors, recounting an anecdote of the great and good engaging in discussion of the *boni iuvenes* (good youths) and

Corellius' apparent withdrawal from politics to his sickbed under Domitian—and even his obstinately continuing life—becomes an act of political defiance. His prolongation of life should be read as a piece of political theater. His seeming retreat from the political center could have been interpreted either as a result of his disenchantment with the regime or as a sign of the severity of his illness. But, by sending out of the room all those who surround him, even his wife, Corellius makes a political statement about the intrusion into his liberty of the Domitianic state, and defies that intrusion by both speaking (to Pliny) about politics and signifying through his dismissal of his household that he is about to engage in conspiratorial political talk. In the same way, Corellius' eventual suicide was an act of freedom and an escape from the tyranny of pain. Though he faced physical infirmity as well as a restriction of liberty in the public sphere and in his own house, Corellius retained his personal freedom.

Titinius Capito was apparently a very different kind of man (*Ep.* I 17). He was an equestrian official of the imperial house who served first in a military capacity in Domitian's wars and then as a senior administrator in Domitian's household. He survived the fall of Domitian and rose further, with a military command in Rome under Trajan (*ILS* 1448). His continued political successes, and Pliny's favorable accounts of him, illustrate the complexity of politics in this period. Pliny praises him here for gaining permission to erect a statue to Lucius Silanus, probably the Lucius Silanus who fell victim to the court politics of the Neronian period. According to Pliny, Capito was known for his reverence of the famous, and even glorified the lives of the most famous (*clarissimi*) through verse, but more remarkable was his domestic reverence for statues of Brutus, Cassius, and Cato, martyrs to the Republican cause.

Capito appears also in VIII 12 where Pliny describes him this way:

Vir est optimus inter praecipua saeculi ornamenta numerandus . . . sollicitarer tamen vel ingenio hominis pulcherrimo et maximo et in summa severitate dulcissimo, vel honestate materiae. Scribit exitus inlustrium virorum in his quorundam mihi carissimorum.

He is the best of men, numbered among the shining ornaments of our age . . . I am encouraged by the talent of the man which is very fine and

---

turning their attention to Pliny. The conversation took place in front of the Emperor Nerva. In VIII 31, Pliny writes to Cornutus Tertullus recommending Claudius Pollio. The letter notes that Pollio had served Corellius when Corellius was engaged in buying land as part of a commission established by Nerva. Corellius was, therefore, clearly still taking an active part in public life in the Nervan period. As consul of C.E. 78, and a former governor of Germania Superior, Corellius was a senior figure in Nerva's Rome.

great and most pleasing in its great severity, and by the honorable nature of his subject matter. For he is writing on the deaths of outstanding men, some of whom were very dear to me. *Ep.* VIII 12

Capito's métier is a peculiar literary genre, a condensed form of biography which has come down to us in the Christian martyr acts and the existence of which may explain why Dio and Tacitus give space to elaborate set-piece deathbed scenes. With his veneration of Republican heroes, his commitment to the legacy of the martyrs who led the opposition to emperors, Capito is a distinctly confusing servant at the heart of the imperial household.

At the start of Book II, Pliny presents us with Verginius Rufus. Rufus played a major role in the events of C.E. 68–70. He defeated the Gallic rebel Vindex and was immediately offered the throne by his troops. He turned down this offer, allowed Galba to obtain the principate, and was promptly rewarded by removal from office. Later, when Otho fell to Vitellius, Rufus was again the choice of the troops in Italy, but, possibly recognizing the inevitability of Vitellius' victory, he fled and lived the rest of his life in the probably unique position of having twice been offered and twice refused the imperial throne.[6] Such decorous refusals made him a dangerous figure for the Flavians, and he seems to have languished in obscurity until the reign of Nerva when he was awarded a third consulship which he shared with the new emperor in C.E. 97.

Pliny does not comment in detail on Rufus' career. Presumably the stories were so well known that there was no need for elaboration. But he does focus on his own relationship with Rufus (who had become Pliny's guardian and political mentor) and on fame. Pliny describes Rufus as the "greatest and most famed citizen" (*maximi et clarissimi civis*), who survived his moment of glory by thirty years, read histories and poems written about him, and thus witnessed his 'posthumous' reputation. He concludes by wondering:

> si tamen fas est aut flere aut omnino mortem vocare qua tanti viri mortalitas magis finita quam vita est. Vivit enim vivetque semper atque etiam latius in memoria hominum et sermone versabitur, postquam ab oculis recessit. Volo tibi multa alia scribere, sed totus animus in hac una contemplatione defixus est. Verginium cogito, Verginium video, Verginium iam vanis imaginibus, recentibus tamen, audio, adloquor, teneo; cui fortasse cives aliquos virtutibus pares et habemus et habebimus, gloria neminem.

---

6. Rufus' behavior seems to have been an issue of considerable historical debate. See Plut. *Otho* 1; 18; Plutarch, *Galba* 6; Tac. *Hist.* I 8; II 51; Dio, LXIII 25 (Xiph. 183 25–184 8 R. St.), who notes that "It is difficult to know whether he did this because he thought it wrong for the soldiers to bestow imperial power, for he said that this was a matter for the senate and people, or because he was completely great-hearted and had no desire himself for imperial office."

if it is right to weep or even to call death what is more the end of the mortality of so great a man than the end of his life. For he lives and will always live and will appear even more widely in the memory of men and in our conversations once he has left our view. I want to write to you about much else, my whole mind is fixed on this one thought. I contemplate Verginius, I see Verginius, now in empty but real dreams I hear, talk to hold Verginius. We have perhaps and will have citizens who are his equal in virtue, but in glory, no one. Pliny, *Ep.* II 1

Rufus has not only achieved the goal of escaping death and securing his own immortality; he has been further assured of that immortality during life.

Pliny returns to the theme in two later letters, VI 10 and the more considered IX 19. The former establishes further links to Rufus. Pliny's mother-in-law owned a house which once belonged to Rufus and which Pliny visited. During the course of this visit, he went to Rufus' tomb, which he found unfinished nine years after Rufus' death. Pliny complains that "his ashes lie neglected and unnamed while his memory and glory circle the world" (*cinerem sine titulo sine nomine iacere, cuius memoria orbem terrarum Gloria pervagetur*), and then he quotes Rufus' epitaph, composed by the man himself, by which he ensured that the "immortal deed" would be remembered:

> Hic situs est Rufus pulso qui Vindice quondam
>   imperium adseruit non sibi sed patriae
>
> Here lies Rufus who, after defeating Vindex, laid hands on power, not for himself but for the fatherland. Pliny, *Ep.* VI 10

In IX 19 Pliny responds to criticism from Ruso, who compares the self-glorification of Rufus unfavorably with the disdain of Frontinus who forbade any monument to be erected to himself. Pliny leaps to Rufus' defense:

> Omnes ego qui magnum aliquid memorandumque fecerunt, non modo venia verum etiam laude dignissimos iudico, si immortalitatem quam meruere sectantur, victurique nominis famam supremis etiam titulis prorogare nituntur.
>
> I think all who have performed something great and memorable are most worthy not just of forgiveness but even of praise if they seek the immortality which they deserve and labor to increase the fame of their glorious name even by their final epitaph. Pliny, *Ep.* IX 19

Pliny's defense is that Rufus was due this honor since it had been hard won. The rest of the argument is less than explicit but if would seem that Pliny is suggesting that such epitaphs are in themselves deserving of praise since publicizing great acts was virtuous.[7] The great act itself is glossed in the retelling of an anecdote. Rufus has received a prepublication copy of a history by Cluvius Rufus. Cluvius has asked for 'factual' corrections from Rufus, but Rufus declines since: *Tune ignoras, Cluvi, ideo me fecisse quod feci, ut esset liberum vobis scribere quae libuisset* ("Do you not know, Cluvius, that I did what I did so that there is freedom for you to write what you wish" [Pliny, *Ep.* IX 19]).

This is a perverse boast since Rufus' actions led indirectly to the Domitianic period, but the defense of *libertas*, a Republican watchword, is Rufus's claim to *fama*. Rufus refused *imperium* for the sake of *libertas*, and worked for the *patria* as an honorable Roman. Although the Republic does not live, we witness nostalgia here for its former glories and we are presented with men who lived as though the Republic were indeed alive. Rufus (and perhaps Pliny) appears to have lived in a paradox.

Pliny found other admirable individuals among the opponents of Domitian, those conveniently—but inaccurately—known as the "philosophical opposition." Pliny's emotional association with this group is clear throughout his letters, but there are few discussions of their activities. One such discussion is IV 22, on Junius Mauricus. Two anecdotes are retold. In the first Mauricus spoke in the Senate on whether a magistrate had the right to suppress the games of the Viennenses. He supported the magistrate's announcement claiming that he wished to abolish the games in Rome as well. As the games were an opportunity for the emperor to display his love for his people, a necessary part of the political apparatus of imperial Rome, this was a proposal hardly likely to win Mauricus imperial (or popular) support. It was a moral statement in the face of public opinion and it almost certainly rested on a view that the games were corrupting the traditional values of the Roman people.

The second anecdote relates to a dinner party held by the Emperor Nerva. Fabricius Veiento was at dinner and in the place of honor. Veiento was an associate of Domitian and although possibly not one of the major players, his membership in the imperial circle meant that he came to be associated with its "crimes." Conversation turned to Catullus Messalinus, a notorious and intimidating prosecutor of the period, whose sins were listed. Nerva wondered aloud as to where he would he be if he had outlived

---

7. Besides, Frontinus' refusal to countenance a monument is subject to irony: such a refusal was in itself a claim to great reputation since the assumption was that reputation would survive with or without a monument.

Domitian, and Mauricus answered "Nobsicum cenaret" ("dining with us"). This was, of course, impolitic since it associated the honored Veiento with Messalinus and, in so doing, placed Nerva, who was honoring him, in a deeply uncomfortable position. The story illustrates the political difficulties of the Nervan period when the wounds of the Domitianic period were not healed and those persecuted by Domitian were back in circulation and in positions of authority alongside their erstwhile prosecutors.[8] Nerva's amnesty was thrown into disarray by just such hostilities. Mauricus' actions were, then, confrontational, though honest; they were the actions of one who would not be cowed by political expediency.

Although Pliny maintained his relationship with Mauricus and family, the most notable portraits of the survivors of that group are of Arria and Fannia. *Ep.* III 16, to Nepos, starts with a notable paradox, at least for Pliny: *adnotasse videor facta dictaque virorum feminarumque alia clariora esse alia maiora* ("I seem to have noted that some deeds and sayings of men and women are the more famous and others the greater" [*Ep.* III 16]). Such a recognition of the fickleness of fame would seem almost a commonplace. Yet in Pliny's moral universe where fame was highly prized, such arbitrary workings were of considerable concern. Pliny goes on to illustrate his point with some anecdotes from a conversation he once had with his friend Fannia about her grandmother, Arria, whose fame rested on her suicide.[9] To this well-known story, Pliny added further stories of Arria's bravery, including, most notably, a story centering on the death of her son.[10]

In *Ep.* VII 19 Pliny discusses what was presumably Fannia's final illness in which she showed, according to Pliny, a courage that recalled the valor of her late husband, Helvidius Priscus, and her father, Thrasea Paetus, both notable victims of imperial persecution. Her valor is further demonstrated by an account of the trial of Senecio, who was being prosecuted for his biography or laudation of Helvidius Priscus. Astonishingly enough, Senecio's defense was that the work was a commission from Fannia, who had lent him diaries for this purpose. Under cross-examination, Fannia corroborated the story, denying in the process that her mother was aware of her actions. This

---

8. The anecdote also neatly illustrates the problems of official forgetfulness. Although Nerva had tried to draw a line under the events of the Domitianic period, there was no forgetting, and Nerva's attempt to declare a revolution, a new time, failed spectacularly.

9. Arria stabbed herself in order to encourage her husband, Caecina Paetus, who had been involved in a conspiracy against the Emperor Claudius, to his death. Her famous last words were: *Paete, nec dolet* ("Paetus, it doesn't hurt").

10. Both Caecina Paetus and son were ill. The boy died and Paetus was in a dangerous condition. Arria continued to nurse Paetus. She completed the funeral arrangements and rites, mourned for her son, but kept his death from his father, showing no grief until Paetus was himself out of danger. Self-control in private is here counterposed to self-control in the public sphere.

resulted in Senecio's death and Fannia's exile. While Senecio and Paetus both appear less than robust under prosecution, Fannia and Arria demonstrate a noble courage. Notably, Pliny also shows that both women displayed the same courage in nonpublic arenas. Because of the deaths or arrests of their menfolk, Arria and Fannia were left as representatives of their family and were able to maintain a family tradition. In so doing, Arria and Fannia appear not just as paradigms of virtue for women, but also for men, and show that even if the great deed cannot be accomplished in public, moral greatness can be reached in private.[11]

In his letters Pliny was engaged, as much as his contemporary Tacitus, in the writing of history. He was preserving for us memories of his age, bringing to light stories that would inform the collective consciousness. There can be no doubt that Pliny, who had lived through the Domitianic period, was aware of the changes in the status of the Roman elite. Although he might imagine himself as a new Cicero, the political circumstances of his career were obviously different. Nonetheless, he still offers a range of admirable individuals who seem connected to Republican traditions. Capito valued the heroes of the Republic. Rufus appears to have behaved politically as if he were still in the Republic, a piece of political fantasizing that looks very much like a restrospective mythologizing of his role. The outspoken Junius Mauricus also gave nothing to the new realities of the imperial age. With Corellius and Arria and Fannia, similar attitudes applied. None of these three were prepared to be intimidated, but all three were forced to display their virtue off the political stage. There is a change from the heroics of the Republican period here, in that by performing away from the public eye, the opportunities for these individuals' virtues to be remembered were greatly reduced. One wonders whether this was one of the primary problems of the imperial age, that virtues exercised in private had less of an audience, unless, of course, they had a Pliny to record their activities. But this privatization of virtue does not, in itself, change the nature of the virtue. These individuals show a deep commitment to their communities and Roman values, to *pietas*. It was thus possible to be great in the imperial age, and to be great in very much the same way it had been possible for Cicero to be great. This modified moral continuity is a very different position on the past than that taken by Tacitus.

---

11. This is reinforced by *Ep.* VI 24. Here Pliny relates an anecdote told to him by an older friend as they were sailing on Lake Como. The friend pointed to a room of a villa which overhung the lake. From this room a *municeps* (townswoman) had thrown herself and her husband into the lake. Pliny was understandably intrigued. The husband had ulcerated genitalia. The wife inspected the ulcers. The disease was sufficiently advanced that she saw no hope. She roped herself to her husband, and she jumped into the lake. Pliny was filled with admiration, but driven to muse at the chance encounter that led to this deed being publicized. As with the stories of the elder Arria, this story is rescued by Pliny and given a place among the *exempla* of the Roman aristocracy.

BREAKING WITH THE PAST: TACITUS AND THE AMBIVALENCE OF REVOLUTIONARY HISTORY

Partly because Tacitus was not prone to theorizing, reconstructing his view of history can be a deeply contentious undertaking. Further, Tacitus' notorious irony is used both to undermine the characters portrayed and also to force the reader to stand outside the text, to take a critical and analytical position on what he or she is being told, and to question continuously the obvious meanings of words and events.[12] T. J. Luce argues that Tacitus was a particularist and not a theorist.[13] The "meaning of history" may also be obscured by the literary structure of the works. Tacitus adopted the traditional approach to structuring a Roman historical work in that he divided the narrative into (sometimes rather loose) annual accounts. The centrality of narrative to ancient historiography means that it sometimes looks like a chronicle, a form which is particularly hard to deconstruct.[14] Yet chronicles, as much as any other literary or historiographical work, are manifestations of a historical theory. Even the choice of an annalistic form, a form which corresponded to the Roman system of dating by years of consuls, was an ideological and literary choice that could be interpreted as signifying a loyalty to Republican-period historiography or to Republican-period political analysis.[15] Yet Tacitus does guide us through the interpretation of the events he sets before us, and also explicitly discusses the meaning of history. Arguably, given the importance of history to Tacitus and his contemporaries, he could hardly avoid producing a theory of history, though those accustomed to the great teleological philosophies of history might have trouble recognizing it as such.

Tacitus' two major works, the *Histories* and the *Annales,* both lack their endings, precisely the points at which one might expect modern historians to allow themselves the liberty of more general remarks about the shape and significance of their work. But, though we have no closures in Tacitus, we do have openings, and starting is at least as important as finishing.

---

12. O'Gorman (2000) 17 writes that "it could be argued that irony in particular is mobilised in relation not only to the principate but also to its critics, suggesting that they examine closely the nature of the principate they criticise *and* the nature of their criticism. The ironical statement therefore not only embodies a particular sceptical attitude on the part of the writer, but also compels the reader to take her political stance in relation to the past."

13. Luce (1986). Of course, particularism is in itself a theory of history.

14. Henderson (1989) points out that the annalistic form had the potential to endlessly defer closure, the *telos* that is so important for giving the historical work its meaning.

15. See Clarke (2002). The point becomes obvious when we consider that the *Histories* opens not with the death of Nero, but with the first January of Galba's principate. For Clarke, Tacitus declares conventional history to be over, but then finds a new stage in which to set history. Ginsburg (1981) 100 suggests that the annalistic form was used to evoke a past age, and its very incongruity was a demonstration of change.

> Urbem Romam a principio reges habuere; libertatem et consulatem L. Brutus instituit. Dictaturae ad tempus sumebantur; neque decemviralis potestas ultra biennium neque tribunorum militum consulare ius diu valuit. Non Cinnae, non Sullae longa dominatio; et Pompei Crassique potentia cito in Caesarem, Lepidi atque Antonii arma in Augustum cessere, qui cuncta dicordiis civilibus fessa nomine principis sub imperium accepit. Sed veteris populi Romani prospera vel adversa claris scriptoribus memorata sunt; temporibusque Augusti dicendis non defuere decora ingenia, donec gliscente adulatione deterrerentur . . . inde consilium mihi pauca de Augusto et extrema tradere mox Tiberii principatum et cetera, sine ira et studio, quorum causas procul habeo.
>
> In the beginning, the city of Rome had kings. L. Brutus instituted freedom and the consulship. Dictators were used as necessary. The power of the decemviri did not last two years and the military tribunes having consular rights lasted a short time. Neither Cinna nor Sulla had long reigns. Pompey and Crassus had power, but lost to Caesar and the arms of Lepidus and Antony fell to Augustus, who with everything exhausted by civil conflict, accepted all under his power in the name of the Princeps. The achievements and failings of the Roman people of old were remembered by outstanding writers and the recording of the time of Augustus does not lack distinguished talents, after which they were deterred by the raging adulation [of the Julio-Claudian emperors] . . . and so it seemed right to me to deal little with Augustus, concentrating only on the end of his period and to move to the reign of Tiberius and the other matters, without anger or prejudice, since I have no reason for such. *Annales* I 1

Tacitus opens the *Annales* by dealing with all Roman history from the foundation of Rome to Octavian in fewer than fifty words. Six words deal with the regal period. Six more introduce the Republic. Sixteen words more and we reach the crises of the late Republic with Cinna and Sulla and within twenty words of that we have the first mention of Augustus. Seven centuries of Roman history are dealt with in half a paragraph. Tacitus then turns to historiography, but quickly resumes his express narrative in I 2 with the defeat of Pompey and Lepidus, the killing of Antony, and a summary of the career of Augustus:

> ubi militem donis, populum annona, cunctos dulcedine otii pellexit, insurgere paulatim, munia senatus magistratuum legum in se trahere, nullo adversante, cum ferocissimi per acies aut proscriptione cecidissent, ceteri nobilium, quanto quis servitio promptior, opibus et honoribus extollerentur ac novis ex rebus aucti tuta et praesentia quam vetera et periculosa mallent.

He seduced the soldiers with gifts, the people with food, and rest with the sweetness of leisure. Little by little he pressed on, annexing to himself the duties of the senate, the magistrates and the law, without opposition, since the most fierce had been slaughtered in battle or through proscription, and the rest of the nobles, somewhat more eager for slavery, were raised up by wealth and honors, and, having gained from the revolution, preferred safety and the present to the old and dangerous. *Annales* I 2

After a brief excursus on the dynastic politics of the Julians, Tacitus reviews the situation at the end of the Augustan period:

Domi res tranquillae. eadem magistratuum vocabula. iuniores post Actiacam victoriam, etiam senes plerique inter bella civium nati. quotus quisque reliquus qui rem publicam vidisset? igitur verso civitatis statu nihil usquam prisci et integri moris. omnes exuta aequalitate iussa principis aspectare.

At home, things were quiet. The magistrates had the same names. The younger men were born after the Actian victory. Even most of the old had been born during the civil wars. How many were there remaining who had seen the Republic? The state had, therefore, been transformed and there was nothing of the original and pure customs. Equality had gone and all looked to the orders of the princeps. *Annales* I 3–4

The transition between Republic and Empire is neither dated nor associated with a single event. Instead, it is described as a process in which Augustus gradually accumulated authority and influence and in which the traditions of Republicanism were eroded.[16] Indeed, the process only seems complete when the politics of the Republic had become a purely historical phenomenon, something of which the Romans of Tacitus' time had no experience.

Annales I–III offers little historical theory, merely noting in I 1 that both the Republic and the Augustan period had received the attention of outstanding historians, but, in *Annales* IV, Tacitus becomes a little more reflective.

Pleraque eorum quae rettuli quaeque referam parva forsitan et levia memoratu videri non nescius sum: sed nemo annalis nostros cum scriptura eorum contenderit qui veteres populi Romani res composuere, ingentia illi bella, expugnationes urbium, fusos captosque reges, aut si quando ad interna praeverterent, discordias consulum adversus tribunos, agrarias frumentariasque

---

16. This treatment differs very considerably from Dio's much later discussion. For Dio, the Principate comes into being with the settlements following the battle of Actium whereas the imperial system is in place by the end of the senatorial debates of 27 B.C.E.

leges, plebis et optimatium certamina libero egressu memorabant: nobis in arto et inglorius labor.

I am not unaware that much of what I retold and what I will tell may seem perhaps minor and of little importance, but no one could compare the annals of our times with the writings of those ancients who concerned themselves with the state of the Roman people. For they had great wars, assaults on cities and the flight and capture of kings or, if they turned to internal matters, they could freely recount the disputes between consuls and tribunes, agrarian and corn laws, the contests between plebs and *optimates*, while I have an inglorious and strictly limited labor. *Annales* IV 32

Although Tacitus distinguished the history of the period of autocracy as being different in nature, he claims continuity with the traditions of Republican historiography in the utility value of history as a means of teaching men to distinguish "honorable from lesser behavior, practicality from wrongdoing" (*Annales* IV 33). This practicality can be seen as an equivalent position to that of the modern utilitarians, but issues of identity and Romanity are profoundly interlinked with the narratives of the past, as Tacitus goes on to show.

This historiographical digression is immediately followed by the story of the prosecution of the historian Aulus Cremutius Cordus in C.E. 25 for his praise of Brutus and Cassius.[17] Although Tacitus gives us little information concerning Cordus' interpretation of Roman history, we are told that Cordus provided Cassius, the tyrannicide, with the epithet "the last of the Romans" (*ultimus Romanorum* [IV 34]). Tacitus gives Cordus a long justificatory speech (IV 34) in which he notes the achievements of writers and historians of the past (Livy, Asinius Pollio, and Messala Corvinus) and claims that he should be able without constraint to "speak of those whom death has put beyond hatred or thanks" (*prodere de iis quos mors odio aut gratiae exemisset* [IV 35]), just as the writers of the past could praise Republican heroes. But this was disingenuous: by calling C. Cassius *ultimus Romanorum*, Cordus asserted that Romanity existed in Republicanism, which, at the very least, may have unnerved a monarch. Cordus is thus asserting that there was a *caesura* in Roman history at the point of the transformation from Republic to Empire, though Tacitus is imprecise in his report of just where that

---

17. The juxtaposition of the digression and Cordus episode has attracted considerable comment. McCulloch (1991) argues that Tacitus sees himself in Cordus, the historian who will be remembered recording the vices of the age. See also Ginsburg (1981) 48–50 and Sage (1991) 3387. By contrast, we follow Martin and Woodman (1989) 169, who note that 4.32 is preparing us for 4.34–35 and argue that Cordus' argument is flawed (183).

caesura should be placed. Further, Cordus connects the *caesura* to a change in the narratives of identity. To be a Roman was to be a Republican, but also, potentially, it was to defend the Roman state through tyrannicide. Yet, the speech concludes: *si damnatio ingruit, qui non modo Cassii et Bruti set etiam mei meminerint* ("Should I be condemned, they will remember not just Brutus and Cassius, but also me" [IV 35]). Cremutius Cordus then left the court and killed himself. By facing down the tyrant and claiming his freedom, if only through his ultimate sacrifice, Cordus claimed an association with that "last Roman." As Cassius had asserted his Romanity and freedom in the conspiracy against Caesar and on the battlefield, so Cordus had laid claim to Romanity in his history, and cemented that claim through his death. We are invited to read Cordus as an *exemplum* and as a victim of tyranny. But Cordus also appears to be a contradiction and an anachronism, consumed by nostalgia for the Republic, and unable to reconcile the lessons of his history with his politics.

Nostalgia for the Republic is something of a theme in *Histories* I, the first half of which concentrates on Galba and his overthrow. Galba's appeal to the Roman elite lies both in his age and in his old-fashioned severity. In this, he represents a notable reaction to the Neronian period with all its iconoclasm and innovation. The account emphasizes how Galba poses as a restorer of tradition and refuses to adopt the political arts of the imperial age such as the courting of popularity, the exercise of patronage to win the loyalty of the court and senate, and the display of generosity to secure the support of the troops. Instead, he relied on old-fashioned moral authority and the display of his personal and political discipline. This policy reached its culmination and disastrous apogee in what was almost the final act of his regime: the adoption of Piso. Piso appears to have been a man who had few enemies and many admirers, but his youth and inexperience meant that he had no individual political authority. He was adopted just as Galba's political position was starting to disintegrate; there was revolt in Germany and unrest in Rome. Galba may or may not have been aware that Otho was gathering support for a *putsch* (even though Tacitus certainly suggests that the conspiracy was well advanced). As Galba was an elderly man, the issue of succession was alive, and as he was also childless, it was clear that he would have to adopt his successor. Galba could have grabbed the opportunity to rescue his regime by associating himself with a powerful individual, thus gaining a whole new source of political support and perhaps military authority (as Nerva was to do in adopting Trajan). At this key moment, Tacitus provides Galba with a long speech in which he (Galba-Tacitus) outlines his view of the imperial system as well as his reasons for adopting Piso, an admirable, aristocratic young man.

In the speech, Galba laments the necessity of imperial rule and claims that the best possible means of discovering the next emperor is adoption, a measure taken by Augustus, who looked only to his own family for suitable adoptees. He claims that he searched through the whole of the available aristocracy before alighting on Piso. There is thus a rejection of the hereditary principle and a claim that the emperor should be appointed by other means, by identifying the "leading man" of the day, a man who is *capax imperii* (capable of rule). What is being advanced here is a new theory of monarchy, one which would potentially free Rome from the rule of men like Gaius, Claudius, Nero, and, as the text can be read as a prediction of the future, Domitian. The speech thus reads like a manifesto, and it is difficult to read it without seeing in it a comment on Nerva's adoption of Trajan in very similar circumstances, a commentary that might at first sight appear to border on the panegyrical. Nevertheless, as ever with Tacitus, the speech is not quite as simple as it seems. The alert may notice that Galba condemns the hereditary principles that made the Roman people "almost the heirloom of a single family under Tiberius, Gaius, and Claudius" (*sub Tiberio et Gaio et Claudio unius familiae quasi hereditas fuimus* [16]) and asks this audience "to call to mind Nero who was made proud by a long line of Caesars" (*sit ante oculos Nero quem longa Caesarum serie tumentum* [16]), seemingly failing to remember that Nero, though indeed descended from a long line of Caesars, was adopted over and above the emperor's natural son. Furthermore, although we might appreciate the sentiments, Galba's complete failure to understand the principate and the political events of which he was a part undercuts our judgment of the speech. In I 5, Tacitus tells us that the urban soldiery had been lost through Galba's meanness. He is supposed to have declared "I choose troops, not buy them" (*legi a se militem, non emi*). When Piso was presented to the troops (I 18), Galba again refused a donative (gift), and Tacitus remarks that he might have maintained the peace even at this stage by a show of liberality. However, "such antique discipline and great austerity was injurious, for now we are not suited to it" (*nocuit antiquus rigor et nimia severitas, cui iam pares non sumus*). Being adopted by a failing emperor effectively made Piso a victim of the imperial regime; Galba was condemning the young man to an early death, just as his politically incompetent choice sounded the death knell of his own regime. The long address that marks the adoption is thus an extended political disquisition and suicide note (*Hist.* I 15–16).

Galba's reign ended in farce. Prematurely believing that Otho's revolt was over, he entered the Forum where he was caught by Otho's troops. As his slaves fled, Galba was thrown from his chair. Tacitus preserves two traditions of the tenor of his last words: he either begs for a few extra days to meet the donative, or offers his throat to the soldiers (I 41). From beginning to end, Galba used the rhetoric of Republican severity but was undermined by the realities of imperial rule. Unable to manipulate the situation, he is a case study of someone who did not understand the *arcana imperii* (secrets of empire), who misread history and the historical *exempla*, ultimately failing to realize that the ways of the Republic were dead. His adoption of Piso is just another example of admirable sentiment and political-historical foolishness.

Tacitus' attitude towards the Republican past is in some ways very clear.[18] That past was gone. The indecent haste with which he covered more than seven centuries of history in the introduction to the *Annales* makes this obvious. It would seem that he is making a distinction between bygone olden times and that past which is more similar to the present (and hence relevant to his contemporaries). He is thus inserting a *caesura* into the history of Rome. Yet, this leaves us with a further problem. The *Annales* commence in C.E. 14, as the first emperor dies. This is possibly the least popular start date for histories of the imperial period, with 49, 44, 31, 28 and 27 C.E. all having much to recommend them.[19] Starting in C.E. 14 suggests that Tacitus viewed that date as being of greater significance than others and only makes sense in the context of a view that the principate did not have a single date of creation, but was formed in a process.[20] But most importantly for our purposes, Tacitus confirms that in his view the Republic is over when it ceases to be part of living memory, when there is no one left alive who can remember its workings. The Republic thus only takes its place within the "olden times" in Tacitus' bipartite division of history when it has ceased to be part of living memory, and thus subject to the arguments of historians. Tacitus' argument becomes historiographic at this stage. He himself presents the decision to start his *Annales* in C.E. 14 as a literary one, the Augustan age having had historians of merit. In both cases, Tacitus distinguishes between the historiographic traditions of the imperial and Republican periods. His argument is that the political structures of the period led to a change in the

---

18. See also Ginsburg (1993).
19. See Syme (1958) 364–73 on the reasons for Tacitus starting in C.E. 14, which Tacitus describes as literary and Syme accepts. Syme also argues that Tacitus had "second thoughts," expressed in *Ann.* III 24 (a passage in which Tacitus suggests that he was intending to turn his attention to the Augustan principate in a later work) on the start date. This was, according to Syme, recognition of a genuine mistake, and that he came to recognize the importance of the fall of the Republic and the emergence of *dominatio* under Augustus. This is implausible since it misreads the passage, which advertises a further work and not an intention to revise the *Annales*. Preliminary readings of his works would probably have allowed Tacitus the opportunity to appreciate any error and restructure his writing.
20. The alternative is to take Henderson's (1989) suggestion on closure seriously for openings and argue that Tacitus was not very concerned when he started. Thus, the *Annales* becomes merely what Tacitus did next after the *Histories*.

way that history could be written. The imperial age was a different epoch and required a different history, a different scripted memory for his contemporaries to lean on. In this, he is with Cordus. He seems to accept Cordus' interpretation of fundamental change in the Augustan period. And yet, faced with the *caesura* at the end of the Republic, Tacitus does not follow Cordus in proclaiming the end of (Roman) history, condemning the true Roman to perpetual exile from the present and a life of nostalgia; he rather asserts that Rome needs a new history for the new age. Galba and Cordus rejected this perceived change in the Roman state and attempted to live the nostalgic fantasy. In so doing, they condemned themselves to death.

Tacitus would thus seem to offer us a revolutionary historiography, in which the Caesarian revolution (by which we mean events from Caesar through Augustus) caused a fundamental breach in the temporal frame, meaning that those of the imperial period needed to live in a different time and that those who wrote about time had to write in a different way. This new imperial Chronos was not, however, the result of a Utopian revolution, and the epoch was marked by inevitable constraints that reduced the freedoms of the previous age. Tacitus does not attempt to disguise this loss of freedom. Rather, it is his acceptance of this characteristic of the epoch that is notable and problematic and which reflects Tacitean ambivalence. The issue is reflected throughout his historical works, but here we concentrate on its presentation in the first books of the *Annales* and in the *Agricola*.

The first books of the *Annales* center on a political struggle in the imperial house, a struggle that is peculiar in that it is undeclared and apparently one-sided. From the very first days of his rule, Tiberius, according to Tacitus, was looking over his shoulder at Germanicus, a rival who refused to be a rival. Germanicus, young, generous, friendly, and open, is the counterpoint to aged, mean, deceitful, closed Tiberius; we can thus see the pair as two different models of imperial leader. Germanicus' early death marked him further as the great lost leader of the empire, while it also provided Tacitus with an opportunity to portray an imperial hero, a man who understood the new age.

Faced with such symbolic overloading of Germanicus, modern historians have worried that his character seems somewhat disappointing.[21] The first major scenes of the *Annales* that feature Germanicus concern the suppression of a mutiny on the Rhine frontier. On hearing of the death of Augustus, the troops on the Rhine and Danube frontiers demanded better pay and conditions and release from service with appropriate benefits once their term (twenty years) had been served. On hearing of the mutinies, Germanicus

---

21. See, for example, Pelling (1993).

left his administrative duties in Gaul and headed to the Rhine camps. There he made a speech proclaiming the virtues of Augustus and Tiberius and demanded that the soldiers make their case. In the clamor that followed, some offered to make Germanicus emperor, at which point he threatened suicide rather than be dishonored by such disloyalty to his uncle Tiberius. In so doing, he demonstrated beyond any reasonable doubt his loyalty to both the political structures and the ideals of empire. His threat of suicide was received with general derision. Eventually, and perhaps more by luck than intention, Germanicus turned the situation around. The soldiers were returned to loyalty and persuaded to round up the ringleaders of the mutiny. These were murdered by the troops, comrade killing comrade to demonstrate loyalty to the emperor and Germanicus. The episode ends with Germanicus arriving at a legionary camp to find the bodies of the massacred. Bursting into tears, he announced that "this was not a cure but a disaster" (*non medicam illud plurimis cum lacrimis sed cladem appellans* [*Ann.* I 49]). Emotional and not entirely successful, he seems an unlikely hero.

In the narrative that follows, the political hostility between Tiberius and Germanicus is often implicit.[22] From II 53 until the death of Germanicus, the narrative concentrates on the conflict between Germanicus and a certain Gnaeus Piso, who can be read as a character set in motion by Tiberius against Germanicus, but who is far from being Tiberius' puppet. Tacitus carefully introduces us to Piso before the narrative turns to the clashes with Germanicus. In II 35 Tacitus details a spat between Piso and Asinius Gallus. Tiberius was to be away from the Senate. Piso, however, suggests that the Senate should continue to sit because that would show that the Roman state could continue to perform its judicial and political functions in the absence of the emperor. Gallus, however, argued that it was unworthy of the dignity of the people of Rome to conduct business other than under the eye of the emperor. According to Tacitus, this was suggested in order to confute the *speciem libertatis* ("show of liberty") by Piso.[23]

Piso reappears in II 43 and this time is given a full introduction.

Cn Pisonem, ingenio violentum et obsequii ignarum, insita ferocia a patre Pisone qui civili bello resurgentis in Africa partis acerrimo ministerio adversus Caesarem iuvit, mox Brutum et Cassium secutus concesso reditu

---

22. Tiberius is mostly a malicious and silent presence, often withdrawn from the narrative, or commenting ironically on the action. See Pelling (1993) on the narrative function of Germanicus.
23. Gallus went on to clash with the emperor by suggesting that magistrates should be elected five years in advance, and posts were to be filled by nomination of the *princeps*. Tacitus claims that Gallus proposed these measures to lay bare the despotic and unconstitutional nature of the government (Tac., *Ann.* II 36).

petitione honorum abstinuit, donec ultro ambiretur delatum ab Augusto consulatum accipere. sed praeter paternos spiritus uxoris quoque Plancinae nobilitate et opibus accendebatur; vix Tiberio concedere liberos eius ut multum infra despectare.

Cn Piso, violent in temper and ignorant of deference, developed his ferocity from his father Piso who in the civil war helped with considerable zeal in Africa the anti-Caesarian party, then followed Brutus and Cassius and, having returned, refused to seek office, until finally he was persuaded by Augustus to take a consulship. But, additionally to his father's spirit, he was also urged on by the nobility and wealth of his wife, Plancina; scarcely did he concede place to Tiberius, but his children he regarded as much below him. Tacitus, *Ann.* II 43

Piso was a Republican, loyal to the point of violence and holding firm to the old traditions well after their time had passed. While some changed their ways when the Republic ended, he continued to emulate his father's loyalty to Brutus and Cassius. Germanicus had already been characterized by a quite different set of adjectives and moral qualities: *civilis* (I 33); *clemens* (I 58); *modestia* (II 26); *munificentia* (II 26); *nobilitas* (II 13); *decus* (II 13); *fama* (II 13); *patientia* (II 13); *comitas* (I 33; I 71; II 13) (polite, forgiving, modest, generous, noble, beautiful, of good repute, durable and patient, friendly) and enjoying the *favor populi* (popularity) (I 7). We are thus presented with a ferocious, impolitic, violent Republican alongside the virtuous (imperial) Germanicus. In C.E. 18 Germanicus was sent to the East to deal with a war brewing on the Eastern frontier, and Piso followed as newly appointed governor of Syria and the second most powerful man in the East.

Germanicus started his journey to the East at Actium where he was also able to call up the "imago" of the battle of 31 B.C.E. and the foundation of the monarchy. The next stop was Athens, which he visited with a single lictor as a mark of respect to the city, and the Athenians honored him in turn, the honors making reference to their great deeds of the past (*Ann.* II 53). Germanicus then traveled through Northern Greece and arrived at Troy which was, according to Tacitus, a reminder of *varietate fortunae et nostri origine veneranda* ("the fickleness of fortune and of our venerable origins"), before he visited the oracle of Apollo at Clarus, which supposedly foretold his early death (*Ann.* II 54). Germanicus' travels resumed the following year (*Ann.* II 59–60) when he visited Egypt. The visit is described as touristic, though he did open the granaries to deal with a famine. He traveled in Greek dress and without guard in emulation of the Republican hero Scipio Africanus, and also visited the great monuments of Egypt. In Thebes (modern Luxor) the priests read to him the inscriptions that enumerated the power of the Egyptian empire, its tribute, its gold, and its manpower.

These stories establish Germanicus as a reader of the past. On the battlefield of Actium, he is able to recall the past (although born long after the battle): Actium was an immediate and powerful memory as the foundation site of the new regime. The visit to Troy could be seen in very much the same way. Germanicus was honoring not just the Homeric epics, but also the mythological foundations of the Roman people and of his family. Significantly, he recalls an Augustan version of history (not the version of early Roman history that we have in the first lines of the *Annales*), in which Romanity springs from Troy and is intimately associated with the rule of the Julians. In this view, the Romans are led from Troy by Aeneas, first ruled by Aeneas' son, Iulus, founder of the Julian *gens,* and the triumph of Augustus was a historic restoration and not an innovation. Nevertheless, alongside this dynastic message, Tacitus has Germanicus reflect among the ruins on the *varietas fortunae*, the fickleness of fortune.

In Troy, perhaps in Athens, and certainly in Egypt, we see Germanicus among the ruins connecting emotionally to a remote past. The pleasure of ruins, which has had and continues to have considerable influence on modern sensibilities, springs not so much from nostalgia, but from the ruin as the sublime. The ruin is a symbol of time and of power, as well as of the failings of human society: the more impressive the original building, the more poignant its destruction. The ruin is a symbol of a previous age, and has thus escaped time, but it is also marked by the destruction of time: the ruin is an element of Chronos, but in manifesting an epoch that has gone, it displays the revolutionary nature of Chronos, always succumbing to Aion, always susceptible to change. It is a signifier of absence, the absence of the people and the society that constructed the building, and an absence of the very functionality of the building; it has been turned into an almost pure sign, stripped of function. But it is also a symbol of the transience of power. In Egypt, Germanicus reads through the lists of the provinces of empire, the huge armies, the gold and other wealth, all of which had gone, and he can see in that transience the eventual fate of Rome and its leaders, to be swallowed by history. At one level, this symbolizes the fate that awaits Germanicus, soon to die in Syria, and that we are all beings unto death, trapped within a Chronos that will collapse, but at another, we see the fate that awaits Rome, the eternal city.

Germanicus' story ends in tears, as it was so frequently punctuated by them. Tacitus provides him with two deathbed orations, one public and one private. Believing himself betrayed and possibly poisoned by the machinations of Piso, perhaps with the backing of Tiberius, Germanicus speaks first to his friends. He calls for revenge, but emphasizes that his father and brother, Tiberius and Drusus, should be the instruments of that revenge. He warns those around him not to turn against Tiberius. Piso was to be the target, and this is in keeping with Germanicus' secret last words:

> Tum ad uxorem versus per memoriam sui, per communis liberos oravit exueret ferociam, saevienti fortunae summitteret animum, neu regressa in urbem aemulatione potentiae validiores inritaret. haec palam et alia secreto per quae ostendisse credebatur metum ex Tiberio, neque multo post extinguitur, ingenti luctu provinciae et circumiacentium populorum.

> Then, turning to his wife, he begged her by his memory and by their common children to control her fierce feeling and submit to the savagery of fortune, and not, once returned to Rome, to annoy the stronger by competition for power. This was open and the rest secret, for it is believed he showed fear of Tiberius and, soon afterwards, he died to great grief in the province and from the surrounding peoples. Tac., *Ann.* II 72

In his last hour, Germanicus showed a profound understanding of the political realities of Rome, warning his wife of the danger that eventually would consume her and most of their children. Tacitus' Germanicus was no romantic and had no illusions about the realities of imperial power and the character of the emperor. Not for him the unrealities of Piso's Republicanism, holding to the traditions of Cassius and Brutus while being the tool of the emperor. Germanicus could see and learn from the birth of the empire and the death of the Republic on the battlefields of Actium, he could understand the origins of Rome in the sack of Troy, and feel the transience of power and empire in the temples of Egypt. Germanicus understood history and his place in it. Germanicus was an open and wholehearted monarchist, a new man for a new age, and a man whose relationship to the past was profoundly different from that of his enemies.

The portrait of Germanicus establishes a complex relationship between Republican and imperial values and between history and an individual's place in history that goes beyond narrowly politically concerns. Germanicus' interpretations of Egypt and Troy were not in the immediate sense political, but in offering a certain understanding of the workings of history, they had political implications. The treatment of these themes within the *Annales* is rather more reflective and difficult than the treatment of time and history that we find in the *Agricola*. The *Agricola* and, indeed, the *Dialogus* appear more concerned with the issues that seem to concern Pliny, in particular the

LIVING WITH THE PAST   165

issue of virtue in the imperial age.[24] Tacitus insists that the route map for political behavior provided by Republican history could no longer work in an imperial age. The very first words of the work express the contrast between what is possible now and what was possible in ancient times, but they also confirm that virtue can still conquer and provide a guide for men who strive for greatness.

> Clarorum virorum facta moresque posteris tradere antiquitus usitatum, ne nostris quidem temporibus quamquam incuriosa suorum aetas omisit, quotiens magna aliqua ac nobilis virtus vicit ac supergressa est vitium parvis magnisque civitatibus commune, ignorantiam recti et invidiam.

> The acts and customs of famous men of old used to be recorded and even in our time, whatever the lack of interest in such matters, sometimes some great and noble manliness conquers and overcomes the envy common to states small and great and the jealousy and ignorance of virtue. *Agricola* 1

That guide, Agricola, is not introduced until the end of chapter 3. After providing the generic background to this particular oratorical and literary form, chapter 2 turns to recent precursors: Arulenus Rusticus' work on Thrasea Paetus and Herennius Senecio's laudation of Helvidius Priscus. Both these publications resulted in the deaths of their authors and the destruction of their books. The *Agricola* comes in the wake of and in contrast to such tales. The contrast is built around 'utility.' Agricola's mother, Iulia Procilla, was praised for disciplining her son when *in iuventa studium philosophiae acrius ultra quam concessum Romano ac senatori* ("in his youth he studied philosophy more keenly than is allowed for a Roman and senator" [*Agricola* 4]). The idea is picked up at the end of the work.

> sciant, quibus moris est inlicita mirari, posse etiam sub malis principibus magnos viros esse, obsequiumque ac modestiam, si industria ac vigor adsint, eo laudis excedere, quo plerique per abrupta sed in nullum rei publicae usum ambitiosa morte inclaruerunt.

> Let them know, whose practice is to admire subversion, that even under an evil emperor it is possible there to be great men, and modesty and deference, if allied to hard work and vitality, excels in praise that fame, which most

---

24. It is also a preoccupation of *Dialogus*, a dramatized discussion of the commonly agreed decline in the standard of rhetoric, which, however, soon becomes a broader reflection on how a post-Republican Roman is supposed to behave (see esp. 25–41).

seek out through sudden, planned death which is of no use to the state. Tacitus, *Agricola* 42

Agricola's achievements were, in contrast, useful, both in the military field, which dominates most of the book, and politically.

> Domitiani vero natura praeceps in iram, et quo obscurior, eo inrevocabilior, moderatione tamen prudentiaque Agricolae leniebatur, quia non contumacia neque inani iactatione libertatis famam fatumque provocabat.

> the nature of Domitian was to be quick to anger, and since he hid it, it was more implacable, but by the moderation and prudence of Agricola, it was softened, because [the latter] did not summon up for himself reputation and death by defiance or empty, ostentatious libertarian gestures. Tacitus, *Agricola* 42[25]

Yet, Agricola did secure recognition. The crowd flocked to his house during his final illness and talked about him throughout the *fora* of the city (43). Agricola is assured of immortality, an immortality secured at least in part because of Tacitus' book.

> Quidquid ex Agricola amavimus, quidquid mirati sumus, manet mansurumque est in animis hominum in aeternitate temporum, fama rerum; nam multos veterum velut inglorios et ignobiles oblivio obruet: Agricola postcritati narratus et traditus superstes erit.

> Everything that we loved about Agricola, everything we admired, survives and remains in the hearts of men for all time, for that is the reputation of his achievements; for most will be forgotten as if they had no glory or nobility but Agricola's story will remain in men's memory, narrated and thus passed to posterity. Tacitus, *Agricola* 46

---

25. Ostentation is also attacked in *Agricola* 40.

> ceterum uti militare nomen, grave inter otiosos, aliis virtutibus temperaret, tranquillitatem atque otium penitus hausit, cultu modicus, sermone facilis, uno aut altero amicorum comitatus, adeo ut plerique, quibus magnos viros per ambitionem aestimare mos est, viso aspectoque Agricola quaererent famam, pauci interpretarentur.

> Agricola, knowing that a military reputation was regarded seriously among the leisured, displayed other virtues and sought out devotedly peace and leisure, and was moderate in habits, easy in speech, and only accompanied by one or two friends so that the majority, who customarily judged a man great by his ambition, having seen Agricola, wondered at his fame, but a few understood. Tacitus, *Agricola* 40

The stories of great men will be passed down and narrated and we see in this concluding sentiment a contrast with the impossibility of narration under Domitian (*Agricola* 2). Memory and what it is possible to remember are not the same as narrated history, but that narration is crucial to embedding memory in public discourse, and Agricola's recountable memory provides an *exemplum* far more useful than the unrecountable memories of the martyrs. The contrast between Domitian's softening under the influence of Agricola and his destruction of senatorial opponents, who continued to behave as if the Republic were real, is instructive. Although the moral blame remains firmly with Domitian, Tacitus accuses the senators killed under him of having brought disaster upon themselves by their defiance.[26] Like Cordus, these men took an impractical position and refused to acknowledge the realities of the imperial age. Tacitus operates a clear distinction between Republican models of behavior, those adopted by a Cato or a Cicero, and those suitable for the present time.[27] Instead of angry nostalgia, he offers new models of behavior for the present.

Still, the Tacitean *caesura* comes at a cost; condemning the Republic to a remote past and breaking with a historical tradition is a considerable act of power, but also of destruction. Breaking with the past is rather more difficult than just announcing that the past is dead. As the past is a *locus* of identity and the narratives of the past flow into the present, breaking with the past requires a reconstruction of identities. But not only is there likely to be disagreement as to the exact relationship of the present to the past, but admitting a *caesura* 'denaturalizes' identities. Once you have one break from the past, it is possible to have another. It starts to become more obvious that identities are constructed, narrated contemporary social artefacts. In which case, any political power can attempt a revolution, establish a new Year One from which the past can once more start. In such revolutions, much is lost. Restarting history often obscures the origins of power and naturalizes current structures. Tacitus' new imperial hero provides a model of accommodation and acquiescence in a brutal and dictatorial regime, an acquiescence that requires a selective forgetting of the past and a silence about much of the present. It establishes the link between silence in the face of oppression and that dictatorial control of the past which is familiar from modern totalitarian regimes.

---

26. Tacitus maintains a very similar position on the major opposition figure under Nero, Thrasea Paetus. Thrasea is generally treated favorably by Tacitus, but in C.E. 59, when Nero informed the senate of his mother's plot to kill him and his subsequent and very unfortunate matricide, Thrasea broke with Nero by walking out of the Senate. Tacitus criticizes Thrasea since his action "brought danger on himself, but did not forward the start of liberty for others" (Tac., *Ann.* XIV 11).

27. Curiatus Maternus' withdrawal from rhetoric and public life in order to prepare and publish Cato, a controversial piece of poetry, is treated at best ambivalently in *Dialogus*.

Yet, as we shall see, the past is resourceful and continuously reemerges. It is written so deep into issues of identity that, in spite of the best efforts of politicians and historians, the past tends to come back to haunt even the great. In this reemergence, this spectral presence, lies the possibility of resistance. The Foucauldian trick of locating resistance in the history of the present enables a resistance which is in part constrained by the episteme of the present, but in so doing, it rejects the possibility of resistance in the knowledge of the revolution by which the present came into being, and ignores the resistant potential that lies in a history of the past.[28] Prerevolutionary history may provide the "voice from outside," the familiar other from which critiques become possible.

HISTORY AND PLACE: RESISTING CAESAR IN TROY AND ROME

One of the clearest examples of history in resistance for us comes from Lucan's *Pharsalia*. Lucan explores many of the same issues as Tacitus and would, indeed, seem to propose or reflect fairly similar historical explanations, but while Tacitean 'pragmatism' might not be the most optimistic or elevating vision of life in the imperial epoch, Lucan's consideration of time and History is, if anything, yet more brutal.

In Book IX of Lucan's *Pharsalia* Caesar visits Troy.[29] The war has been won, but the triumphant Caesar cannot rest until he has captured or killed Pompey. Chasing Pompey, Caesar heads east, aiming for Egypt. On his rather roundabout route, he passes Troy and stops to view the site. His pilgrimage to Troy is marked by a display of reverence for a space brimming with history, which culminates in the impulsive erection of a turf altar to the Lares of Troy and a promise to restore the city (9. 961–99). Caesar's visit recalls Aeneas' tour of the site of Rome guided by King Evander in *Aeneid* VIII. Yet while Aeneas was eager to inscribe himself into a Roman tradition and to understand the future place that would be Rome, Caesar's own wander around the fields that were Troy brings him into collision with archeology. Caesar fails to comprehend a site in which, we are told, every stone brims with history (9. 970–73). Thickets veil the city's remains (9. 969); Caesar stumbles over Hector's grave and crosses a stream where the mighty river Xanthus once flowed, without even noticing (9. 974–77). Unable to contain his annoyance at the ignorance of the ruler of the world, Caesar's guide

---

28. One could read volumes II and III of the *History of Sexuality* as providing that resistant "voice from the outside." See chapter 1 for our understanding of Foucault's histories.

29. On the visit to Troy, see Gowing (2005) 89–92 on the Trojan episode, who argues that Lucan here produces an anti-Virgilian reading of Troy to undercut the ideology of the imperial regime.

exclaims: "*Herceas... non respicis aras*"? ("have you no regard for the Hercean altars?"). Archeology becomes the first point of resistance to the Caesars.[30]

Caesar's lack of respect for history had already been demonstrated in his treatment of Rome. In Book III, he allows his troops to loot the temple of Saturn, which Lucan turns into a reversal of the historic processes of conquest and imperial expansion by which that treasury had been filled:

> Eruitur templo multis non tactus ab annis
> Romani census populi, quem Punica bella,
> quem dederat Perses, quem victi praeda Philippi,
> quod tibi, Roma, fuga Gallus trepidante reliquit,
> quo te Fabricius regi non vendidit auro
> quidquid parcorum mores servastis avorum,
> quod dites Asiae populi misere tributum
> victorique dedit Minoia Creta Metello. 3.156–63

> The wealth of the Roman people untouched for years, that the Punic Wars and Perses and the booty of the defeated Philip had yielded, the gold which the Gaul in cowardly flight left to you, Rome, the gold for which Fabricius would not sell you to the king, was dragged from the temple. Whatever the customs of our thrifty forefathers had amassed, the tribute that the wealthy Asian people sent and Minoan Crete gave to victor Metellus was seized.

Caesar is thus engaged in the unmaking of history as well as in a destruction of historic proportions. Instead of an epic of historic foundation, we are in an epic of the actual destruction of history.[31]

With Pompey's flight from Rome and as Caesar's army approaches, the disintegration of the city reaches its culmination:

> Ergo, ubi concipiunt, quantis sit cladibus orbi
> constatura fides superum, ferale per urbem
> iustitium; latuit plebeio tectus amictu
> omnis honos, nullos comitata est purpura fasces.
> Tum questus tenuere suos, magnusque per omnes
> erravit sine voce dolor. . . . 2. 16–21

---

30. It is interesting to speculate as to whether Tacitus was aware of this passage while writing about Germanicus in Troy. The contrast between the imperial Germanicus interpreting the monuments, and seeing in it an omen of destruction, and the imperial founder failing to read the ruins and seeing in them an omen of his greatness is striking.

31. In the *Aeneid*, Aeneas is portrayed fleeing a burning Troy with his household goods and family members so that Troy can be reborn in Italy. The parallel scene in the *Pharsalia* (2. 728–31) has Pompey fleeing Rome with gods and family to meet his eventual destruction.

So when they realized how great were the disasters for the world that the words of the gods predicted, a gloomy suspension of government afflicted Rome. Every magistrate hid behind the plebeian cloak, purple accompanied none of the rods of office. Then they held back their complaints, and great voiceless grief pervaded all.

This breakdown of political order, government, and the conventions of everyday life suggests that Rome is on the verge of collapse. In their turmoil, the people recall memories and traditions to provide reassurance. Yet, even the memory of Caesar misleads, becoming more frightening than the past reality, and when the people turn to religion, a special kind of ritualistic memory, that too fails them.[32] Prophets are summoned from Etruria, the locale of ancient religious lore (1. 584). Arruns, the oldest of these, orders a procession and the frightened citizens solemnly participate in a ritual of purification (1. 592ff). Well-ordered lines parade around the walls of Rome, reminding everyone of past landmarks, ancient divine decrees, and mystic verses. The connection between tradition, identity, and place is reestablished. The Roman community is renewed by reconnecting with the places which memorialize the traditions of the nation. The well-ordered and preordained ritual, the regulated dress and posture, the familiar route, the religiously approved gestures all display a collective knowledge and offer the possibility of an 'appropriate' narrative by which to control and counter the anarchy that threatens.[33] Yet the omens terrify Arruns and hastily he withdraws. Figulus takes over (1. 639ff) and predicts the imminent destruction of Rome. All the tradition does is to emphasize it own breach. Although a reassuring and appropriate narrative is offered, it fails; History predicts its own end.

Memory, though, is not so easily suppressed. Early in Book II, the elderly of Rome turn to their memories:

> . . . At miseros angit sua cura parentes,
> oderuntque gravis vivacia fata senectae
> servatosque iterum bellis civilibus annos.
> Atque aliquis magno quaerens exempla timori
> "Non alios" inquit "motus tunc fata parabant,
> Cum post Teutonicos victor Libycosque triumphos
> Exul limosa Marius caput abdidit ulva." 2. 64–70

---

32. Caesar appears not as the older ones could remember him, but greater, wilder, and more pitiless (1. 478–80). See Gowing (2005) 83 on the problematic character of these memories. *Religio* has few of the Protestant associations of religion, instead reflecting ritual practices in which collective identities and memories are performed.

33. For more reflection and debate on the public character of meaning embodied in rituals of commemoration and their regulating force, see Connerton (1989); Middleton and Edwards (eds) (1990).

Miserable parents have their own sorrow: they hate their tenacious life that brought them to an oppressive old age, and preserved them to see civil war for a second time. And someone said, seeking a precedent for this great fear: "The Fates gave rise to a similar tumult when Marius, victor from his Teutonic and Libyan triumphs, as an exile, covered his head in marshy reeds."

The elders, the holders of memory, remember that this is not the first time that civil war has threatened Rome (2. 68–233). Yet this is more than a horror story repeated. A precedent is located for Caesar's invasion and hence he is incorporated within a historical line, to be turned into a historical occurrence that can, like the last civil war, be survived. Religious ritual and historical memory form sites of resistance in this moment of extremity, and memory, and perhaps even nostalgia, become an exercise of collective power, perhaps the last source of power available to the citizens of Rome. Yet, although the factual accuracy of the memories is of secondary significance compared to the use of the memories as an attempt to control the past and what is to come, these memories offer a false interpretation of past and present.[34] For Caesar is no Marius. He will not simply go away in the end, leaving the Republic to continue, marked but not destroyed by its traumas. Instead, this civil war will be transforming, leading to a period of monarchy, and eventually to Nero, with whom Lucan opens his epic. These memories are inappropriate and similarly fail. For within this remembering, there is also a longing for death, a death that will end the memories of trauma and their fragile resistance to the coming age.

These true memories falsely applied multiply the ambivalences of the late first-century reception of the Republican past. Reading Lucan against Tacitus there is, at some levels, a stark contrast, but in others a similarity. Both Lucan and Tacitus present us with a Republican past which is severed from the present by a revolutionary act, but that past resonates as part of the collective memory that informs identity. It is to that collective memory that Pliny clings in his self-identification with Cicero, but which Tacitus rejects. But Lucan finds in that memory strength to resist. That resistance is integral to the *Pharsalia*. In the memory of the revolution and the madness of Caesar there is a recollection that the principate is built on trauma. Augustan and Tiberian representations of their rule as a restoration of the Republic, traditional rather than revolutionary, established an interpretation of history as an element central to the principate. Both Tacitus, in claiming that the Republic ends when the resistant (true) memory of it dies, and Lucan, in conceiving of Caesar the revolutionary, deny that version of history. But in

---

34. For a sociopsychological approach to conversational remembering, see Middleton and Edwards (1990b).

that denial, the history of the Republic becomes subject to dispute. In being put to death in the narratives of Lucan and Tacitus, the Republic becomes a powerful specter that haunts in its separation, and the act of separation exists as a scar on the present. In these histories of the present, the accuracy of the representation of the past becomes almost beyond question, the least interesting issue at stake.

Pierre Nora argues that "collective memory simplifies; sees events from a single, committed perspective; is impatient with ambiguities of any kind; reduces events to mythical archetypes."[35] Individual memory is, of course, central to allow us to operate within society, memorizing social and behavioral codes but also establishing our narratives of identity. We remember who we are and how we are. But as Ricoeur (1994) points out, those memories need to be narrated and given social-symbolic ratification in language and narrative. Memories, even individual memories, are often collective. And as individual memory depends on socially secured narrative, so collective memory depends on a collective narration, mythic in function and perhaps historical in form, but different from history.[36] Whereas history is subject to the authority of the historian, and thus almost inevitably an elitist discourse, collective memory speaks of communal identity; therefore, even an oppressed, silenced community can hold together through its shared memories; even inaccurate memories or poor historical analyses offer a respite from the tyranny of the present. Such collective memory is thus in the service of the present, a gesture of power *by* the living, and thus *about* the living.[37]

This link between psychological identity and collective memory explains the full trauma that faced Lucan's Roman population and the defiance that rested in their act of collective memory. If Caesar's invasion was a year zero for Rome, then they were (as Cordus would put it) the *ultimi Romanorum*. The old were attempting to recall a past, a shared past, in which Caesar could be incorporated. They were struggling to put forward a rhetoric in which Rome survived the invasion. But this is always a political strategy and it was not just the (fictional) Roman crowd who knew this. The (fictional) Caesar himself offers his own version of Roman history when, standing in front of the soldiers in Book I, he offers them a common history: *"Bellorum o socii, qui mille pericula Martis mecum" ait "experti decimo iam vincitis anno"* ("'Partners in war,' he said, 'victors for ten years now, having suffered a thousand dangers in warfare . . .'" [1. 299–300]).[38] The speech provides a version of

---

35. As quoted in Wertsch (2002) 19.
36. See Nora (1989) with an extensive discussion of what he views as the conflict between history and collective memory; see also Wertsch (2002) 10–66.
37. See, indicatively Hosbawm and Ranger (eds) (1983); Confino (1997).
38. Bruner and Fleisher Feldman (1995) and Robinson (1995) deal explicitly with the strategic

Roman history in which Caesar emerges against the elderly Pompey as the new power, a man who represents the independence of Rome against the tyrant. Pompey becomes the heir of Sulla, driving Rome towards civil war, turning against the loyal and victorious armies who had fought so bravely in Gaul, a man who neglected Roman citizens and instead elevated pirates who were loyal to him. In Caesar's history, Pompey becomes a threat to constitutionalism and the rule of law, perverting justice by sending troops into the forum to ensure a guilty verdict. The last hope, the last bastion of freedom is Caesar, whose death would complete Pompey's triumph, but whose victory would resurrect liberty. The oddity of the speech is not that it is materially wrong (indeed, its factual content is broadly correct), but that the interpretation of the motives of the participants is so plainly perverse. Caesar, the destroyer of so much that is historic, deploys history in his cause.

Time and again in the epic Caesar reminds his soldiers of their common expeditions to the North and West, playing on their collective memory. The theater of bonding reaches its climax just before the battle at Pharsalus:

> O domitor mundi, rerum fortuna mearum,
> miles, adest totiens optatae copia pugnae.
> Nil opus est votis, iam fatum accersite ferro.
> In manibus vestris, quantus sit Caesar, habetis.
> Haec est illa dies, mihi quam Rubiconis ad undas
> promissam memini, cuius spe movimus arma. 7. 250–55

> Soldier, conqueror of the world, arbiter of my destiny, here is the opportunity for battle so often hoped for. There is no need of prayers—now summon fate with the sword. It is in your hands how great Caesar will be. This is the day, promised to me by the waters of the Rubicon, in the hope of which we went to war.

Now, the war has come not for the liberation of Rome, but for the greatness of Caesar and his soldiers. Caesar gives himself over to his soldiers, his fate in their hands, but he also makes it understood that it is *their* fate that is at stake. Moreover, not only does Caesar offer his soldiers the position of rulers of the world; he goes on to de-Romanize their opponents. Pompey's eastern alliances allow Caesar to turn the conflict into a battle for Rome against a foreign enemy.[39] Caesar's troops thus become the embodiment of Rome,

---

features of social as well as individual remembering, and with the ways in which people often enter groups at will through a special selection of autobiographical memories.

39. Cf. here Roller (2001) 17–63 where he distinguishes between two distinct approaches dividing Roman aristocracy in the mid-first century C.E., which, he argues, are exemplified in the

possibly a new Caesarian Rome. Yet world conquest seems not to be enough. Caesar also offers his troops control over history: *haec acies victum factura nocentem est. . . . Nunc pugnate truces gladioque exsolvite culpam* ("The loser in this battle will be made a criminal . . . fight with ferocity now and with the sword dissolve any blame" [260–62]). The victor will determine history; Pompey's troops will come to be blamed in Caesarian discourses and guilt for the war will be reassigned. There appears to be a historical relativism here: he who controls the present, controls the past, and there is no absolute arbitration of historical or divine truth to govern collective memory.

For the purposes of the battle speech, Caesar is given a moment of rhetorical self-effacement. *Non mihi res agitur, sed, vos ut libera sitis turba, precor gentes ut ius habeatis in omnes. Ipse ego privatae cupidus me reddere vitae plebeiaque toga modicum conponere civem* ("Not for me have we engaged in war, but so that you, I pray, may have rights above all peoples so that you are a free crowd. I myself desire to return to ordinary life and to be a normal citizen in plebeian toga" [7. 264–67]). Caesar places the soldiers and the community center stage: *Me fortuna meorum commisit manibus* ("Fortune has placed me in the hands of my own army" [7. 285–86]). His plan is their plan, their right, and their responsibility, and so he spends the greater part of his speech addressing their duty, their role, and their future (7. 285–339). This outburst of collectivism sits uncomfortably with the isolationist, Nietzchean hero of other passages, but it makes sense as an attempt to develop a new narrative of the war by which to bind the soldiers to the collectivity of the Caesarian regime. All along, his greatness (mentioned right at the beginning of his speech) is what is really at stake; it is his destiny that is ultimately being delayed (7. 295–96), but his memoirs establish a collective memory and simplify the tortured progress from the Rubicon to Pharsalus, turning the "liberation" of Rome into a personal triumph and the shared dream of his troops. Such perversions of history and attempts to reform and abuse the collective memory depend for their success on the willingness of the audience to listen and to adopt the new memories. In Book I, the soldiers waver (1. 352ff). His history does not match their history. Love of the country and the ancestral gods has some hold over them, but, ultimately, Caesar's new collectivity rises up and they abandon their traditions, their private histories, and their families for Caesar. Caesar's new history triumphs. At Pharsalus, the Caesarian troops rush eagerly to battle following his speech, fighting to conquer the world and to invent a guiltless, new past.

Lucan explores a malleable past, emphasizing the ambivalences of memory. Anxious to ground the world that whirls around them, parents and

---

"assimilating" and "alienating" viewpoints adopted by the Pompeians and the Caesarians, respectively.

elders of the *Pharsalia* scour the past for resemblances with the present. Even Tacitus' invokes memory as a *locus* of resistance to the tyranny of Domitian in *Agricola* 2, for when all are silenced by the tyrant, the memory remains free. The mind can still reminisce in private; memory remains a threat to the tyrant since it has the potential to resurface, but even if it lurks beyond representation, it remains a present, if unspoken, accusation. Such resemblances would reassure that beneath the unrecognizable (and thus terrifying) surface it has all been seen, and survived, before. That is, when a community is threatened, the collective memory becomes a force which defends not only against the assault on the community and its political identity, but also against the psychological damage that this assault could bring with it.

If memory is one of the rare arenas in which a resistant identity can be asserted and preserved, then control of memory becomes a powerful political weapon, as can be seen from the history and politics of virtually every modern state and national group. Maurice Halbwachs places collective memory at the heart of social formations and, by doing so, also demonstrates the strong grip it holds over the individual.[40] As Halbwachs claims, "Society obligates people not just to reproduce previous events but also to 'touch them up,' shorten them, complete them, . . . give them a prestige that reality did not possess."[41] In so doing, the collective memory turns into a 'perfect' narrative, its ambiguities are eased, its injustices simplified, and the narrative becomes more powerful, its messages more true, and less easy to resist. Yet, this would seem to simplify the processes at work. A dominant hegemonic ideology will always be able to impose its version of history and make its collective memories powerful. The Halbwachs model suggests that resistance must depend on a struggle to replace one collective, 'perfect' memory with another, and in so doing establish a competition between two similarly constructed ideologies. This seems to us to be a reaction to modern political debates in which versions of history are made to do key ideological work so as to, for instance, establish the truth of liberalism, the inevitability of communism, and the originality of ethnic identity. It seems largely true that historians, for all their careful scholarship, have limited effects on these ideological encounters. Yet, our classical texts emphasize the power dynamics. Memory is a poor defense against tyranny, since Caesar speaks another history, another memory, and it is that history that threatens to become dominant. There is, it seems to us, in this multiple duplicitous history a

---

40. Halbwachs (1980). McAdams (2004) discusses extensively the self that emerges through redemptive memories and their role in identity formation. Fivush (2004) further discusses the subtle dilemmas between self as an active agent and self as part of a communal conscience that underlies most efforts at remembering.
41. Halbwachs (1980) 51.

powerful resonance with Tacitean histories. The division between Republic and Empire in Lucan is between two forms of memory; our reading of Tacitus suggests that it is with the death of Republican memory that the Empire will begin. Caesar's soldiers and Germanicus are trapped within this brutal imperial history and the old of Rome, despairing of their situation and attempting to read Caesar into their memories, installing him in their histories, ultimately fail, since Caesar is too great to belong and they have outlived their time. Collective memory has imprisoned them in a falsity and a bygone age. In this memory, there is resistance, but there is also a longing for death.

Cordus is thus disingenuous in the extreme. To suggest that the memories he recalls of the Republican heroes are beyond hatred is to claim that the past is somehow apolitical, and that the specter that he puts onto the contemporary stage has no power. His opposition is a commitment to death and an admission that he has lived beyond his time.[42] Instead of a futile dispute between perfect histories, our texts appear intent on messing up that perfection, and on refuting the ideological simplicity of collective memories. In this argument, memory does not fight memory for hegemonic truth, for all memories have truth; what matters is how useful and appropriate those memories are. History is subsumed by the present, and the tyrants who control the present ultimately control the past. Real resistance lies in exhibiting that control.

TRAVELLING TO FORGET: SPACE AND MEMORY IN THE *THEBAID*

In problematizing memory, our texts also offer the theoretical possibility of an absence of memory and of a revolutionary moment that could make memory anew. It is this possibility that we find explored in the *Thebaid*. As the work unfolds, we find the participants trapped in a world working through the implication of the Oedipal curse, the past dominating the present. But this determining temporal frame exists also within a spatial frame: the *Thebaid* has a very specific landscape in which halls, cities, and wastelands become mnemonic zones in which history is physically manifested. It is these spaces that cement the epoch of disorder that afflicts Thebes, and it is in escape from those spaces that there is a faint hope of resisting that epochal doom.

---

42. Cordus may be foolish, but the moral responsibility for his death still rests firmly with Tiberius. Cf Tacitus on the martyrs as discussed above.

In the prologue of the *Thebaid*, Oedipus emerges from a self-imposed isolation to curse his children and call destruction upon his city.[43] He is disheveled and blind, a wretched, destructive individual. Oedipus' companion is the Fury Tisiphone, whose presence brings the Underworld into Oedipal Thebes.[44] Tisiphone is an eerie escort to Oedipus in his living death.[45] In bringing the Underworld into the city, one of the foremost spatial boundaries is breached; but if place is disturbed, so is time. Dangerous pasts haunt a family and city. The curse that Oedipus calls upon his own flesh and blood continues the Oedipal tragedy and the subsequent fragmentation of family and city across the generations. Central to this tragic beginning are acts of remembering and forgetting. Oedipus rants as a "forgotten" man, conveniently put aside to no-man's-land by his sons. They never call; they never visit; they never provide a guiding hand for the old and blind father. He is a forsaken past but a memory that haunts the present.[46]

Oedipus' abdication left his son-kings alternating in power and exile.

 . . . alterni placuit sub legibus anni
exsilio mutare ducem. Sic iure maligno
fortunam transire iubent, ut sceptra tenentem
foedere praecipiti semper novus angeret heres. 1. 138–41

It was decided under a law to exchange leader and exile in alternating years. Thus, they order by a malign law the transference of fortune so that the new

---

43. Hill (1990) notes the close parallels between the opennings of the *Aeneid* and the *Thebaid*. After the invocation of the muse, Virgil and Statius present us with two despairing heroes, but whereas the heroic Aeneas fears for his men and harbors doubts as to his historic destiny, Oedipus curses his progeny.

44. Tisiphone is a more terrifying "companion" deity than Venus in the *Aeneid*. Her "chance" encounter with Oedipus at 1. 88–90, *Talia dicenti crudelis diva severos advertit vultus. Inamoenum forte sedebat Cocyton iuxta* . . . ("The cruel goddess turned her gloomy gaze towards him. She was sitting, *as it chanced*, by dreary Cocytus . . . "), suggests her haunting of the city, and "the chance" of the encounter (a rather peculiar suggestion) has a quality of randomness, of lack of control very different from the fateful, planned destinies of the *Aeneid*. Her mission recalls that of the Fury Allecto from Books VII and XII of the *Aeneid*, whose function was to drive on the war and hasten the destruction of Turnus. Jupiter's use of Furies creates an unsettling alliance between the forces of light and evil, but Allecto's presence is always controlled and temporary (*Aen.* 12. 845–52).

45. *Illum indulgentem tenebris imaeque recessu sedis inaspectos caelo radiisque penates servantem tamen adsiduis circumvolat alis saeva dies animi, scelerumque in pectore Dirae* ("As he indulged his darkness in the depths of his abyss, keeping to his retreat beyond the gaze of sky and sun, round him on tireless wings hovered the mind's fierce day, and in his heart his crimes' avenging Fury" [1. 49–51])

46. This would appear to be a further classical and Oedipal example of the Freudian return of the repressed, which is a consistent theme of this chapter. See also Armstrong (2005), esp. 134–40 in which it is shown that Freudian analysis uncovered not just the repression in the subconscious, but the repression of the past.

heir always angered the holder of the scepter in the prospect of the rapidly approaching transfer.

This alteration created a palace that was home to no sibling, plagued by a perpetual, prospective absence that slowly reduced it to a ruin, a symbolic manifestation of the decay of the house of Oedipus:

> Et nondum crasso laquearia fulva metallo,
> montibus aut alte Grais effulta nitebant
> atria, congestos satis explicitura clientes;
> non impacatis regum advigilantia somnis
> pila, nec alterna ferri statione gementes
> excubiae nec cura mero committere gemmas
> atque aurum violare cibis: sed nuda potestas
> armavit fratres, pugna est de paupere regno. 1. 144–51

> And then no heavy gold shone on yellow-panelled ceilings, no halls were raised up on high columns from the Greek mountains, sufficiently vast for the crowd of clients; no spears watched over the restless dreams of Kings, no groaning watch took turns on station; none cared to fill the gem encrusted wine-bowl or dirty the gold plates with food. Naked power gave arms to the brothers; battle was joined over a pauper realm.

The decay of the palace, the home of the Theban kings, is made more poignant by the desire for a homeland that dominates archetypal epic narratives. In *Aeneid* 8, Aeneas finds his ultimate home at the site of Pallanteum. In the *Odyssey*, a faithful servant's orchard, the palace's main hall, and the old conjugal bed are places of memory and are crucial to Odysseus' reintegration with the history of Ithaca. But in Thebes, there is a continuous cycle of regression and progression as the brothers swap exile and kingship. Centrality and marginality alternate, and as the palace is in continuous transition, its walls lose their luster.

The power of history even imprisons the gods. In an extraordinary council of the gods, convened in Book I, histories of past slights fuel bitterness and encourage recriminations. Juno rhetorically demands the destruction of Samos, Mycenae, Sparta, and other places as a condemnation of memory, the destroyer of the world:

> quod si prisca luunt auctorum crimina gentes
> subvenitque tuis sera haec sententia curis,
> percensere aevi senium, quo tempore tandem

terrarum furias abolere et saecula retro
emendare sat est? 1. 266–70

Since if the nations must expiate the original crimes of their founders, and this proposal to list the sins of generations past has come so late onto your agenda, what distance in time is enough to efface the world's madness and correct the ages past?

If there is no escape from history and memory, no means of forgiving and forgetting, and, thus, no way of starting afresh, historical determinism robs individuals of their freedom, condemning them to destruction.

It is in this bleak, historically determined environment that we find Polynices, Prince-abdicate and King-in-waiting, brooding on his temporary nonexistence:

Interea patriis olim vagus exsul ab oris
Oedipodionides furto deserta pererrat
Aoniae. Iamiamque animi male debita regna
concipit, et longum signis cunctantibus annum
stare gemit . . .
. . .
nunc queritur ceu tarda fugae dispendia. 1. 312–16; 320

Meanwhile the son of Oedipus, an exile drifting for long time away from his land, secretly roams Boeotia's empty lands. Already he reflects darkly on his promised reign and groans that the long year stands still and the constellations linger in the sky . . . now he complains at the slow waste of exile.

Life in this temporal and spatial hiatus is unbearable, Robbed of an identity that he must resume in a year, but trapped by a future of endlessly repeated negation, he searches for an escape and, led by Fury or Fate, he heads to Argos (1. 324–28). Leaving the "lonely wasteland," Polynices passes mythically liminal places, the wild woods "filled with screams of Theban frenzy" where Pentheus was slaughtered by the Bacchic women, both an uncomfortable omen of death for the kings of Thebes and a site of memory in the wilderness. The journey takes Polynices beyond these places of memory, and as he crosses into the Peloponnese, the transition from one landscape of memories to another, new land is marked by an outbreak of the sublime, a turning over of order, of place, and of time:

Sed nec puniceo rediturum nubila caelo

> promisere iubar, nec rarescentibus umbris
> longa repercusso nituere crepuscula Phoebo:
> densior a terris et nulli pervia flammae
> subtexit nox atra polos. Iam claustra rigentis
> Aeoliae percussa sonant, venturaque rauco
> ore minatur hiemps, venti transversa frementes
> confligunt axemque emoto cardine vellunt,
> dum caelum sibi quisque rapit. 1. 342–50

But no cloud promised the return of brightness to a reddening sky, no dusky light glimmers, reflecting the sun as the shadows grow thin. Dark night, denser at the ground, pierced by no ray, covered the poles. And now the passes of barren Aeolia are struck and resound and the coming storm threatens and bellows; the roaring winds hurl themselves on the crossings and pull at the axes as the hinges of the world give way while each seizes for itself the sky.

Space and time lose their familiar dimensions. Polynices wanders through the forests and mountains, unable to understand a place that offers neither refuge nor any known sign:

> Ac velut hiberno deprensus navita ponto,
> cui neque Temo piger neque amico sidere monstrat
> luna vias, medio caeli pelagique tumultu
> stat rationis inops . . .
> talis opaca legens nemorum Cadmeius heros
> adcelerat . . .
>   . . .
> . . . dat stimulos animo vis maesta timoris. . . . 1. 370–75; 376–77; 379

As a sailor, caught in a wintry sea, for whom neither the lazy Great Bear nor the moon's friendly light show the way, stands without plan in the midst of the tumult of sky and sea . . . so the Cadmeian hero passing through lightless forests sped up . . . the sad force of fear gives energy to his heart.

The storm sweeps away groves and trees, washes rocks from the hills, creates rivers and waterfalls, floods the marshes, and drenches the hero; he arrives in Argos soaked and unrecognizable as if the flooded streams have washed away his identity as well as the dirt (earth). Whereas all the places of Boeotia had significance, the legendary places of Argos do not produce the same recollections, and he comes to rest at an unknown palace gate. But no sooner has he settled for the night when a competitor for the doorstep (Tydeus) appears and they fight for this limited shelter from the weather (1. 401–20). The clamor draws the attention of the old King Adrastus, who makes his way to the gate and roundly castigates the strangers (1. 431–43). Invited by the king to declare their identity, Tydeus volunteers his lineage but makes it clear that he is desperate to escape it and is grateful to be in front of Adrastus' palace: *maesti cupiens solacia casus monstriferae Calydonis opes Acheloiaque arva deserui; vestris haec me ecce in finibus ingens nox operit* ("desiring comfort in my sadness, I left the wealth of Calydon, home of monsters, and Achelous' meadows. You see, a great night covers me here as I am on your threshold" [1. 452–55]). Polynices is more coy and reluctant to advertise his patrilineage and homeland: *nec nos animi nec stirpis egentes—ille refert contra, sed mens sibi conscia fati cunctatur proferre patrem* ("'I too do not lack spirit and ancestry,' the other retorts, but conscious of fate hesitates to name his father" [1. 465–67]).

Haunted by their homelands, the two warriors are both proud of, and disturbed by, their pasts. Yet, their random meeting and resulting encounter with Adrastus turn into an unexpected opportunity to step out of the cycle of memory and retribution; the Argive king offers the two enemies a break with the past, and an opportunity to start again:

> Immo agite, et positis, quas nox inopinaque suasit
> aut virtus aut ira, minis succedite tecto.
> Iam pariter coeant animorum in pignora dextrae.
> Non haec incassum divisque absentibus acta;
> forsan et has venturus amor praemiserit iras,
> ut meminisse iuvet. 1. 468–73

> Now come and lay aside the threats which night or virtue or anger, unexpected, prompted and come inside. Now let your hands come together as a pledge of your spirits. These events are not without meaning and the gods are not absent. Perhaps future love may have sent this anger as a vanguard so that it will give pleasure as a memory.

Breaking with a destiny determined by the past, Adrastus offers a new way to consider those memories. Instead of remembering their strife, Adrastus suggests that their common need and the violence they exacted upon each other should form the basis and source of friendship: a surprising suggestion, but one that actually comes to pass. The benevolent king can make such memories sources of affection; a shared past, even one in hostility, becomes a source of unity.

Having established peace, Adrastus moves everybody into the light of his hall, where he can inspect his guests freely. As soon as he has the chance to examine their clothes and weaponry, he realizes that the two warriors' rough dress, a deliberate disguise of noble line and identity, provides the answer to a previously undeciphered riddle given to him by Apollo, that a pair in wild beasts' guise were going to be his sons-in-law (1. 490–92). And the two fleeing heroes acquire stronger ties with the place; they are not only inscribed in its present but turn out to be part of its legends, included in the divine foretellings of the city.

The activity in the Argive palace is a palpable expression of the fruitful energy of the city. In contrast to the royal halls of Thebes, Adrastus' palace is filled with light, wealth, comfort and food. Couches are covered with fine-spun purple and coverlets glistening with gold, tables are polished, gilded lanterns dispel the dark (1. 512–24). History is strong there too, but a history that seems to provide hope. As soon as the men are washed and welcomed, Adrastus gives them a lesson in the history of the city, drawing on the representations that appear all around the elaborately adorned hall. Introduced to the historic riches of the city and offered its princesses as brides and a new lineage as joint heirs to Adrastus (who has no male offspring), the two men, now friends, find a new home and new histories to which they can belong. The quintessential quest of the epic hero seems to have come to an end for them; they have arrived.

But for all the hope and honors he receives, Polynices is still haunted by his own past and is distanced from the community. He finds memories contaminating the Argives' celebration. As Adrastus engages with his guests' pasts, Polynices loses heart:

> Deiecit maestos extemplo Ismenius heros
> in terram vultus . . .
> "non super hos divum tibi sum quaerendus honores
> unde genus, quae terra mihi, quis defluat ordo
> sanguinis antiqui: piget inter sacra fateri." 1. 673–78

> Straightaway the Ismenian hero turned his sad gaze towards the ground. . . . "You must not now, amidst these divine honors, seek after my family, my land, and what class of ancient blood runs in my veins. I am reluctant to speak amid these sacred rites."

Adrastus reacts by drawing Polynices out of his self-pity. As he explains, rumors from Thebes have brought the story of Oedipus to Argos. But, he argues, Fate has allowed them to move from their old communities. They carry their traditions and their histories with them and, upon entering Argos, their sorrow also enters the city. Their stories are now part of the narratives that permeate the great hall of Argos. Since they are received in the Argive palace, they become part of that building's representational system, inserting themselves within the histories and protocols of their guest-palace. Among the Argives, they both change, and are changed by the communal space that they have entered.[47] Polynices' analysis would seem to be right (and so it eventually turns out), but Adrastus makes a startling claim: that here, in Argos, the past can be put to rest:

> . . . ne perge queri casusque priorum
> adnumerare tibi: nostro quoque sanguine multum
> erravit pietas, nec culpa nepotibus obstat. 1. 688–90
>
> So do not carry on with your lament, nor list as yours the fates that befell your ancestors. *Pietas* has also often deserted our line, but no blame stands in the way of the descendants.

The king speaks as if Juno's injunction to end the feuds of history had come to pass, and in his denial of tradition, his sentiments have a sacrilegious but humane quality. Adrastus offers Polynices a future without the burden of memory.[48] He believes that the past is not at liberty to dictate the future. Adrastus offers Polynices a new future, a future built into the traditions of Argos, cemented by marriage to Argia, the king's daughter. In full awareness of the complexities and ambivalence of remembering, Adrastus offers Polynices and Tydeus the option of forgetful memory in which identities can be reforged as an act of will and the prison of the past escaped. In this option lies hope and freedom, but in the course of the *Thebaid*, that hope and freedom is spectacularly withdrawn. History triumphs in the last instance.

CHRONOS AND AION: TIME AND ITS ENTRAPMENTS

In Adrastus' offer and the eventual triumph of History we have a dramatization of one of the abiding problems of modern philosophy, a problem that

---

47. For a discussion of plurality in communities and intercommunal selves, see Worthington (1996).
48. Memory as a cause of sorrow is central to Homer's *Odyssey*. One of the most famous *loci* of that epic is Odysseus overwhelmed by grief at the banquet of the Phaeceans in Book VIII. In *Odyssey* IV Helen used a potion of lethe, the balm of forgetfulness, to calm troubled minds, on which see Bergren (1983).

besets Kant, Hegel, Marx, and Heidegger: the problematic nature of time as an ontological force. Yet, this seemingly quintessentially modern problem seems reflected in our ancient texts. To find our way through this problem, we turn to Gilles Deleuze, notably his proposal that we see time in two forms: Chronos and Aion.

> In accordance with Chronos, only the present fills time, whereas past and future are two dimensions relative to the present in time. . . . There is always a more vast present which absorbs the past and the future. . . . Chronos is an encasement, a coiling up of relative presents. . . . Inside Chronos, the present is in some manner corporeal. . . . The present measures out the action of bodies and causes. The future and past are rather what is left of passion in a body. . . . In accordance with Aion, only the past and future inhere or subsist in time. Instead of a present which absorbs the past and future, a future and past divide the present at every instant and subdivide it ad infinitum into past and future, in both directions at once. . . . Whereas Chronos was inseparable from the bodies which filled it out entirely as causes and matter, Aion is populated by effects which haunt it without ever filling it up. . . . Whereas Chronos was inseparable from circularity and its accidents—such as blockages or precipitations, explosions, disconnections, and indurations—Aion stretches out in a straight line, limitless in either direction. Always already passed and eternally yet to come, Aion is the eternal truth of time: pure empty form of time, which has freed itself of its present corporeal content and has thereby unwound its own circle, stretching itself out in a straight line. It is perhaps all the more dangerous, more labyrinthine, and more tortuous for this reason.[49]

Time as Chronos is an encasing device that frames and fills the present. It provides the frame for the structures of thought and thus the structures of society. Chronos works within memory, collective and personal and, Deleuze argues, is fixed and immobilized. Memory—Chronos would thus exist with a fixed space, a place which is marked and operates as a mnemonic that imprisons, but also provides a home in which understanding can be achieved. Chronos is always present and always in the present. Aion, however, is a stretched line that extends infinitely, cannot be reckoned, cannot be controlled, and cannot encompass anything within it, as it is only a stretched line. The line reaches to the future and to the past; it can connect all time, human and nonhuman, and runs through Chronos and all Chronoi as a connecting thread. But the connection is only temporal, enclosing none of

---

49. Deleuze (1990) 162–68

the frameworks and scaffolding of society and thought that are maintained in Chronos.

Memory is a key to being. Being takes place in time and we understand time through memory as we understand being through time. To forget is to undo some sense or part of being, and to forget all is to cease to be, at least as we would recognize it. Yet time exists as Chronos and Aion, as affixed structure and dynamic line. One could argue that as Polynices leaves Thebes, he abandons Chronos and breaks with the space in which the frame of Chronos exists. Such a transition is temporal and spatial, moving the hero from the spaces of memory and thus the frame of his being, space and time, is transformed. This trauma is marked by the metaphysical crisis of the storm, the great event, the temporal and spatial disturbance through which the hero has to fight to reach a new land. That transformation is elemental and personal; the hero, and the world are thoroughly soaked as if the grim memories, the earth by which he is marked, can be washed from his body.[50] But when Polynices reaches Adrastus' palace, he is forced to come to terms once more with his past. His being, his identity, is caught up in the past, and when he is asked about his identity, he has to face the fact that memory and identity are so closely linked that even in this new land any claim to identity must bind him once more to memory, a memory that is already present in the rumors that have crossed from Thebes ahead of him. Chronos creeps into the palace to absorb him. And yet, Adrastus offers him a way out. Chronos is not all-encompassing; there is also Aion. Adrastus claims that the future is not bound by the past, and because of this Polynices can *make* his own identity, *without* rejecting the past. This, radically, offers Polynices not just the chance of being, but also of becoming afresh.

In his consideration of space and memory, Maurice Blanchot looks for and celebrates any sign of rupture. For Blanchot forgetfulness, or what could be termed illegible memory, is a condition to be cherished rather than deplored. Incomprehension, obliqueness, and forgetfulness work in language by creating pauses which allow fragments of speech, memory, and thought to float separate from each other. In this incomprehension and separation is a space of freedom. Romantically attached to the fragment, Blanchot celebrates its logic—or the lack thereof.

---

50. Polynices is only one case of this phenomenon in the *Thebaid*. The Argive widows accomplish a similar journey to Athens in Book XII, a journey which, it has been argued, has the potential at least to allow them to develop new identities. For more on this, see Braund (1996). In the same book, Argia's alternative journey into the night scorns historical continuum and official voices and duties and frees her as an individual to grieve for her spouse.

The interval, fissure, interruption, discontinuity; each of these betokens a blank, empty space "all the more empty as it cannot be confused with pure nothingness. . . . " It is precisely from nothingness that Blanchot delivers the interval, discovering in this space of discontinuity the source of energy, a motivating force that advances discourse throughout, however, making its progress direct or easy. To interrupt discourse would be to divide it, but the intermission thus occasioned ensures a breathing space through which discourse can be given impetus and acquire plurality whilst new interactions spring up to form a dialogue . . . an infinite conversation, *l'entretien fini*.[51]

If Chronos is all-encompassing, a complete structure of society, then to forget is to make a tear in the fabric of society and thus to allow opportunities for change to emerge. Alternately, one could, like Polynices, embrace exile. Exile establishes the individual as marginal, both from the home society and from the new society. But marginality destabilizes inside/outside within a wider process of spatialization of politics and culture.[52] This "radical opportunity" suggests that embracing marginality is a constructive act, and not just an act of resistance: it is in marginality that the individual has freedom from Chronos and its social constraints. What is offered to Polynices in Argos is a life of exile within a new community, a marginality built into the fabric and traditions of the Argive society. The spatial and temporal exile has the opportunity of a new family, a new identity, and all its possibilities of freedom and renewal. But that opportunity stretches beyond the individual, since a willingness to accept the other for what it is, to honor the other within society and provide it with a place allows society to embrace the exilic opportunity. Adrastus' offer to Polynices suggests a radical difference between Thebes and Argos. In Thebes, History (as Chronos) dominates. Argos is similarly faced with difficulties, but is open to change, open to the outsider and the new traditions that he brings. This is a community which has a place for the other, and because of its fluid relationship with the past, it has an uncertain and open future. The Theban community is complete—and sick. Adrastus' community is incomplete—and healthy.[53]

The hope of an escape from History that Adrastus provides is born from the nature of memory and history. We have seen the close interweaving of memory, time, and place in the formation of identity. Yet, although time

---

51. Barakońska and Nitka (1999) 101.

52. The sociology of space has been the center of considerable recent debate. Gayatri Spivak and bell hooks, for instance, write on the potential of spatial discontinuities to dismantle binaries that would entrap thought. See, e.g., Spivak (1987); bel hooks (2000). Spatial division is central to the politics of identity, on which, e.g., see Soja and Hooper (1993).

53. See the discussion of Nancy's "inoperable community" in chapter 4.

and space are in some senses absolute, with an existence independent of any human perception, time and place are also cultural and psychological artefacts. Time as Chronos is a construct. Individuals can argue about the meaning and nature of Chronos and assert their preferred meanings. Yet, if Chronos can be narrated in an act of power, then the power of Chronos is in some sense illusory; individuals can escape by creating new narratives. Adrastus presents Argos as being not imprisoned by History, and Polynices is presented with the chance to *become* again. He can enter another noble family, lead another great people, inhabit other great halls. Exile in Argos provides Polynices with a freedom that would be impossible in Thebes. Similarly, Lucan's Pompey in the *Pharsalia* needed to be freed from History to become again. Pompey's reemergence as the great man happens in exile, on the island of Lesbos in the company of Cornelia, away from Rome and all its memories. Exile seems to bring freedom. And yet both Pompey and Polynices are dragged back from their exiles, recalled by History which, eventually, they cannot escape. Six books and three years later, Polynices will be standing again in front of Thebes, pounding against its walls, recalled by the epic flow of time (the working of Chronos). Similarly, in the previous chapter, we repeatedly discovered lovers meeting on beaches or at dawn, in interstitial places and times in which the personal could exist, but when day comes, the city and its demands encroach. Is this where the fairy tale ends and escape to Aion proves to be but an illusion? After all, Adrastus may have offered Polynices respite in Argos, but this was part of a time that was already predicted by the oracle, already part of the Chronos that was fixed. In both epics, the audience would know this even as they saw new hope in exile. The force of a history already lived and of a fate fixed by the gods ensured that hope would inevitably be extinguished. The historic and epic bindings of time (the workings of Chronos) dictated their future, and Aion (the open-ended and infinite flow of time) was an illusion. In the end, their identities were beyond their control. The offer of an exilic escape, a home away from the prison of history, becomes a false freedom. Even the powerful, who think they might be able to control time, struggle in vain to escape its clutches. In this context, Chronos becomes fate, a hidden, directing, all-encompassing power, against which the efforts of individuals are as nothing.

This sense of the sublime workings of time brings us to Germanicus and Caesar among the ruins. Ruins are symbols not just of time, but of place. Wandering in the ruins places the contemporary in the old and allows the individual to be relocated into a different, other place and thus escape the contemporary in nostalgic reverie. But ruins are both survivors of time and victims of it. They symbolize the past as real and present, but in a special form since that which is present is only a remnant of the past. Ruins thus show a past that is dead, and this is the lesson that Germanicus seems to draw from Troy. The past of the great city is gone, turned to piles of stones, and his emotional connection with that ruination leads him to reflect on the fickleness of fortune, and realise that the past will claim him and Rome. Before time, the individual is as of nothing; time is a sublime force that sweeps away the great: empires, cities, and—alongside them—individuals.[54] Germanicus accepts History as inevitable, indeed as inevitable as death. As an accurate reader of History, Germanicus is a fatalist.

Lucan's Caesar at Troy presents a limited contrast. A sublime force himself, Caesar resists and provokes the sublime. His encounter with Troy is elemental. The very stones resist his understanding and encroachment, yet he proclaims his control over the site by erecting an altar and making a speech. Although Caesar may generate narratives that attempt to change collective memory, the past offers resistance, and just as the old of Rome used their memories to ward off the approaching disaster, so do the stones hold back their secrets from the dominant power. But at best the combat between Troy and Caesar is a draw; the stones may resist and hold back their secrets, they may symbolize the fracturing and end of epochs and eventually destruction of all that Caesar will make, but Caesar asserts his imperial Chronos. Lucan's Cato had a choice between staying loyal to a nostalgic version of the past up to the point of death, or adapting to new imperial traditions. He chose to become the defender of the great tradition of Republicanism and to reside within the Republican temporal frame, but that resistance was his and his followers' doom. The past offered no escape from History.

Ultimately, the literature of the first century C.E. appears to lack optimism. Its characters are imprisoned by history in their presents, presents that, for people like Pliny, appear to reduce them and threaten their capacity to achieve greatness. Tacitus offers his contemporaries a choice between adapting to the practical realities of the new age (following the course of Agricola) and thereby winking at despotism, or retreating to a nostalgic and fatal reverie for a Republican past. Polynices' struggle with time and tradition would raise difficult questions for (Statius') contemporaries. Could late first-century C.E. Romans follow Polynices across an equivalent mountain range and escape their historical frame? And if they could, would they, like Polynices, find themselves back in the same place, still part of the empire, three years later? In yesteryear's Thebes, Polynices may have managed to walk across a mountain range and find for himself a new world, but in the first century C.E., sailing away from Rome would not only be to risk a potentially terrifying elemental transformation, a loss of identity and a self-effacement

---

54. Cf Ovid *Metamorphoses* 15. 418–30.

with limited hope of success, but would present rather daunting practical problems.[55]

The desire for new narrative traditions, and hence different sources of identity, demands a break, a significant narrative moment around which the tradition can fracture. Revolutions (by definition), peace treaties, scientific discoveries, wars can all be classed as such moments. These cruces in the historical memory can become points of conflict, potential *caesurae* in the historical memory, but also real *caesurae* in the interpretations that create different and alternate traditions. One side may argue that after this point everything changed, while another can argue that everything remained the same, simply sustained by different structures. It is the plethora of potential points of change that makes the historiography of the contemporary West so extraordinary and so very different from other traditions, and it is this very plethora of change points that devalues the place of history in our identities. If everything is perpetually made anew, what is the importance of the past? But in the minimizing of the past, the present becomes all-embracing. A false dichotomy operates between this perpetual present and this absent past. Although one might argue that the resurrection of the past, which is such a prevalent feature of contemporary politics and the so-called "ethnic revival," is in opposition to modernity, it is in historical terms a feature of it. The present is presented not simply as a dislocation from tradition, but as a superficial manifestation of time in which identities cannot be manufactured. The Chronos of the present is so narrow and alienating that identities must be constructed in the remembrance of the past.

There would seem to be absolutely no guarantee, as many would fondly hope, that these manifestations of traditional identity will simply fade away as modernity takes hold. Similarly, although the Republicans of the imperial Roman elite may have seemed anachronistic and steeped in a hopeless nostalgia, there seemed to be no guarantee that the survival of empire would lead to its acceptance and to the adoption of new traditions by the die-hard Republicans, especially if those new traditions required, as the traditional elite would see it, their own extinction. Further, although it often is possible to find a tear in the past, the moment from which we can exile ourselves from the binding of Chronos and think that we have discovered the possibilities of Aion, an open-ended future freed from the past, we then finds ourselves in a very frightening place, a land without signs. Thus, revolutions frequently rush to the old when the world becomes too terrifying. In this, the ancients seem more realistic and do not set up the choice as one between

---

55. For example, Lucan's Pompey considers flight to Parthia, but the prospect of life among the barbarians and the fear of the sexual exploitation of Cornelia by the Parthian king close off that option (8. 210–455).

unquestioning familiarity and the wild unknown. Adrastus does not ask Polynices to forget and erase; instead, he gives his soon-to-be son-in-law an alternative tradition and an alternative narrative, the traditions and narrative of Argos in which he can find a home. But neither Adrastus nor Argia ask him to choose between the old and the new. In the infinite, straight line of Aion, Argive furnishings (similar to those in Adrastus' great hall) can meet with Theban memorabilia, haunting Polynices' memory and identity without ever filling them up. Later in the epic, we see him marching back against Thebes, a proud leader of the Argives, and at the same time a fugitive scorned by Thebes. His fate, gods, and the inexorable force of history recall him from exile; and yet he does not quite return—or else, it is not the Polynices who abandoned Thebes in Book 1 who stands again in front of the walls of the city three years later. The Polynices who eagerly awaits a meeting with Eteocles is still the brother of a usurper, the son of a demented old king, and the leader deprived of his (Theban) army; and yet he is now also the beloved husband of a princess, cherished son-in-law of a widely respected king, and leader of another devoted army, the Argive one. Polynices in front of the walls of Thebes is suspended between identities and traditions that vie for him, an antagonism played out in Book XII through the image of Argia and Antigone, wife and sister, respectively, initially warring and ultimately joined in love and grief over Polynices' body. Polynices is a man engraved in the past and transformed and liberated in the present. Thebes is at the same time Polynices' home and birthplace, as well as a hostile, remote location that separates him from his hearth and next of kin. If space defines identity, as we have contended, Polynices is now himself a crux, a lacuna that defies complacent interpretation and understanding, but also in that interstitial place between communities, Polynices can make ethical decisions, and Argia, in her giving over of Polynices to Thebes, can show a loyalty to the other, born of her two communities (and histories) (see pp. 85–87).

For Polynices and Argia the option is not a choice between revolution or conservatism, but an ethical requirement to honor the past in the present. Forgetting is not the solution, even if it were possible, since by forgetting we risk the past reemerging to haunt us in dangerous new ways; Oedipus was forgotten and emerged anarchically to restart the tragedy of the *Thebaid*. The Thebans would have done a much better service to themselves and their children had they laid a guiding hand on the shoulder of the blind old king. Rather than seeing memory and forgetting as utilitarian issues, to remember is ultimately an ethical issue. Should one forget a departed loved one, a parent, a grandparent, or a great-grandparent, one loses them afresh, consigning them to a second and more final death. Remembering them revives them in the personal and collective past that we share and then bequeath to the next generation. This applies not just to all who have lived in the past. De Certeau (1988) 1 draws on Michelet, the great French Romantic historian, who claimed that in writing the history of France, he revived the unquiet dead, gave them their place on the stage, and then consigned them once more to their tombs, their identities reasserted. By so doing, the author came to find peace. Remembering becomes our duty to the others, but those others include ourselves, bound into our identity by the narratives of memory.

Between the prisons of memory and the dangers of forgetting, there seems an aporia in our texts. Blanchot's fragmentary memories, a partial forgetting, seem somehow an incomplete solution, and the freedoms of exile are for Polynices and probably for those contemporary Romans who withdrew from the social fray, ultimately illusory. The past comes back. But that memory is ethical. As Tacitus urges his contemporaries to preserve the memories of those who suffered under Domitian (*Agricola* 2), so the memories of Polynices are ultimately honored by his new family.

This loyalty to the event brings us to Alain Badiou.[56] Like Nancy, Badiou questions the ethics of consensus and unitary logic and offers an ethics of disharmony. The event ruptures normality and pushes the boundaries of what is thought to be possible. For Badiou, the event is a trauma in a society's belief system (its habitus). But, given the prevalence of events, the habitus requires some means of healing and recovery; tissues can form over the trauma, though perhaps retaining the memory (the scars) of the trauma. In the very moment that an event happens, people attempt to give that event meaning and discourses are employed to emplot the event. That emplotting is part of the healing of the wound, part of the process of transforming what is irrational and extreme into a means of affirming the rational. By contrast, Badiou argues for the ethical necessity of fidelity to the incomprehensibility of the event in order to preserve its potential to surprise and unsettle ideas, ideologies, and identities.[57] Badiou argues that engagement with the event needs the event to be sustained, nourished in incomprehension and discord. Individuals must be faithful to the event. Yet, this may come at some considerable personal and social cost, reliving traumas and denying the power of narratives to heal and bring peace. Badiou, and in this we find an echo of Lacan, proffers a politics of alienation, an alienation that can be liberating but deeply uncomfortable, so uncomfortable that one wonders whether we can truly live in such an immediate relationship to the event.[58] The ethical stance *vis à vis* the past is to show loyalty to the event,

---

56. For more on Badiou's work on ethics vs. aesthetics and the place of the event within it, see, e.g., Badiou (2005); Hallward (2003).

57. Cf. here Hallward (2003) 128–30.

58. In psychoanalytical terms, one wonders whether this is a refusal of a 'cure.' Once the history

after all, and by remaining wary of those narratives that explain it away, we can approach the event afresh again and again.

In Badiou and Lucan, we are encouraged to live in the scars of History: forgetting the event, disregarding history, imposing narratives, all seem to fail. Cato 'forgets' that the Republic is over but his resistance is misconceived. Those who live in the past have no place in the present, and cannot change that present. Cato, the stones of Troy, and the old of Rome are, as much as the philosophical opposition castigated by Tacitus, an honorable irrelevance. Yet, there would seem to be an aporia here between a resistant past and a collaborationist present, corresponding to the bipolar modernist division between past and present, between the all-encompassing Chronos and nostalgic self-delusion. It is these two 'perfect' collective memories that ultimately offer no choice, and are rejected in Tacitus, Lucan, and Badiou. If utilitarian forgetfulness seems unlikely to help us find our way through the maze, exile is also only a partial solution. A Romantic attachment to exile ignores the fact that, in the last instance, History triumphs. Germanicus, a knowing victim of History, does allow Troy to affect him, and comes to understand more about time and history as a consequence. Collective memory, as was noted above, is vulnerable to strengthening by simplification, whereas historical debate (not about the odd fact here and there, but about the meaning and structure of history) inevitably complicates. Complicating, raising doubts, questioning the relationship and meaning of the tradition for the present, all weaken the hold of the tradition and loosen the bindings. A continued awareness of the trauma of the event and of the artificiality of collective memories form the basis of critique. In this, the antique approach seems thoroughly Foucauldian: the best hope of escape from the tyranny of the present is a critical history of that present. Yet, there is also here a sense that the real revolution might be to step, even momentarily, outside History, and view History from its traumas. The prison of History is shaken in remembrance of the scars of History, and not in the certainties of new revolutionary memories or in the nostalgia of the old.

---

is uncovered, to continue to live in the trauma of the event would seem to invite neurosis.

6

Imperial Dreams

BEING ROMAN IN A WORLD EMPIRE

NATION AND EMPIRE

Throughout this book we have been exploring the relationship between the symbolic economy and individuals. We have searched for fissures and the incompleteness of symbolic economy, and looked at how that economy is restructured or even denied in a series of 'scenes.' A wish for, and concern with, distance from the symbolic economy has been an abiding observation of ours in our studies. The symbolic economy itself, though, is a convenient reification of a complex world of social and ideological engagements, and as such must also be a simplification. An untidiness in the symbolic economy is inevitable, and is surely a feature of all relatively complex societies. Yet those societies do not fragment, and, as we have noted, symbolic economies display a surprising resilience in the face of the disparate pressures to which they are subjected. In part, this resilience must relate to politics, the workings of power within a society to enforce social norms. One might see political power as ultimately enforcing a symbolic economy by making it more difficult to escape from or reject that economy than it is to maintain an imperfect existence within it. And this poses a methodological problem. We have written this history from the individual, from the lowest levels at which the symbolic economy is manifest, and progressed towards larger and larger spatial entities, until, in this chapter, we will look at the Empire itself. But this approach entails a micro-economic analysis, and the problem with micro-economics is that it can lose the bigger picture, the macro-economic factors that shape the economic world in which we operate. We operate locally, but in a global context. Further, through the various scenes, our analysis has concentrated on particular ideas. But ideas in themselves have no geographical or social spread. They exist in the texts and are iterated in their reading. Yet a symbolic economy has to exist in time and space; it needs a territory, and although we have rigorously avoided delineating that territory within the chapters so far, our symbolic economy has had as strong a spatial aspect as it has had a temporal manifestation (one may think, for example, of Polynices' exile, or Pliny's domestic isolation).

Our difficulty with this problem is in part historiographical. Since the rise of the nation state, there is an assumption that symbolic economies and political organizations will be coterminous. The symbolic economy defines the ethnic unit, which defines the nation, which is, in normal circumstances, the highest level of political organization. This relationship can be seen as a modern phenomenon, though there is a general recognition that the correlation between a symbolic economy and political organization is not necessarily closely tied (thus one can have quite developed and separate sub-cultures within a nation state). Nevertheless, that association of political and cultural units is not peculiar to modern sensibilities.[1] When people write "Rome," there is an assumption of a shared culture that either encompasses the territory of the polity, or tends towards an encompassing of that territory. Roman "civilization" is associated firmly with the Roman Empire; hence, the very extensive literature on "Romanization," in which the perceived problem is a state (Empire) which does not have a unified symbolic economy (culture). The arguments over the extent of acculturation are political since a shared symbolic economy is seen to increase the legitimacy of the state. Further, the nation state becomes the political force which fixes the symbolic economy.[2] One could, therefore, imagine writing this book the other way around: seeing identity as primarily a feature of the political extension of Rome, and move from the Empire to the city to the individual, from the macro-economic to the micro-economic, tracing the impositions of the polity on the individual. Yet, merely because the Roman 'nation' (we use the term

---

1. There is considerable debate in the sociological literature on the origins of nationalism. See, for instance, Gellner (1983) and Smith (1981; 1986), and the summary in Bentley (1987). Although Smith (1986) argues that the idea of a nation is primordial, it is generally agreed that the importance of nationalism and ethnicity varied according to social and political circumstances. The debate has been confused by rather careless assumptions about the role of ethnicity and nationalism in historical societies, since the "expert" evidence of contemporary historians about past societies tends to impose contemporary assumptions of the importance of ethnicity into the historic evidence, which are then taken as evidence of the primordial nature of the nation.

2. Gellner (1983) 1–38 sees the modern state's need of an educated population as the origin of a drive towards cultural homogenization. Such cultural policies link ethnicity and the modern state.

advisedly) is imagined, we see no reason to see the idea of that 'nation' as the master-idea, in awe of which all other imagined communities must make their space. Similarly, although it may be convenient for political discourse to see the nation as the level at which identities are fixed, there is very little reason to believe that modern identities are determined by the nation, and, as a multinational couple, we would deny that determination. In some ways, this is the myth of ethnicities and nation states: that they are primordial, territorial, and integral, when they are always invented symbolic communities in whose collective memories histories are simplified for the benefit of political powers and political coherence. Yet, such a myth is rarely generated by the state or the political machinery itself; rather it is generated by those who wish to locate themselves within the mythic culture of the state and thus discover the meaning of the nation. We would argue that this discourse of nationalism is a feature of an individual, psychological need to associate the nation with a symbolic economy, rather than a 'natural' feature of a political structure that determines the symbolic economy.[3] To write history from the perspective of the nation would seem to us merely to reinforce this highly questionable prejudice.

Yet, to deny that the polity or the 'nation' affixes the symbolic economy is not to ignore the importance of state political power and the spatiality of a symbolic economy.[4] Even in radical geographical traditions, the organization of space is seen as fundamental to the establishing and fixing of identities. For Henri Lefebvre, revolution could only occur in circumstances of radical spatial change, while David Harvey and Ed Soja have argued that contemporary urban geography, rather than being open, malleable, and capable of infinite reinterpretation, merely represents the flexibilities of late-stage capitalism.[5] In a crucial parallel for our arguments below, the multiculturalism of space within the contemporary city, the ability of groups of all sorts to create spatial identities (urban villages) in which their identities can be expressed, and the cultural eclecticism of much modern architecture all exist within a broader and determining symbolic (and real) economy. Although these groups might at first sight seem oppositional to the 'mainstream,' part of the reaction to the norms of the capitalist economy, these subordinate groups are, in fact, integral to, produced by, and delimited within the capitalistic system.[6] In critiquing that capitalistic globalization, one of the problems

---

3. Smith (1981) argues that writers and intellectuals, the controllers of political discourse, are the most likely sources for nationalist sentiment.
4. Somers and Gibson (1994) 61 sees the politics of identity as an "ontological narrative [which] embeds identity in time and spatial relationships."
5. See the influential studies of Lefebvre (1991); Soja (1989); Harvey (1990).
6. See Castells (1977).

is the absence of an 'outside,' since the system is all-encompassing, which means that the spatial organization is both naturalized and appears inevitable, a feature of the workings of History.

We can read that globalism in our epics. Polynices seems to find exile in the new spaces of Argos, but the old spaces, and the workings of History, drag him back; Pompey too has a glimpse of a hopeful future in internal exile in Lesbos, but History is not to be denied, working in Argos and Lesbos as it worked in Thebes and Rome. Yet, there is a clear difference to between Argos and Thebes, as there is between Lesbos and Rome. History may work in both places, but the local apparitions of History are very different. The parallel would seem to be between the city and the Empire: what is possible in Lesbos is subordinated, eventually, to the workings of the Caesarian Empire, while Adrastus in Argos might assert the independence of his city, but it is Jupiter's Empire that encloses his city in History. As the symbolic economies are enclosed in space, we find an awareness of a multilayering of space, and a consequent multilayering of the symbolic economies.

In this chapter, we will follow this link between History and space, tracing this multilayering of the symbolic economy. The complexity of this spatial organization contrasts with an ideological bipolarity, so often accepted by modern scholars (and fundamental to the Romanization debate) between barbarian and citizen. That bipolarity is a "structural given" within our ancient texts, and carries with it a strong sense of 'inside' and 'outside,' but the multilayering of the spatial aspects of the symbolic economy weakens that polarity, and in that weakening there is an undermining of the fundamental polarities of Roman political organization. If there is no clear division between what is 'inside' and 'outside,' and significantly no clear understanding of the criteria on which the division between 'inside' and 'outside' is made, the association of a particular space with a particular symbolic economy, one that one might perhaps wish to name "Rome" for example, becomes problematic.

We argue that in Silius Italicus' portrayal of Hannibal, an archetypal barbarian, we find a peculiar ambivalence about the anti-hero, an ambivalence that carries through to a pervasive uncertainty about the moral status of old Rome, and of new Rome. The epic appears more confident of the continued influence of the barbarian in contemporary Roman society than it is of the lasting legacy of its virtuous Roman hero, Scipio. Hannibal comes to haunt the future of Rome, a specter of a barbarian other, but in the treachery of the Italian allies and the luxurious life of Capua, there lies a picture of the future of Rome. Even though there is no doubt where Silius' sympathies lie, the barbarian is absorbed within the historical narrative of Rome as the Roman is obscured. In Tacitus' *Germania* and *Agricola* we are repeatedly encouraged to view the Empire from the outside, though, problematically, not as barbarians. Tacitus establishes a "third place" in this bipolar universe of Roman and barbarian. From this "third place" we are alienated from an Empire to which, equally clearly, we are meant to lend our support.

We seek to understand this ambivalent position through comparison with modern imperial structures. The idea of Rome is in dispute in these texts, and in that dispute there emerges a distancing from the imperial state. There was a 'lack' in the ideology of the Roman Empire. In the vast spaces of Empire, what holds together the spaces is a very thin, insubstantial, symbolic economy. Although it has very considerable power, this insubstantial quality means that it is only able to bind weakly. In that weakness though, lay both the success of the Roman Empire and its ultimate vulnerability. The 'lack' allowed other elements of the symbolic economy relatively free play, but also made it vulnerable to alternative ideologies which provided individuals with new meanings.

SYMPATHY FOR THE DEVIL: HANNIBAL THE HERO

In the late first century C.E., the Roman poet Silius Italicus produced a new epic version of the second Punic War. We have a brief obituary notice for Silius in Pliny, *Epistle* 3.7, which depicts a bookish devotee of Virgil who achieved the consulship under Nero, but then lived in retirement, writing and collecting art and houses. Silius was the last consul to be appointed by Nero and the last of the Neronian consuls to die. Thus, his death represented the passing of an age. His life can be read as a manifesto for comfortable nostalgia. Following in a literary tradition that had shifted from Virgil's epic of Roman foundation to Lucan's story of destruction, a return to the Punic War was a literary and historical homecoming. The Second Punic War was Rome's Great Patriotic War; Livy describes it as *bellum maxime omnium memorabile* ("the most memorable war in history").[7] Here, at least, one could expect a comfortable and safe story of the triumph of Roman values. Yet, as we saw in the previous chapter, devotion to the old ways was difficult to separate from a political stance. The past was far from a safe, foreign land. The comfort of Silius dissolves in a persistent unease, an unease that centers on an absence. Like Virgil, against whose epic we are surely meant to read the *Punica,* Silius opens his epic in Carthage, but whereas the *Aeneid* commences with Aeneas worrying about the destiny of Rome, Silius' most obvious

---

7. Livy, *Ab Urbe Condita* 21.1.1. This is obviously a *topos* of historiography, but Livy backs his assertion with an elaborate catalogue of evidence.

Roman hero, Scipio, does not appear until Book XI. The main character of the Silian narrative is, instead, a Carthaginian, Hannibal.

The poem establishes familiar polarities. Hannibal is a character faithless, ferocious, and cunning:

> Ingenio motus avidus fideique sinister
> is fuit, exsuperans astu, sed devius aequi.
> armato nullus divum pudor; improba virtus
> et pacis despectus honos; penitusque medullis
> sanguinis humani flagrat sitis. (1. 56–59)

> By nature he was hungry for action and a betrayer of his promises, a master in cunning but a strayer from justice. Once armed, he had no shame before the gods; his virtue was impious, and he looked down on the honor of peace; and a thirst for human blood burned deep within him.

We witness Hannibal as a boy receiving his most important lesson: that the Romans are a hated nation, awaiting punishment for the grief and destruction of the first Punic War. As the years pass, Hannibal's father, Hamilcar, is killed, as is his son-in-law, Hasdrubal, and the young Hannibal becomes the leader of the Carthaginians. His first strategic decision is to break the treaty imposed on the Carthaginians at the end of the First Punic War and to attack the Saguntines, Rome's Spanish allies.[8]

Yet, on the battlefield of Saguntum, Hannibal is far from a straightforward figure. Read against the *Aeneid,* he recalls for us both the heroic founder of the Roman nation and Aeneas' enemy, Turnus.[9] This confusion is particularly obvious in his duel with Murrus.[10] When the two men meet, Hannibal, seeing his enemy charging him, seizes a huge rock and hurls it:

> Haec inter cernens subeuntem comminus hostem
> praeruptumque loci fidum sibi, corripit ingens
> aggere convulso saxum et nitentis in ora
> devolvit, pronoque silex ruit incitus ictu. 1. 488–91

> Meanwhile, seeing his enemy come close, and realising that he could trust his position on the overhanging ground, he shook the rampart and tore out

---

8. See Dominik (2003) 477 n. 14 on the historicity of the breaking of the treaty.

9. See Feeney (1991) 302–12 and Hardie (1993) *passim.* For an intertextual reading of the *Punica* against the *Aeneid* see Pomeroy (2000) esp. 153–60.

10. As in the *Aeneid,* there is a delay in the duel being joined as Murrus looks for Hannibal (1.426) in the field. In *Aeneid* 12, it was Aeneas who searched for Turnus.

a huge boulder and hurled it at the head of his enemy as he rose up; and the stone flew quickly downwards.

Extreme physicality, like this, stays in the mind. If Hannibal was able to shake a boulder out of the rampart, Turnus in *Aeneid* 12 was hardly a lesser hero in brutal strength:

nec plura effatus saxum circumspicit ingens
saxum antiquum ingens, campo quid forte iacebat,
limes agro positus litem ut discerneret arvis.
vix illum lecti bis sex cervice subirent,
qualia nunc hominum producit corpora tellus;
ille manu raptum trepida torquebat in hostem
altior insurgens et cursu concitus heros. *Aeneid* 12. 896–902

Without a word more he looked round and his eyes lit on a stone, a huge old stone which for years had been lying there on the plain as a boundary mark between fields, to prevent disputes about ownership. Hardly could twelve strong men, of such physique as the earth produces nowadays, pick up and carry up on their shoulders. Well, Turnus pounced on it, lifted it, and taking a run to give it more impetus, hurled his stone from his full height at Aeneas.

Turnus missed, but Hannibal strikes. A shaken Murrus resumes the fight, but Hannibal menaces him; his eyes darken and his heart fails at the realization of his impending death: . . . *velut incita clausum agmina Poenorum cingant et cuncta paventem castra premant, lato Murrus caligat in hoste* ("It seemed as if the Punic column is rapidly surrounding him, and he fears that the whole camp presses on a him. Murrus' eyes grow dim before his powerful foe" [1. 497–99]). Now, roles are reversed. Murrus' faint heart brings to mind Turnus' fear and hesitation in *Aeneid* 12. 916–17, which enabled Aeneas to pierce him with a spear.[11] For a moment, Murrus takes the place of Turnus, and, for that moment, Hannibal becomes again Aeneas.

This same swapping of roles continues throughout the battle. Warriors from both sides meet heroic deaths. Prominent among these is the death of an ally of Hannibal, Asbyte, a maiden warrior who recalls Camilla, the Volscian ally of Turnus in the *Aeneid*. Enraged by her death, Hannibal makes his presence felt in the battlefield with rattling arms and a dazzling shield:

---

11. *Aen.* 12. 916–17: . . . *Rutulos aspectat et urbem / cunctaturque metu letumque instare tremescit* ("He gazed at the city, the Rutuli; faltered with fear; trembled at the weapon menacing him").

> namque aderat toto ore ferens iramque minasque
> Hannibal et caesam Asbyten fixique tropaeum
> infandum capitis furiata mente dolebat.
> ac simul aerati radiavit luminis umbo,
> et concussa procul membris velocibus arma
> letiferum intonuere, fugam perculsa repente
> ad muros trepido convertunt agmina cursu. 2. 208–14

For Hannibal approached with anger and threats written all over his face; he grieved for slaughtered Asbyte, and was filled with anger at the unspeakable trophy of her head. And, as soon as his shield shone with a bronze glitter, and the arms struck by his rapid movements thundered death far and wide, the column, as if suddenly struck, turned to flight towards the walls of the city in rout.

The terror of Hannibal's arrival recalls Aeneas' entrance into the battle on his return from Pallanteum in *Aeneid* X. A similar light had enveloped the Trojan leader, a light that restored courage to his men and demoralized Turnus' army.[12] In the thick of battle, Silius blends Aeneas into Turnus and both into Hannibal: the barbarian carries in him elements of both the Italian Turnus and the Trojan Aeneas, the foundational elements of the Roman nation.

Following the sack of Saguntum, Hannibal embarks on a tour of the local tribes, sends for omens to the oracle of Jupiter Ammon, and worships at Hercules' altars, where he admires the depiction of the twelve labors on the doors of the temple (3. 1–60). But he has little time for this: his thoughts and his heart are with his wife and child, and he rushes to meet them (3. 61–62). Tender declarations of love and shared tears as the two lovers spend their last night together render this relationship elegiac.[13] Yet Imilce was "attached to Hannibal with an affection full of memories" (*imbuerat coniunx memorique tenebat amore* [3. 65]), and, as she reminds him in 3. 113, "no hardship can overcome chaste love" (*castum haud superat labor ullus amorem*). Imilce emerges not as the fickle, coquettish *puella*, but as the *matrona*, the respectable Roman woman. Imilce, a Carthaginian aristocrat with an

---

12. *Aen.* 10. 260–64: *Iamque in conspectu Teucros habet et sua castra / stans celsa in puppi, / clipeum cum deinde sinistra / extulit ardentem. clamorem ad sidera tollunt / Dardanidae e muris, spes addita suscitat iras, / tela manu iaciunt.* ("And now, as he stood high up in the stern-sheets, Aeneas held his Trojans and their encampment in view: so he lifted his shield with his left hand and made it flash. The Dardanians upon the walls raised a great shout; their fighting spirit revived at this new hope, their fire was redoubled").

13. Looking ahead in the text, the couple's painful parting at the seashore in the end of this all-too-brief encounter (3. 127–57) will also remind us of the heart-rending partings of many of Ovid's *Heroides*, in this elegiac retelling of the Greek myths.

illustrious ancestry (*atque ex sacrata repetebat stirpe parentes* [3. 106]) should remind us of Dido, but whereas Dido struggled against destiny and against the historic mission of her man, Imilce refuses to delay the course of fate.[14] In her compliance, Imilce jars with Dido and reminds us of Creusa, Aeneas' soft-spoken Trojan wife. Ultimately, Hannibal has to leave Imilce, as Aeneas left Dido and Creusa, but Hannibal does not desert his wife or lose her in a burning city. He makes provisions for her, as a loyal and responsible lover.[15] As this elegiac interlude draws to an end, Mercury is recruited by the Father of Gods to stir the sleeping leader (3. 162–82), upbraiding him with the same sharpness he had deployed on Aeneas in Libya in *Aeneid* 4. 554–70. Disturbed by this dream, Hannibal, like the Trojan hero, stirs his sleeping camp and preparations for war commence.

Categorizing Hannibal is difficult. He slips between epic models and flirts with an elegiac persona. This may reflect his "crafty," "untrustworthy" personality, but he does not show the dissimulation of Lucan's Caesar. It seems to us that Hannibal in Silius' epic escapes from the role designated to him by history, that of archetypal villain. Nevertheless, Hannibal never becomes Aeneas; the identification is always fleeting and his barbarity repeatedly asserts itself. For instance, in the Carthaginian sojourn in Capua in Book XI we are given a detailed account of the city's luxury and decadence (11. 28–54) and watch Hannibal and his army succumb to the effeminate pleasures of music and art (11. 259–368; 11. 37–482). Yet Hannibal's interlude in Capua recalls Aeneas' sojourn in Carthage, where he was similarly lulled into oriental, effeminate ways (*Aeneid* 4. 259–76).[16] In this pattern of allusion, the archetypal 'other' is not that different, not that foreign and it becomes possible to imagine Aeneas as Hannibal, and to see Rome in the Carthaginian.[17] As Hannibal departs from Imilce to engage with his destiny,

---

14. *Punica*, 3. 114–15: *sin solo aspicimur sexu, fixumque relinqui, cedo equidem nec fata moror* ("But if you judge me by sex alone, and are determined to leave me, I yield indeed and will not delay the course of destiny"). In Ovid's *Heroides*, Dido asks Aeneas for a delay in true elegiac fashion: *Heroides* 7. 175–78. Cf. Spentzou (2003) 174–78.

15. In this aspect of his presentation, Hannibal ultimately "looks back" to the archetypal doomed conjugal bond, that of Hector and Andromache in the *Iliad*.

16. Both leaders receive new armor in the course of the epics. Aeneas' armor, though, was a gift of honor, ordered from a god (Vulcan) by a goddess (Venus), while Hannibal was given his shield by the Gallicians (2. 395–456), whose generosity was provoked by fear that they would be the next target of Carthaginian aggression. Aeneas' shield is devoted to the future of Rome and therefore takes us beyond individual fears or hopes, while Hannibal's armor focuses on the Carthaginians' past history, especially that of his own *gens*; cf. Gale (1997) esp. 189.

17. This ambivalence extends to relation with the divine, and to history. In Book 1, as Murrus braces himself to face the charging Hannibal, he prays to Hercules, the founder of his motherland, for help (1. 505–7). Hannibal claims that Hercules will recognize the more worthy warrior and will thus come to Hannibal's assistance instead (1. 508–14). Similarly, as Hannibal forces his soldiers to cross the high Alps in Book III, he invokes Hercules' support as a fellow spirit of transgression (3.

both he and she look Roman, and in some ways he appears as a more humane Aeneas, not so blinded by a commitment to the State as to forget his love. There is a loosening of absolutes in the text as we read it. Ethnic and political identifications, with all the moral certainties therein contained, are slipping. Even in this most patriotic of epics, loyalty to the state is not the only virtue, and Roman readers can have sympathy with, and even see themselves in, their historic enemy.

Hannibal's prominence accentuates the obvious lack of a viable Roman hero in the early books of the *Punica*. Various Romans seem candidates, notably Regulus (Book VI), Fabius Cunctator (Book VII), Paulus (Books IX and X), and Marcellus (Books XII and XIV), and this shifting cast offers a problematic collective heroism. Such fluidity in leadership was a feature of Republican politics, though it is somewhat foreign to the epic tradition.[18] Yet this multiplicity has consequences, since if all the Roman aristocracy comes to be judged by the heroic standard set by Aeneas, when individuals fall short, it reflects on all of Rome. The multiple representatives of virtue create not solidarity drawn from shared responsibility, but fragility and precariousness.

This precariousness emerges towards the end of Book I. The Roman senators are summoned by the consul to decide on Rome's policy on the siege of Saguntum:

> Concilium vocat augustum castaque beatos
> paupertate patres ac nomina parta triumphis
> consul et aequantem superos virtute senatum.
> facta animosa viros et recti sacra cupido
> attollunt; hirtaeque togae neglectaque mensa
> dexteraque a curvis capulo non segnis aratris;
> exiguo faciles et opum non indiga corda,
> ad parvos curru remeabant saepe penates. 1. 609–16

The consul called the august council—the Fathers happy in chaste poverty, with names born from triumphs—a senate equaling the gods in virtue. Brave deeds and a sacred passion for right raised up these men; their togas

---

500–15). Yet in Book II, Hercules weeps with compassion for Saguntum's plight, pitying the city he founded and appealing to Fides for help (2. 475–92) and later Hercules shows loyalty to the Romans (e.g., 15. 78–9; 17. 649–50).

18. Helzle (1996) 231–300; Wilson (1993); and Hardie (1993), *passim* and esp. 8–10, 24–25, 38–39, 69–71, 96–97, have been challenged by this "multiple heroism," though Feeney (1986) defends the concept.

were rough; their meals careless, their hands quick to the sword from the crooked plough; at ease with little, desiring no riches, they often returned to simple households from the triumphal chariot.

Silius reinforces this reverent introduction with an elaborate description of the scenes portrayed on the doors and walls of the temple where the Senate convened: proud memories of victorious battles and glorious spoil accumulated in the course of Rome's expansion (617–29). Once the issue of Saguntum is debated, however, opinions differ. Cornelius Lentulus and Fabius Maximus see Rome's position and future in contrasting ways and hold opposite views. Nagging questions surface: which of the two is the worthy keeper of Rome's traditions? Who is more capable of leading Rome's cause to a successful resolution? Can virtue be represented in two diverging paths?[19] The inconclusive debate contrasts with the *Aeneid*'s often painful but always energizing certainties. In the *Aeneid*, Roman destiny is always fixed, but in Silius the future seems contingent and negotiable, a course to be debated rather than divinely inspired.[20]

This uncertainty contrasts with the situation in Saguntum, and the Saguntines become a focus of old-fashioned virtues and heroism, a kind of surrogate Rome in Spain.[21] Silius stresses the Italian blood of the Saguntines. For example, Daunus comes from Apulia and fights bravely, though he has insufficient moral or physical strength to overpower Hannibal (1. 440–51). Murrus is of mixed Rutulian, Spanish, and even Greek blood (1. 476–79), and is thus representative of the cosmopolitan citizenry of the late first century C.E. He is also slaughtered by Hannibal. Moreover, the Saguntines' dutiful and loyal conduct is a reminder of the legendary qualities of old

---

19. Pomeroy (2000) 160–62 sees in the multiplicity of leaders a collective ethos of self-effacing and civic-minded senators essential to the functioning of the Roman Republic. Contrast Tipping (1999), who sees the *Punica* as exposing the transgressive, self-promotion of individuals of the late Republic.

20. Silius' rewriting of Aeneas exposes the latent strains in Aeneas' supra-individual personality (a phrase borrowed from Hardie [1993] 4), strains that were mostly confined within disturbing and unsettling similes and metaphors in the *Aeneid* (see Lyne 1987). The *Aeneid* is filled with prophecies of nationhood, signifiers of Rome's collective and historic triumph, such as Jupiter's prophecy in Book I and Anchises' Roman prophecy in Book VI. Scipio also visits the underworld, but instead of the triumph of his family and city, he receives a particularly bleak vision of the destiny awaiting Rome. Silius' Jupiter confirms that he plans to test the Romans' endurance with war, because they have forgotten their glorious history (3. 572–84), and he predicts that Rome will be famed, but for its calamities rather than its triumphs (3. 584–85). Even when Jupiter looks further into the future and predicts better days (3. 592–629), his emphasis is on the glory and success of the future emperors, a nod towards *panegyric*, a form replete with ambiguity and dissimulation.

21. The fate of Saguntum parallels that of Troy, whose encounter with the imminence of annihilation is a paradigmatic epic *topos*. See Hardie (1993) 81–82.

Rome, which the Romans of Hannibal's time seem to have abandoned; they dither and calculate as their Spanish allies face destruction.[22]

This is a world in which the boundaries between Romans and barbarians are eroded.[23] Roman self-representation reaches a crisis just after the Roman humiliation at the battle of Cannae in Book X. As Book XI begins, several Italian peoples defect. Silius exposes their faithlessness (11. 1–27); fiercest of all, the Samnites are eager to reignite old feuds, the Bruttians are fickle, the Apulians treacherous, the Hirpini vain, and so forth. A first-century C.E. Roman poet constructs a list of Italian barbarians in marked contrast to the Virgilian vision of an Italian-Roman empire carefully promoted in the *Aeneid*.[24] At the center of the confusion, we have Capua, a city both Italian and Greek and, incidentally, the foremost city of the region where Silius made his home. Capua was an early defector to the Carthaginian cause, but Capua itself contrasts with Carthage. Rather than a barbarian city, it is a city of luxury, and therefore a dark reflection of Silius' contemporary Rome.[25]

This absence of clear polarities extends even into Scipio's greatest hour of success. As he looks down at the massacre in the battlefield of Zama and the size of the disaster dawns upon him, it is Hannibal who addresses a warning to Rome:

> decedesque prius regnis quam nomina gentes
> aut facta Hannibalis sileant. nec deinde relinquo
> securam te, Roma, mei; patriaeque superstes
> ad spes armorum vivam tibi. Nam modo pugna
> praecellis, resident hostes: mihi satque superque,
> ut me Dardaniae matres atque Itala tellus,
> dum vivam, expectent nec pacem pectore norint. 17. 609–15

> You shall fall from power before the peoples cease to speak of the name or achievements of Hannibal. Nor do I leave you, Rome, safe from me. Surviving my country, I will live in the hope of a war against you. You triumph in just this battle, but your enemies remain. Enough, and more than enough for me, if the Dardanian mothers and the land of Italy look out for me, while I live, and do not know peace of mind.

---

22. For an extended exploration of these parallels, see Dominik 2003, *passim* and esp. 476–85.
23. As explored in Tipping (1999).
24. For Virgil's allegiance to Italy, see Ando (2002) 123–42.
25. For more on the mirroring games between Rome, Capua, Carthage and the other cities in Silius, see Cowan (forthcoming).

The image of the defeated Hannibal accompanies the victor of Zama on his return to Rome. The picture of the fleeing Hannibal is included in the processional images at Scipio's triumph and attracts the greatest attention from the crowd (17. 643–44); Hannibal becomes a perverse sort of *triumphator,* building himself into Roman history. He thus mirrors Scipio in the procession, providing a potential for transgression at the very moment of triumph.[26] In his proclamation of an enmity that will survive his death, Hannibal not only takes his place as the eternal, mythic barbarian, but remains a transgressive presence in Roman history: not accepting his condemnation and defeat, or even his death, he eludes the control of the imperial state. Hannibal asserts a freedom lost to the Roman conquerors. As the defeated Hannibal survives in eternal opposition, so is Scipio Africanus lost to Rome. In Book XV, Scipio chooses Virtue over Pleasure, a choice that establishes him as a representative of old Roman values, rejecting personal satisfaction (and the road to tyranny thereby implied) for the values of community. Yet in so doing, he distances himself both from the future Rome and from his contemporaries, who debate, fail, and act without moral certainty. Scipio stands apart from Rome's present and future, while Hannibal is written into Rome's future in an eternal oppositional freedom.

We cannot easily read Silius' poem as a critique of his contemporary society and a glorification of lost Republican values. The epic and its heroes lack simplicity and the moral universe that they inhabit, one which we might think was open to very simple dichotomies, lacks clarity. We could read the *Punica* as another example of disengagement from a remote past, or at least of an uncertainty about the role and significance of that past for contemporary Romans. Yet, Hannibal complicates the problem, for he is the implacable enemy and is, as such, the justification for permanent Empire. The point of Empire is to keep the Hannibals "Outside" so that "Insiders" may be able to rest safe in their beds. But in the texts of the long first century, not just with Silius, but notably with Tacitus, there is a sense that "we Romans" may in fact be barbarians, descended not from Scipio, but from the Africans he conquered, and if the barbarian is within, then the Roman might just be outside the boundaries, geographical and chronological, of contemporary empire. Hannibal, admirable in many ways, horrific in others, both is and is not Aeneas. Contemporary Rome both was and was not Silius' Capua. The old Roman aristocracy shared some similarities with Silius' fellow senators, but existed at an obvious distance from Silius' contemporary world. The struggle in Silius' *Punica* is neither for ancient Rome, nor for modern Rome, nor for the world of the barbarian. In the *Aeneid* and also in

---

26. Cf. here Tipping (1999) 274–78.

the *Odyssey,* there is an overwhelming sense of the search for a home, a place where the struggles of the epic will be rendered peaceful, but in Silius one has first to wonder where that home may be, in old Rome, in Saguntum, in Capua, in the Rome that will come, or in Carthage, with Imilce. While most epics have a hero in search of a home that is known and will be known, the *Punica* is an epic without a home, without the grounding so essential to give meaning to the hero's quest.

FIGHTING FOR SLAVERY: ETHICS AND ETHNOGRAPHY IN TACITUS

In the *Germania,* and to a lesser extent the *Agricola,* Tacitus tried his hand at ethnography. Ethnography ancient and modern has a mixed reputation, partly because of its tendency to 'invent' the barbarian, and, in so doing, to create a series of polarities that establish or at least reaffirm the identity of the 'home' nation. Nevertheless, most ethnographic texts are complex in their depiction of the studied peoples. Inevitably, the writers bring their preconceptions and obsessions to the treatment of a foreign people, and thus ethnography will tell us as much about the culture of the individual writing the account as (hopefully) about the subjects of that account. Tacitus' ethnography is no different; it operates as a discussion of, and reflection on, contemporary Rome, as well as a consideration of the Germans and Britons.

The "local interests" of Tacitus can be seen in his focus on the sexual morality of the Germans:

> Quamquam severa illic matrimonia, nec ullam morum partem magis laudaveris. . . . Ne se mulier extra virtutum cogitationes extraque bellorum casus putet, ipsis incipientis matrimonii auspiciis admonetur venire se laborum periculorumque sociam, idem in pace, idem in proelio passuram ausuramque. Hoc iuncti boves, hoc paratus equus, hoc data arma denuntiant. Sic vivendum, sic pereundum: accipere se, quae liberis inviolata ac digna reddat, quae nurus accipiant, rursusque ad nepotes referantur.
>
> Ergo saepta pudicitia agunt, nullis spectaculorum inlecebris, nullis conviviorum inritationibus corruptae. Litterarum secreta viri pariter ac feminae ignorant. Paucissima in tam numerosa gente adulteria, quorum poena praesens et maritis permissa: abscisis crinibus nudatam coram propinquis expellit domo maritus ac per omnem vicum verbere agit; publicatae enim pudicitiae nulla venia: non forma, non aetate, non opibus maritum invenerit. Nemo enim illic vitia ridet, nec corrumpere et corrumpi saeculum vocatur. Melius quidem adhuc eae civitates, in quibus tantum virgines

nubunt et eum spe votoque uxoris semel transigitur. Sic unum accipiunt maritum quo modo unum corpus unamque vitam, ne ulla cogitatio ultra, ne longior cupiditas, ne tamquam maritum, sed tamquam matrimonium ament. Numerum liberorum finire aut quemquam ex adgnatis necare flagitium habetur, plusque ibi boni mores valent quam alibi bonae leges.

Their marriage code, however, is strict, and no element of their customs deserves more praise. . . . For the woman is advised in the very rituals that inaugurate her marriage to be virtuous and not be the cause of conflicts, that she comes to be his partner in labors and dangers, and to share his sufferings and risks in peace as in war. They symbolize this with a team of oxen, a horse ready to ride, and the gift of arms. So she must live and bear children. She is receiving something that she must hand over intact and in a proper state to her children, which her daughters-in-law receive in time and bequeath to her grandchildren.

Thus the reputation of women is protected, and they live uncorrupted by the enticements of spectacles or the incitements of dinner parties. Neither men nor women know of secret letters. There is so little adultery given the size of the population, and the penalty for adultery is imposed by the husband. After cutting her hair, he drives her out of his house, naked in the presence of close relations and beats her through the village. There is no pardon for prostitution. Neither beauty, youth, nor wealth find her a husband. For No one laughs at vice, or calls it "of-the-age" to seduce or be seduced. Better still in some states only virgins marry, so that one event brings to a conclusion the hopes and prayers of a woman. She takes one husband in the same way that she has one body and one life and neither thinks beyond him, nor desires further than him, for they love not so much the husband as the state of matrimony. It is held to be vicious to limit the number of children or kill those born after the heir. Good morals are more powerful there than good laws elsewhere. *Germania* 18–19

The vices listed, adultery, relaxed attitudes to sexual promiscuity, serial monogamy, infanticide (and possibly contraception), are those that were regarded as symptomatic of the decay of Rome from its period of archaic virtue. The phrase *Nemo . . . saeculum vocatur* suggests that adultery was "of the age" and hence marks an implicit difference between contemporary Rome and archaic Rome and Germany. The polarity between Rome and Germany is made more complex by the association of these Germanic virtues with the old Romans. Tacitus implicates his readers in his moral judgments. The most obvious contrast here is with Livy. In his *Praefatio* he complained about the decline of moral values, but claimed that his "bitter comments . . . are not likely to find favor" and that "we can neither endure our vices, nor face the medicines necessary to cure them," implying at least that he was in a minority position. Tacitus shows no such concern; for him contemporary Roman sexual behavior is immoral; Rome is thus debauched, but Tacitus and his audience are not. We have a Rome from which Tacitus and his friends can exclude themselves, creating a distance between observer and observed. Ellen O'Gorman (1993) calls this an "assignation of otherness to elements of one's own society" which masks the polarities of Roman versus barbarian. In O'Gorman's view the otherness of the barbarian in the *Germania* is not undermined by the ideal qualities of that barbarian (it remains a structural certainty), but is paralleled by the 'otherness' of Roman society.

Although Tacitus finds many things about the Germans to praise, such as their attitude towards kings,[27] he also emphasizes the strangeness (that "structural otherness") of German society in, for instance, the presence of women on the battlefield and their role in logistical support.[28] Equally strange and foolish was Germans' prodigious consumption of alcohol:

> Tum ad negotia nec minus saepe ad convivia procedunt armati. Diem noctemque continuare potando nulli probrum. Crebrae, ut inter vinolentos, rixae raro conviciis, saepius caede et vulneribus transiguntur. Sed et de reconciliandis in vicem inimicis et iungendis adfinitatibus et adsciscendis principibus, de pace denique ac bello plerumque in conviviis consultant, tamquam nullo magis tempore aut ad simplices cogitationes pateat animus aut ad magnas incalescat. Gens non astuta nec callida aperit adhuc secreta pectoris licentia ioci; ergo detecta et nuda omnium mens. Postera die retractatur, et salva utriusque temporis ratio est: deliberant, dum fingere nesciunt, constituunt, dum errare non possunt.
>
> . . .

---

27. Tacitus, *Germania* 7, claims that the Germans chose their kings on account of their nobility, and their generals for their valor. Power was not absolute, and commanders led by example. Their leaders were thus subject the judgment of the community, more Republican than imperial leaders. Tacitus contrasts German kingship with Domitian, whose involvement with Germany was such that his presence lurks within the ethnography, an absolute monarch who did not cover himself in military glory, almost an anti-type for Germanic kingship.

28. *Germania* 7: quodque praecipuum fortitudinis incitamentum est, non casus, nec fortuita conglobatio turmam aut cuneum facit, sed familiae et propinquitates; et in proximo pignora, unde feminarum ululatus audiri, unde vagitus infantium. Hi cuique sanctissimi testes, hi maximi laudatores. Ad matres, ad coniuges vulnera ferunt; nec illae numerare aut exigere plagas pavent, cibosque et hortamina pugnantibus gestant ("It is an especially powerful incitement to bravery that the cavalry and infantry units are not mustered by chance, but by family or clan. Close to them, too, are their wives, so that they can hear the shrieks of their women or the wails of their children. These women are the most revered witnesses, these the greatest supporters. The men bring their wounds to their mothers and wives, and the women do not fear to weigh up and examine the gashes and they bring food and encouragement to the warriors").

> Si indulseris ebrietati suggerendo quantum concupiscunt, haud minus facile vitiis quam armis vincentur.

When dealing with business, they often retire to a feast, but always armed. To drink all day and all night is not considered disgraceful. The quarrels that inevitably arise over the drinks are seldom settled by argument, but more often by violence and death. Nevertheless, they often decide at a feast the reconciliation of feuds, the arrangement of marriages, the elevation of leaders, and even on peace or war thinking that at no other time is the spirit so sincere or so prone to noble sentiments. The people are not cunning or sufficiently artful to not open the secrets of their hearts in such undisciplined circumstances. Thus, the minds of all are laid bare and unprotected. On the next day they reconsidered, and a sound account is taken of both discussions. They debate when they are incapable of fabrication but they decide when they cannot err. . . . If you indulge their drunkenness by supplying them with as much as they desire, they will be conquered more easily than by arms. *Germania* 22–23

Tacitus also comments on gambling customs:

> Aleam, quod mirere, sobrii inter seria exercent, tanta lucrandi perdendive temeritate, ut, cum omnia defecerunt, extremo ac novissimo iactu de libertate ac de corpore contendant. Victus voluntariam servitutem adit: quamvis iuvenior, quamvis robustior adligari se ac venire patitur.

They play at dice—surprisingly enough—when they are sober, making it serious; and they are so reckless in their desire to win, however often they lose, that when everything is gone they stake their bodily liberty on a last decisive throw. A loser willingly undergoes slavery: even though he may be younger and stronger, he allows himself to be bound and sold. *Germania* 24

Instead of noble savages against whom Romans can measure their fall from grace, the *Germania* critiques German society for its lack of restraint and injustice. Untrammeled liberty threatens their community.

> luitur enim etiam homicidium certo armentorum ac pecorum numero recipitque satisfactionem universa domus, utiliter in publicum, quia periculosiores sunt inimicitiae iuxta libertatem. *Germania* 21

Even homicide can be atoned for by a fixed number of cattle or sheep, the compensation being received by the whole household. This is to the advantage of the community: for private feuds are most dangerous when there is liberty.

In a crucial concluding chapter, Tacitus ascribes the defeat of the Bructeri to German failings:

> pulsis Bructeris ac penitus excisis vicinarum consensu nationum, seu superbiae odio seu praedae dulcedine seu favore quodam erga nos deorum; nam ne spectaculo quidem proelii invidere. Super sexaginta milia non armis telisque Romanis, sed, quod magnificentius est, oblectationi oculisque ceciderunt. Maneat, quaeso, duretque gentibus, si non amor nostri, at certe odium sui, quando urgentibus imperii fatis nihil iam praestare fortuna maius potest quam hostium discordiam.

> The Bructeri were defeated and almost destroyed by an alliance of neighboring tribes, either through hatred of their domineering pride or the desire for booty, or a special favor given to us by the gods. We were even permitted to witness the battle. More than 60,000 fell, not by Roman swords or javelins, but—more splendid still—as a spectacle before our delighted eyes. Long, I pray, may the peoples persist, if not in love for us, certainly in hating one another; since as fate is driving our empire, fortune can probide us with nothing better gift than emnity among our foes. *Germania* 33

Tacitus attributes the destruction of the Bructeri to base motives (hatred, pride, greed). Violence and passion conspire to bring destruction, with Tacitus and the Romans looking on. Ultimately, in spite of some positive qualities, Tacitus depicts the Germans as morally flawed, definitely strange, and politically naïve. Although Tacitus and his audience appear to stand apart from contemporary Roman society, the destruction of the Bructeri offers a unified Roman state the opportunity to celebrate. Ethical and political issues lurk within this text: the character of imperialism, the importance of *libertas*, and the nature of Rome as opposed to the barbarians. There is clearly an "us" in this text, but the character and ethical status of that "us" are obscure.

The *Germania* would seem to refuse simple polarities since, although the Germans are clearly read through Roman lenses, the portrayal is nuanced and complex. The Germans are not just a "mirror" to the imperial power in opposition to which Roman identity can be constructed. In the 'othering' of Rome, Tacitus and his audience are put in a "third place," but there is no doubt on which side of the border that place is located. Tacitus celebrates Roman victories, and the Germans are not a "familiar other," combining Roman and non-Roman characteristics. As in his treatment of time, the historian remains engaged with his contemporary society and does not retreat into nostalgia or spatial-cultural isolation.

The complexity of this position is also exposed in the *Agricola,* in which the ethical position of the barbarian opposing Roman imperial expansion is more fully explored and is counterpoised to the role of Agricola as an *exemplum* to the imperial age. Agricola's actions extended the reach of a morally corrupt, tyrannical empire. Understanding Agricola's position as ethical requires engaging with Tacitean ambivalence about the Empire and with the pragmatism which is such an important feature of Tacitean politics.

One of the more startling episodes in the *Agricola* is the speech of the British leader Calgacus (*Agricola* 30–32). Rousing his troops for the crucial battle against Agricola and his army at Mons Graupius, the battle which was the culmination of Agricola's conquest of Britain, Calgacus delivers a thorough critique of Rome and Roman imperialism. Not only is Calgacus' rhetoric fiery and seemingly persuasive, more vibrant in its imagery than the parallel speech that Agricola delivers to his own troops, but the specific charges made against the Romans by Calgacus are supported by the text of the *Agricola*. Calgacus accuses the Romans of a megalomaniacal desire for world conquest that pushes Roman power to its furthest limits; Agricola's strategic aim, as stated in *Agricola* 27, was indeed to reach the *terminum Britanniae* ("the very edge of Britain"), which in itself foreshadows Agricola's ambitious plan to take control of Ireland (*Agricola* 24). Calgacus claims that the sea offers no retreat or respite from Rome; *Agricola* 25 and 28 confirm Roman mastery of the sea lanes. Calgacus notes the historic precedent of successful rebellion, a rebellion reported in *Agricola* 16. Calgacus uses the case of Usipi, mutinous tribesmen recruited into the Roman army, as evidence of the fragile loyalty of the Roman forces; the mutiny is reported in *Agricola* 28. Calgacus attacks the destructive corruption, financial and sexual, of Rome; such corruption is detailed in *Agricola* 13 and 19, and in an anonymous speech on the verge of the Boudiccan rebellion in *Agricola* 15. This litany culminates in a startling characterization of the Romans:

> Raptores orbis, postquam cuncta vastantibus defuere terrae, mare scrutantur: si locuples hostis est, avari, si pauper, ambitiosi, quos non Oriens, non Occidens satiaverit: soli omnium opes atque inopiam pari adfectu concupiscunt. Auferre trucidare rapere falsis nominibus imperium, atque ubi solitudinem faciunt, pacem appellant.

> Ravagers of the world, after exhausting all lands with their destruction, they search the sea. If an enemy is wealthy, they are consumed by greed, if poor, by a need for glory, which neither East nor West has sated. For they

are only people who are equally aroused by wealth and poverty. To robbery, butchery and rape, they give the false name "empire," and where they make a desert, they call it "peace." *Agricola* 30

Yet even here, in the midst of rhetorical flights and apothegmatic conclusions, Calgacus recalls Tacitus' own summary of the impact of cultural change in Britain: *Idque apud imperitos humanitas vocabatur, cum pars servitutis esset* ("This was called 'culture' among the ignorant when it was part of their enslavement" [*Agricola* 21]).

Calgacus' speech summarizes the depiction of Roman imperialism in the *Agricola*, thus making it tempting to associate Tacitus with the views expressed by Calgacus. Rather uncomfortably, at this moment of Roman triumph, it appears to be the enemy of Rome, and not its hero, Agricola, who delivers the most accurate summation of the nature of Roman rule. At the very least, we have Tacitus speaking in the voice of the colonized, showing his ability to imagine himself on the other side of the ethnic and political divide. Tacitus' Calgacus is convincing as one of the very few subaltern voices in Roman literature.

Others have, of course, wrestled with its particular difficulty.[29] Katherine Clarke argues that Tacitus allows the Romans to appear as barbarian brigands while Calgacus and his men are repositories of Roman *virtus* and proper Latin usage. The process of acculturation results in an exchange of identities.[30] Agricola's victory is his crowning achievement, a dramatic high point of the work, but that victory entails the enslavement of these seeming British-Romans. Thus, the ethics of the *Agricola* and of Agricola himself become questionable. Clarke attempts to escape from this bind by seeing two Romes in conflict: "Calgacus is representative of the fact that Old Rome is to be found in the most remote parts of the Empire, or even beyond the Empire's bounds."[31] Rather than seeing the war as a conflict between Roman and barbarian, good and bad, Clarke argues that the conflict represents an inevitable clash of eras and is almost an allegory for political and cultural change in Rome. Locating the story in Britain, the little-known island in the ocean, creates a space separate from Rome in which Agricola can shine and traditional Roman virtues can be expressed. Britain is a place for political fantasies, a literary "other place and time"; it serves Tacitus as the "future"

---

29. D. Braund (1996) 168–69 suggests that Calgacus is in error because he is out of date: Agricola has reformed Roman government. Yet, this ignores the endemic nature of the corruption of Roman government.

30. Clarke (2001).

31. Clarke (2001) 106. In a rather similar way, one could argue that Saguntum in the *Punica* was representative of "Old Rome." Yet, the very process of locating Roman identity at a great distance from Rome itself and among the barbarians is both peculiar and potentially significant.

serves writers of science fiction, a world in which the concerns of the characters can be played out free from the confusing trappings of contemporary society.[32] Yet, Clarke's reading would seem to worsen the ethical position of Agricola himself. Tacitus' Agricola is the servant of imperialism and plays an active role in the extension of tyranny, but he is also the instrument of History's juggernaut, a man who serves the demands of a teleology in which the old virtues are necessarily lost. Clarke's interpretation radicalizes Tacitus' realism by making the activities of his hero amoral. History and power are on Agricola's side and nothing else matters. Yet Tacitus' Agricola is not Lucan's Caesar. Tacitus was not an amoralist who valued the efficient use and accumulation of political power above all else. He existed in a morally complex universe where understanding good and evil was difficult and required the sophisticated understanding of history that he himself could provide. Whatever else we may doubt, Agricola is shown as an ethical individual: even if he eventually served an immoral emperor (Domitian), Agricola's cause was just. Clarke, it seems to us, cannot have the answer to Calgacus' speech.

In important respects, Calgacus' analysis is correct; that analysis is supported in the rest of the text and the complaints about Roman rule would appear to relate to what moderns might call the deep structures of Roman power and its intrinsic oppressive nature. Yet, Calgacus makes a fundamental error: he misunderstands and misrepresents the nature of the Roman Empire. This error emerges not so much in the speech, with its claims to liberty (of which more later), but in a typically Tacitean contrast between words and action. Calgacus predicts that the Roman army will disintegrate due to its multi-ethnic nature. Further, the behavior of the Britons, both on the battlefield and in defeat, shows that they are not worthy defenders of an old-world freedom and virtue.

Calgacus' key evidence for the fragility of the Roman Empire is the revolt of the Usipi, detailed in *Agricola* 28. The Usipi were Germans who were enrolled into the army to serve in Britain. They were given a Roman centurion to lead them and a small number of Roman soldiers who were presumably there to inculcate discipline and model behavior. They were to be acculturated into the Roman army. Something, however, went wrong. The centurion and his Roman soldiers were murdered and the Usipi commandeered some boats and set sail for home. Unfortunately, they could not navigate and relied on three kidnapped sailors to do this for them. When one of these escaped, the Usipi killed the other two; but then had no way of getting home. Without a realistic alternative, the Usipi became pirates but

---

32. It seems to us that the political "realism" of the account would argue against a strong temporal disassociation of Britain from the rest of the Empire.

with mixed success. Reduced to starvation, they turned to cannibalism and drifted over to Germany, where some were enslaved and ended up back in the Roman slave markets; thus the survivors were able to retell their story for the amusement of their new Roman masters. The Usipi combined barbarity, piracy, cannibalism, and, finally, servitude. Calgacus saw the Usipi as model Roman provincials and assumed that when Agricola's provincial troops came under pressure they would act in a similar way. But the Usipi were failed provincials, who rejected the tutelage of Rome and degenerated as a consequence.

Calgacus' second error lies not so much in his judgment of his enemy, but in his confidence in the virtue of his own men. As the Romans gained the upper hand on the battlefield, the British lost discipline and rationality (*Agricola* 37). The battle itself became incoherent. In various parts of the field, the Britons displayed contrasting behaviors. Some bravely charged superior forces, inevitably meeting their deaths. Others fled from inferior forces and were cut down in their rout. Eventually they rallied in the woods, but then lost all hope and fled in disorderly fashion, making them easy victims of the disciplined Romans. When the Romans called off the pursuit, some of the British warriors returned home (but burned their own houses in rage). Others went into hiding, but immediately abandoned their retreats. Some met to attempt a rally, but just as hastily deserted. Some murdered their own wives and children (*Agricola* 38). We do not see here the virtues of the old Romans, a people disciplined in their defense of freedoms and ancestral traditions, but disorder, indiscipline, irrationality, inconsistency, and rage, suicidal tendencies, wild bravery, and brazen cowardice. Calgacus and his men do not represent old Roman virtues, the last island of freedom whose loss is to be mourned, but *barbaritas;* they, not the Romans who defeat them, most closely resemble the Usipi.

The failings of the Britons, like those of the Usipi and those of the Germans in the *Germania,* mean that they cannot be used as models for Roman behavior; we are not presented with the noble savage so much as a savage who may, from time to time, do something noble. The Germans and Britons, very much like Silius' Hannibal, can stand outside Roman culture and offer critiques or provide a perspective on Rome, but there is, in the end, no doubt that Tacitus stands with Agricola, as Silius stands with Scipio, in cheering the victories of Rome.

But if Calgacus is wrong about the Romans and their army, there is little doubt that he is right that the *imperium* of Rome meant the end of freedom, which leaves Agricola's ethical role in doubt. There is, as Clarke argues, a possible chronological argument, but Agricola's achievements go beyond correcting an anachronism (tidying up time) and thus fulfilling a teleological requirement for Roman imperial conquest. While, as we have argued, it seems that Tacitus foresaw death for those who refused to live in the present and face the pragmatic changes of the imperial epoch, Britain existed beyond the Empire, and beyond its chronological parameters. Agricola's conquests may have been the work of History, but that does not free him from ethical responsibility. Agricola is no Caesar. Instead, this forcible exchange of liberty for servitude must have an ethical quality which to us is obscure and we need to understand how service to an Empire of Servitude can be seen as justified.

Agricola 21 discusses the politics of acculturation in the Roman empire:

> Sequens hiems saluberrimis consiliis absumpta. Namque ut homines dispersi ac rudes eoque in bella faciles quieti et otio per voluptates adsuescerent, hortari privatim, adiuvare publice, ut templa fora domos extruerent, laudando promptos, castigando segnis: ita honoris aemulatio pro necessitate erat. Iam vero principum filios liberalibus artibus erudire, et ingenia Britannorum studiis Gallorum anteferre, ut qui modo linguam Romanam abnuebant, eloquentiam concupiscerent. Inde etiam habitus nostri honor et frequens toga; paulatimque discessum ad delenimenta vitiorum, porticus et balinea et conviviorum elegantiam. Idque apud imperitos humanitas vocabatur, cum pars servitutis esset.

> The following winter was spent on schemes of improvement. For since the men were dispersed and primitive, they were easily roused to war, and he wished to make them quiet and peaceful through comforts. Privately, he encouraged, and publicly he helped so that they built temples, fora, and houses. He praised the eager, and castigated the slow. Thus, desire for honor supplanted force. Now, indeed, he educated the son of the chiefs in liberal arts and preferred the talent of the British to the studiousness of the Gauls, so that instead of rejecting Latin, they desired eloquence in it. Even our clothes were honored and the toga was often worn; and little by little, they were given up to the seductions of moral weakness, the porticos, the baths, the elegant entertainments. This was called "culture" among the ignorant when it was part of their enslavement. Tacitus, *Agricola* 21

Humanitas, suggestive of "civilization," "living like a human" (as opposed to an animal), or "culture," is identified with living in the city by the ignorant ones. In exchange for freedom, the empire offers the barbarians an escape from dispersal and warfare, with the added bonus of the accoutrements of Roman culture. Although Tacitus condemns Roman imperialism, the alternative—anti-social dispersal and violence and living like Calgacus and his people—is not attractive. Unfortunately, Tacitus does not tell us what true *humanitas* is or where it is located. The engagement with Roman culture is not depicted as a falsity, an assumption of an unreal 'imitation' of Romanity on the edge of the Empire by which to seduce the provincials, but rather as an adoption of customs and institutions at the heart of Roman culture. It is that culture which demanded the loss of individual liberty. The barbarians' enslavement was not a result of the loss of their own culture, in a kind of shameful political trick on the part of Agricola, but was an integral part of their adoption of Roman customs: Agricola was making Romans.

Calgacus made the assumption that if someone was German, African, or British, he could not be Roman. They would thus not risk their lives for their conquerors, for the foreigners who led them. In this, he was spectacularly wrong. The extent of Calgacus' error is demonstrated by the battle. The victory was achieved not by the legions, which remained as a tactical reserve, but by the allied troops, the very forces that Calgacus had claimed would fragment (*Agricola* 35).[33] These allied troops chased the Britons across the battlefield, showed courage and resourcefulness, displayed the discipline characteristic of Roman troops, and emerged as representatives of Roman values. The *Agricola* can thus be seen as a story of imperial integration. Calgacus, and one presumes at least some of Tacitus' audience, found the transformation from barbarian to Roman accomplished by the troops to be somewhat unlikely. Yet Tacitus represents it as real and fundamental and this problem takes us to the heart of a debate about the nature of Roman ethnic identity.

Outside the *Agricola*, perhaps the most explicit Tacitean discussion of Roman ethnicity comes in *Annales* XI 23–25, for C.E. 48. This is a Tacitean version of a debate in which the emperor Claudius argued for the inclusion in the Senate of the leaders of certain tribes from Central and Northern Gaul (Gallia Comata).[34] This aroused opposition since the Gauls were historic enemies of Rome; the Gallic sack in the fourth century B.C.E., Gallic raids into Italy, and the wars to take control of Gallia Cisalpina were some of the darkest moments of Roman history. Nevertheless, Claudius argued that the Romans were not consanguineous. They had different origins and were the

---

33. It is puzzling for conventional accounts that Tacitus attributes the victory not to the "core" troops of the Roman legions, but to the auxiliaries. One could see this as another element of Agricola's virtue: that he was out to preserve Roman lives (though Roman generals were not notably squeamish) or even as a reflection of historical fact. We, however, would read this as a central element in the ideology of the text. We see it as a demonstration of the superiority of the provincial Romans over the barbarians.

34. Unusually, we have a documentary version of Claudius' speech: *ILS* 212. Whereas the Tacitean account covers the oration in summary, the inscription was a verbatim account, from which we have little more than the introduction.

creation of a political union of various peoples. For Claudius, the incorporation of outsiders into Rome could be traced back to the time of Romulus, with most cases resulting in gradual assimilation; the natural conclusion was that, in time, the Gauls would seem to be Roman too. Claudius's ancestor Clausus had joined Rome in the eighth century B.C.E, just as the Gauls were now being invited to join Rome. Thus, the people of Gallia Comata were no different from the Etruscans and the Volsci, the Sabines and Greeks of Southern Italy.³⁵

The antiquarianism of the speech is characteristic of Claudius and recalls three rather odd episodes from earlier in *Annales* XI. XI 11 tells us that Claudius held the secular games a mere sixty-four years after those held by Augustus. Secular games were supposed to be held when all those who had the chance to see the previous set of games had passed on, but Claudius engaged in an arcane chronological dispute with Augustus as to how the time between the secular games should be calculated. In the same year, he decided to introduce three new letters into the Latin alphabet, an innovation that failed. His decision was based on research into the formation of alphabets, which he decided was an evolutionary process and one that should continue (XI 13–14). In XI 15, Tacitus tells us that Claudius introduced a college of *haruspices* (diviners) to preserve the "oldest Italian skill" (*vetustissima Italiae disciplina*) which was specifically the preserve of leading Etruscans. Interspersed with these stories are accounts of Claudius' attempts to restore the morals of Rome, of the adulteries of his wife Messalina, and of the rise of Nero. Claudius's antiquarianism strikes an odd note. While Rome lurched towards debauchery, the emperor attempted to reform the alphabet; while his wife was (allegedly) wildly promiscuous, Claudius studied ancient Italian arts of prophecy. His antiquarianism is everywhere read as a foolish inability to see what was under his nose, an indication that he was living in a remote past and not in the moral abyss of contemporary Rome. It is very tempting to read his oration on Gallic citizenship in the same way.

As with Calgacus' speech, we are faced with an oration which is not necessarily wrong in any detail, but where the context calls the analysis into question. The opposing case is made anonymously. This senatorial voice argues that Italy could provide enough senators, and that the memory of a completely Roman senate was a glorious and well-established tradition that other Italians followed. Should the Gauls of Gallia Comata be allowed in the Senate, there would be no room for the poor senators of Latium. Rich provincials would inevitably replace old senatorial families. Both sides had

---

35. Roman identity is presented primarily a matter of legal status, even though Tacitus *(Annales* XI 24) gives Claudius a clause in which he makes reference to the mixing of "customs, arts, and families." Cf. Giardina (1994).

an argument from history, and it would seem that both sides agreed about the "facts." Claudius uses history to suggest that there are no fixed traditions of the Roman people and that the boundaries of Rome were continuously moving, while the anonymous senator argues that there was a core Roman people who shared a past and a land (Italy). Like most ethnicities, these ethnic origins are located in a distant antiquity and disputes over its nature are, in fact, arguments about history. The anonymous senator offers a Virgilian view of Romanity in which the Roman people were formed through the union of Italians and Romans (Trojans). Claudius rejects this. It is his view of history and of Roman identity as a continuously expanding category that inevitably triumphs. Imperial history overcomes Republican history and imperial models of Roman identity replace Republican understandings.

Calgacus' error was a failure to understand that being Roman was possible for the Gauls, Germans, and Britons who served in Agricola's army. Yet, this still does not offer an answer to the basic problem: why was it better to be subject to the imperial demoralization of luxurious Rome rather than remain a barbarian? Tacitus acknowledges the weaknesses of Rome, but still stands on the Roman side of the border, exulting in the slaughter of barbarians.

The idea of Rome that we find in Claudius' oration on the Gauls was, of course, the one that came to dominate because of the political authority that lay behind it, but it is also the idea of Rome that lies on the surface of the *Agricola*. Both reflect an open vision of imperial identity, in which there was acculturation; there was also considerable scope for the different peoples of the Empire to assimilate and to begin a journey towards Roman identity. It is on that path the Agricola sets the eager people of Britain. Yet, there is an inherent confusion in the Claudian account. The vision of Empire that Tacitus puts in Claudius' mouth is in many ways radical, in that it offers a prospective vision of Rome that extends far beyond the city, beyond Italy, and into the provinces. But in wrapping that policy in archaisms, Claudius misrepresents his radicalism. In making the Gauls Roman, Claudius rejects a substantial element in the Roman historical tradition (or Rome's collective memory). In that tradition, Rome and Italy were formed in conflict with the Gauls (as Gaul was formed in conflict with Rome). He also rejects the romanticized vision of the anonymous senator (and wonders whether the romanticism was meant to undercut the opinions given) and his Virgilian vision of a Rome and Italy unified by common values. As with his restoration of ancient Italian religious practices, Claudius fails to notice that in his archaism he is driving out the values of the old order. By his decisions, the poor Italian senators who had provided the moral backbone of the Roman state were to be pushed out, and that living connection with the past was to be lost. It was thus a step in the dissolution of a tradition, even as Claudius thought that he was maintaining a tradition. Even as Claudius attempted to restore archaic Rome, he was creating a new Empire in which the historic enemies of Rome would sit in a Senate from which the historic Romans would be excluded. Those Latin old Romans were lost in the vastness of this new Empire.

IMPERIAL FRAGMENTS

We find in these Roman imperial texts a structural analogy with the problems of modern imperial identity. Although there are, of course, radical differences between the Roman and modern experiences of empire, we find that the similarities lie in a problematization of the nature of empire and in the relationship between the ideological structures of empire and other levels of the symbolic economy.

The politics of the nation emerged with the modern era alongside that other great modern notion 'civilization' and with the development of European imperialism. In the 'discovery' of non-European peoples, a unitary ladder of civilization emerged in which various nations occupied different chronological development rungs. In understanding history and geography in this way, late eighteenth- and nineteenth-century intellectuals developed the idea of a cultural unit which had a shared past, shared values, and a shared political structure. The nation thus emerges as an imaginary community with a supposedly shared imaginary. In its essence, the nation is defined both positively (in shared values) and negatively (against those 'outside' who do not share those values) and with the 'othering' of the 'outside' and the shared values of the 'inside' the qualities of the citizen are established.[36] But there is no simple duality. The complexity arises in part from the varying degrees of 'otherness' and in part from the very process of 'othering' as an act of power. Postcolonial writers have emphasized the importance of the African and Oriental in the formation of European identity. Yet, in the process of self-definition, the 'other' is incorporated. This is in part because there is always an 'excess' in every identification that refuses assimilation, and an identification with the values of the citizen leaves an 'excess' of non-citizen values. As we have explored throughout the previous chapters, this excess encourages alienation, but in that alienation from the hegemonic symbolic economy there is an encouragement to identify with the other. Further, the

---

36. On the negative definition of ethnicity, see Yelvington (1991); Parsons (1975); Glazer and Moynihan (1975).

artificiality of the 'othering' means that the colonized are never quite what the colonizers believe them to be; they are always reacting to the discourses of the colonizers, or not accommodating the mythic role which these discourses have scripted for them. In these circumstances, the encounter with the other is always likely to unsettle colonial discourses. To accommodate the realities on the ground to the parameters of the discourse takes a great act of power and that power is applied to both the colonized and the colonists.

In creating the imperial citizen, modern discourses established divisions in time and space. The modern man who came to run the empire deployed the available technologies of power to advance the modernity of empire. In making the modern world, a temporal division operated between the world that was, and is, modern and that which was following the teleological path towards modernity. In this we find some parallels with Clarke's argument about Calgacus' speech and the issues of time therein. But that spatial-temporal division between the old world and that which must come was also a division between public and private within the symbolic economy. The symbolic economy relies upon a memory that embeds its workings: it is difficult to imagine a symbolic economy that has no historic depth. Yet, the modern always claims to be severing itself from tradition, turning all that is solid into air, in a continuous process of revolutionary change. The space of tradition is the space of privacy, in which the continuous revolution of modernity is allowed pause. In this space, religious belief, sexual behaviour, family ties, and friendships are allowed play, whereas in the public arena, the disciplines of modernity should have hegemony. As postcolonial writers have maintained, that idealized division between the rationalist, secular public world and the 'cultural' private world survived the end of European colonialism and remains a dominant feature of the liberal system.

The continuous revolutions of the modern seem to us to have had a paradoxical effect. They have created a global system, an imperial symbolic economy, but the content of that symbolic economy is slight. To put it in terms of our previous chapter, the modern Chronos has a very limited scope, but an extended territory. Thus, modern man is placeless and stateless, moving through the global village, either virtually or corporally. Because modern man can be anywhere in this global village, he is perpetually nowhere; there is no place for him. This dislocation in modernity is not just a feature of global corporatism, high-class tourism, and borderless cyberlands, but also of mass migrations and the consequent reduction in political and communal integration. The displacing of individuals takes people out of the spaces of their symbolic economies, and in so doing reduces their identities, perhaps even to the level of what Agamben terms Homo Sacer,[37] the bare man,

---

37. Agamben (1998).

rootless, stateless, rightless, and frequently "illegal." From this derives the systemic alienation in modernity and also the psychological requirement to create traditions and identities in nostalgia, which are often paper-thin in a postmodernist mode. Yet, this perpetual alienation and achievement of identity is not inimical to modernity but allied with it. The politics of the nation emerged not in opposition to the modern imperial paradigm, but at that same time. The modern man can exist in the global village precisely because all identities are allowed there; supported by modern technologies, reinforced by discourses, and always confined by the enabling modern. Yet, precisely because all cultures are allowed within the modern (within limits), the modern can be presented as apolitical, secularist, uninterested in the worlds of subaltern cultures, provided that the field is left clear for the untrammelled operation of modernity. In its proclaimed disinterest in cultural values, modernity reduces man to the Homo Sacer, the unit of life. 'Culture,' 'religion,' 'family,' and all that builds identity must happen off stage, in private. We are all, then, living in a 'third space,' neither barbarians outside the Empire, nor in an Empire which has no space for us.

In this position, we recognize our shared 'alterity' to the modern world, and face a political choice. We may embrace the shared experience of alterity, allow barriers to decay, and trust to new emergent, social formations in which the integrity of those others is recognized, or to reject the 'other' in order to reinforce our own specific alterities. In so doing, we could reject the polarities of citizens and barbarians, polarities which bring the Homo Sacer into existence. But this would run against the rhetoric of political powers who seek to reassert simplified polarities and collective memories and to establish narratives of identities in spite of all experience to the contrary. It seems to us that the myths of nation are maintained in full consciousness of their mythic quality, in part because there is no viable alternative. It is this consciousness of falsity that renders the rhetoric uncertain; it is a similar uncertainty which we detect in the rhetoric of Roman and barbarian in our ancient texts.

We have uncovered a considerable reluctance in Silius and Tacitus to work entirely within the dichotomies of Roman and barbarian. That reluctance was manifested in a presentation of the barbarian as having some admirable, or Roman, qualities, and also in a contrary presentation of the Roman as being far from ideal. Neither typology appears comfortable in the texts. There is a disassociation from the polarities and from the myths that should build the community of Rome, and in this disassociation there is a third space, not entirely comfortable with Rome, but not barbarian. It is this partial disassociation which seems to us to allow Agricola a certain ethical space. For in bringing the Britons into the Empire, Agricola does not enforce a demoralization, but instead establishes conditions in which the Britons could find that third space. They share the same slavery as Tacitus and Agricola, but they are also in a position to perceive that place as slavery, and hence disassociate themselves from the imperial symbolic economy. Further, the nature of that symbolic economy, the bathhouses, the dinner parties and the public architecture, is also very slight, offering again an analogy with the modern imperial systems: it is in the technology of Roman life, not its myths and stories, that Rome now lies. To become Roman requires visiting the baths, a step not too difficult and not too destructive. Here lies the paradox which allows Agricola an ethical position. Agricola offers a technology of living that seems superior to that which the Britons had previously enjoyed, and the world of liberty in which they live is depicted as being fundamentally flawed. Here we may also think of the Germans: They exchange that liberty for the culture of Rome and resultant slavery, but that slavery is better than the freedom they previously enjoyed, and, in any case, the requirements of the enslaved are slight. The price of belonging to Rome is worth paying in part because it allows the option not to belong, to remain, like Agricola, ethically self-sufficient and to be good in a bad empire.

Our reading of the Claudian debate is then crucial to this position. The anonymous senator offers a Virgilian view of Rome, a view which, in our sense, could be called 'nationalistic.'[38] It is a myth that attempted to bind together a group formed of the peoples of Italy. But this was an insufficient myth for the imperial age and may even be said to be, like the modern notions of nation, in creative tension with the notions of empire. The emperor's personal political authority extended far beyond the boundaries of Italy. The emperor was as glad to patronize provincial elites as he was to provide support for the elites of Italy; the state provided security and financial benefits (control of taxation for instance) to urban elites wherever they lived. To invest in these political benefits, local elites needed to become part of the Roman nation, but in achieving that extension of Roman identity, the Italianate conception of Rome ceased to hold sway. It is this shift that we see taking place in the Claudian debate.

It seems to us that this was not an idea that emerged from Claudius' antiquarian research, but a stage in the political evolution of the idea of Rome: instead of a Rome based around a myth of shared Italian past, what emerges in the first century is a Rome centred on loyalty to the emperor. Although the elites of Italy may have wished otherwise, the most obvious symbol of Empire was the emperor himself, and it is the image of the Emperor that is the most obvious unifying element in the material culture of the Empire. This identification of state and emperor can be seen in the panegyrical poems of Statius: the emperor is a divine symbol, a conqueror of the barbarians, a

---

38. See Ando (2002) and Gruen (1993), esp. pp. 28–50.

man-god who surpasses all previous symbols of Roman history and greatness.[39] It is possible to read such sentiments ironically, but ironic readings are contingent on naïve readings. Agricolan loyalty to Domitian, the uneasy quiescence which Tacitus defends, becomes loyalty not so much to the despised man, but to the position and the symbolism of that position, which meant Rome.

Our readings of the ancient texts suggest to us that the idea of Rome that emerges in the first century is not a nationalistic myth, a dream with power to bind. Instead Rome has the symbolic minimalism of the modern imperial dream. But like the modern imperial symbolic, it seems to us that it allows space for other symbolic layers, like that Italico-Roman myth of Virgilian epic. Rome existed alongside other identities, binding them into a greater whole.[40] Yet, this is not to diminish the power of Roman identity. Neither Tacitus nor Silius, nor those soldiers who fought for Rome at Mons Graupius had seemingly any lack of commitment to the Roman cause. The power of this reduced idea of Rome is reflected in Tacitus' description of it as *humanitas*, being human. The alternative is, inevitably, not being human: being a barbarian. Although Rome lacks a transcendent idea, the alternatives to Rome, the Germans, the historic Carthaginians, the Caledonians, do not appear attractive. Even if Agricola is a servant to a failed state, it is a

---

39. In *Silvae* I 1, Statius, writing on an equestrian statue of Domitian erected in the Forum, compares Domitian favorably with Aeneas and Hector (13), and with Mars (18). The steed is a symbolic of mythic power and of great natural force, which Domitian only can control (54), that master being a "star" (55). Domitian is Germanicus, conqueror of the Dacians (55–57). In the second half of the poem, the mythic hero Curtius rises to acclaim the statue (74–75) and then compares his own act of self-sacrifice in saving Rome (riding his rather unfortunate horse into a chasm that was opening in the floor of the Forum as an act of dedication to the gods) unfavorably with those of Domitian (79–81). Statius proclaims the immortality of the statue, its immortality matching that of Rome, and of the gods, who will welcome Domitian eventually. We are told that the statue is a gift of senate and people (91–100). Thus, emperor, senate and people, Roman human and divine, ages past and ages to come, are bound together in praise of the emperor and his statue. Similar themes are visible in other Statian panegyrics. In IV 2 Statius feasts with the *regnator terrarum orbisque subacti,/ magne parens . . . spes hominum, . . . cura deorum* ("ruler of lands, conqueror of the world, the great parent, the hope of men, and the care of the gods" [1.14–15]). Domitian shines with a visage that barbarians and unknown tribes would have recognized (38–45). Statius offers us an empire that is held together by the person of the emperor.

40. One of the issues that have puzzled historians is the seeming continuity of local ethnic traditions and indeed a perceived revival of those traditions in the late first and early second centuries within the context of what appears to have been a rapid cultural and political homogenization of Italy. Bradley (2000), for example, shows that ancient Umbria in this period displayed both cultural change and ethnic continuity. He argues that "what this requires us to do . . . is disentangle ethnic identity from culture and politics." It seems to us, rather, that this survival and perhaps revival reflect the "incomplete" nature of *Romanitas* as a nationalistic ideology. It thus created very little friction with preexisting ethnic customs (as long as they could be assimilated within the Roman system) and provided the conceptual space in which individuals could revive and explore local identities. See also Lomas (1991; 1995).

better failed state than the alternatives. Even if the dream of Rome is hardly credible, Rome is a state in which it is more possible to be human. This is achieved by adopting that "third place" which is not quite assimilated into any ideological system, in which Roman is served, from where it might just be possible to live ethically.[41]

Tacitus, it seems to us, offers a Faustian pact, that is, an ethical position which is in service to a corrupt regime, but which saves itself by assuming a distance from that regime. That pact is justified by the absence of a viable alternative. Rome is the least bad option. This is a familiar line. Parts of the modern symbolic economy are frequently justified by this pragmatism. We know that the system is not perfect, that it is unfair in many ways and produces or tolerates economic inequalities and injustices on an extraordinary scale, but what is the alternative? As a minimalistic justification of Empire, it is an argument that works, but only until there is an alternative. The empty heart of the imperial symbolic is always longing for the idea that will fill its void.

---

41. See, here, Žižek (2000) 70–124 and his vision of the "ticklish subject," the individual who is never quite content with his or her identifications.

7
Epilogue

This book is an experiment in reading without rules. We read across genres and, to a certain extent, across periods. We read in conjunction with texts of modernity, and texts of contemporary philosophy. We read open to connections and resonances. We read to explore texts which surprise and even shock. We read the literature not as explorations, mappings so to speak, of a known landscape on which we can create a palimpsest of commentaries that establish firm meanings, but as experiences of a foreign country in which the unknown and possibly unknowable are emphasized. We are familiar with experiencing the foreign country that is the past through the texts, but we seek to restore the ancient experience of alterity, in which our texts seem to display a distancing, or alienation, from ancient contemporary life. It is that alterity that is central to our interpretation. In that distancing, which allows the Romans to see themselves as living in a foreign land, we find resonance and understanding. For that distancing would in part seem to echo the contemporary experience of modernity, but also the modern experience of antiquity.

It seems to us that a great deal of classical scholarship is anxious to maintain a distance between antiquity and the history of the present, focusing on the particularity and peculiarity of ancient societies. This perception is based on a conception of the past as divided into semi-discrete blocks; although antiquity was continuously rediscovered, it was never relived. Antiquity thus has a discrete presence within modernity, always there, but always other. And yet, that would seem to correspond to our desultory experience of the modern, as we argued in the last chapter. The representation of modernity as new, as tearing apart all that is old, both denies historical roots and, in its self-representation, creates a fundamental breach with the 'remote' past but also with the immediate past, with the past of memory. The relevance of classics to the modern would seem to exist in reception, but not in analogy. Classical scholars (are expected to) fear anachronism and are aware of the differences that divide us from the past. They thus honor those differences as culturally fundamental almost as a point of ideology. In terms of historical method, attempting to understand antiquity on its own terms, however naïve, would seem a scientific and defensible position; certainly a safer stance than its alternatives. In this book, however, we have argued for connections; we have argued that we should explicitly read antiquity as moderns, through the understandings of the world that modernity provides us with. We honor the historical specificity of antiquity, but suggest that it is necessary and inevitable that we connect those ancient texts with the texts of Modernity. In so doing, we honor the resonances that make antiquity a place of fascination. For us, the selves that were constructed in antiquity were not so different and the differences in the symbolic economy, striking though they are, do not render the ancients unassailably foreign. The past may be a foreign country, but it is filled with people recognizable, familiar, and compatriots in the human condition.

Thus, in this engagement of the classical and modern, we argue for the relevance of, and a relationship to, classics not in the sense that the classics are received in the modern and thus form part of the archeology of knowledge of the modern, nor in the sense that the classical is part of the archeological substratum of modern society (put a spade into the contemporary soul or modern politics and out will pop classical Athens).[1] We do not see the classics as a nostalgic refuge from the modern and still less as a spiritual Eden from which the modern has so sadly departed and from which it can be judged and found wanting. Rather we find in antiquity a resonance with, and a difference from, modernity that allows critical reflection. In honoring the differences, we find similarities. That familiarity comes not just from a contingency that makes the texts part of the history of the present. Our argument is for an analogous working of the ancient individual in his or her society. As the history of the past gives perspective on the present, so does the history of the present allow us to see more clearly the past. That communication, the conversation that we have been able to establish in this book, seems to us to be in itself of significance, not just as a reassertion of the importance and relevance of classics in the modern world, and thus as a denial of the absoluteness of the divisions between past and present and

---

1. Though, in not making these arguments, we are not necessarily disputing their validity.

of the uniqueness of the modern, but as a demonstration that to honor the strangeness of the past does not mean that we are unable to draw experience, knowledge, and understanding from that past.

Yet, in exploring the fissures in our texts, our intention has been to defamiliarize antiquity. We do not see the texts as in any way safe, or at least part of a safely encoded world in which the scholar can work away happily and in confidence that the insecurities and uncertainties of modernity are remote. Rather than quietly archiving away the discordant voices within the established categories of systematic thought, locating them within genres and typologies, establishing the traditions in which they can comfortably rest, we listen to their incoherence: the anger, the grief, the puzzlement, the doubt, the fear, the nostalgia. Our readings are more raw, seeking to understand the discomfort of the texts and to explore why they should discomfort us as much as they do. One can read Statius *Silvae* for his literary invention, his wit, his bejeweled use of language, his irony and inversions, for the display of intellectual and artistic brilliance, but when he grieves and his tears wash away his words, then what use is all his skill? We can see in Lucan a clever, angry, oppositional text, subverting imperial conventions, but in the blood and violence, in the hopelessness of Cato, the megalomania of Caesar, and the love of Pompey, we have more complicated, subtle, disturbing messages of life in an imperial age. Tacitean rhetoric and artistry, his narrative energy and damning analysis make the *Annales* especially a work of historiographic brilliance, but without the sense of a satisfactory answer to many of those big political questions that resonate through the work, culminating in that powerful question of what was *humanitas* in contemporary life. In Silius, Lucan, and Tacitus, History is a dangerous and difficult phenomenon. And for Pliny, the man who seems so comfortable in his luxury and so complacent in his friends, we have such uncertainties that he seems obliged to display to us his bedroom and explain to us that no subversion takes place within those walls. He is a man so confident in himself that he hides away in the dark seeking his immortality while his household celebrate the Saturnalia, and finds it necessary to force the hedges round his villa to proclaim his identity, just in case anyone (and perhaps Pliny himself) might forget.

Across so many texts, and so many areas of life, there is a pervasive uncertainty. Technologies of friendship, the place of tradition, the function of history, the nature of society and an individual's place in it, the meaning of conjugality all generate concern. The contours of these problems may easily be mapped, and the landscape imagined, but description is rather more straightforward than explanation. The problems afflicting the texts do not appear to stem from a single point of crisis. It is obvious that the rise of the imperial state underpins much of what we have been discussing, but that imperial state was in itself a complex phenomenon, reacting to, as well as producing, ideological issues. The emergence of the Emperor as the dominant figure has traditionally been seen as the epoch-making event, but it would seem simplistic to trace the debates in Roman society back to this constitutional issue, and indeed to invest overly in constitutionalism as the motor of historical development. Although the loss of power was undoubtedly felt by at least some within the senatorial order, and this was a particular vocal group well represented in our surviving material, those affected were a very small element within Roman society. The analogy with modernity helps here. The issues of modernity are clearly interlinked, but multi-causal. Although many reductionist analyses have been applied, from Marxism to Neo-liberalism, the multidimensionality of the issues of modernity would appear to render an explanation dependent on constitutional form both crude and implausible. Given the nature of our texts, and, indeed, much of the surviving political thought from antiquity, it is tempting to make all societal issues flow from the imperial court. However, it seems rather more plausible, as we argued especially in chapter 2 and, as, we think, follows from our analyses of the histories of the "great men," to see the imperial court as equally caught up in the ebb and flow of history, subject to its entrapments and anxieties. It makes rather more sense to see, for instance, the innovations of the Neronian court as responses to the shifting certainties of Roman society rather than as causes of that uncertainty.

Our project, then, retains a Foucauldian element in refusing a reductionist emphasis on sovereignty and instead maintaining a focus on "biopower," the way in which power is deployed in society to create, maintain, and discipline the self.[2] It seems to us that all societies must maintain these biopolitical regimens in order to function, and it follows that freedom, in anything but a narrowly constitutional definition, is almost inconceivable. Freedom from the biopolitical regimen, in which power is most felt, would entail a level of psychic and social anarchy that would render existence problematic for the individual and for society. The "Great Man" who can step beyond convention and enact the voice of History, is, on this view, either a delusion or, in many senses of the word, insane; this insanity is dramatized by our ancient sources. Nonetheless, it seems to us that the Foucauldian project, in exposing the artificiality of the regimens of biopolitical control, has that freedom return in alienation. If we can choose between biopolitical regimens, if they no longer bind and we are aware of their artificiality, do we

---

2. See Agamben (1998), who argues that (early) Foucault saw a fundamental distinction between modernity and antiquity in that modernity included "bare life" within the regime of politics, and that this position is in need of correction. Arguably, that correction occurs in Foucault (1985; 1986), and would allow us to deploy the concept of "bio-power" in relation to antiquity.

not immediately stand in alienation from the biopolitical regimen, a regimen that no longer enjoys credibility?

It follows from our argument that all societies are at all times in tension. The tension stems from a psychological alienation, which we presume would vary in intensity in different societies, from the emergences of the Real which act as a perpetual threat to the individual and society, and, additionally, from the competition between individuals (the natural friction) within society. The principal difference between societies would seem, in a Foucauldian analysis, to be aesthetic.[3] If, ultimately, we are mapping "the human condition" as reflected in the literature of our period, then, it seems to us, our work has considerable value since it reduces the uniqueness of the modern and reinforces a transhistorical humanity. We, however, lay claim to a closer analogy with the modern. Much of the response to the modern centers on the prevalence of change, an assumption that, in this work, we are engaged in partially undermining. We see in our texts not just a response to historical change (a fact which all Roman historiography appears acutely aware), in which what was old and trusted seemed no longer to apply; we think that there is a great deal more going on than an awareness that the old discourses of identity might no longer apply, that the Virgilian-Augustan Golden Age (itself mythic in this context) could not be relived in an age seemingly debased. Instead, we see an awareness of the pervasive and flawed nature of the biopolitical regimen, that individuals are controlled by that regimen, and that not only is that control discomforting (in representing a limitation on freedom), but escape from it is unlikely. Throughout our chapters, we have found characters seeking moments of escape and redemption, but they are continuously reclaimed by the regimen. We use a variety of terms, but whether we describe this regimen as the biopolitical order, the symbolic economy, or History, that order stalks the imperial world, destroying Republican nostalgia, dragging lovers from island or domestic exile, or annexing frontier tribes to the Roman way. The problem is not that Roman order is broken, but that the biopolitical system is so powerful that subversion or escape is impossible, which is one of the major conclusions of our last chapter.

In many ways our ancient texts respond to the dominance of the imperial regimen in more subtle and realistic ways than their modern counterparts. Although historiographical and critical traditions seek to uncover opposition and subversion (and sometimes portray the Empire as more politically united as a result of the absence of obvious, organized oppositional forces), one would be hard pressed to produce ancient texts that called for revolution

---

3. We use 'aesthetic' in its postmodern sense which would enclose notions of the ethical.

or even counterrevolution. Complaints about the Empire may be many and can be recovered from our texts. Laments of the loss of liberty and contempt for despotism are common, but in the face of the juggernaut of History that brought about Empire, these laments have little obvious political result: they lament something that cannot, in the real world of rational, commonsense people, be changed. For all the alienation we have detected, we find no urge to revolution in our texts, and this absence cannot just be the result of a political (self-)censorship. Unlike so much modernist political radicalism (but perhaps in modes similar to political debates of the last two decades), our texts lack Utopianism. The traditions of the Platonic Republic seem very distant from the political thought of our period. What survives and opposes the historical juggernaut is not Utopian militancy (and we may think of Tacitus' seeming skepticism in the face of Republican traditionalists), but—and this appears repeatedly—the individual human bond, the bond of love. We see this survival in the stories of grief, in the palace of Argos, in the mourning on the fields of battle, in Pompey on Lesbos. These narratives of affect allow a distancing from the narratives of History, providing moments of resistance and redemption. Instead of revolutions, these minor revolts are assertions of distance from the symbolic economy; they survive the crushing of the individuals as scars or marks in the symbolic economy, as memories that cannot easily be assimilated. The stones resist. The memory of love lives on. These minor revolts have a spectral presence, like the ghost of a loved one who refuses death. It is in that refusal to be subsumed within the symbolic economy that an assertion of humanity is preserved. The question is not Utopian—there are no Platonic perfections, no waiting for the Messiah who will solve all problems—but rather how to live more humanly in these times. It takes us back to Tacitus and his consideration, one of the few explicit considerations in all Roman literature, of what it was to be Roman. In the *Agricola* he notes that the unwary identified *humanitas* with a material culture, when that culture, that biopolitical order, was servitude. But, and by implication, *humanitas* lay elsewhere; not with the Roman and certainly not with the barbarian; not in the identification with empire or a nostalgic reverie, but in some other place of personal, socially alienated ethics. The ethical community could only be found in the disengagement from society.

THAT IS THE PARADOX the Romans of the first century c.e. faced. In finding the spectral presence of humanity outside the symbolic economy, in the gaps and fissures in History, there is both hope and potential for change.

Bibliography

Adorno, T and Horkheimer M. (1979) *Dialectic of Enlightenment*, tr. J. Cumming (London and New York).
Agamben, G. (1998) *Homo Sacer: Sovereign Power and Bare Life*, tr. D. Heller-Roazen (Stanford).
Ahl, F. (1976) *Lucan: An Introduction* (Ithaca).
Ando, C. (2002) "Vergil's Italy: Ethnography and Politics in First-Century Rome." In D. S. Levene and D. P. Nelis (eds.) *Clio and the Poets. Augustan Poetry and the Traditions of Ancient Historiography* (Leiden and Boston) 123–42.
Armstrong, I. (2000) *The Radical Aesthetic* (Oxford).
Armstrong, R. H. (2005) *A Compulsion for Antiquity: Freud and the Ancient World* (Ithaca and London).
Badiou, A. (2001) *Ethics: An Essay on the Understanding of Evil*, tr. P. Halliward (London and New York).
———. (2005) *Handbook of Inaesthetics*, tr. A Toscano (Stanford).
Barakońska, L. and Nitka, M. (1999) "The Forgetful Memory of Blanchot." In W. Kalaga and T. Rachwal. (eds.) *Memory, Remembering, Forgetting* (Frankfurt).
Bartsch, S. (1994) *Actors in the Audience: Theatricality and Doublespeak from Nero to Hadrian* (Cambridge, MA and London).
———. (1997) *Ideology in Cold Blood. A Reading of Lucan's* Civil War (Cambridge, MA and London).
Bassett, E. L. 1966. "Hercules and the Hero of the *Punica*." In L. Wallach (ed.) *The Classical Tradition: Literary and Historical Studies in Honor of C. Caplan* (Ithaca) 258–73.
Batinsky, E. (1993) "Julia in Lucan's Tripartite View of the Republic." In M. Deforest (ed.) *Woman's Power, Man's Game* (Wauconda, IL).
Behler, E. (1996) "Nietzsche in the Twentieth Century." In B. Magnus and K. M. Higgins (eds.) *The Cambridge Companion to Nietzsche* (Cambridge) 281–322.
Beike, D. (2004) (ed.) *Self and Memory* (New York and Hove, UK).
Benhabib S. (1994) "The Critique of Instrumental Reason." In S. Žižek (ed.) *Mapping Ideology* (London, New York) 66–92.

Bentley, G. C. (1987) "Ethnicity and Practice." *Comparative Studies in Social History* 29: 24–55.
Benvenuto, B., and R. Kennedy. (1986) *The Works of Jacques Lacan: An Introduction* (London).
Bergren, A. (1983) "Language and the Female in Early Greek Thought." *Arethusa* 16: 69–95.
Bergson, H. (1912) *Matter and Memory*, tr. N. P. Paul and W. S. Palmer (London).
Bourdieu, P. (1977) *Outline of a Theory of Practice* (Cambridge).
———. (1990a) *In Other Words: Essays towards a Reflexive Sociology* (Oxford).
———. (1990b) *The Logic of Practice* (Cambridge).
Boyle, A., and W. J. Dominik. (eds.) (2003) *Flavian Rome. Image, Culture, Text* (Leiden).
Boyle, A. (2003) "Reading Flavian Rome." In A. Boyle and W. J. Dominik (eds.) (2003) 1–67.
Bradley, G. (2000) *Ancient Umbria: State, Culture and Identity in Central Italy from the Iron Age to the Augustan Era* (Oxford).
Bradley, K. R. (1991) "Dislocation in the Roman family." In idem, *Discovering the Roman Family* (New York and Oxford) 125–55.
Braund, D. (1996) *Ruling Roman Britain: Kings, Queens, Governors and Emperors from Julius Caesar to Agricola* (London and New York).
Braund, S. (1996) "Ending Epic: Statius, Theseus, and a Merciful Release?" In *Proceedings of the Cambridge Philological Society* 42: 1–23.
Brennan, T. (1998) "The Old Stoic Theory of Emotions." In Sihvola and Engberg-Pedersen (1998) 21–72.
Bruner, J., and C. Fleisher Feldman (1995) "Group Narrative as a Cultural Context of Autobiography" in Rubin (ed.) 291-317.
Cascardi, A. (1992) *The Subject of Modernity* (Cambridge).
Castel, R. (1994) "'Problematization' as a mode of Reading History." In J. Goldstein (ed.) *Foucault and the Writing of History* (Oxford, Cambridge, MA) 237–52.
Castells, M. (1977) *The Urban Question: A Marxist Approach* (London).
de Certeau, M. (1988) *The Writing of History*, tr. T. Conley (New York and Chichester).
Champlin, E. (1991) *Final Judgements: Duty and Emotion in Roman Wills 200 B.C.–A.D. 250* (Berkeley and Oxford).
Chanter, T., and E. Ziarek (eds.) (2005) *Revolt, Affect, Collectivity. The Unstable Boundaries of Kristeva's Polis* (New York).
Chartier, R. (1994) "The Chimera of the Origin: Archaeology, Cultural History, and the French Revolution." In J. Goldstein (ed.) *Foucault and the Writing of History* (Oxford and Cambridge, MA) 167–86.
Clarke, K. (2001) "An Island Nation: Re-reading Tacitus' *Agricola*." *JRS* 91: 94–112.
———. (2002) "*In arto et inglorius labor*: Tacitus's anti-history." In A. Bowman, H.M. Cotton, M. Goodman, and S. Price (eds.) *Representations of Empire: Rome and the Mediterranean World* (Proceedings of the British Academy, 114) (Oxford) 83–103.
Classen, C. J. (1998) "Tacitus—Historian between Republic and Principate." *Mnemosyne* 41: 93–116.
Cohen, D., and R. Saller (1994) "Foucault and Sexuality in Greco-Roman Antiquity." In J. Goldstein (ed.) *Foucault and the Writing of History* (Oxford and Cambridge, MA) 35–59.
Collingwood, R. G. (1994) *The Idea of History*. Rev. ed. (Oxford, and New York).
Confino, A. (1997) "Collective Memory and Cultural History." *American Historical Review* 102.5: 1386–1403.

Connerton, P. (1989) *How Societies Remember* (Cambridge).
Conte, G. B. (1986) *The Rhetoric of Imitation. Genre and Poetic Memory in Virgil and Other Poets* (Ithaca).
Cooper, J. (1992) "An Aristotelian Theory of the Emotions." In A. Rorty (ed.) (1992) 238–57.
Cornell, D. (1992) *The Philosophy of the Limit* (New York).
Cowan, R. (forthcoming) *Indivisible Cities: Mirrors of Rome in Silius Italicus.*
Crotty, K. (1994) *The Poetics of Supplication: Homer's* Iliad *and* Odyssey (Ithaca).
Davidson, A. I. (1994) "Ethics as Ascetics: Foucault, the History of Ethics and Ancient Thought." In J. Goldstein (ed.) *Foucault and the Writing of History* (Oxford, Cambridge, MA) 63–80.
Deleuze, G. (1990) *The Logic of Sense*, tr. M. Lester with C. Stivale (London).
Deleuze, G., and F. Guatarri (1984) *Anti-Oedipus: Capitalism and Schizophrenia*, tr. R. Hurley, M. Seem, and H. R. Lane (London).
Detwiler, B. (1990) *Nietzsche and the Politics of Aristocratic Radicalism* (Chicago and London).
Dreyfus, H. L. (2003) "'Being and Power' Revisited." In A. Milchman and A. Rosenberg (2003a) (eds.) *Foucault and Heidegger: Critical Encounters* (Minneapolis) 30–54.
Dietrich, J. (1999) "Thebaid's Feminine Ending." *Ramus* 28.1: 40–53.
Dominik, W. J. (2003) "Hannibal at the Gates: Programmatising Rome and Romanitas in Silius Italicus' Punica 1 and 2." In A. J. Boyle and W. J. Dominik (eds.) *Flavian Rome. Culture, Text, Image* (Leiden and Boston) 469–97.
Eagleton, T. (2005) *Holy Terror* (Oxford).
Edwards, C. (1997) "Self-Scrutiny and Self-Transformation in Seneca's Letters." *Greece and Rome* 44: 23–38.
Edwards, C., and G. Woolf (eds.) (2003) *Rome the Cosmopolis* (Cambridge).
Eldred, K (2000) "Poetry in Motion: The Snakes of Lucan." *Helios* 27: 63–74.
Fantham, E. (1999) "The Role of Lament in the Growth and Death of Roman Epic." In M. Beissinger et al. (eds.) *Epic Traditions in the Contemporary World. The Poetics of Community* (Berkeley and London) 221–36.
Feeney, D. (1986) "Epic Hero and Epic Fable." *Comparative Literature* 38: 137–58.
———. (1991) *The Gods in Epic. Poets and Critics of the Classical Tradition* (Oxford).
Fivush, R. (2004) "The Silenced Self: Constructing Self from Memories Spoken and Unspoken." In Beike et al. (eds.) (2004): 75–93.
Fletcher, J., and A. Benjamin. (eds.) (1990) *Abjection, Melancholia, and Love. The Work of Julia Kristeva* (London and New York).
Fortenbaugh, W. W. (2003) *Aristotle on Emotion. A Contribution to Philosophical Psychology, Rhetoric, Poetics, and Politics and Ethics* (London).
Foucault, M. (1977) *Discipline and Punish: The Birth of the Prison*, tr. Alan Sheridan (London).
———. (1978) *The History of Sexuality I: Introduction* (London).
———. (1984) *The Foucault Reader*, ed. P. Rabinow (London).
———. (1985) *The Use of Pleasure: The History of Sexuality II* (London).
———. (1986) *The Care of the Self: The History of Sexuality III* (London).
———. (1987) *The Final Foucault*, eds. J. Bernauer and D. Rasmussen (London and Cambridge, MA).
———. (2002) *Archaeology of Knowledge*, tr. A. M. Sheridan Smith (London and New York).
Frede, D. (1992) "Mixed Feelings in Aristotle's *Rhetoric*." In A. Rorty (ed.) (1992) 258–85.

Frier, B. W. (1985) *The Rise of the Roman Jurists* (Princeton).
Fukuyama, F. (2002) *The End of History and the Last Man* (New York).
Gale, M. 1997. "The Shield of Turnus: Aeneid 7.783–92." *Greece and Rome* 44: 176–96.
Ganiban R. (2007) *Statius and Virgil. The* Thebaid *and the Re-interpretation of the* Aeneid (Cambridge).
Geertz, C. (1973a) "Internal Conversion in Contemporary Bali." In C. Geertz, *The Interpretation of Cultures* (New York) 170–89.
———. (1973b) "Ritual and Social Change: A Javenese Example." In C. Geertz, *The Interpretation of Cultures* (New York) 142–69.
Gellner, E. (1983) *Nations and Nationalism* (London).
Giardina, A. (1994) "L'identità in compiuta dell' Italia romana." In *L'Italie d'Auguste à Dioclétien, Colloque d'École française de Rome*, 198 (Rome) 1–89.
Gibson, A. (1999) *Postmodernity, Ethics, and the Novel. From Leavis to Levinas* (London and New York).
Gibson, B. (2006) "The *Silvae* and epic."In Nauta et al. (eds) (2006): 163–83.
Giddens, A. (1984) *The Constitution of Society: An Outline of the Theory of Structuration* (Berkeley and Los Angeles).
———. (1991) *Modernity and Self-Identity: Self and Society in the Late Modern Age* (Cambridge).
Gill, C. (1996) *Personality in Greek Epic, Tragedy, and Philosophy: The Self in Dialogue* (Oxford).
———. (2006) *The Structured Self in Hellenistic and Roman Thought* (Oxford).
Ginsburg, J. (1981) *Tradition and Theme in the Annals of Tacitus* (New York).
———. (1993) "*In maiores certamina:* Past and Present in the Annals." In T. J. Luce and A. J. Woodman (eds.) *Tacitus and the Tacitean Tradition* (Princeton) 86–103.
Glazer, N., and D. P. Moynihan. (1975) "Introduction." In N. Glazer and D. P. Moynihan (eds.) *Ethnicity, Theory and Experience* (Cambridge, MA) 1–29.
Gowing, A. *Empire and Memory: The Representation of Roman Republic in Imperial Culture* (Cambridge and New York).
Gray, J (1995) *Liberalism*. 2nd ed. (Buckingham).
Green, A. (1999) *The Fabric of Affect in the Psychoanalytical Discourse*, tr. Alan Sheridan, The New Library of Psychoanalysis 37 (London and New York).
Gross, E. (1990) "The Body of Signification." In Fletcher and Benjamin (eds.) (1990) 80–102.
Gruen, E. S. (1993) *Culture and National Identity in Republican Rome* (London).
Haidu, P. (1992) "The Dialectics of Unspeakability: Language, Silence, and the Narratives of De-subjectification." In S. Friedlander (ed.) *Probing the Limits of Representation* (Cambridge, MA).
Halbwachs, M. (1980) *The Collective Memory*, tr. F. Ditter and V. Y. Ditter (New York).
Hallett, J. (1973). "The Role of Women in Roman Elegy: Counter-Cultural Feminism." *Arethusa* 6: 103–24.
Hallward, P. (2003). *Badiou: A Subject to Truth* (Minneapolis and London).
Hammer, D. (2008) *Roman Political Thought and the Modern Theoretical Imagination* (Norman).
Hand, S. (ed.) (2000). *The Levinas Reader. Emmanuel Levinas* (Oxford).
Hardie, P. (1993) *The Epic Successors of Virgil. A Study in the Dynamics of a Tradition* (Cambridge).
———. (2006) "Statius' Ovidian poetics and the Tree of Atedius Melior (*Silvae* 2.3)." In Nauta et al. (eds.) (2006) 207–221.

Harvey, D. (1990) *The Condition of Postmodernity: An Enquiry into the Origins of Cutural Change* (Oxford).
Heidegger, M. (1993) *Basic Writings from Being and Time (1927) to the Task of Thinking (1964)*, ed. D. F. Krell (London).
Helzle, M. (1996) *Der Stil ist der Mensch: Redner und Reden im romischen Epos* (Stuttgart).
Hemelrijk E. A. (1999) *Matrona Docta: Educated Women in the Roman Elite from Cornelia to Julia Domna* (London).
Henderson, J. (1989) "Livy and the Invention of History." In A. Cameron (ed.) *History as Text. The Writing of Ancient History* (Chapel Hill, NC) 64–85.
Hershkowitz, D. (1995) "Pliny the Poet." *Greece and Rome* 42: 168–91.
———. (1997) "'*Parce metu, Cytherea*': 'Failed' Intertext Repetition in Statius' *Thebaid*, or, Don't Stop Me If You've Heard This One Before." *Materiali e Discussioni per L'Analisi Di Testi Classici* 39: 35-52.
———. (1998) *The Madness of Epic. Reading Insanity from Homer to Statius* (Oxford).
Hill, D. (1990) "Statius' *Thebaid*: A Glimmer of Light in the Sea of Darkness." In A. Boyle (ed.) *The Imperial Muse: Ramus Essays in Roman Literature of the Empire* (Bendigo) 98–118.
Hobsbawm, E., and T. Ranger (eds.) (1983) *The Invention of Tradition* (Cambridge).
Hoffer, S. E. (1999) *The Anxieties of Pliny the Younger. American Classical Studies* 43 (Atlanta).
Hong H., and E. Hong (eds.) (2000) *The Essential Kierkegaard* (Princeton).
hooks, bel (2000) *Feminist Theory: from Margins to Center* (Cambridge, MA).
Inwood, B. (1997) "'Why do fools fall in love?'" In R. Sorabji (ed.) *Aristotle and After* (London) 55–69.
Janan, M. (1994) *"When the lamp is shattered": Desire and Narrative in Catullus* (Carbondale and Edwardsville).
Johnson, W. R. (1987) *Momentary Monsters. Lucan and his Heroes* (Ithaca, NY).
Joughin, J., and S. Malpas (2003) *The New Aestheticism* (Manchester).
Kant, I. (1987) *Critique of the Aesthetic Judgement*. Vol 2, tr. W. S. Pluhar (Indianapolis, IN).
Kaster, R. (2005) *Emotion, Restraint and Community in Ancient Rome* (Oxford and New York).
Kearney, R. (2003) *Strangers, Gods, and Monsters. Interpreting Otherness* (London and New York).
Keith, A. (2000) *Engendering Rome. Women in Latin Epic* (Cambridge).
Kristeva, J. (1982) *Powers of Horror: An Essay in abjection* (New York).
———. (1987) *Tales of Love*, tr. Leon S Roudiez (New York).
Lacan, J. (1977) *Écrits: A Selection*, tr. A. Sheridan (London).
———. (1981) *The Four Fundamental Concepts of Psychoanalysis: The Seminar of Jacques Lacan. XI*, tr. A. Sheridan (New York, London).
Laclau, E., and L. Zak (1994) "Minding the Gap: The Subject of Politics." In E. Laclau (ed.) *The Making of Political Identities* (London).
Lechte, J. (1990) *Julia Kristeva* (London and New York).
Lechte, J., and M. Margaroni (2004) *Julia Kristeva. Live Theory* (London and New York).
Lefebvre, H. (1991) *The Production of Space* (Oxford).
Lendon, J. E. (1997) *Empire of Honour: The Art of Government in the Roman World* (Oxford).
Leonard, M. (2005) *Athens in Paris: Ancient Greece and the Political in Post-War French Thought* (Oxford).
Lévi-Strauss, C. (1969) *The Raw and the Cooked* (New York).

Liebeschuetz, W. (1966) "The Theme of Liberty in the *Agricola* of Tacitus." *Classical Quarterly* 16: 126–39.
Lomas, K (1991) "Local Identity and Cultural Imperialism: Epigraphy and the Diffusion of Romanisation in Italy." In *Papers of the Fourth Conference of Italian Archaeology 1: The Archaeology of Power 1* (London) 231–39.
———. (1995) "Urban Elites and Cltural Definition: Romanization in Southern Italy." In T. J. Cornell and K. Lomas (eds.) *Urban Society in Roman Italy* (London) 107–20.
Lovatt, H. (1999) "Competing Endings: Re-reading the End of Statius *Thebaid* through Lucan." *Ramus* 28.2:126–51.
———. (2005) *Statius and Epic Games: Sport, Politics, and Poetics in the* Thebaid (Cambridge).
Luce, T. J. (1986) "Tacitus' Conception of Historical Change: The Problems of Discovering the Historian's Opinions." In I. S. Moxon and A. J. Woodman (eds.) *Past Perspective in Greek and Roman Historical Writings* (Cambridge) 143–55.
———. (1993) "Reading and Response in the *Dialogus*." In T. J. Luce and A. J. Woodman (eds.) *Tacitus and the Tacitean Tradition* (Princeton, NJ) 11–38.
Luhmann, N. (1986) *Love as Passion. The Codification of Intimacy* (Oxford).
Lyne, R. O. A. M. (1987) *Further Voices in Vergil's Aeneid* (Oxford).
Lyotard, J-F. (1988) "The Sublime and the Avant-Garde." In *The Inhuman* (Stanford) 89–107.
McAdams, D. (2004) "The Redemptive Self: Narrative Identity in America Today." In Beike et al. (eds.) (2004).
Martin, R. H.,and A. J. Woodman (1989) *Tacitus Annals Book IV* (Cambridge).
Mayer, R (2001) *Tacitus, Dialogus de Oratoribus* (Cambridge).
Matier, K. (1989) "Hannibal: The Real Hero of the Punica." *Acta Classica* 32: 3–17.
Megill, A. (1985) *Prophets of Extremity: Nietzsche, Heidegger, Foucault, Derrida* (Berkeley, Los Angeles, London).
Middleton, D., and D. Edwards (eds.) (1990a) *Collective Remembering* (London).
———. (1990b) "Conversational Remembering: A Social Psychological Approach." In Middleton and Edwards (eds.) (1990) 23–45.
Milchman, A., and A. Rosenberg (2003a) (eds.) *Foucault and Heidegger: Critical Encounters* (Minneapolis).
———. (2003b) "Toward a Foucault/Heidegger Auseinandersetzung." In Milchman and Rosenberg (2003a) 1–29.
Miller, Paul Allen (2005) "The Art of Self-Fashioning, or Foucault on Plato and Derrida." *Foucault Studies* 2: 54–74.
———. (2007) *Postmodern Spiritual Practices: The Construction of the Subject and the Reception of Plato in Lacan, Derrida, and Foucault* (Columbus).
Mitchell, D. R. (2001) *Heidegger's Philosophy and Theories of the Self* (Aldershot, Burlington, Singapore, Sydney).
Montiglio, S. (2000) *Silence in the Land of Logos* (Princeton, NJ).
Morford, M. "How Tacitus Defined Liberty." *Aufstieg and Niedergang der römischer Welt* II 33.5: 3420–50.
Nancy, J-L. (1991) *The Inoperable Community*, ed. by P. Connor, tr. P. Connor et al. (Minneapolis and Oxford).
———. (2000) *Being Singular Plural* (Stanford).
Nauta, R., H-J van Dam, and J-L Smolenaars (eds.) (2006) *Flavian Poetry* (Leiden).
Newlands, C. (2002) *Statius' Silvae and the Poetics of Empire* (Cambridge).
Nora, P. (1989) "Between Memory and History: Les lieux de mémoire." *Representations* 26: 7–24.

Nussbaum, M. (1994) *The Therapy of Desire* (Princeton, NJ).
O'Gorman, E. (1993) "No place like home: Identity and Difference in the *Germania* of Tacitus." *Ramus* 22: 135–54.
———. (2000) *Irony and Misreading in the Annals of Tacitus* (Cambridge).
Owen, S. G. (1909) "On Silius Italicus." *Classical Quarterly* 3: 254–57.
Pagan, V. (2000) "The Mourning After: Statius' *Thebaid* 12." *American Journal of Philology* 121: 423–52.
Parsons, T. (1975) "Some Theoretical Considerations of the Nature and Trends of Change in Ethnicity." In N. Glazer and D. P. Moynihan (eds.) *Ethnicity, Theory and Experience* (Cambridge, MA) 53–83.
Pelling, C. (1993) "Tacitus and Germanicus." In T. J. Luce and A. J. Woodman (eds.) *Tacitus and the Tacitean Tradition* (Princeton, NJ) 59–85.
Pichon, R. 1924. *Histoire de la littérature latine*. 12th ed. (Paris).
Pollmann, K. (2001) "Statius' *Thebaid* and the Legacy of Vergil's *Aeneid*." *Mnemosye* 54.1: 10–30.
Pomeroy, A. J. 1989. "Silius Italicus as Doctus Poeta." *Ramus* 18:119–39.
———. 2000. "Silius' Rome: The Re-writing of Vergil's Vision." *Ramus* 29: 149–68.
Radice, B (1963) *The Letters of the Younger Pliny* (London).
Ransom, J. S. (1997) *Foucault's Discipline: The Politics of Subjectivity* (Durham and London).
Reynolds, J. (2006) *Understanding Existentialism* (Chesham).
Ricouer, P. (2004) *Memory, History, Forgetting*, tr. K. Blamey and D. Pellauer (Chicago, London).
Robinson, J. (1995) "Perspective, Meaning, and Remembering." In Rubin (ed.) 199–217
Roller, M. (1998) "Pliny's Catullus: The Politics of Literary Appropriation." *Transactions of the American Philological Association* 128: 265–304.
———. (2001) *Constructing Aristocracy. Aristocrats and Emperors in Julio-Claudian Rome* (Princeton and Oxford).
Rorty, A. (ed.) (1992) *Essays on Aristotle's Rhetoric* (Berkeley).
Rossi, A. (2000) "The *Aeneid* Revisited: The Journey of Pompey in Lucan's *Pharsalia*." *American Journal of Philology* 121: 571–91.
Rostagni, A. (1964) *Storia della letteratura latina* (Turin).
Rubin, D. (ed.) (1995) *Remembering our Past. Studies in Autobiographical Memory* (Cambridge).
Rudich, V. (1993) *Political Dissidence under Nero: The Price of Dissimulation* (London, New York).
Sage, M. M. (1991) "The Treatment in Tacitus of Roman Republican History and Antiquarian Matters." In H. Temporini (ed.) *Aufstieg und Niedergang der römischer Welt* II 33.5: 3385–3419.
Safranski, R. (1998) *Martin Heidegger: Between Good and Evil*, tr. E. Osers (Cambridge, MA and London).
Sartre, J.-P. (1958) *Being and Nothingness: An Essay on Phenomenological Ontology* (London).
Schacht, R. (1983) *Nietzsche* (London, New York).
Sherwin-White, A. N. (1966) *The Letters of Pliny: A Historical and Social Commentary* (Oxford).
Sihvola, J., and T. Engberg-Pedersen (eds.) (1998) *The Emotions in Hellenistic Philosophy* (Kopenhagen).
Smith, A. D. (1981) *The Ethnic Revival* (Cambridge).
———. (1986) *The Ethnic Origin of Nations* (Oxford).

———. (1998) *Julia Kristeva. Speaking the Unspeakable* (London).
Smolenaars, J. J. L. (2006) "Ideology and Poetics along the Via Domitiana: Statius *Silvae* 4.3." In Nauta et al. (eds.) (2006) 223–44.
Soja, E. W. (1989) *Postmodern Geographies: The Reassertion of Space in Critical Theory* (London).
Soya E., and B. Hooper (1993) "The Spaces that Difference Makes." In M. Keith and S. Pile (eds.) *Place and the Politics of Identity* (London and New York) 183–205.
Somers, M. R., and G. D. Gibson (1994) "Reclaiming the Epistemological 'Other': Narrative and Social Construction of Identity." In C. Calhoun (ed.) *Social Theory and the Politics of Identity* (Cambridge, MA) 37–99.
Spargo, Clifton R. (2004) *The Ethics of Mourning: Grief and Responsibility in Elegiac Literature* (Baltimore, MD).
Spentzou, E. (2003) *Readers and Writers in Ovid's Heroides. Transgressions of Gender and Genre* (Oxford).
Spivak, G. (1987) *In Other Worlds: Essays in Cultural Politics* (London).
Stavrakakis, Y. (1996) *Split Subject and Split Object. Towards a Generalisation of the Lacanian Logic of Lack* (Colchester).
Stavrakakis, Y. (1999) *Lacan and the Political* (London and New York).
Striker, G. (1992) "Emotions in Context: Aristotle's Treatment of the Passions in the *Rhetoric* and his Moral Psychology." In A. Rorty (ed.) (1992) 286–302.
Syed, Y. (2005) *Vergil's* Aeneid *and the Roman Self. Subject and Nation in Literary Discourse* (Ann Arbor).
Syme, R. (1958) *Tacitus* (London).
Taylor, C. (1989) *Sources of the Self: The Making of the Modern Identity* (Cambridge).
Taylor, M. (2000) *Journeys to Selfhood* (New York).
Thomas, Dylan (1971) *The Poems of Dylan Thomas* (London).
Tipping, B. (1999) "*Exemplary Roman Heroism in Silius' Punica.*" D.Phil. diss., Oxford University.
Toews, J. E. (1994) "Foucault and the Freudian Subject: Archaeology, Genealogy and the Historicization of Psychoanalysis." In J. Goldstein (ed.) *Foucault and the Writing of History* (Oxford, Cambridge, MA) 116–34.
Toohey, P. (1992) *Reading Epic. An Introduction to the Ancient Narratives* (London and New York).
Tosh, J. (1991) "Domesticity and Manliness in the Victorian Middle Class; the Family of Edward White Benson." In M. Roper and J. Tosh (eds.) *Manful Assertions: Masculinities in Britain since 1900* (London, New York) 44–73.
Trouillet, M. R. (1995) *Silencing the Past: Power and the Production of History* (Boston).
Valente, J. (2003) "Lacan's Marxism, Marxism's Lacan (From Žižek to Althusser)." In J.-M. Rabaté (ed.) *The Cambridge Companion to Lacan* (Cambridge) 153–72.
Van Dam, H-J (2006) "Multiple imitation of Epic Models in the *Silvae*." In Nauta et al. (eds.) 185–205.
Veyne, P. (2003) *Seneca. The Life of a Stoic*, tr. David Sullivan (New York and London).
Wallace-Hadrill, A. (1988) "The Social Structure of the Roman House." *Papers of the British School at Rome* 56: 43–97.
———. (1994) *Houses and Society in Pompeii and Herculaneum* (Princeton).
Wertsch, J. (2002) *Voices of Collective Remembering* (Cambridge).
Williams B. (1997) "Stoic Philosophy and the Emotions: Reply to Richard Sorabji." In R. Sorabji (ed.) *Aristotle and After* (London).
Williams, G. (1978) *Change and Decline: Roman Literature in the Early Empire* (Berkeley, Los Angeles, London).

———. (1986) "Statius and Vergil: Defensive Imitation." In Bernard, D. (ed.) *Virgil at 2000: Commemorative Essays on the Poet and His Influence* (New York) 207–224.

Wilson, M. 1993. "Flavian Variant: History. Silius' Punica." In A. J. Boyle (ed.) *Roman Epic* (London).

Woolf, G. (2003) "The City of Letters." In C. Edwards and G. Woolf (eds.) *Rome the Cosmopolis* (Cambridge).

Worthington, K. (1996). *Self as Narrative: Subjectivity and Community in Contemporary Fiction* (Oxford).

Yelvington, K. (1991) "Ethnicity as Practice? A Commentary on Bentley." *Comparative Studies in Social History* 33: 158–68.

Žižek, S. (1991) *Looking Awry: An Introduction to Jacques Lacan through Popular Culture* (Boston).

———. (2000) *The Ticklish Subject. The Absent Centre of Political Ontology* (London, New York).

———. (2004) "From Antigone to Joan of Arc." In *Helios* 31: 51–62.

Index

Abascantus, 96–97
abject, 56–57, 71, 87–88
Actaeon, 40n26, 78
Actium, 155, 162, 163, 164
Adrastus, 111, 112, 114–15, 116–17, 139, 181–83, 185, 189–90
adultery, 109, 134–35, 206–8
aesthetics, 13, 15, 16, 229
Agamben, Giorgio, 220–221, 228n2
agency, 13, 15, 18, 37, 132
Agricola. *See* Tacitus, *Agricola*
Aion, 144–45, 184–85, 187
Aletes, 78–79, 102
alienation, 5–6, 16, 19, 30, 37, 55, 72, 121, 132, 134, 191–92, 219, 221, 225, 228–29
alteriority, 104–6
amator exclusus, 107, 109, 124–25
amicitia, 29, 30–37, 43, 64, 90, 131
Amphiarus, 115–16
anger, 69–71, 103, 105–106
Antigone, 17, 81–82, 85–87, 190
Antigone, 17, 87
apatheia, 67–69
Argia, 84–87, 106, 111, 112–17, 136, 139–40, 183, 185n50, 190
Argos, 86, 111, 179, 180–83, 186–87, 190, 196, 230

Ariminum, 59
Arria, 151–52
Arruns, 170
Arulenus Rusticus, 165
Asbyte, 199–200
Asinius Gallus, 161
Athens, 162
Atedius Melior, 93–95, 97, 103
Augustus, 31, 32, 66, 154–55, 217. *See also* literature, Augustan
authenticity, 16, 19, 21, 22, 62–63, 93, 97–98, 103

Bacchante, 75, 179
Badiou, Alain, 145, 191–92
barbarians, 23, 106, 113n8, 189n55, 196–97, 200, 204–5, 206, 208–16, 218, 221–23, 230
Bartsch, Shadhi, 46, 56
bedroom, 25, 32, 38, 41, 110, 111–14, 116–18, 119, 120, 124, 131, 135–36, 138–39, 178, 227
Blanchot, Maurice, 145, 185–86, 191
body, the, 16, 46, 56, 63, 87–88, 98, 130–31. *See also* embodiment
Borgia, Cesare, 62
Bourdieu, Pierre, 37n20, 37n21

Britons, 206, 213–16, 222
Bructeri, 210
Brundisium, 48, 52
Brutus, 65, 118, 147, 156–57, 162, 164

Caesar, 65; of Lucan, 30, 44–64, 80, 87n25, 88, 137, 140, 168–76, 187–88, 213, 227
Caesarism, 30, 60–64, 80
Calgacus, 211–16, 220
Caligula, 28, 69
Calpurnia (wife of Pliny), 107–8, 124–31, 137, 138
Calpunia Hispulla, 125–26, 128–30
Calpurnius Fabatus, 127–31
Calvisius Rufus, 141
Capaneus, 116–17, 134
Capua, 196, 201–2, 204, 206
Carthage, 198, 223
Cassius, 147, 156–57, 162, 164
Cato, 4, 44n33, 56, 111, 118–19, 121n20, 123–24, 135–36, 137, 140, 147, 167, 188, 192, 227
Catullus Messalinus, 150
Cesare. *See* Borgia, Cesare
Cicero, 65, 66–67, 142–43, 152, 167
civilization, 7, 40, 215–16, 219–20. See also *humanitas*
Chronos, 144–45, 160, 163, 183–89, 220
classics, 8, 13–15, 225–27
Claudius, 28, 136, 216–18, 222
Cluvius Rufus, 150
Codrus, 136–37
collectivity, aristocratic, 36–37
communism, 63
community, 9, 20–22, 29, 38, 39, 47, 50–51, 51n38, 52, 55, 68, 69, 71–72, 75, 78, 84, 92, 94, 97, 117, 124, 175; Roman, 44
Comum, 32, 126
consolatio, 89–90, 93–98, 100n38, 103
conjugality, new, 111–12, 124, 131–32, 137. *See* marriage
Cordus, Aulus Cremutius, 156–57, 160, 167
Corellius Rufus, 146–47

Cornelia, 111, 120, 121–24, 136, 138, 187
Cottius, 92
court, imperial, 27–28, 33–34
Cremutius Cordus. *See* Cordus, Aulus Cremutius
Creon, 81, 82–84, 87, 88
crowd, the, 28–29, 50, 53, 54, 62, 75, 76, 77, 97, 103, 109, 116–17, 121, 122, 134, 135–36, 166, 172, 174, 178, 205

Daunus, 203
dawn, 112, 116–17, 118, 121, 141, 187
death, 6, 16, 18, 48, 53–54, 61, 68, 70–71, 75–80, 87–88, 93, 106, 118
delatores, 33
Deipyle, 114
Deleuze, Gilles, 144–145, 184
democratic moment, 74, 88, 105
Dido, 113, 201
discontent, 62–64
discourse, 5, 11–12, 15, 16, 19–20, 22, 24–25, 99, 137, 220. *See also* society, code of
dissimulatio, 34
docta puella. See elegy, mistress in
dominatio, 30, 31–32, 43, 44, 64
Domitian, 2, 23, 30, 31, 32–33, 34n16, 96–97, 146–47, 150, 151, 158, 166–67, 175, 191, 208n27, 213, 223
dreams, 18, 102, 113, 136, 140, 149, 178, 201; of empire, 223–224; of Pompey, 121, 123, 136, 140

Egypt, 88n29, 136, 162–63
elegy, 84, 98, 105n50, 107–10, 126, 143, 200–201; mistress in, 98, 108–10, 120, 123–25, 130–31, 137; personification of, 108–9; and teaching of love, 126
embodiment, 16, 63, 87, 100–101. *See also* body, the
emperor, 36–37, 39, 90, 160, 222–23, 227

epic, 2, 23–24, 47, 55–56, 59–60, 72–73, 89, 143, 206
Epictetus, 68–69
Eteocles, 75, 79–82, 102, 112, 190
ethics, 16, 21, 69–72, 104–6, 111, 121, 123–24, 132, 134, 190–91, 213, 230
ethnicity, 189–90, 194–95, 213–19, 223n40
ethnography, 206, 208–11
Euphrates (philosopher), 145–46
event, 2, 58n47, 80, 82, 88, 99, 103, 105–6, 144–45, 172, 175, 181, 185, 191–92, 228
exile, xiii, 36, 82, 85, 86, 111, 112, 117, 121, 152, 160, 171, 177–79, 186–92, 194, 196, 229

factionalism, 33
false consciousness, 5–6
fama, 164–67. *See also* Pliny and *fama*
family, 52
Fannia, 151–52
fascism, 63, 64
Foucault, Michel, 10–16, 19, 21, 124, 168, 228–29; *Discipline and Punish*, 11; *History of Sexuality* 10–11, 13–15; "What is Enlightenment?," 12–13, 15
funeral, 77–79, 84–87, 90, 94–96, 97
freedom. *See* liberty
Freud, Sigmund, 14–15, 63, 177n46
fundamentalism, 21
Fundanus, 90–91, 93

Galba, 157–59
Gallus, 66–67
games, 150
Gaul, 50, 141, 161, 169, 173, 215, 216–19
genealogy, 22; of ideas, 12; of the modern, 21; of texts, 5
Germanicus, 160–64, 176, 187–88
Germans, 206–11, 222
Giddens, Antony, 37
Gill, Christopher, 9

Glaucias, 93–96, 97, 103
globalism, 196, 220–21
Greek, writers, 23
grief, 7, 68–69, 72–97, 99, 101–4, 230

halls, 79, 178, 182–83
Halbwachs, Maurice, 175
Hannibal, 50, 196, 198–205, 214
Helen of Troy, 113, 140
Helvidius Priscus, 141, 151
Hercules, 40
Herennius Senecio. *See* Senecio
heroism, 3, 30, 40, 44, 60–64, 72–73, 80, 116, 117, 148, 202
Hipsipyle, 117n12
history, 6, 7, 8; 11–12, 14–15, 25, 55, 56, 60, 62–64, 75, 106, 111, 119n13, 122, 143, 144–45, 152–57, 167, 171–76, 178–79, 182–83; end of, 62–63, 167, 169–70, 196, 219, 227, 230; and ethnicity, 218–19; and ideology, 175–76; and power, 175–76, 213; of the present, 12, 13, 15, 144–45, 168, 176, 226; and resistance, 156–60, 168–69, 171, 175–76; and theory, 153; triumph of, 63, 111, 136–37, 140–41, 187–88, 192, 214–15, 229. *See also* past, the; Pliny and *fama*
Holocaust, the, 58n47, 70–71, 105–6
Homo Sacer, 220–21
horror, 6, 25, 70–71, 75, 87, 102
houses, 29, 32, 33, 38–39, 75, 147
humanitas, 212, 215–16, 223, 227, 230
hunting, 40

Ide, 76–77
identity, 16, 56, 74, 104, 167–68, 185–87, 221–22; collective, 78, 105n51, 172; Roman, 3, 157, 187–89, 212–13, 216–19, 223
ideology, 22, 64, 102; and conflict, 2, 5, 175–76; end of, 63–64; and modernity, 19; sublimation by, 7, 79; and uncertainty, 5, 227–28

Ilerda, siege of, 48–49
Imaginary, the, 17–18, 20
Imilce, 200–201, 206
imperialism, 6, 25, 111, 196–97, 210–222
individualism, 30, 37n22, 49–50, 55, 60–64, 132
intertextuality, 23–24
Iulia Procilla, 165

Johnson, W. R., 4
Junius Mauricus, 150–51
Juno, 178–79

Kant, Immanuel, 12, 57
Kearney, Richard, 56–58
Kierkegaard, Søren, 60–61, 62
Kristeva, Julia, 56n40, 57, 72, 87, 92, 103, 135, 138

Lacan, Jacques, 14n32, 16–22, 132, 191
Laelius, 51–52
lament, 73, 83–86
Latin, silver. *See* literature, silver
leadership. *See* politics, and leadership
legacies, 31, 34; hunting of, 34, 37, 91
Lesbos, 111, 121–24, 140, 196, 230
Levinas, Emmanuel, 104, 112, 132
Lévi-Strauss, Claude, 37n21
liberalism, 30, 62, 220
liberty, 10n14, 12, 13, 16, 21, 22, 36, 43, 57, 63, 68, 69, 71, 73, 102, 105, 108, 118, 147, 150, 154, 157, 160, 161, 167n26, 173, 179, 183, 185–87, 191, 205, 209–10, 213–16, 222, 228–30
literature, 35, 65–67, 88–89, 130–31, 142; Augustan, 3, 4, 108–9, 126; history of, 24; of the late first century, 5, 8; silver Latin, 4
Livy, 3, 156, 197, 207–8
Longinus (Ps), 56n39
love, 50, 52, 98, 99, 103, 105, 107–14, 116–24, 125–27, 134–40; and ethics, 112–14, 122–24, 134–36, 227, 230; hidden, 134–36; and poetry, 65–67, 98, 107–11, 116–17; on stage, 135–36
Lucan, 4, 5, 6, 22, 23, 24, 30, 44–56, 63–64, 102, 111, 135–37, 140, 144, 227; *Pharsalia* I 33–64, 60; *Pharsalia* I 129–57, 44–46; *Pharsalia* I 296–386, 50–52, 174; *Pharsalia* I 186–226, 46–47; *Pharsalia* I 484–635, 59; *Pharsalia* I 673–95, 75; *Pharsalia* II 289–391, 118–19; *Pharsalia*, III 156–63, 169; *Pharsalia* IV 253–381, 48–49; *Pharsalia* V 244–370, 52–55; *Pharsalia* V 476–702, 48; *Pharsalia* V 722–815, 120; *Pharsalia* VII 250–96, 173–74; *Pharsalia* VIII 1–158, 122–24; *Pharsalia* IX 961–99, 168. *See also* Caesar, of Lucan
Lyotard, Jean-François, 58

Macedo, murder of, 39–40
Maeon, 76, 79–80, 88, 102
Marcia, 119
Marius, 170–71
marriage, 25, 55, 99, 108, 111–12, 119, 123–32, 134–40, 206–7; marriage, lineage, 126
Marxism, 5, 14n31, 63
masculinity, 3, 5, 108, 130–131, 139
Melampus, 115
Melior. *See* Atedius Melior
memory, 25, 84, 167, 184–87, 190–92, 220, 226; collective, 152, 170–76, 195, 218, 221; and forgetting, 176–77, 189–91; and place, 179–81. *See also* history
Menoeceus, 82–84
Menoetes, 86
Mistress. *See* elegy, mistress in
monarchy, 5, 81–84
Mons Graupius, 211, 214, 216, 223
mourning. *See* ritual, of grief
Murrus, 198–99, 203
muses, 108–9
Musonius Rufus, 124

Naevius, 50
Nancy, Jean-Luc, 20–21, 71, 112, 132–34
Nero, 2, 27–28, 29, 60, 66, 69, 70–71, 171, 197
networks, social, 30–33, 36–37, 124, 131–35
Nerva, 66, 146n5, 150–51, 157, 158
Nietzsche, Friedrich, 16, 62–64
nihilism, 16, 21, 25, 64, 103
nostalgia, 144, 197, 221, 227; for the Republic, 150, 157–60, 192, 229
Nussbaum, Martha, 69–71

Odysseus, 40, 51n38, 178, 183n48, 206
Oedipus, 81–82, 84, 176–78, 190; and Freud, 14
opposition, 3, 5, 49, 205, 229–30; literary, 105, 110, 227, 229; political, 31, 141, 146–48, 150, 155, 167n26, 176, 192, 216; to society, 61, 72, 130, 132, 133, 135, 138, 189, 230
Otho, 148, 158
otium, 141, 145n4, 146

past, the, 5, 21, 22, 134, 181, 183, 197, 226; as locus of identity, 167–68, 184–87; Republican, 55, 96–97, 134n36; Theban, 78–79, 83, 186. *See also* history
pastoral, 42n27, 43, 44, 115, 136
Paulinus, Valerius, 141
Pharsalus, 75, 88, 111, 121, 173, 174
Philetos, 95n36, 96n37
pietas, 50, 90–98, 102, 125–27, 152
Piso (adopted heir of Galba), 157, 159
Piso, Gnaeus, 161–62, 163–64
Pliny, 6, 30–32, 34, 36, 38–44, 64, 102, 124–31, 138, 139, 141–52, 197, 227; *Epistles* 2, 6, 23; *Ep.* I 1, 143; *Ep.* I 2, 143; *Ep.* I 6, 40; *Ep.* I 10, 145–46; *Ep.* I 12, 146; *Ep.* I 17, 147; *Ep.* II 1, 148–49; *Ep.* II 17, 38, 42–43; *Ep.* II 20, 91; *Ep.* III 1, 39n23; *Ep.* III 14, 39–40; *Ep.* III 16, 151; *Ep.* IV 1, 126; *Ep.* IV 2, 91; *Ep.* IV 7, 91–92; *Ep.* IV 19, 125–26; *Ep.* IV 22, 150; *Ep.* V 3, 65–66; *Ep.* V 6, 40–41, 43n30; *Ep.* V 16, 90–91; *Ep.* VI 10, 149; *Ep.* VI 24, 152n11; *Ep.* VII 4, 66–67; *Ep.* VII 5, 107–8, 124–25; *Ep.* VII 19, 151–52; *Ep.* VIII 10, 128–30; *Ep.*VIII 11, 128–30; *Ep.* VIII 16, 39, 89–90, 92–93; *Ep.* IX 2, 142–43; *Ep.* IX 7, 43; *Ep.* IX 13, 141–42; *Ep.* IX 19, 149–50; *Ep.* IX 36, 38–39; *Ep.* IX 40, 39n23; and history, 6; home of, 38–39, 40–43; and *fama,* 141–43, 148–52; *Panegyricus,* 31, 34n16, 36, 40, 64
politics, 5, 20–21, 25–26, 29, 55, 82, 101, 145–46, 193; and leadership, 134, 202–3, 208–9; Roman, 33–34, 64; withdrawal from, 35–36, 146–47, 167
Polynices, 81–82, 84–87, 111, 112–14, 116, 136, 139, 179–83, 185–91
Pompey, of Lucan, 4, 44–45, 47n37, 50, 75, 88n29, 111, 118, 119–24, 136, 138, 139–40, 173, 227, 230
Priscilla, 96–97
psychoanalysis, 14–22

rape, 46, 54, 212
rationality, 8, 55, 57, 69–71, 72, 98, 220
Real, the, 17–19, 20, 21, 72, 75, 81, 82, 87, 92, 93, 101, 102, 103, 105, 229
redemption, 103, 230
Regulus, 91–93
representation, crisis of, 30, 34
Republic, fall of, 2, 147, 154–56, 172; legacy of, 24, 144; traditions of, 23, 143, 152. *See also* nostalgia; Tacitus and the Republic
Republicanism, 119, 155, 156–57, 164, 188, 189
revolution, 22, 37, 64, 71, 101–2, 103n45, 135–36, 190, 195, 220, 230; Caesarian, 144, 160, 171–72, 189, 192

ritual, 72, 99–101; of grief, 74, 77–78, 80, 94, 99, 102, 170. *See also* funeral
Romanization, 194–95, 215–19
Rome, city of, 3, 53–54, 74–75, 168, 204, 206–8, 218; community of, 111, 221–22; destruction of, 52, 54, 56, 118, 163, 169–70; idea of, 194–98, 221–24; march on, 120–21, 169–70; personification of, 46; and Pompey, 120–21; traditions of, 5, 50, 137–38, 150, 218
Rubicon, 46–47
ruins, 47n36, 163, 169n30, 187–88

salutatio, 28–29, 32
Saguntum, 198, 200, 202–4, 206
Sardus, 142
Sartre, Jean-Paul, 16
Scipio Africanus, 198, 203, 204–5
Sejanus, 28
self, 9–22, 61, 131–33; destruction of, 74, 90–91, 94–95; fashioning of, 13; history of 10, 21; objective-participant model of, 8
Semiotic, 72, 87, 92, 100–101, 102n43, 103
senate, 31, 33, 34, 52, 63n59, 122, 148n6, 150, 155, 157, 161, 167n26, 202–3, 206, 217, 219, 223n39
Seneca, 28–29, 30, 35–36, 37, 68–71, 105–106; *ad Marciam,* 68; *ad Polybium,* 68; *de Ira,* 69, 98; *de Tranquillitate Animi,* 35–36; *Epistle* 9, 36; *Epistle* 55, 35; *Epistle* 63, 68; *Epistle* 68, 35
Senecio, Herennius, 151–52, 165
sex, 67, 98, 108, 109–10, 112–13, 119, 125, 206–8, 211
silence, 38, 40, 50, 58, 59, 73, 82, 115, 175
slaves, 38, 39–40, 66–67, 89–90, 92–93, 95, 108, 125, 136, 214
society, 19–20; codes of, 5, 18, 37, 72, 80, 97, 117, 137; formation of, 132–35, 175; and self, 18–19,
60–62, 131–33; structure of, 37, 133–34. *See also* utopia
Silius Italicus, 6, 23, 196, 197–98, 203–6, 223, 227
Spurinna, 39n23
state, 2–3, 26, 39, 92, 139, 146, 147, 155, 157, 160, 161, 194–95, 197, 210, 218, 222–24, 227; devotion to, 3, 44, 46, 47, 87, 97, 202; resistance to, 105
Statius, 4n3, 102, 222–23; grief and, 7; *Silvae* 6–7, 23, 106, 227; *Silvae* I 1, 223n39; *Silvae* I 2, 108–10; *Silvae* I 3, 41n27; *Silvae* II 1, 93–96; *Silvae* II 2, 42n28; *Silvae* II 4, 95n35; *Silvae* II 6, 95n36; *Silvae* IV 2, 223n39; *Silvae* IV 3, 43n31; *Silvae* V 1, 96–97; *Silvae* V 3, 97–98; *Thebaid,* 6, 23–24, 73, 91, 102, 106; *Thebaid* I 312–79, 179–81; *Thebaid* II 319–74, 112–14; *Thebaid* III 33–93, 79; *Thebaid* III 114–209, 76–78; *Thebaid* XI 587–761, 81–82; *Thebaid* XII 60–104, 83–84; *Thebaid* XII 188–423, 84–86
Stella, 108–10, 135
stoicism, 67–71, 72
sublime, 55, 56–59, 187
suicide, 70–71, 76, 79–81, 95, 96, 146–47, 151–52, 157
Symbolic, the, 17–19, 20, 21, 56, 72, 75, 100–101, 102n43, 103, 105–6, 132, 138n39, 139
symbolic economy, 19–20, 22, 62, 64, 72, 80, 97, 98, 99, 101, 102, 105n51, 132, 135, 139–40, 193–97, 220, 222, 224, 229–30; and territory, 194–97

Tacitus, 2, 4, 6, 23, 24, 142, 144, 153–68, 171–72, 191, 223; *Agricola,* 164–67, 196–97, 211–16, 221–22; *Agricola* 1–4, 165; *Agricola* 21, 212, 215–16; *Agricola* 28, 213–14; *Agricola* 30–31, 211–16; *Annales,* 153, 159–60, 227; *Annales* I 1–4, 154–55; *Annales* IV 32–35,

155–57; *Annales* XI 23–25, 216–19; *Dialogus,* 164, 165n24; *Germania,* 196–97, 206–211; *Germania* 7, 208n27–28; *Germania* 18–19, 206–8; *Germania* 21–24, 208–10; *Germania* 33, 210; *Histories,* 27, 153; *Histories* I 15–16, 157–58; and the Republic, 154–60
terror, 4, 29, 30, 33, 44, 50, 58–59, 64, 75, 80
theory, in classics, 8
Theseus, 40
Thessander, 116, 117
Thomas, Dylan, 71
Thrasea Paetus, 151, 167n26
topiary, 41, 43
totalitarianism, 64, 138n39
Tiberius, 32, 66, 160–61, 164
Tifernum, 127
time, 184. *See also* Chronos
Tiro, 66–67, 98
Tisiphone, 177
Titinius Capito, 147–48
Tradition. *See* past, the
Trajan, 31, 40, 147
trauma, 19–20, 64, 72, 81, 99–100, 102, 105, 191–92
Troy, 47n36, 50, 59, 162, 163, 164, 168–69, 187–88, 192, 203n21
Turnus, 45–46, 47n36, 198–99, 200
Tydeus, 75, 114, 181–82

Underworld, 81, 95, 177
Usipi, 211, 213–14
utilitarianism, 156, 165, 190
utopia, 10n14, 20–21, 71, 136, 160, 230

Vatia, 35
Venus, 108
Verginius Rufus, 65, 148–50
Vespasian, 28, 32
Vestricius Spurinna, 92
villas, 35, 38–39, 41–43, 64, 227
Vindex, 149
violence, 21, 45–46, 56
Violentia, 108–10
Virgil, 43, 197, 218, 222; *Aeneid,* 3, 23–24, 44–46, 50, 55, 58n38, 59, 98, 108, 113, 168, 197, 198–200, 203, 204, 205–6
virginity, 97, 110, 206–7
Vitellius, 27, 29, 148
Voconius Rufus, 142
Vulcan, 108

Wiesel, Elie, 70–71
wills, 31, 89
witchcraft, 77
withdrawal. *See* politics, withdrawal from

www.ingramcontent.com/pod-product-compliance
Lightning Source LLC
Chambersburg PA
CBHW030109010526
44116CB00005B/172